Praise for *Climate of Corruption*

Larry Bell's *Climate of Corruption* details a timely, compelling narrative concerning the hijacking of science and demonization of carbon by political power brokers and eco-evangelists.

—Joseph D'Aleo, former Weather Channel director of meteorology and weather producer for ABC's *Good Morning America*

Larry Bell has uncovered through outstanding investigative reporting why and how this scam has been so successful for nearly 20 years now. He describes in precise detail the dozens of constituencies that benefit so much through access to money and power through this crime against humanity . . . And to what end?" Larry makes clear to what end: to make evil people rich and powerful and just plain folks all the poorer.

—Jay Lehr, science editor, *Environment and Climate News*

Those of us fortunate enough to have traveled in space bet our lives on the competence, dedication, and integrity of the science and technology professionals who made our missions possible . . . In the last twenty years, I have watched the high standards of science being violated by a few influential climate scientists, including some at NASA, while special interest opportunists have dangerously abused our public trust . . . This important book shines light on the self-serving agendas and shady political dealings behind the global warming hoax that we absolutely must change while there is still time.

—Walter Cunningham, Apollo 7 astronaut

Larry Bell connects the dots between indisputable scientific frauds, carbon regulation and marketing scams, and bogus green energy charades. He makes a convincing case that alarmist climate crisis rhetoric is far more political than scientific.

—Michael J. Economides, editor-in-chief, *Energy Tribune* and professor, University of Houston

More praise for *Climate of Corruption*

Larry Bell has cut through the heavily funded bad science of global warming advocates, the outrageous claims of politicians and scare threats from extremist environmentalists to explain the truth about Earth's climate and the man made and natural forces that change it. This book is very readable, clearly presented, detailed and documented, so you know Larry Bell is giving us the real story. He has done an amazing job of sorting it out and putting it in proper perspective.

—John Coleman, meteorologist and founder of The Weather Channel

CLIMATE OF CORRUPTION

Politics and Power Behind the
Global Warming Hoax

Larry Bell

GREENLEAF
BOOK GROUP PRESS

Published by Greenleaf Book Group Press
Austin, Texas
www.gbgpress.com

Distributed by Greenleaf Book Group LLC

For ordering information or special discounts for bulk purchases, please contact Greenleaf Book Group LLC at PO Box 91869, Austin, TX 78709, 512.891.6100.

Design and composition by Greenleaf Book Group LLC and Alex Head
Cover design by Greenleaf Book Group LLC
Illustrations by Larry Bell

Publisher's Cataloging-In-Publication Data (Prepared by The Donohue Group, Inc.)
Bell, Larry (Larry Spencer)
    Climate of corruption : politics and power behind the global warming hoax /
Larry Bell.—1st ed.
    p. ; cm.
    Includes index.
    ISBN: 978-1-60832-083-7
    1. Climatic changes—Popular works. 2. Climatic changes—Political aspects. 3. Global warming—Popular works. 4. Global warming—Political aspects. 5. Hoaxes. I. Title.
QC902.8 .B45 2011
363.738/74   2010932186

Part of the Tree Neutral® program, which offsets the number of trees consumed in the production and printing of this book by taking proactive steps, such as planting trees in direct proportion to the number of trees used: www.treeneutral.com

Printed in the United States of America on acid-free paper

10 11 12 13 14 15   10 9 8 7 6 5 4 3 2 1

First Edition

TreeNeutral®

CONTENTS

Foreword ix

Preface xi

Some Deserved Words of Appreciation xvii

Abbreviations and Acronyms. xix

Introduction: The Big Climate Crisis Lie 1

SECTION ONE: SETTING THE RECORDS STRAIGHT

Chapter 1   The Chicken Little Syndrome. 13

Chapter 2   Cooking the Climate Books 29

Chapter 3   Forcing Factors and Fictions. 47

SECTION TWO: POLITICAL HIJACKERS OF SCIENCE

Chapter 4   Feverish Climate Claims 61

Chapter 5   UN Political Science Lessons 85

Chapter 6   Contrails over Copenhagen 99

SECTION THREE: CARBON DEMONIZATION SCAMS

Chapter 7   Cap-and-Tax Daisy Chain. 125

Chapter 8   Climate as Religion. 143

Chapter 9   Getting a Real Grip on "Green" Energy. 155

SECTION FOUR: RETAKING AMERICA'S FUTURE

Chapter 10   Reenergizing Free Enterprise 187

Chapter 11   Demanding Truth and Accountability 215

Chapter 12   Exercising US Exceptionalism 237

Notes 255

Index 281

About the Author. 297

Dedicated to Al Gore, whose invention of the Internet made this book possible, and whose invention of facts made it necessary

FOREWORD

W hat a timely book! Larry Bell's insightful overview of global warming hysteria will open the eyes of many who still believe in the science as propagated by the United Nations' Intergovernmental Panel on Climate Change (IPCC) and in the promises of politicians to save them from climate disasters. After two decades of corrupt science, we are finally able to learn the truth about the politics behind the conspiracy among a small group of influential scientists to manufacture a global warming scare from data that showed none.

Many would place the beginning of the global warming hoax on the Senate testimony delivered by James Hansen of NASA during the summer of 1988. More than anything else, this exhibition of hyped alarm triggered my active skepticism about the man-made warming scare. This skepticism was further amplified when I acted as a reviewer of the first three IPCC reports, in 1990, 1996, and 2001. Increasingly, claims were made for which there was no evidence; in some cases the "evidence" was clearly manufactured. For example, the 1996 report used selective data and doctored graphs. It also featured changes in the text that were made *after* the scientists had approved it and before it was printed. It caused Dr. Frederick Seitz, a world-famous physicist and former president of the US National Academy of Sciences, the American Physical Society, and the Rockefeller University, to write in the *Wall Street Journal*: "I have never witnessed a more disturbing corruption of the peer review process than events that led to this IPCC report."

All throughout, politicians loudly proclaimed that "the science is settled" and proceeded to construct regulatory schemes to limit the emission of greenhouse gases (GHGs) and—in the process—to control energy. The capstone to all this fraudulent behavior must surely be the "cap-and-trade" legislation passed by the US House of Representatives in 2009. It has nothing to do with climate; instead, it is a giant tax scheme that redistributes income from citizens who use energy, whether electricity heat or motor fuel, to the favored few. It has been estimated that this legislation has provided a livelihood to some two thousand or more lobbyists and has placed a corresponding burden on the rest of the population.

By now, the international climate business has degenerated into a scheme to transfer resources from developed to developing nations. Or as cynics put it, "from the poor in rich countries to the rich in poor countries."

The truth is that there is no evidence for any significant human impact on global climate, and that there is nothing in a practical sense we can do to affect global climate. And, as Larry Bell points out, a somewhat warmer climate with increased levels of carbon dioxide in the atmosphere would be beneficial overall to Earth's inhabitants, especially to those in developing nations who depend on agriculture for a living. *Climate of Corruption* brings a breath of fresh, cool air to the overheated climate debate.

—S. Fred Singer
Former director of the US National Weather Satellite Service,
professor emeritus at the University of Virginia,
and coauthor of *Unstoppable Global Warming*

PREFACE

Regarding climate science there is at least one certainty: There is absolutely no reason to believe that Earth is any warmer now than it was during past periods when life flourished—times when agriculture was abundant, pyramids and cities were built, and world citizens became connected in trade and culture.

The March 2006 *Time* magazine cover story "Global Warming: Be Worried, Be Very Worried" warned of impending climate doom that would result in melting polar caps, rising oceans, and other catastrophes. If any worry is warranted, think about the next overdue Ice Age that scientific "experts" predicted only a few decades earlier. Then hope that the cooling period we are currently experiencing will only be brief. Understand that the real impetus behind the cooked numbers and doomspeak of the global warmers has little to do with the state of the environment and much to do with shackling capitalism and transforming the American way of life in the interests of global wealth redistribution ("social justice").

Is this all a conspiracy? It really isn't in the conventional sense, where a diabolical network of people and organizations unite to hatch intentionally malevolent plans. Let's assume that most of the entities and individuals discussed in this book truly believe they are pursuing righteous causes, even when we happen to strongly disagree with their viewpoints and priorities. Maybe we can hope that some of them will cut us the same slack.

But then, what about when those people and institutions we rely upon for important public information knowingly violate our trust? For example, by perpetrating unwarranted fear campaigns and by politically attacking and marginalizing those who challenge and expose factual errors, omissions, and uncertainties we need to know about. Should we excuse them even when they believe such actions are guided by superior moral authority? Absolutely not! These are clear acts of deception and corruption.

Obviously, this book addresses controversial topics, and readers have a right to know something about the person who wrote it. First, I am not a climate scientist and have never even played one in the movies. And although Houston is my chosen home, I have never been associated with "Big Oil"—or "little oil" either, for that matter. Nor am I connected with scientific funding, business organizations, or lobbies on either side of the issues. Few people within any such camps will know who I am, nor do they have any real reason to.

I have written some articles about climate, energy, and technology that were published in the *Energy Tribune*, an international magazine. This was done by invitation, and for small stipends, yet never was I influenced in any way regarding what I would write about or say. I would have cheerfully written them free of charge, but please don't tell the magazine.

In short, I am a space guy. My field is space architecture, which deals with planning and designing space stations and habitats for future lunar and Mars missions. I also undertake research and planning for extreme environments on Earth, such as polar, desert, underwater, and disaster facilities. This interest extends to working to prevent our entire planet from becoming an extreme environment.

My background and interests emphasize a holistic perspective regarding basic principles that govern how natural and technical systems work, how they are connected, and how they can be managed to support the most complex systems of all—us humans. This, in fact, is how this project really got started. I was innocently exploring some research and notions about "Spaceship Earth"—considering what we might possibly learn from nature about how to design artificial, closed climate and energy systems operating beyond our planet. Some space guys think about those kinds of things. In any case, that inquiry revealed much more than I bargained for.

Quite early in my investigation, I recalled a comment offered by S. Fred Singer when he visited my office several years ago to exchange ideas on a totally different space-related matter. During our meeting, he observed that satellite temperature recordings of the Earth's lower atmosphere were cooling more rapidly, relative to the surface, than greenhouse theory predicts. It would be expected that carbon dioxide (CO_2) would warm the lower atmosphere first, which would then radiate heat back to the surface, the reverse of what was being observed. I certainly had no reason to doubt him. Fred is an internationally recognized climate physicist and former

Distinguished Research Professor at George Mason University. He served as the first director of the US National Weather Satellite Service and also as vice chairman of the US National Advisory Committee on Oceans and Atmospheres. In addition, he has written numerous publications about climate, energy, and environmental issues, including a recent *New York Times* best seller, *Unstoppable Global Warming*, coauthored with Dennis T. Avery.

Although I didn't think all that much about Fred's casual observation at the time, it piqued a mild interest, and my later investigations have amplified questions regarding numerous climate change hypotheses, most particularly in regard to alarmist assertions, which have no real basis in science. My subsequent conclusions will now qualify me as a global warming skeptic and doomsday denier. This is not intended to suggest that I don't believe that climate change occurs or that it isn't abnormally warm right now. Compared with Ice Ages that have historically dominated Earth's climate about 90 percent of the time, we can be very grateful we are blessed with conditions more favorable for the lives we enjoy.

Yes, climate change is real, occurring with regular and irregular cycles and for lots of reasons. Scientists know about many of them, but much less about how these dynamic causes and effects interact or what combined results will occur at any given time. No one, not anyone, can even begin to reliably predict what Earth's global climate will be a decade or multiple decades hence, much less whether the impacts will be positive or negative with regard to all God's creatures—us included. Nor has anyone or any science conclusively demonstrated that human activities have caused or are causing climate change for better or worse, or if so, which activities, and with how much influence. Any claims of certainty to the contrary are bogus. Accordingly, and specifically, assertions that human CO_2 emissions are the root of climate crisis, or that such a threat exists, are challenged as factually unsupportable alarmism.

One unfortunate fact we can count on is that we are facing a global energy supply dilemma that has no simple solution. Answers do not lie with much-touted "renewable" energy sources, because they all lack sufficient potential capacities to make much overall difference. And for all their advertised "greenness," absolutely no options are immune from environmental activist opposition. Yet fossil fuels (coal, oil, and natural gas—particularly coal) are regarded as real villains, and a predicted global warming apocalypse will be their curse. (The term "fossil fuels" often will be referred to hereafter simply as "fossils.") Even resistance to the scourge of disaster risks previously associated with nuclear power now pales in comparison.

Global warming hysteria centered upon fossil-fuel CO_2 emissions is being advanced and exploited by powerful alternative energy marketers and carbon-trading interests. Aided and abetted by climate science hijackers, their aggressive lobbying campaigns have been extremely consequential. CO_2, which sustains plants that nourish us with oxygen and food, has come to be popularly characterized as a polluting menace. Initiatives to develop vital oil and natural gas reserves are being delayed, while options with scant potential dominate public media and legislative attention.

Inescapable evidence shows that human activities are impacting Earth's environment, typically not for the better. Air, water, and land pollution are an expanding global reality. Environmental scientists who study such matters play important roles in pointing such things out and helping us to do better. That purpose is not well served, however, by exaggerated statements calibrated to get maximum attention. Alarmism is not conducive to sound judgment or worthy of public respect, whatever the motives.

There can also be no doubt that fossil fuel depletion is a very real and serious problem, and while nuclear development is essential, it is most unfortunate that there are presently no complete or perfect remedies. Yet, given our proven history of human innovation, progress, and resilience, we have every reason to believe that solutions will ultimately be realized.

I had never planned to write this book—or any book. First, after family and friends witnessed the amount of research I had compiled—and were relentlessly exposed to my ever-deepening passion about the topics—they insisted that I do so. Eventually, I realized that I had to, like it or not. This decision was motivated by the fact that, like many of you, I am a parent who cares about the future of my children and the generations who will follow. I want them to inherit a clean, healthy planet, along with means to obtain energy sufficiency essential for comfortable lifestyles and economic opportunities. Conservation must be a big part of all solutions.

We clearly need to develop better alternatives, and to begin doing so now. In the meantime, we must also develop and expand access to resources that will enable those transitions; we must not be misled by hyperbole regarding sustainable replacement options that can only serve as supplements at best. Misguided, climate hysteria–induced, knee-jerk energy policies won't help get us where we need to go.

Each of us must determine whether or not we regard ourselves to be true environmentalists. I believe that environmentalism is not so much defined by what we are against as by what we are for, and neither fear nor guilt are prerequisites. Environmentalism need not be strident or perpetually confrontational. An environmentalist identity cannot really be owned, only practiced.

SOME DESERVED WORDS OF APPRECIATION

The preparation and production of this book turned out to be a much larger enterprise than I originally expected, and I am grateful to many people who supported its realization. My wife Nancy's early encouragement to undertake the project and continued belief in its value has been essential throughout the process. Major typing assistance afforded by my sons, Aaron and Ian, has transcribed my hand-printed draft jottings into legible text.

My esteemed colleague Professor Olga Bannova has been an ever-willing sounding board for ideas and a constructive critic for narrative. Two of our graduate students, Harmon Everett and Michael Fehlinger, contributed to manuscript production as author-compensated consultants. It should be noted that neither the book nor any perspectives it presents are in any way implied to represent publications or views of my employers: the University of Houston, the Gerald D. Hines College of Architecture, or the research center that I direct within the university. Nor is the book used as a text or designated information resource for any courses that I teach or supervise.

The wonderfully competent, dedicated, and enthusiastic Greenleaf Book Group team has contributed in all ways imaginable to make this project a successful and pleasurable experience. Editors Bill Crawford and Linda O'Doughda offered innumerable structural and literary suggestions to make it a greatly improved product. Graphic designer Brian Phillips produced the attractive and engaging jacket artwork, also collaborating with Design Manager Sheila Parr on internal book layout. Others, including Production Manager Chris McRay, Marketing Associate Katelynn Knutson, and Distribution Manager Kristen Sears, planned and coordinated numerous aspects of production and market promotion.

Thank you all.

ABBREVIATIONS AND ACRONYMS

ACEEE	American Council for an Energy-Efficient Economy
ACP	Alliance for Climate Protection
AMO	Atlantic Multidecadal Oscillation
ANWR	Arctic National Wildlife Refuge
AWEA	American Wind Energy Association
bbl/d	barrels per day
CAFE	corporate average fuel economy
CAP	Center for American Progress
CBO	Congressional Budget Office
CCS	carbon capture and storage
CCSP	Climate Change Science Program
CCX	Chicago Climate Exchange
CDA	Center for Data Analysis
CFCs	chlorofluorocarbons
CFL	compact fluorescent lighting
CO_2	carbon dioxide
CRU	Climate Research Unit
CSP	concentrating solar power
CSR	corporate social responsibility
DOE	Department of Energy (US)
DOI	Department of the Interior (US)
DSCOVR	Deep Space Climate Observatory
ECX	European Carbon Exchange
EGS	enhanced geothermal system
EIA	Energy Information Administration
EPA	Environmental Protection Agency (US)
ESA	Endangered Species Act

EU	European Union
EUV	extreme ultraviolet
FCCC	Framework Convention on Climate Change
FWS	Fish and Wildlife Service (US)
GCR	galactic cosmic ray
GCM	general circulation model
GDP	gross domestic product
GHG	greenhouse gas
GIM	Generation Investment Management
GISS	Goddard Institute for Space Studies
GSAM	Goldman Sachs Asset Management
GW	gigawatt
ICAP	International Carbon Action Partnership
ICE	Intercontinental Exchange, Inc.
IEA	Institute of Economic Analysis
IGCC	integrated gasification combined cycle
IMF	International Monetary Fund
IPE	International Petroleum Exchange
IPCC	Intergovernmental Panel on Climate Change
IPPR	Institute for Public Policy Research
kW	kilowatt
kWh	kilowatt-hour
LIA	Little Ice Age
MW	megawatt
MWP	Medieval Warm Period
N_2O	nitrous oxide
NASA	National Aeronautics and Space Administration
NCEE	National Center for Environmental Economics
NGO	nongovernmental organization
NIEO	New International Economic Order
NOAA	National Oceanographic and Atmospheric Administration
NRDC	Natural Resources Defense Council
OMB	Office of Management and Budget
OSI	Open Society Institute
PDO	Pacific Decadal Oscillation
ppm	parts per million
PTC	production tax credit
RCMP	Royal Canadian Mounted Police

RPS	renewable portfolio standard
SO_2	sulfur dioxide
STATS	Statistical Assessment Services
UCS	Union of Concerned Scientists
UNCED	United Nations Conference on Economic Development
UNEP	United Nations Environment Programme
USCAP	United States Climate Action Partnership
USGS	United States Geological Survey
UV	ultraviolet
VAT	value added tax
WCED	World Commission on Environment and Development
WMO	World Meteorological Organization
WTO	World Trade Organization
WWF	World Wildlife Fund

Introduction

THE BIG CLIMATE CRISIS LIE

LARRY BELL

*Spaceship Earth reporting . . . all systems functioning
. . . thermal controls optimum. Thank you, God.*

Conscientious environmentalism does not require or benefit from subscription to hysterical guilt over man-made climate crisis claims. Perhaps some may argue that unfounded alarmism is justifiable, even necessary, to get our attention to do what we should be doing anyway: for example, conserve energy and not pollute the planet. Hey, who wants to challenge those important purposes?

But what about examining motives? For example, when those who are twanging our guilt strings falsely portray polar bears as endangered climate victims to block drilling in Alaska's Arctic Natural Wildlife Reserve (ANWR), and when alarmists classify CO_2 as an endangering pollutant to promote lucrative cap-and-trade legislation and otherwise unwarranted alternative energy subsidies. What if these representations lack any sound scientific basis? Is that okay?

The Hot Spin Cycle

Cyclical, abrupt, and dramatic global and regional temperature fluctuations have occurred over millions of years, long before humans invented agriculture, industries, automobiles, and carbon-trading schemes. Many natural factors are known to contribute to these changes, although even our most sophisticated climate models have failed to predict the timing, scale (either up or down), impacts, or human influences. While theories abound, there is no consensus, as claimed, that "science is settled" on any of those theories—much less is there consensus about the human influences upon or threat implications of climate change.

Among these hypotheses, man-made global warming caused by burning fossils has been trumpeted as an epic crisis. CO_2, a "greenhouse gas," has been identified as a primary culprit and branded as an endangering "pollutant." This, despite the fact that throughout Earth's history the increases in the atmospheric CO_2 level have tended to follow, not lead, rising temperatures. It should also be understood that CO_2 accounts for only 0.04 of 1 percent of the atmosphere, and about 97 percent of that tiny trace amount comes from naturally occurring sources that humans haven't influenced.

The big lie is that we are living in a known climate change crisis. Climate warming and cooling have occurred throughout the ages. Is the Earth warming right now? Probably not, but what if it is? It might be cooling next year. The models that predict a crisis are speculative at best, and two recent events have cast even more doubt on their accuracy. One relates to undisputable evidence that influential members of the climate science community have cooked the books to advance their theories and marginalize contrary findings. The other problem is evidence provided directly by Mother Nature herself that the global climate appears to have entered a new cooling cycle.

Public exposure of hacked e-mail files retrieved from the Climate Research Unit (CRU) at Britain's University of East Anglia revealed scandalous communications among researchers who have fomented global warming hysteria. Their exchanges confirm long-standing and broadly suspected manipulations of climate data. Included are conspiracies to falsify and withhold information, to suppress contrary findings in scholarly publications, and to exaggerate the existence and threats of man-made global warming. Many of these individuals have had major influence over summary report findings issued by the United Nations' IPCC. This organization has been recognized as the world authority on such matters, and it shares a Nobel Prize with Al Gore for advancing climate change awareness.

Among the more than three thousand purloined CRU documents is an e-mail from its director, Philip Jones, regarding a way to fudge the data to hide evidence of temperature declines: "I've just completed Mike's *Nature* [journal] trick of adding the real temperatures to each series for the past 20 years [i.e., from 1981 onward] and from 1961 for Keith's *to hide the decline* [emphasis mine]." "Mike," in this instance, refers to climatologist Michael Mann, who created the now infamous "hockey stick" chart that has repeatedly appeared in IPCC reports, as well as in Al Gore promotions, to portray accelerated global warming beginning with the Industrial Revolution—hence, caused by humans. The chart has been thoroughly debunked thanks to careful analyses by two Canadian researchers who uncovered a variety of serious problems. Included are calculation errors, data used twice, and a computer program that produced a hockey stick out of whatever data was fed into it.[1]

Some of the e-mails reveal less than full public candor about what scientists don't know about past temperatures. For example, one from Edward Cook, director of tree ring research at the Lamont-Doherty Earth Laboratory, to CRU's deputy director Keith Briffa on September 3, 2003, admitted that little could be deduced regarding past Northern Hemisphere temperatures from the tree ring proxy data Mann used: "We can probably say a fair bit about [less than] 100-year extra-tropical NH temperature variability . . . but honestly know f**k-all [expletive deleted] about what the [more than] 100-year variability was like with any certainty."

Correspondence leaves no doubt that the members of the network were concerned the cooling since 1998 they had observed would be publicly exposed. In an October 26, 2008, note from CRU's Mick Kelly to Jones, he comments, "Yeah, it wasn't so much 1998 and all that I was concerned about, used to dealing with that, but the possibility that we might be going through a longer 10-year period of relatively stable temperatures . . ." He added, "Speculation but if I see this possibility, then others might also. Anyway, I'll maybe cut the last few points off the filtered curve before I give the talk again as that's trending down as a result of the effects and the recent cold-ish years."

Another e-mail to Michael Mann (which James Hansen at NASA was copied on), sent by Kevin Trenberth, head of the Climate Analysis Section of the US National Center for Atmospheric Research, reflected exasperation concerning a lack of global warming evidence: "Well, I have my own article on where the heck is global warming. We are asking here in Boulder where we have broken records the past two days for the coldest days on record. We had four inches of snow." He continued, "The fact is that we can't account for the lack of warming at the moment, and it is a travesty that we can't . . . the data is surely wrong. Our observing system is inadequate."[2]

Trenberth, an advisory IPCC high priest and man-made global warming spokesperson, didn't waste a publicity opportunity to link a devastating 2005 US hurricane season to this cause. After ignoring admonitions from top expert Christopher Landsea that this assumption was not supported by known research, Trenberth proceeded with the unfounded claim that dominated world headlines.

Clearly, members of the CRU e-mail network used their considerable influence to block the publication of research by climate crisis skeptics, thus preventing inclusion of contrary findings in IPCC reports. In one e-mail, Tom Wigley, a senior scientist and Trenberth associate at the National Center for Atmospheric Research, shared his disdain for global warming challengers, common among global warming proponents: "If you think that [Yale professor James] Saiers is in the greenhouse skeptics camp, then, if we can find documentary evidence of this, we could go through official [American Geophysical Union] channels to get him ousted."[3]

Possibly one of the most serious and legally hazardous breaches of professional accountability is seen in an e-mail from Jones to Mann concerning withholding of taxpayer-supported scientific data: "If they ever hear there is a Freedom of Information Act now in the UK, I think I'll delete the file rather than send it to anyone." He then asks Mann to join him in deleting official IPCC-related files: "Can you delete any e-mails you may have had with Keith re: AR4 [the IPCC's Fourth Assessment Report]?" A different e-mail from Jones assures Mann of the way some troublesome contrarian research will be handled: "I can't see either of these papers being in the next IPCC report. Kevin and I will keep them out somehow, even if we have to redefine what the peer-reviewed process is!"

A Jones letter to his colleagues instructed them, "Don't any of you three tell anyone that the UK has a Freedom of Information Act." Still another stated, "We also have a data platform act, which I will hide behind."

The CRU fallout is spreading: It now includes broader allegations by a Russian scientific group that climate-change data obtained from that country has been cherry-picked to overstate a rise in temperatures. Russia accounts for a large portion of the world's landmass, and incorrect data there would affect overall global temperature analyses.

Two things are clear from the CRU emails: (1) Perpetrators of climate science fraud have routinely conspired to exaggerate temperature increases since the Industrial Revolution, and (2) these same perpetrators virtually ignored comparable and even warmer times that preceded this period, as well as prolonged temperature declines since this period, that contradict greenhouse theory and model predictions. Other explanations that conform much more closely to observed fluctuations have been dismissed or aggressively attacked. These practices have produced unsupportable alarmist statements trumpeted in the world press that continue to influence multitrillion-dollar US and international policy decisions—decisions based upon a contrived crisis of hysteria . . . a climate of corruption.

Chilling News for "Warm-Mongers"

The climate is always changing, in long and short cycles, and mankind has survived and thrived in conditions that have varied greatly from what they are right now.

It is apparent that our planet is once again experiencing a global cooling trend, just as it did quite recently between 1940 and 1975, when warnings of a coming new ice age received front-page coverage in the *New York Times* and other major publications. NASA satellite measurements of the lower atmosphere, where warming greenhouse models predicted effects would be greatest, stopped rising as a decadal trend after 1998 *despite increased levels of CO_2*. Measurements recorded by four major temperature-tracking outlets showed that world temperatures plummeted by more than 1 degree Fahrenheit (1°F) during 2007. This cooling approached the total of all the warming that had occurred over that past 100 years. In other words, temperatures worldwide and collectively never rose more than 1°F in a century. 2008 was significantly colder than 2007 had been. Although models predicted that the year 2008 would be one of the warmest on record, it actually ranked fourteenth coldest since satellite records commenced in 1979, and the coldest since 2000.[4]

If ordinary citizens don't receive or heed scientific reports, many may legitimately question global warming assertions from direct experience. Take the year 2007, for example. North America had the most snow it's recorded in the past 50 years. A Boston storm in December dumped 10 inches of snow, more than the city typically receives in that entire month, and Madison, Wisconsin, had the highest seasonal snowfall since record keeping began.[5] Record cold temperatures were recorded in Minnesota, Texas, Florida, and Mexico.

Those trends continued into the following 2 years. During October 2008, Oregon temperatures mid-month dipped to record lows, and Boise, Idaho, received its earliest-ever recorded snowfall. December 2008 witnessed 3.6 inches of snow in the Las Vegas Valley, the most to have fallen at that time of year since 1938, when record keeping began. Houston witnessed its earliest-ever recorded snowfall on December 4, 2009.[6]

A blizzard on February 20, 2010, broke a Washington, DC, 110-year-old annual snowfall record of 55 inches as well as seasonal records in Baltimore and Philadelphia.[7] Then, on February 26 and 27, another storm that pummeled New York City for 2 days broke a monthly snowfall record (37 inches) in Central Park that had stood for 114 years; the previous record for February was 28 inches in 1934, and the largest for any month was 30.5 inches in March 1896.[8]

Most people's perceptions about warming and cooling trends depend on where they happen to reside and the time range they have experienced for reference. During July 2010, those throughout New England witnessed temperatures among the ten warmest recorded during that month in about a century, while temperatures in southeastern US states registered below normal. Simultaneously, Los Angeles broke a coldest July day record set in 1926, Australia since 1966, and the southern cone of South America saw the coldest July in half a century.[9] Freezing temperatures in eastern Bolivia (normally above 68°F) killed millions of fish in three major rivers, characterized there as an environmental catastrophe.[10]

Going back to 2007, Baghdad saw its first snowfall ever recorded, and China experienced its coldest winter in 100 years. Record cold temperatures were also recorded in Argentina, Chile, and yes, even Greenland. The end of 2007 set a record for the largest Southern Hemisphere sea ice expanse since satellite altimeter monitoring began in 1979, it was about 1 million square kilometers more than the previous 28-year average. In 2008, Durban, South Africa, had its coldest September night in history, and parts of that country experienced an unusual late-winter snow. A month earlier, New Zealand officials at Mount Ruapehu reported the largest snow accumulation ever.[11]

According to records collected by NASA, the National Oceanographic and Atmospheric Administration (NOAA), and the Hadley Centre for Climate Change,

2008 was cooler than 2007, making it the coldest year thus far of the 21st century. And this has occurred while atmospheric CO_2 levels have continued to rise.[12]

This picture is far different from much of the information presented in the media. As a case in point, a 2008 Associated Press report claimed that the 10 warmest days recorded have occurred since the time of President Bill Clinton's second inaugural in January 1997. The report quoted James Hansen, who heads NASA's Godard Institute for Space Studies (GISS); Hansen is a principal adviser to Al Gore and has been a primary source of much global warming alarmism. NASA later issued corrections. In reality, the warmest recorded days—in descending order—occurred in 1934, 1998, 1921, 2006, 1931, 1934, 1953, 1990, 1938, and 1939. As Jay Lehr, a senior fellow and science director at the Heartland Institute, stated on CNN's *Lou Dobbs Tonight* program in December 2008, "If we go back in really recorded human history, in the 13th century we were probably 7 degrees Fahrenheit warmer than we are now."[13]

Bear in mind that monthly, annual, decadal and much longer temperature fluctuations are fundamental aspects of Earth's dynamic climate history. Also remember that incredibly complex and interactive mechanisms and effects of those changes are geographically distributed in ways that confound global generalization. Most recently, NOAA's National Climatic Data Center reported that March, April, May and June of 2010 set records for the warmest year worldwide since record-keeping began in 1880. However, June was actually cooler than average across Scandinavia, southeastern China, and the northwestern US according to the same report.[14]

NOAA ground stations reported the June average to be 1.22°F higher than normal, while NASA satellite data showed the average to be only 0.79°F above a 20-year average. This made June 2010 the second warmest in the short 32-year satellite temperature record, and the first six months of 2010 were also the second warmest. So what can we really deduce from all of this to predict a trend? Not much of anything, and certainly nothing to be alarmed about.

Climate, Carbon, and Conspirators

So, who stands to gain from climate science corruption? There are many culprits, and they are becoming ever more powerful. Principal among these are certain agenda-driven federal government regulatory agencies, alternative energy and environmental lobbies, and yes, the UN and other organizations that seek global resource and wealth redistribution. Many of these organs of misinformation are joined at a common colon.

The IPCC has long served as the authoritative source of alarmist climate change predictions cited in media and activist warm-mongering campaigns. A richly funded example is Al Gore's Alliance for Climate Protection (ACP), which has routinely enlisted celebrities in advertising for united action against a "climate crisis." In reality, the IPCC only conducts literature reviews, although many of the publications it selectively cites are produced by the same influential people that author its reports. Moreover, illuminating CRU e-mails revealed that a small group within that organization actively worked to prevent research findings that contradicted their biases from being published in leading journals, hence blocking dissenting views from being reviewed and cited in IPCC reports.

Global warming doom-speakers and promoters of fossil energy alternatives are united behind carbon-capping politics. Climate change alarm drives the development and marketing of technologies that are otherwise uncompetitive without major government support. Unwarranted climate fear, combined with legitimate public concern about fossil-fuel depletion and dependence upon foreign oil, is promoted to justify to taxpayers and consumers the use of more costly energy options. Media campaigns portray images of dying polar bears as fossil fuel–generated carbon casualties to support arguments against drilling in ANWR and, by association, other national oil and natural gas reserves. Fossil-fuel prices rise higher, assisted by massive CO_2 sequestration costs and de facto cap-and-trade taxes, so consumers pay more, making alternatives seem all the more attractive.

Does it seem remarkable that the US Environmental Protection Agency (EPA) applied a global warming argument to declare that CO_2, the natural molecule essential for all plant life, is a "pollutant"? Might that possibly have to do with a larger agenda supported by the EPA and other organizations, such as wind and solar power lobbies and prospective carbon brokers, to limit fossil fuel use by requiring costly carbon sequestration, in turn making alternatives more price competitive, justifying subsidies, and supporting cap-and-trade schemes? But of course, those purposes wouldn't fall within EPA responsibilities, would they? And they wouldn't make any sense at all if man-made carbon emissions didn't pose a dire climate threat.

Yet consider the implications of the suppressed EPA "Internal Study on Climate" report that was kept under wraps, its author silenced, due to pressure to support the agency's agenda to regulate CO_2. Alan Carlin, a senior research analyst at the EPA's National Center for Environmental Economics (NCEE), had stated in that report that after examining numerous global warming studies, his research showed the available observable data to invalidate the hypothesis that humans cause dangerous global warming. He concluded, "Given the downward trend in temperatures since 1998 (which some think will continue until at least 2030), there is no particular reason to rush into decisions based upon a scientific hypothesis that does not appear to explain most of the available data."[15]

After serving with the EPA for 38 years, Alan Carlin was taken off climate-related work and was forbidden from speaking to anyone outside the organization on endangerment issues such as those in his then-suppressed report. A then-proposed "endangerment finding" under the Clean Air Act would enable the EPA to establish limits on CO_2 and other GHG concentrations as threats to public health, directly supporting cap-and-trade carbon regulations. That finding is now in force.

Bowing to pressure from global warming alarmists, the US Department of the Interior (DOI) placed polar bears on its Endangered Species Act list in 2008. Reported threats of massive melting in their habitats prompted this action. While the act's purview doesn't extend to actually regulating GHGs, there is little doubt that the classification establishes the species as poster cubs for the man-made global warming movement. It also supports environmentalist opposition to oil and gas drilling in ANWR.

But are polar bear populations really declining, as tragically depicted in Al Gore's film, *An Inconvenient Truth*? Apparently not, according to Mitchell Taylor, manager of Wildlife Research for the Government of the Canadian Territory of Nunavut, which monitors these conditions: "Of the thirteen populations of polar bears in Canada, eleven are stable or increasing in number. They are not going extinct [nor do they] even appear to be affected at present . . . [It is] silly to present the demise of polar bears based on media-assisted hysteria."[16]

Cap-and-trade legislation, a major priority of President Barack Obama's administration, has no defensible purpose without a supporting global warming rationale. It also makes no sense from an economic standpoint. It will place onerous cost burdens upon energy consumers, continue to drive businesses overseas, and offer no real climate or environmental benefits whatsoever. Such legislation will multiply the price of electricity by dramatically increasing coal plant construction and operating costs for CO_2 sequestration. While intended to make such "renewables" as wind and solar more attractive, even this legislation won't make them competitive without large tax-supported subsidies. A new stock exchange would then be created that treats ("bad") carbon as a valuable ("good") commodity, providing billions of profits for operators.

Al Gore, now a very wealthy "green energy" proponent, strongly lobbies for carbon-emission trading through a London-based hedge fund called Generation Investment. He cofounded the company with David Blood, former head of investment management at Goldman Sachs, which in turn is a large shareholder in the Chicago Climate Exchange, a "voluntary pilot agency" established in 2003 to advance trading in US carbon emissions. Both organizations are working hard to persuade governments to block new power plants that use fossils. Gore exuberantly told members at a March 2007 Joint House Hearing of the Energy and Science Committee: "As soon as carbon has a price, you're going to see a wave [of investment] in it . . . There will be unchained investment."[17]

Perhaps the most serious public deception perpetrated by this "war against climate change" (e.g., the carbon enemy) is the notion that cleaner, sustainable options are *available* in sufficient abundance to replace dependence upon fossil resources that currently provide about 85 percent of all US energy. Regrettably, this is broadly recognized not to be the case at all. Ironically, many of the same groups that champion environmental and human causes are inhibiting progress toward vital solutions.

Extravagantly funded media campaigns continue to advertise a "climate change crisis," despite obvious evidence that the Earth began cooling once more at least a decade ago. Meanwhile, America's energy and industrial progress is being held hostage by political and legal pressures applied by groups that no one elected to represent us, and industries and other businesses that provide jobs and revenues are being driven overseas. And, as artificially manipulated energy costs continue to add unsustainable burdens to already out-of-control government borrowing and spending deficits, those impacts will fall hardest upon people who can least afford them.

Section One

Setting the Records Straight

Global Temperatures Over Past 12,000 Years

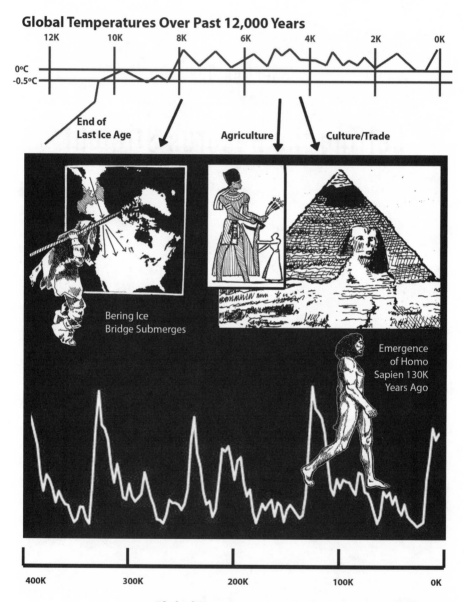

12K 10K 8K 6K 4K 2K 0K

0°C
-0.5°C

End of
Last Ice Age

Agriculture

Culture/Trade

Bering Ice
Bridge Submerges

Emergence
of Homo
Sapien 130K
Years Ago

400K   300K   200K   100K   0K

Global Temperatures Over Past 400,000 Years

Larry Bell

Chapter 1

THE CHICKEN LITTLE SYNDROME

Global Temperatures Over Past 1,000+ Years

Global Temperatures Over Past 120 Years

Former vice president (now Nobel laureate) Al Gore, *Time* magazine, and numerous other sources have proclaimed that the climate debate has officially ended. The Earth is warming, the consequences are dire, and humans—along with our technologies of destruction—are the cause. Our only hope, it seems, is to implement extremely stringent cap-and-trade legislation to drastically reduce horrifically polluting carbon dioxide (CO_2) emissions spewing from fossil-fueled smokestacks and to switch to clean energy alternatives that are claimed to be most assuredly abundant.

As I mentioned earlier, *Time*'s March 2006 cover proclaimed, "Global Warming: Be Worried, Be Very Worried." Polar ice caps are melting faster than ever; rising waters will flood coastal communities; more and more areas are being devastated by droughts; and by any measure, Earth is at the tipping point—all because of us.

Fear and guilt are powerful motivators for those who care, and most of us really do. Some who purport to be even more caring and knowledgeable about basic concerns we all share have become adept at pulling our guilt strings. Their tactics are often most effective when, with a pretense of superior moral authority, they project really horrific consequences onto that guilt. This brands doubters as deniers of inconvenient truths recognized by all truly smart and informed experts. Maybe you have heard some of that.

A basic tactic used by calculating "hysteria hypesters" is to treat propaganda as obvious fact. The Institute for Public Policy Research, a British think tank, has advocated a way to induce "mass behavior change" to combat global warming by nurturing a new "common sense": "[We] need to work in a more shrewd and contemporary way, using subtle techniques of engagement . . . The facts need to be treated as being so taken for granted that they need not be spoken . . . It amounts to treating climate-friendly activity as a brand that can be sold. This is, we believe, the route to mass behavior changes."[1]

Just how well are those guilt and scare tactics succeeding? An emerging market for "eco-therapists" who specialize in treating "eco-anxiety" suggests that those tactics are working quite well. For instance, a February 16, 2008, *New York Times* article reported that more than 120 of these specialists are now listed in the field of "ecopsychology" to help people who are excessively worried that their own carbon emissions are causing global warming. The International Community for Ecopsychology's definition refers to that term as "a synergetic relationship between planetary and personal well-being" and states that "the needs of one are relevant to the other." Some schools, including Lewis & Clark College in Portland, Oregon, have created courses on counseling such patients. Sarah Edwards explained to *Fox News* in April of that year that eco-anxiety (manifested in feelings of fear, grief, anger, confusion, and depression) caused her shoulder pain, fibromyalgia, and fatigue. Her reasoning may go pandemic: A British independent news source has reported that eco-anxiety has been blamed for symptoms ranging from overeating and bulimia to depression and even alcoholism.[2]

This seems to raise another threat for Mr. Gore to consider: Is it possible that rising CO_2 levels are making people crazy?

All this might seem comical if not for the fact that a number of people are deeply troubled with alarm and guilt about human impacts upon climate change. A particularly tragic case involved an Argentine family. In March 2010, Francisco Lotero and Miriam Coletti shot two of their children before killing themselves after making an apparent suicide pact over fears about effects of global warming. Although their 2-year-old son, Francisco, died instantly, their unnamed 7-month-old infant daughter remarkably survived.

Galloping Glaciers

This isn't the first time that prominent news publishers, supported by scientific experts, have warned us about perils of uncorrected climate changes. On October 7, 1912, for example, the *Los Angeles Times* alerted readers, "Fifth Ice Age Is on the Way: Human Race Will Have to Fight for Existence in Cold." By August 9, 1923, the situation had already become desperate, causing the *Chicago Tribune* to declare on its front page, "Scientist Says Arctic Ice Will Wipe Out Canada." A complementary story posited that huge parts of Asia and Europe were also threatened. The world soon appeared to be warming again by the 1930s, however, causing some scientists and news reporters to suggest that CO_2 might be the cause.

By the 1940s, it became apparent that global mean temperatures had begun to fall once again, which through the 1970s led to concerns that the Earth was once more heading toward a new Ice Age. Advancing glaciers presented renewed threats to human settlements in Alaska, Iceland, Canada, China, and the Soviet Union.

In 1973, *Science Digest* concluded, "At this point we do not have the comfortable distance of tens of thousands of years to prepare for the next Ice Age, and that how carefully we monitor our atmospheric pollution will have direct bearing on the arrival and nature of this weather crisis." Consequently, the scientists warned, "Once the freeze starts, it will be too late."[3]

In a June 1974 article titled "Another Ice Age?" *Time* observed, "When meteorologists take an average of temperatures around the globe, they find the atmosphere has been gradually cooler for the past three decades . . . and the weather aberrations they are studying may be the harbinger of another Ice Age."[4]

The March 1, 1975, cover of the respected *Science News* magazine depicted the city of New York being swallowed by an approaching glacier and announced, "The Ice Age Cometh." The threat was clear and urgent: "Again, this transition would induce only a small change in global temperature—two or three degrees—but the impact on civilization would be catastrophic." The *New York Times* followed suit with a headline story: "Scientists Ponder Why World's Climate Is Changing; A Major Cooling Widely Considered to Be Inevitable."[5]

The prestigious National Academy of Sciences agreed with this view. In 1975, it issued a warning that there was a "finite possibility that a serious worldwide cooling could befall the Earth within the next 100 years."[6] Popular publications echoed and amplified the alarm. The title of a book by science writer Lowell Ponte, published that same year, pretty much summed up the crisis: *The Cooling: Has the Next Ice Age Already Begun? Can We Survive It?* He warned that "global cooling presents humankind with the most important social, political, and adaptive challenge we have had to deal with for 110,000 years."[7] *The Genesis Strategy*, published a year later, had a similar message. Noteworthy is that the author, Stephen Schneider, has subsequently changed his course of concern 180 degrees and has now become a prominent global warming authority. The same shift of position is true for Crispin Tickell, who wrote *Climate Change and World Affairs* (published in 1977), an influential book of that period.

A New Crisis Emerges

By the late 1970s, observed rising world temperatures heralded the coming of new media sensations. Climate model calculations, including some at Princeton's Geophysical Fluid Dynamic Laboratory, began to predict that substantial global warming could result from increasing atmospheric CO_2 levels. At the time, those projections were generally regarded to be an interesting but largely academic exercise, even by many of the scientists involved. But about 10 years later the theory gained worldwide attention following testimony in 1988 by NASA's James Hansen before then-Senator Al Gore's Committee on Science, Technology and Space. When queried by Gore (D-TN), Hansen stated that he was 99 percent certain that temperatures had in fact increased, and that there had been some greenhouse warming, although he made no direct connection between the two. This observation was consistent with concerns about a particularly warm summer that year in some US regions.

The scheduling and staging of Senator Gore's hearings were carefully orchestrated. As later recounted by his co planner Senator Timothy Wirth (D-CO) in an interview with PBS *Frontline*: "We called the Weather Bureau and found out what historically was the hottest day of the summer…so we scheduled the hearing that day, and bingo, it was the hottest day on record in Washington, or close to it…we went in the night before and opened all the windows so that the air conditioning wasn't working inside the room."[8]

Although the general response within the small community of scientists engaged in large-scale climate research was critical regarding use of highly uncertain model results as a basis for determining important public policy decisions, many did agree that increased atmospheric CO_2 levels could possibly have influenced the changes in temperature. Their agreement, however, did not warrant the greatly exaggerated claims that began to appear in the popular US and European media by early 1989 that "all scientists" agreed that warming was real and had catastrophic potential.

Scientists who took issue with these "objective facts" were often subjected to painful consequences. Lester Lave, a professor of economics at Carnegie Mellon University, reported that he was dismissed from one of the hearings for even suggesting the global warming issue was controversial. The late Reginald Newell, a meteorology professor at MIT, believed that he had lost National Science Foundation funding for data analyses that were failing to show net warming over the past century because reviewers suggested his results were dangerous to humanity.

As the Cold War ended in the late 1980s, the Union of Concerned Scientists, an organization originally devoted to nuclear disarmament, actively turned its attention to the new cause. In 1989, they circulated a much-publicized petition that was published in the *New York Times,* urging recognition of global warming as a potentially great danger to mankind. Seven hundred scientists, including many members of the National Academy of Sciences and some Nobel laureates, signed that petition. Merely three or four of the signers, however, had any involvement with climatology.

The article helped to solidify the desired public perception that all scientists agree with the global warming disaster scenario.[9]

In specific reference to the petition, the president of the National Academy of Sciences warned its members at their 1990 annual meeting not to lend their credibility to issues about which they have no special knowledge. His warning came too late: Exaggerated claims based upon meager scientific evidence had already become the gospel for a new religious fervor. Claudine Schneider, a US congresswoman from Rhode Island, expressed the tenets of the new orthodoxy at a 1989 Tufts University global warming symposium when she said, "Scientists may disagree, but we can hear Mother Earth, and she is crying." What caring person would want that? After all, scientists are people too.

Political pressures on global warming dissidents increased when Senator Gore admonished skeptics in a featured *New York Times* op-ed piece and associated "true believers" with Galileo. In another article, he compared the warm summer of 1988 to *Kristallnacht*, which ushered in the Holocaust.

Well-known entertainment figures joined politicians and activist groups to rally more followers: In 1989, Robert Redford proclaimed at a meeting he hosted at his Sundance, Utah, ranch that it was time to stop the research and begin acting (a subject he was more familiar with). Barbra Streisand financially supported the research of Michael Oppenheimer (at the Environmental Defense Fund), who was a global warming activist, not a climatologist. Meryl Streep presented an impassioned public television appeal to stop warming. There should be no doubt that their pleas were truly sincere and caring. Perhaps this applies to many others termed "skeptics" (agnostics) and, even worse, "deniers" (atheists) as well? Can't they be sincere and caring environmentalists, too?

Wages of War

The April 2008 cover feature of *Time* drew a direct and unseemly parallel between US involvement in World War II against Nazi Germany and Japan and the current battle against climate change. The famous image of five American Marines raising a flag at Iwo Jima following a terrible 35-day battle during which sixty-eight hundred American soldiers were killed was changed to depict the Marines planting a tree, and the caption read, "How to Win the War on Global Warming."

Climate war marketing has become a large business, and it's becoming much bigger with substantial help from an organization founded by Al Gore, called the Alliance for Climate Protection (ACP). The alliance has launched a $300 million climate crisis media campaign over a 3-year period to promote GHG reductions through a new international treaty, US legislation, and other initiatives. Advertisements are already appearing in nationwide television, print, radio, and online media, targeted to diverse audiences. As Al Gore stated, "NASCAR fans, churchgoers, labor-union members, small businessmen, engineers, hunters, spokesmen, corporate leaders, you name it—where public opinion goes, federal policy will follow." An example is an early television segment, narrated by William H. Macy, showing footage of American soldiers storming beaches at Normandy during World War II, a civil rights march, and a Moon landing. The message links these critical points in history to an urgent need for action now: "We can't wait for someone else to solve the climate crisis. We need to act, and we need to act now. Join us. Together we can solve the climate crisis."[10]

And the solution? Although the message doesn't quite tell us, it's actually very clear: We should all support the war against climate change. And the answer, of course, is to support carbon cap-and-trade legislation and alternative energy subsidies.

Although major donor sources are not known, it is understood that large ACP contributions have been provided by from such billionaire luminaries as George Soros; CNN founder Ted Turner; Sun Microsystems cofounder Vinod Khoska; and Apple CEO Steve Jobs. (Mr. Gore sits on Apple's board of directors.)[11] Al Gore is contributing his salary as a partner in the venture capital firm of Kleiner Perkins Caufield & Byers to the alliance, along with his Nobel winnings ($750,000) and proceeds from his movie and his book, *An Inconvenient Truth.* This does not include the investment income he garners from Kleiner (much greater than salary and taxed at lower than ordinary income rates), yet his strong personal commitment to alliance's goals is irrefutable. There should be no doubt regarding his genuine dedication to the cause.[12]

At least you have to give Al Gore credit for putting his money where his mouth is, while also feeding it from profits he receives from the climate change war. For example, he has invested $35 million with the Capricorn Investment Group, a firm that *Bloomberg News* says puts clients' assets into hedge funds and invests in "makers of environmentally friendly products." Capricorn was founded by billionaire Jeffrey Skoll, who produced Mr. Gore's "documentary," *An Inconvenient Truth.* That's quite a large sum for someone whose estimated total assets in 2000 were between $800,000 and $1.9 million.[13]

Since his nonelection to the presidency, Mr. Gore has been very successful as an eco-multimillionaire, with an estimated net worth well in excess of $100 million. In addition to his six-figure speaking gigs, he signed on as an adviser to Google in 2001—before it went public—and received stock options now reportedly valued at more than $30 million. When he joined Apple's board in 2003, he received stock options believed to be valued now at about $6 million. In 2004, Mr. Gore and some partners purchased the Canadian news network *News World International (NWI)* for $70 million and renamed it *Current TV*. His investment partners were former Goldman Sachs senior director Philip Murphy (Democratic Finance Committee chair); Richard Blum (husband of California senator Dianne Feinstein); Sun Microsystems cofounder Bill Joy; and Bill Pittman, former AOL Time Warner CEO.[14]

Fast Money, in an article titled "Al Gore's $100 Million Makeover," quotes Philip Murphy's recollections of the time in 2003 when Mr. Gore was struggling to launch the *Current TV* cable network and also starting a hedge fund (now with more than a billion dollars in assets) called Generation Investment Management (GIM). According to Gore, both were created with a desire "to incorporate sustainability values into the financial-services work I was doing." Murphy had introduced Gore to his GIM partner, David Blood, formerly with Goldman Sachs, and "they were asking, 'can this make money? Can this be a business?'" Apparently, the answer was (and still is) strongly affirmative.[15]

Good News! It's Terrifying—and It's Our Fault!

Government, corporate, and private climate change research funding depends upon delivering results the sponsors want. What if it turned out that climate change follows natural cycles, and for good or for bad, we don't have a lot to say or do about it? That would qualify as a true climate change disaster for thousands of scientists, administrators, and their families, whose work and lives have come to depend upon causes that are anthropogenic (resulting from the influence of human beings on nature; hereafter used interchangeably with "man-made").

Let there be no mistake: As most of us recognize, environmental scientists are among Earth's most dedicated and caring inhabitants—people who are as principled and ethical as humans come. Few, if any, selected their profession for its financial potential, and their education and competencies warrant true respect. Many are associated with universities and others with government agencies. They write scholarly papers; compete for publishing opportunities in selective journals; present peer-reviewed papers at global conferences; spend countless hours writing grant proposals; and yes, participate in the United Nations' IPPC scientific working groups. Okay. Enough pandering.

The stark reality is that climate sciences have become strongly politicized over the global warming issue. Some of the strongest proponents of human-caused climate change theories in Congress, for example, are among the strongest supporters of those funding programs. Government agencies that receive and distribute these funds find it necessary to demonstrate that threats are real and urgent in order to justify budgets and demonstrate public benefits. Philanthropic organizations routinely give out large sums of research money on the same alarmist basis. An example is the MacArthur Foundation, which earmarks $500,000 no-strings-attached grants for climatologists who speak out about global warming threats.[16]

An inescapable fact is that climate change politics has had apparent partisan leanings. Climate Science Watch (a nonprofit public interest education and advocacy project "dedicated to holding public officials accountable for the integrity and effectiveness with which they use climate science and related research in government policymaking") has been strongly critical of US Climate Change Science Program (CCSP) cutbacks under Republican influences since the program peaked in 1995. That was when Republicans gained control of both houses of Congress. In February 2002, the first year the George W. Bush administration gained major influence over the federal budget, interagency climate research budgets were reduced to 1993 levels. Then, after the 2006 election cycle brought a new Democratic majority in both the House and the Senate, the dynamic changed to restore more funding to the "starved" climate programs and create new ones through twelve different 2008 bills approved by the Senate Appropriations Committee. Various Office of Management and Budget (OMB) reports projected CCSP increases of $155 million for February 2007 and $282 million for 2008.[17]

A National Academy of Sciences/National Research Council analysis report reviewing CCSP funding cutbacks under the Bush-Cheney administration wasn't positive; it concluded that "U.S. capability to monitor trends, document the impacts of future climate change, and further improve prediction and assimilation models . . . will decline even as the urgency of addressing climate change increases." This conclusion is not surprising. The National Academy of Sciences has always enthusiastically supported expensive climate research programs, and it has taken strong stances supporting both global cooling and global warming models, shifting positions in concert with weather patterns. The academy, along with the numerous institutions it represents, depends upon billions of federal dollars to fund thousands of research projects, tens of thousands of PhD degrees (along with many more associate positions), and dozens of professional journals that publish the results.[18]

Democrats and Democrat-backed institutions are almost invariably the ones who support the United Nations' efforts to use global warming to promote worldwide wealth redistribution. It is ironic to see IPCC political officials challenging the objectivity of scientists who don't subscribe to their clearly demonstrated and well-documented biases. A case in point is when their "Climate Change 1995 Summary for Policymakers" report stated they had found a "human fingerprint" as evidence of anthropogenic global warming. The author of that particular science chapter, a US government employee, finally publicly admitted to having made "backroom" changes under pressure from top US governmental officials. The report had been edited to remove five different statements—all of which had been approved by the panel's scientific consultants—that had specifically said no such evidence had been found. The IPCC, to this day, has never offered real evidence to support its assertion that humans are causing global warming.[19] Yet without humans as the cause of global warming, there is no way to develop widespread support for the global warming funding bonanza.

US Climate Science: Growth of a New Industry

Global warming, aka climate change, has been a natural blessing to government agencies and researchers that undertake climate science research. Growth of US government funding in this new industry has been phenomenal: It increased from $209 million in 1989, when the subject first began to heat up following then-Senator Gore's 1988 Committee on Science, Technology and Space hearings, to a proposed $1.446 billion (in 2005 dollars) in 2008. That's nearly a 200 percent rise. The largest player in this arena in 2008 was NASA ($816 million in 2008), followed by the National Science Foundation ($145 million), the US Department of Commerce and NOAA ($163 million), and the US Department of Energy (DOE; $122 million). Comparatively paltry budgets were awarded to the US Department of Agriculture ($55 million), the DOE's Office of Health, Safety and Security ($47 million), and the EPA ($17 million), plus a few others.[20]

Notably, the EPA's climate budget has since become much more generous, with $112 million included by the Obama-Biden administration for FY 2010.

That's only part of it. According to a 2007 press release by the White House Office of Science and Technology, the US was already spending about $5 billion per year on climate research through various programs. This was more than twice the amount spent on sending humans to the Moon during the Apollo program (about $2.3 billion per year). But then, the Moon doesn't have a climate to study, and even if it did, we probably couldn't blame the Industrial Revolution for changing it.[21]

Climate change began to capture the attention of US security organizations following the Yom Kippur Arab-Israeli war of 1973 because of this nation's increasing concerns about continued dependence upon foreign oil imports. This provided the foundation for expanded government investment in science programs that connected energy priorities with environmental issues that have broad public appeal and support. "Saving the planet" has become a popular theme to justify expanding budgets.[22]

NASA brought satellite Earth surface and atmospheric sensing capabilities to climate science research, applying technologies and expertise from the Mercury and Gemini programs of the 1960s. Its 2008 climate change research budget in constant 2005 dollars was more than thirty-five times larger than was reported in 1989, but it was reduced in 2006 by about 6 percent below the 2005 level.

One of the casualties of NASA's climate science cutbacks was the Deep Space Climate Observatory (DSCOVR) satellite proposed in 1998 by then-Vice President Gore for Earth observations. Republican critics derided the $100 million system, nicknamed "GoreSat," as an "overpriced screensaver" with unfocused purposes; it has since been held in storage at the cost of $1 million per year.

The most outspoken critic of NASA's priorities and the Bush-Cheney administration's climate change policies was James Hansen (who, as I mentioned earlier, was Gore's star global warming testifier at his 1988 Senate hearings). In his capacity as director of GISS, Dr. Hansen expressed his disagreement very strongly during a 2004 speech at the University of Iowa, where he also publicly announced his support for the presidential campaign of Senator John Kerry (D-MA). In 2001, Hansen had been the recipient of a $250,000 award from the Heinz Foundation, headed by Senator Kerry's wife, Teresa Heinz, a circumstance that made the political endorsement by a prominent NASA civil servant appear particularly suspect.

Hansen was never the least bit hesitant about speaking out against the Bush administration and NASA policies regarding global warming in general and their lack of support for aggressive GHG abatement measures in particular.[23] In a January 29, 2006, interview published in the *New York Times,* he charged that NASA public relations officials had pressured him to allow them to review future public lectures, papers, and postings on the GISS website. This followed a December 6, 2005, presentation he gave to the American Geophysical Union, during which he stated that the Earth's climate is approaching a tipping point that will result in the loss of the Arctic as we know it, with sea levels rising as much as 80 feet and thus flooding coastal areas. He warned that this could be halted only if GHG emissions are reduced within the next 25 years.[24]

And that was the good news. In a paper titled "Is There Still Time to Avoid Disastrous Effects?" presented at a Climate Change Research Conference held in Sacramento, California, on September 13, 2006, Hansen added hellfire for the damned: "Melting ice caps will raise sea levels by between 32 and 78 feet, forcing millions to seek refuge; increasingly violent weather patterns will cause major destruction and as the land dries up, bush fires will be more frequent."

After the master of disaster claimed to have received threats of recrimination for continuing to speak out, he was offered support by two organizations. One was the Government Accountability Project, a Washington, DC, law firm that volunteered legal support in a suit against NASA. The other was George Soros through his Open Society Institute (OSI), as part of its Politicization of Science program. (Yes, that's what they really call it!) As reported in a September 24, 2007, editorial published in the *Investor's Business Daily,* titled "The Soros Threat to Democracy," OSI may have supported Hansen to the tune of up to $750,000 out of that fund. Dr. Hansen has denied receiving any money, and there is no proof that he did. Yet he was listed as an "OSI grantee" in the "2006 Soros Foundation Network Report." George Soros, like Al Gore and John Kerry, was not a big George W. Bush fan.

The Science Unanimity Myth

Widely circulated statements that scientists unanimously agree about global warming and human contributions to it or the importance and consequences of it are patently false. The apparent purpose of such claims is to discredit those with opposing viewpoints, deriding them with contempt previously reserved for those who deny the Holocaust, the dangers of tobacco, and the achievements of NASA's Apollo program. Al Gore has little tolerance for unbelievers, as evidenced in this statement:

"Fifteen percent of the population believes the Moon landing was staged in a movie lot in America, and somewhat fewer believe the Earth is flat. I think they should all get together with the global warming deniers on a Saturday night and party."[25]

"Scientific consensus" representations attached to scary climate projections have played well to legitimize highly speculative research conclusions useful to justify additional funding, sell newspapers, and enhance television audience ratings. But several petitions and surveys involving science communities present a far from unified picture.[26]

- In 1992, a "Statement of Atmospheric Scientists on Greenhouse Warming" that opposed global controls on GHG emissions drew about 100 signatures, mostly from American Meteorological Society technical committee members.[27]

- In 1992, a "Heidelberg Appeal," which also expressed skepticism on the urgency of restraining GHG emissions, drew more than 4,000 signatures from scientists worldwide.[28]

- In 1996, a "Leipzig Declaration on Climate Change" that emerged from an international conference addressing the GHG controversy, was signed by more than 100 scientists in climatology and related fields.[29]

- In 1997, a survey of American state climatologists (the official climate monitors in each of the fifty states) found 90 percent agreed that "scientific evidence indicates variations in global temperatures are likely to be naturally occurring and cyclical over very long periods of time."[30]

- In 2001, the American Association of State Climatologists concluded that "climate prediction is complex, with many uncertainties; the AASC recognizes climate prediction is an extremely difficult undertaking. For time scales of a decade or more, understanding the empirical accuracy of such prediction—called verification—is simply impossible, since we have to wait a decade or more to assess the accuracy of the forecasts."[31]

- In May 2007, a survey of 530 climate scientists by the Heartland Institute revealed that only about one-half agreed that "climate change is mostly the result of anthropogenic causes," and only one-third of those agreed that "climate models can accurately predict conditions in the future."[32]

- In April 2008, the results of a survey of 489 scientists, conducted by the Statistical Assessment Service (STATS), indicated that most (74 percent) believed that some human-induced greenhouse warming has occurred, up from 41 percent reported in the 1991 Gallup survey. Only 41 percent of those polled, however, said they were directly involved in any aspect of global climate science.[33]

- In 2008, a US Senate minority report issued by Senator James Inhofe (R-OK) presents the testimony of 650 climate-related scientists from around the world who strongly challenge global warming crisis claims. They include a Nobel laureate and former IPCC study participants.

- In March 2009, more than 600 skeptical people attended a conference organized by the Heartland Institute in New York City to protest cap-and-trade regulations favored by President Obama that would roll GHG emissions back to 1990s levels. President Vaclav Klaus of Czech Republic delivered the keynote speech. Speaking again the next day to Columbia University faculty and students, he reaffirmed his strong opposition to a concept that global warming is man-made. "The problem is not global warming . . . by the ideology which uses or misuses it—it has gradually turned the most efficient vehicle for advocating extensive government intervention into all fields of life and for suppressing human freedom and economic prosperity."[34]

Scientific questions and disputes will never be resolved by opinion poll tabulations. If that were the case we might now be fleeing in seal-oil fueled snowmobiles the ravages of the miles-thick glaciers predicted a few decades ago. Yet it is disingenuous to suggest that the debate is over. Or if it is, that will come as a big disappointment to those with a few remaining contrary opinions that they may be required to abandon by majority vote. In fact, some man-made warming proponents are attempting to discredit skeptical scientific opinions out of existence altogether.

For instance, in a December 2004 article titled "Beyond the Ivory Tower: The Scientific Consensus on Climate Change," published in the journal *Science*, Naomi Oreskes, a University of California–San Diego history professor, reported that her search of the Internet under the term "climate change" turned up 928 studies, based on which she cheerfully concluded that there was complete scientific agreement.[35]

Few, if any, scientific papers claim to "refute" the theory of human-induced warming, and a search under the term "climate cycles" rather than "climate change" would have produced a different result. Hundreds of studies have been published that discuss potentially important and dominant natural forces that influence global warming and cooling over both short and very long periods, including solar climate-forcing factors (hereafter referred to at times simply as climate forcings).[36]

Issues of debate cannot be resolved by claims that a consensus among authorities has settled the matters so long as a minority, even a small one, believes otherwise. Objective science and progress have always been advanced by those who have proven that simple lesson.

If global warming crisis skeptics and deniers are heretics, they may perhaps take some comfort in the fact that their numbers are rapidly growing. This is particularly true in the US. A 2010 Gallup poll indicates that the percentage of respondents who said they worry "a great deal" about global warming was only 28 percent, down from 33 percent in 2009 and 41 percent in 2007, when worry peaked. Global warming ranked last of eight environmental issues listed in the survey.[37]

Gallup also conducted a 2010 poll that asked the question "Thinking about what is said in the news, in your view is the seriousness of global warming generally exaggerated, generally correct, or generally underestimated?" In just 4 years the percentage of Americans who believe global warming has been exaggerated has grown by 60 percent, constituting 48 percent of the respondents.[38]

Chapter 2

COOKING THE CLIMATE BOOKS

Departing from responsible science recipes.

LARRY BELL

N o one can confidently forecast global, national, or even regional weather conditions that will occur months or years into the future, much less predict climate changes and impacts that will be realized over decadal, centennial, and longer periods. Nevertheless, this broadly recognized limitation has not dissuaded doomsday climate predictions that have captured worldwide media attention. Such postulations attach great credence to extreme speculations, incomplete data, and overly simplistic computer models that have never demonstrated accuracy. Given the huge uncertainties, and under great pressures to produce definitive conclusions, modelers hedge many projections with probabilistic language that gets them off the hook of accountability. The pronouncements are typically cast as percentile chances that something or other may happen, or simply that such an event is more or less likely to happen than not. Truly alarming possibilities are usually treated as most newsworthy.

Fog in the Crystal Ball of Climate Forecasts

Scientists who study climate change phenomena generally fall into two professional camps. *Meteorologists* tend to recognize the inherent, almost biological complexity of the overall climate system and view it as resilient and "self-healing." As a group they are usually more skeptical about the importance of global warming and less confident about climate model results. *Physicists*, on the other hand, are accustomed to reducing the behavior of a physical system (e.g., climate) to a minimum number of mathematical equations in order to study it. They have a simpler view of climate forcings, and they tend to have more confidence in models as predictive tools.[1]

Even the most sophisticated climate models must be simplified to run on present-day computers, which aren't nearly fast enough to handle all known processes with a high level of definition. Not even really big, three-dimensional general circulation models (GCMs), which are capable of tracking more than 5 million different variables at any given time, can do the trick. Those variables include climate influences associated with these factors, among hundreds of others: upper atmosphere jet streams; deep ocean currents; variations in radiant energy from the Sun; amounts of solar radiation reflected back to space by ice sheets and glaciers; seasonal vegetation patterns; atmospheric GHG and aerosol changes; eddies in the oceans that transfer heat laterally; and numbers, types, and altitudes of clouds.[2]

Since GCMs must process enormous amounts of complex data, they require very expensive supercomputers that only wealthy national governments can afford. Prominent US systems are located at NASA's GISS, the US National Center for Atmospheric Research, NOAA's Geophysical Fluid Dynamics Laboratory, and Britain's Hadley Centre. Yet with all their computing power, even the EPA urges caution in taking results too literally: "These complicated models are able to simulate many features of the climate, but they are still not accurate enough to provide reliable forecasts of how the climate may change."[3]

Very small model errors associated with reference data, or underlying assumptions regarding climate-forcing mechanisms and interactions, can yield very large errors in outputs. Such errors are inescapable and expand rapidly as a function of the projected forecast period. Because the accuracy cannot be tested prior to that yet-unrealized future time, results are compared with those yielded by other modelers for general validation, although all these may be very wrong.

Roy Spencer, a principal research scientist at the University of Alabama, Huntsville, and former senior scientist for climate studies at NASA, observes that results of the one or two dozen climate modeling groups around the world often reflect a common bias. One reason is that many of these modeling programs are based upon the same "parameterization" assumptions; consequently, common errors are likely to be systematic, often missing important processes. Such problems arise because basic components and dynamics of the climate system aren't understood well enough on either theoretical or observational grounds to even put into the models. Instead, the models focus upon those factors and relationships that are most familiar, ignoring others altogether. As Spencer notes, "Scientists don't like to talk about that because we can't study things we don't know about."[4]

Joanne Simpson, who recently died at age eighty-six, developed some of the first mathematical models of clouds in attempts to better understand how hurricanes draw power from warm seas. Ranked as one of the world's top meteorologists, she believed that global warming theorists place entirely too much emphasis upon faulty climate models, stating: "We all know the frailty of models concerning the air-surface system . . . We only need to watch the weather forecasts."[5]

Another prominent scientist, Syun-Ichi Akasofu, is a staunch critic of certain parts of the United Nations' IPCC 2007 AR4 report "Summary for Policymakers." He determined that IPCC computer models could not duplicate observed temperature patterns in Arctic regions. Although the CO_2 forecasts did indicate a warm Arctic condition, they were lower than actually reported, and colder areas were absent. Dr. Akasofu stated, "If fourteen GCMs cannot reproduce prominent warming in the continental Arctic, perhaps much of this warming is not produced by greenhouse effect at all."[6]

Spencer coauthored a report of a scientific study that was published in *Science Daily* at the end of 2007. In the report he asserted that IPCC's computer models may be wildly overestimating man-made global warming due to a lack of understanding of the important roles that clouds play: "All leading climate models forecast that as the atmosphere warms there should be an increase in high-altitude cirrus clouds, which would amplify any warming caused by man-made GHGs . . . To give an idea how strong this enhanced cooling mechanism is, if it was operating on global warming it would reduce estimates of future warming by over 75 percent."[7]

NASA's GISS director, James Hansen, seems to have been well aware of this model problem when his organization, along with MIT, published a paper in the February 28, 2001, issue of the *Bulletin of the American Meteorological Society*. The authors of that paper explained that the Pacific Ocean "may be able to open a 'vent' in its heat-trapping cirrus cloud cover and release enough energy into space to significantly diminish the projected climate warming . . . This newly discovered effect—which is not seen in current prediction models—could significantly reduce estimates of future climate warming."[8]

Graeme Stephens of Colorado State University's Department of Atmospheric Science warned in a January 2005 paper, published in the *Journal of Climate*, that computer models involve simplistic cloud feedback descriptions: "Much more detail on the system and its assumptions [is] needed to judge the value of any study. Thus we are led to conclude that the diagnostic tools currently in use by the climate community to study feedback, at least as implemented, are problematic and immature and generally cannot be verified using observations."[9]

A peer-reviewed climate study that appeared in the July 23, 2009, edition of *Geophysical Research* is critical of IPCC modeling tendencies to fudge climate projections by exaggerating CO_2 influences and underestimating the importance of shifts in ocean conditions. The research indicated that influences of solar changes and intermittent volcanic activity have accounted for at least 80 percent of observed climate variation over the past half century. Study coauthor John McLean made this observation:

> When climate models failed to retrospectively produce the temperatures since 1950, the modelers added some estimated influences of carbon dioxide to make up the shortfall . . . The IPCC acknowledges in its fourth Assessment Report that [El Niño-Southern Oscillation] ENSO conditions cannot be predicted more than 12 months ahead, so the output of climate models that could not predict ENSO conditions were being compared to

temperatures during a period that was dominated by those influences. It's no wonder that model outputs have been so inaccurate, and it's clear that future modeling must incorporate the ENSO effect if it is to be meaningful.[10]

Even Kevin Trenberth, an exposed party in the University of East Anglia CRU "Climategate" scandal, has admitted that the IPCC climate models failed to duplicate realities. In 2007 he stated, "None of the models used by the IPCC are initialized to the observed state and none of the climate states in the models correspond even remotely to the current observed climate."[11]

Human CO_2 Fingerprints and Footprints

One reason why anthropogenic influences upon global climate change are extremely difficult to model is that there is no reliable way to separate human sources from natural ones. More generally, atmospheric measurement records are very short and exist against a background of other natural variables that have other unknown effects. For example, satellite spectral analyses of North Atlantic oscillations reveal a randomly varying climate pattern with little evidence of a persistent long-term trend influenced by man-made CO_2 contributions. Models have been shown to under-predict natural climate variations on decade-long to century-long timescales; to incorrectly predict variances over timescales in which anthropogenic CO_2 levels would be expected to rise; and to under-predict changes due to short-term natural influences. Such influences include volcanic eruptions, stratospheric ozone variations, sulfate aerosol changes, and solar change events.

It is important to realize that global temperatures and atmospheric CO_2 levels have fluctuated greatly over hundreds, thousands, and millions of years, long before humankind lit cave fires or Icelandic Vikings tended cattle, sheep, and goats on previously warm Greenland grasslands. In most cases, the temperature changes led, rather than followed, changes in atmospheric CO_2 levels—not the other way around.

Records of CO_2 levels and temperatures bear this out.

During the 149 years between 1812 and 1961 there were three periods when average CO_2 concentrations were higher than those when temperatures peaked in 2004. Circa 1820, they reached about 440 parts per million (ppm). Around 1855, they were about 390 ppm, and they returned to about 440 ppm in 1940 when man-made CO_2 emissions were nearly 30 times higher than they were in 1880 (such emissions are even higher than that now).[12]

Based upon a variety of proxy indicators, such as ice core samples, atmospheric CO_2 levels have remained relatively low over the past 650,000 years, even during the six previous interglacial periods when global temperatures were as much as 9°F warmer than the temperatures we currently enjoy. If this is true, might we legitimately wonder what accounted for those nonhuman greenhouse influences? It would seem to suggest that anthropogenic CO_2 contributions may have no discernible influence upon climate, or that proxy data is often inaccurate—or both.

Maurine Raymo, an MIT associate professor of earth, atmospheric, and planetary sciences, published a paper in the April 1988 issue of the journal *Nature*, suggesting that the Earth has endured huge climate swings on a number of occasions over the past 1.5 million years.[13] Records from ice cores and ocean sediments show that atmospheric CO_2 concentrations over this period have fluctuated greatly throughout Earth's history due to several natural causes. Levels of CO_2 rise and fall seasonally in response to warming and cooling effects of plant growth cycles. GHGs and aerosols emitted from volcanic eruptions, along with probable Earth orbit, solar changes, and other contributors, have combined heating and cooling effects. In turn, these forcing factors affect ocean temperatures, which influence evaporation rates (rainfall and plant growth) and the amount of atmospheric CO_2 absorbed and released. More CO_2 is dissolved at ocean surfaces, particularly in polar regions where water is coldest. Aerobic respiration by plants and animals breaks down glucose into CO_2 and water, while photosynthesis reverses the process. Huge deposits of limestone, marble, and chalk, mainly composed of calcium carbonate, are eroded by ocean water to produce CO_2 and carbonic acid. Climate change is thus very natural.[14]

Looking back over several million years in Earth's history, it is challenging to imagine that major global temperature swings can be attributed to man-made CO_2, or any CO_2 for that matter. It is apparent that past CO_2 levels have been high at times when global temperatures were low, and vice versa. During the eras when dinosaurs thrived, global temperatures ranged between 72°F and 77°F, a blistering 20 degrees higher than today's average between 54°F and 57°F.[15] So far as we know, none of those creatures, flatulent as they may have been, would have been responsible. And there is no evidence that they burned coal or drove SUVs.

Around 600 million years ago (during the Cambrian period of the Early Paleozoic era), atmospheric CO_2 levels were believed to be about 7,000 ppm, compared with the 379 ppm in 2005![16] Then, approximately 480 million years ago (between the Ordovician and Silurian periods), those levels gradually dropped to 4,000 ppm over about 100 million years, while average temperatures remained at a steady 72°F. The CO_2 levels later jumped rapidly to 4,500 ppm during the Late Ordovician period, and guess what! Temperatures dove to an estimated average similar to today, even though the CO_2 level was around twelve times higher than it is at present. Yes, as CO_2 went up, temperatures plummeted.

About 438 million years ago, atmospheric CO_2 dropped from 4,500 ppm to 3,000 ppm, yet according to fossil records, world temperatures shot rapidly back up to an average 72°F. So, regardless of whether the CO_2 levels were 7,000 ppm or 3,000 ppm, temperatures rose and fell independently.[17]

Also, over the past 600 million years there have been only three periods, including now, when Earth's average temperature has been as low as 54°F. One was the Late Ordovician period; the other occurred about 315 million years ago, during a 45-million-year-long cool spell called the Late Carboniferous period. Most of our planet's coalfields date back to that time. Both CO_2 and temperatures shot back up at the end of it, just as the main Mesozoic dinosaur era was beginning. CO_2 levels rose to between 1,200 ppm and 1,800 ppm, and temperatures again returned to the average 72°F that Earth seemed to prefer.[18]

Around 180 million years ago, CO_2 rocketed up from about 1,200 ppm to 2,500 ppm. And would you believe it? This coincided again with a big temperature dive from 72°F to about 61°F. Then, at the border between the Jurassic period when T. rex ruled and the Cretaceous period that followed, CO_2 levels dropped again, while temperatures soared back to 72°F. Average temperatures remained at that high level until long after the dinosaurs became extinct.[19]

Perhaps you'll wish to ponder this question: Given that over most of Earth's known climate history, the atmospheric CO_2 levels have been between four and eighteen times higher than they are now—throughout many times when life not only survived but also flourished; times that preceded humans; times when CO_2 levels and temperatures moved in different directions—how much difference will putting caps on emissions accomplish? Consider also that about 97 percent of all current atmospheric CO_2 derives from natural sources.

Throwing the Public a Curve

The IPCC's 2007 AR4 report "Summary for Policymakers" asserted that atmospheric GHGs (read as CO_2) "now far exceed preindustrial values over the past 650,000 years." That report appears to reflect some short-term memory deficiencies. It is not accurate, as the authors claim, that CO_2 in the preindustrial era was about 25 percent lower than it is now. As evidenced by the more than ninety thousand direct CO_2 measurements taken in America, Asia, and Europe between 1812 and 1961, concentrations have been much higher than the approximate 380 ppm level we see today.[20]

With such weak evidence, how did organizations find a way to convince the public that atmospheric CO_2 levels are skyrocketing? As it turned out, IPCC representations of postindustrial influences on climate change were heavily based upon a very misleading, unpublished, non-peer-reviewed research report submitted by the author. A now-infamous "hockey stick" graph that illustrated the report's conclusions has since been thoroughly debunked, yet it was repeatedly highlighted in IPCC summary reports. It was also used as the main visual in the Clinton-Gore administration's report "National Assessment of the Potential Consequences of Climate Change" (2000) and again featured in Al Gore's *An Inconvenient Truth*—both the movie and the book.

The graph's creator was none other than Michael Mann, later exposed as a principal inner-circle member of the Climategate network revealed through hacked CRU e-mails. When Mann produced the graph, he was a young PhD at the University of Massachusetts and the IPCC report lead author, who selected his own non-peer-reviewed paper for inclusion. Arguably, this flawed study has done more to advance the concept of global warming hype than all others combined.

Mann's research produced curves representing changes in atmospheric CO_2 levels over time frames ranging from 300 to 10,000 to 400,000 years. All showed that low preindustrial concentrations soared up to about 370 ppm at the end of the 20th century, obviously (it appeared) due to human influences. Temperature change graphs superimposed over the CO_2 curves made that connection clear and dramatic.[21]

Mann's early temperature data was taken from several different proxy records, particularly tree rings. More recent records were based upon official surface readings taken since 1980. They included some measured in what are termed "urban heat islands" influenced by buildings, paving and other infrastructure developments, which probably inflated the warming change. He eliminated substantial temperature fluctuations that occurred during the Medieval Warm Period (MWP; about 950 to 1300 AD) and the Little Ice Age (LIA; 1500s to 1800s), reinforcing the premise that temperatures were quite stable for approximately 900 years prior to 1910, and then they rocketed upward. The results were impressive.[22]

Issues arose after two Canadian non–climate scientists trained in statistics began to wonder if the chart wasn't maybe too stunning. Steve McIntyre, a metallurgy and data analysis expert, and Ross McKitrick, an economist from the University of Guelph, asked Mann for sources of the original data, and after repeated requests, they finally obtained an incomplete response. They learned that the Mann temperature proxy studies had given heaviest weight to tree ring data from fourteen Sierra Nevada mountain sites in California based upon ancient slow-growing, high-elevation bristlecone pine trees that wouldn't have reflected a strong 20th-century growth spurt attributable to warming as had been assumed. On the other hand, early high CO_2 levels could have been a fertilizing growth factor, since the trees can live 5,000 years. After eliminating the problematic tree data and repeatedly recalculating, the distinctive hockey stick shape flattened.

McKitrick commented on this circumstance regarding issues of corporate transparency: "The failure of the IPCC to carry out . . . independent verification or to audit studies may be partly explained by the lack of independence between the chapter authors and the original authors. Professor Mann was lead author of the chapter relying on his own findings, a lack of independence that would never be tolerated in ordinary public offering of securities."[23]

Russia: A New Cold War

A report titled "How Warming Is Being Made: The Case of Russia" alleges that the CRU and England's Hadley Centre for Climate Change, the UK's two top climate research organizations, have improperly selected Russian climate data to bolster warming claims. Issued by the Institute of Economic Analysis (IEA), an independent Moscow-based group, the report shows that the Russian data used for analyses came from just 25 percent of the country's meteorological stations and omitted about 40 percent of its landmass. Those chosen stations tended to be closer to large population centers, which tend to be warmer.

According to the IEA's president, Andrei Illarionov, "The IEA report concludes that it is necessary to recalculate all global temperature data in order to assess the real rate of temperature change during the last century. Global temperature data will have to be modified because the calculations used at Copenhagen by the United Nations Climate Change Conference analysts are based upon Hadley-CRU research."[24]

McIntyre notes that a March 2004 CRU e-mail tends to confirm an intentional suppression of Russia's Siberian climate records that has been suspected for some time. A communication from CRU's director, Phil Jones, to Mann states, "Recently rejected two papers (one for JGR and [one for] for GRL) from people saying CRU has it wrong for Siberia. Went to town in both reviews, hopefully successfully. If either appears [in the journals] I will be very surprised, but you never know with GRL."[25] (JRL refers to the *Journal of Geophysical Research*, and GRL to the *Geophysical Research Letters*.)

In response to this charge of data manipulation, the United Nations' World Meteorological Organization (WMO; aka Met Office) offered a denial, stating in part, "These [Russian stations] are distributed around the globe and provide a fair representation of changes in global temperatures over land. We do not choose these stations and therefore it is impossible for the Met Office to fix the data." Dave Britton, spokesman for the Met Office, stated that while it would publish station data as soon as it could, this may take a while because that data came from climate centers in many countries, some of which may not be willing to give up their intellectual property.[26]

Intellectual property? Is climate change a proprietary investment?

Confused Carbon Conceptions

Popular conceptions about anthropogenic CO_2 contributions to global warming promulgated by the IPCC for media dissemination are very misleading, for several reasons.

1. The actual amount attributable to human sources is extremely tiny relative to the atmospheric total, with incalculably small net greenhouse influences.
2. History shows that those miniscule amounts have fluctuated between much higher and lower relative concentrations than now, long before industrial societies existed and yet when life on Earth flourished.

3. These fluctuations generally followed, rather than preceded, global temperature changes, often by hundreds and even thousands of years.

4. No one can say just how warm is "normal," although interglacial periods, such as our present one, are certainly abnormally more wonderful than glacial periods that last about ten times longer.

5. There is absolutely no evidence to support catastrophic scenarios projected by those who simultaneously ignore predictable warming benefits.

Al Gore's description of GHGs in both his movie and his book titled *An Inconvenient Truth* refers to these gasses producing a "thickening" of the atmosphere. This gives the impression that human activities are really filling up the air with copious quantities of CO_2 that are enveloping the planet in a dense, heavy insulating blanket of massive proportions. A realistic image is very different.

For every 1 million molecules in the atmosphere, only about 380 of these are CO_2. The vast majority—about 368—of these CO_2 molecules are from natural land and sea sources, while only about 12 are believed to come from human activities, which include fossil-fuel burning and cement industries.

It is estimated that atmospheric CO_2 has been growing at a rate of about 0.4 percent per year since 1974. Let's assume, for example, that all this increase is attributed to humans. Now imagine that instead of CO_2 molecules, we are thinking of a medium-size city with a population of about a hundred thousand people. At this rate, it would require about 5 years to add one new person. That is how much the city's urban density would "thicken."

Of all GHGs, water vapor comprises about 70 percent of the total by volume, while CO_2 constitutes somewhere between 4.2 and 8.4 percent. If we assume that humans are responsible for about 0.12 percent of the greenhouse effect, that would probably amount to less than 0.02°F of warming over the past hundred years. That includes all CO_2 emission sources. On a molecular basis, methane, another GHG, is about twenty-three times more efficient at producing atmospheric warming than is CO_2; it is also accumulating in the atmosphere more rapidly.

A common misconception is that all or most CO_2 emissions from human activities accumulate steadily in the atmosphere with a proportional greenhouse effect. Yet, on average, the surface environment absorbs about half of those CO_2 emissions. In addition, each unit of CO_2 increase generally produces half the warming effect of the preceding one, and the atmosphere can become saturated to stop further effects.

Discerning Influences

The IPCC's Second Assessment Report, "Climate Change 1995," asserts that "the balance of evidence suggests a discernible human influence [on warming]," but it doesn't really explain which human influence(s) are discernible. We are left to assume it is referring to GHG emissions (primarily CO_2) due to the attention directed toward them, along with some mention of deforestation. Development of cities, growth of agriculture, construction of highways, and other possible influences are difficult to model. The main suspect, of course, is CO_2.

About 80 percent of the recorded atmospheric CO_2 rise during the 20th century that has been attributed to greenhouse warming occurred *after* an initial major rise in global surface temperatures. Temperature increases in the Northern Hemisphere since the 1970s have occurred mostly during cold seasons. Most of the current warming occurred before 1940 and declined afterward, until the 1970s, despite a large surge of CO_2 during that cooling period. The Earth has warmed only slightly since the 1940s.

Historical surface measurements, along with "proxy" evidence obtained from mountain glaciers, tree-growth rings, ocean coral layers, and other biological indicators, suggest that global average temperatures had risen about 0.9°F during the early part of the 20th century, before most GHGs had been added to the air by human activities. The temperatures peaked by around 1940 and then cooled until the 1970s. Since that time, little or no surface temperature increases have been observed.[27]

On the other hand, about 80 percent of the atmospheric CO_2 increases (those that might be attributed to human sources), entered the air after 1940, a time when temperatures were either cooling (prior to the 1970s) or increasing very little (after this period). If this is accurate, anthropogenic contributions since the 1970s would be only about 0.18°F.

But what if atmospheric CO_2 levels continue to rise, and perhaps even double the present level of about 380 ppm? Some models predict that they might, which has led to concerns about disastrous temperature levels in the future. Typical GCM estimates predict that such a doubling might produce an increase in the range of 2.7°F to 8.1°F, but with very high levels of uncertainty subject to large errors. These numbers are not at all consistent with observed CO_2 doubling effects from natural causes. For example, influences of volcanic eruptions suggest a "sensitivity " (impact) of only 0.54°F to 0.9°F for a doubling, and a variety of biological and other feedback yields a sensitivity of about 0.72°F if doubled.[28]

The IPCC's Third Assessment Report, "Climate Change 2001," acknowledged that climate is naturally variable, and human influences couldn't be conclusively pinpointed or quantified: "The fact that the global mean temperature has increased since the late 19th century and that other trends have been observed does not necessarily mean that an anthropogenic effect on the climate has been identified. Climate has always varied on all timescales, so the observed change may be natural."[29]

Yet the report still went on to blame people for recent warming in even stronger terms than before: "There is new and stronger evidence that most of the warming that occurred over the last 50 years is attributable to human activities . . . In light of new evidence and taking into account the remaining uncertainties, most of the observed warming over the past 50 years is likely to have been due to the increase in greenhouse gas concentrations."

The selection of "the last 50 years" as a benchmark is interesting because the IPCC report then deleted temperature records from weather balloons (past 41 years) and satellites (past 21 years) that did not reveal substantial warming. In addition, about half of that period (from 1950 to 1975) recorded cooling, not warming. Records also show that areas of Greenland have become colder during the last half century, particularly in the southwestern coastal region, as have surface temperatures in the nearby Labrador Sea. This information is based upon studies conducted by Edward Hanna at Britain's University of Plymouth and John Capellan of the Danish Meteorological Institute, using data obtained at eight Greenland weather station sites and three stations recording sea surface temperatures.[30]

The IPCC's Fourth Assessment Report, "Climate Change 2007," specifically asserts that global temperatures during the past 50 years are the warmest in the past 1,300 years due to fossil burning, although neither statement can be proven. The Medieval Warm Period, which was well documented in earlier IPCC summaries but disappeared in the hockey stick graph, was warmer than the 20th century, when temperatures peaked about 1940 and changed little from the 1990s on. Again, about 80 percent of that 20th-century increase occurred before the end of that 1940 peak.

If humans are responsible for warming (or cooling) changes during the 20th century, then who or what caused similar changes before we allegedly messed up the climate balance before that time? And why do temperatures continue to periodically fluctuate downward at times when our greenhouse contributions should theoretically cause steady increases—as the IPCC's own report "Climate Change 1990" observed? According to that report, "The upper troposphere shows there has been a rather steady decline in temperatures since the late 1950s and early 1960s in general disagreement with model simulations that show warming at those levels when the concentrations of GHGs is increased."[31]

Changing Climate: From What to What?

Satellites can now provide new information about the dynamics of weather systems, global atmospheric and surface temperature changes, atmospheric composition, cloud and rainfall patterns, sea and ice level measurements, and other data that wasn't available a few decades ago. One of the numerous reasons this is important is that to understand climate change, we must know what benchmarks it is changing from. This is a fundamental problem because before the advent of satellites (i.e., prior to 1979), which observe the entire Earth and its atmosphere, all we have to compare changes to are surface recordings at scattered sites that used now-antiquated instruments and methods. In addition, some later developments at many of those sites have produced localized heat island pockets of warming effects that have been inflated and projected onto regional and global scales.

We still don't really know how cool (or warm) it was at the beginning of the last century. Early temperatures were recorded using liquid-in-glass thermometers that were both difficult to calibrate and read and unreliable due to glass shrinkage. Most measurements were conducted in the Northern Hemisphere, typically in or near small towns, often with thermometers placed in direct sunlight or on walls of buildings that blocked, absorbed, and/or reflected radiation. Not all were continually monitored or recorded at the same time of day. Over time, large buildings were constructed next to many of these thermometers and cities grew up around them. Weather stations were developed—often located at airports where aircraft engines contributed heat.[32]

NOAA operates a surface network of 1,221 temperature monitoring stations across the US. So we might assume that the government has a pretty good handle on temperature changes, right? Maybe not. Anthony Watts, a former TV meteorologist who distrusted the data, organized a large volunteer effort to visit most of those stations and photographically document compliance with official installation standards. Direct surveys of 1,003 of those stations revealed that only 11 percent met basic requirements.[33]

From early times until today, many regions—remote polar regions in particular—have had spotty surface temperature monitoring. Measurements of sea temperatures are recorded at floating buoys and on board cooperating ships. The ship measurements rarely occur at the same locations and often employ nonstandard procedures, sometimes using buckets or engine intake water, which is obtained from levels lower than the buoys. US compilers of global temperatures don't recognize ship measurements as being acceptably reliable.

How much exactly has the Earth warmed during the past hundred years or so? Nobody really knows for sure because nobody knows what the temperature was before satellites entered the scene.

And as far as the future is concerned, scientists know virtually nothing about that either. Global climate forecast models are really nothing more than informed, but highly speculative, guesses produced by untested methods, which are easily manipulated to comply with preconceived expectations. Even in regard to local weather predictions, the ability to really forecast beyond about 10 days is unrealistic. This is because of what is known as a "butterfly effect," in which very small events, analogous to the flutter of a butterfly's wings, mix together with compounding complex influences that become manifested a few days or weeks later in unpredictable ways.[34] Climate models are no different, and they have never demonstrated an ability to predict changes even 10 years ahead, much less 100 years or more.[35]

Setting the Thermostat: How Cool Do We Want It?

Former NASA administrator Michael Griffin got in hot water with some "environmentalists" for remarks he made in May 2007. During an interview broadcast on National Public Radio's *Morning Edition*, he commented:

> I have no doubt that global—that a trend of global warming exists . . . I'm not sure it's fair to say that it is a problem to wrestle with . . . to assume that is a problem is to assume that the state of the Earth's climate today is the optimal climate, the best climate that we could have or ever have had, and that we need to take steps to make sure it doesn't change . . . First of all, I don't think it's within the power of human beings to assume that the climate does not change, as millions of years of history have shown. Second, I guess I would ask which human beings—where

or when—are to be accorded the privilege of deciding that this particular climate that we might have right here today is the best climate for all other human beings. I think that's a rather arrogant position for people to take.[36]

Mr. Griffin's remarks were taken by some to suggest that NASA was backsliding on its roles in collecting and analyzing satellite climate data. Philip Clapp, president of the National Environmental Trust, a nonpartisan watchdog group, thought that the comments conflicted with his own organization's science findings. "The science performed by NASA, as well as scientists around the world, shows that global warming is no longer an environmental issue. It's a rapidly advancing disaster. Millions of people across the world will face hunger, flooding from a rise in sea levels, and water scarcity. To try to hide that by saying we don't know what the climate should be is ignoring the science of his own agency."[37]

So NASA appears to have a new mandate: Verify that there definitely is a climate crisis based upon doomsday scenarios projected by your employee, James Hansen, and other alarmists, regardless of what the actual data shows. Forget about large temperature shifts that predated modern human history, and assume we are responsible. After all, what else do we pay you for?

It's Official Now: No More Global Warming

The term "global warming" has now been replaced in sophisticated circles with the more PC, acceptable term "climate change." Since the distinctions tend to be somewhat confusing, please accept the following clarification as a public education service for those discriminating readers who actually care to be up to date on such matters.

To begin this short tutorial, global warming—as commonly used by Al Gore and in the press—is a euphemism for unnatural (man-made) and dangerous heating of the Earth that human beings are causing through CO_2 emissions we release into the atmosphere. It does not generally refer to natural warming periods that have been interspersed with cooling and very cold events throughout billions of years. It also doesn't refer to those natural changes plus any additional, yet unknown, influences humans have contributed. You probably already knew that.

So what exactly does "climate change" mean? Perhaps we can find out by referring to an official definition cooked up by the UN and its IPCC.

Article 1 of the United Nations' Framework Commission on Climate Change (FCCC) makes it clear that the organization's definition of the term is about human, not natural, causes. Here, climate change is a "change of climate which is attributed directly or indirectly to human activity that alters the composition of the global atmosphere and which is in addition to natural climate variability observed over comparable time periods."

In any case, if some of you haven't followed all this, you needn't worry too much. What it all comes down to is that humans are causing global warming, climate change, and lots of variability through our "unnatural acts."

There can be little doubt that our ancestors and we ourselves have affected our planet and its ecosystems in many ways that are not entirely for its good. Examples of those ways include, but are not limited to, deforestation, and soil erosion caused by improper land management; atmospheric particulates, sulfates, and other pollutants produced from industry and vehicle exhaust; and the release of toxic wastes into soils and water. There is, however, no clear scientific evidence that atmospheric CO_2 resulting from human activities has produced or will produce dangerously deleterious effects upon global climate or temperatures. Meaningful impact projections using current climate models are not yet possible. Forecast methods that attempt to include all suspected influences over exceedingly short-term (much less inter-annual, decadal, and centennial) timescales produce only highly speculative guesses.[38]

Chapter 3

FORCING FACTORS AND FICTIONS

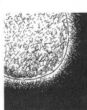

1. Active Sun   **2. Heliosphere**   **1. Inactive Sun**   **2. Heliosphere**

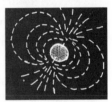

4. Atmosphere   **3. Magnetosphere**   **4. Reflecting Clouds**   **3. Magnetosphere**

Hot

1. Active sunspot periods produce high solar wind pressures.

2. Solar winds create the heliosphere that blocks cosmic rays from space.

3. Some cosmic rays are blocked by the Earth's magnetosphere.

4. Solar radiation passes through the atmosphere, producing warming.

Not

1. Periods of low sunspot activity reduce solar wind pressures.

2. More cosmic rays from deep space enter the magnetosphere.

3. The magnetosphere blocks some, but not all, cosmic rays.

4. Cosmic rays enter the atmosphere, creating clouds that reflect radiation.

There is certainly nothing new about cyclical, often abrupt climate changes, most particularly those that occur during relatively brief interglacial periods, such as the one we currently have the great fortune to enjoy. To appreciate just how lucky we are to live in the present, consider climate cycles from a big-picture historical perspective. Over the past 400,000 years, much of the Northern Hemisphere has been covered by ice, up to 3 miles thick, at regular intervals lasting about 100,000 years each. Much shorter interglacial cycles, like our current one, lasting anywhere from 12,000 to 18,000 years, have offered reprieves from the bitter cold. From this perspective, there can be no question that current temperatures are indeed abnormally warm.

The average temperature of our planet has been gradually increasing on a fairly constant basis over the past 18,000 years or so since it began thawing out of the last Ice Age. By about 12,000 to 15,000 years ago, Earth had warmed enough to halt the advance of the glaciers and cause sea levels to rise. About 8,000 years ago, an ice bridge across the Bering Strait became submerged, cutting off migrations of people and animals to North America.[1]

A short review of recent history (at least according to Earth's large-scale calendar) may provide some perspective. Let's start with a period from about 750 BC to 200 BC, before the founding of Rome, when temperatures had dropped from a previously warmer time. A resulting cooler, drier climate caused river and lake levels to drop in Egypt and Central Africa. The Tiber River froze, and snow remained on the ground for long periods almost unimaginable now. European glaciers advanced, and water that became trapped in them and other ice sheets caused sea levels to drop somewhat also.[2]

Then the climate warmed up again. Grapes were first reported in Rome about 150 BC, and soon grapes and olives were being cultivated in large abundance further north in Italy than would have been possible during earlier centuries. By about 350 AD, the climate became milder in the northern regions, and tropical regions became much wetter. Heavy rains in Africa caused high-level Nile floods, and Central America and the tropical Yucatan experienced similar conditions. By the late 4th century, the climate may have been warmer than it is now.

As the glaciers continued to melt, the sea may have risen slightly, possibly 3 feet or less, evidenced by the remains of ancient harbors in Naples and the Adriatic that are now about that depth below water. North Africa (now Tunisia, Algeria, and Morocco) was moist enough to grow grain, and the area experienced a large population expansion. But those good times were to end for a while. By around the 9th century, conditions began to cool again, and ice formed once more on the Nile.[3]

But then, guess what! At about the beginning of the 10th century, it began to become warmer. A decline in high winds and fierce storms favored more shipping, and trade fairs began to occur in about 1000 AD. The Norse colonized Greenland and caught codfish and seals in ice-free seas.

Conditions during this MWP, also referred to as the Medieval Climate Optimum, witnessed an estimated 50 percent population growth in Europe (about 5.5 million by 1300 AD), evidence that year-round food crops were abundant. Mountain passes stayed open longer during summers, enabling luxury goods—such as spices from Oriental caravans, sugar from Cyprus, and Venetian glass—to be traded for English wools and Scandinavian furs. The warm times were good times. Thousands of temples were constructed in Southeast Asia, including Angkor Wat, which suggests very favorable weather for agriculture and labor.

Consider that as recently as 1,000 years ago Icelandic Vikings on Greenland's southwestern coast were raising cattle, sheep, and goats in grasslands. Then, around 1200, temperatures in Greenland began to drop, and the settlements were abandoned by approximately 1350. Atlantic pack ice began to grow around 1250, and shortened growing seasons and unreliable weather patterns, including torrential rains in Northern Europe, led to the Great Famine of 1315–1317.[4]

Beginning about 1300, weather became unstable and unpredictable, with warm and dry summers in some years, cold and wet summers in others. Storms and high winds increased in the North Sea and the English Channel, making the shipping industry hazardous. Grain failures occurred throughout Europe in 1315, and catastrophic rains affected huge areas, ranging from Ireland to Germany and north into Scandinavia.[5]

Then, starting around the year 1550, climate shifts began to turn increasingly dreadful, and between the years 1690 and 1700, food shortages claimed millions of lives. Hubert Lamb, founder of the Climate Research Unit at the University of East Anglia, described the shift this way: "In the middle of the 16th century, remarkably sharp changes occurred. And over the next 150 years or more, the evidence points to the coldest regime—though accompanied by notably great variations from year to year and from one group of a few years to the next—at any time since the last major Ice Age ended 10,000 years or so ago."[6]

Although temperatures have been generally mild over the past 500 years, we should remember that significant fluctuations are normal. Remember, the Little Ice Age brought frigid weather to the Northern Hemisphere between the 16th and 19th centuries, when Alpine glaciers advanced to gradually engulf farms and villages by the mid-17th century (the LIA mentioned in chapter 2). The Thames River and New York Harbor froze over by 1780, and sea ice closed shipping harbors in Iceland, where an estimated one-third of the population perished.

Some widely publicized reports ignore or minimize mention of the MWP and LIA, dismissing them as rather erratic regional, rather than global, phenomena. They are wrong to do so. The first of these was clearly global, and the second was hemispheric, if not worldwide.[7]

The current CO_2 increases we have witnessed most dramatically during the first half of the 20th century have followed a 300-year warming trend, during which surface temperatures have been recovering from chills of the LIA. History shows us that lagging atmospheric CO_2 increases can be expected due to natural releases of gases from oceans as the temperatures have risen.[8]

The past century witnessed two distinct periods of global warming. The first occurred between 1900 and 1945, and the second, following a slight cool-down, began quite abruptly in 1975. That second period rose at quite a constant rate until 1998, and then stopped and began falling again after reaching a high of 1.16°F above the average mean. Between 2001 and 2008, the temperature anomaly declined, averaging out at 0.86°F above the mean. Although this represents only a short change over a long period of warming, global anomalies had risen steadily from around 1.10°F below the mean in 1910. While still not enough to prove a trend, it does tend to throw cold water on notions of a climate catastrophe in progress. About half of all estimated warming since 1900 occurred before the mid-1940s despite continuously rising CO_2 levels.

As Donald Easterbrook, a geology professor of Western Washington University, has observed, "Two cycles of global warming and two cycles of global cooling have occurred during the past century, and no matter what the causes, we cannot escape the conclusion that the Earth is in for global cooling in the next two to three decades."[9]

None other than East Anglia CRU director Phil Jones has admitted that there has been no statistically significant warming trend for at least 15 years. He has also admitted that temperatures during the Middle Ages may have been higher than they are today.[10]

The Uncertain Nature of Climate

As we all must recognize, it is impossible to reliably forecast weather events over days and weeks, much less accurately predict climate changes and causes typically measured over multiple decades. Climate forcings are too poorly understood, the variables too numerous, and their interactions too dynamic and complex, for confident modeling. But given the fact that Earth's climate has been fluctuating long before mankind discovered the benefits of harnessing fire, it is logical to assume that many influences—and clearly the most dominant ones—involve naturally occurring, sometimes cyclical, events.[11]

Key among these natural climate forcings are believed to be changes in the Earth's orbital eccentricity around the Sun, along with its slow axial "wobble" over many thousands of years, called Milankovitch cycles. These conditions influence the amount of sunlight received on the surface of the Earth, and they seem to correspond with glacial and interglacial cycles. Short fluctuations within interglacial periods appear to be linked to other influences. They include periodic, cyclical variations in solar outputs; natural changes in ocean currents; seasonal effects of cloud cover, precipitation, and vegetation growth; and occasional volcanic eruptions producing warming GHGs, along with dust and aerosols that block sunlight to cause cooling.

Variations in Earth's orbital path around the Sun occur in 21,000-year cycles as gravitational influences of other planets, the Moon, and the Sun pull Earth closer or farther away from the Sun. Variations in the direction of Earth's axis (the wobble) occur in roughly 26,000-year cycles. Variations in Earth's axial tilt between 22.1 degrees and 24.5 degrees (currently 23.44 degrees) occur in 41,000-year cycles.

Earth's orbital path and axial tilt cycles affect climate patterns in the two hemispheres significantly. Current Southern Hemisphere summers and winters are more extreme than in the Northern Hemisphere due to a 6.8 percent differential solar exposure. Also, the Earth is closest to the Sun during southern summer and farthest away during southern winter. Gradually, Northern Hemisphere winters will become slightly warmer as Earth becomes closer to the Sun during northern winter—southern summer. About 7,000 years ago, when Earth's axis was 24.14 degrees, the Sahara Desert was a very different place, with lakes, rivers, grasslands, and patches of jungle. Then, over a 3,400-year period, it became gradually transformed into what we find today. Better times will eventually return, since massive amounts of water remain trapped underground.[12]

Many scientists believe that Pacific Decadal Oscillation (PDO) and Atlantic Multidecadal Oscillation (AMO) ocean cycles associated with El Niño and La Niña conditions, in combination with solar activity variances, have had important climate influences during the past century. These factors may account for much of the observed warming trends of the period from 1910 through the 1930s, cooling from the 1940s to the 1970s, and warming during the decade between 1980 and 1990. Solar activity cycles of about 11 years and 200 years may modulate the effects of galactic cosmic ray (GCR) magnetic fields, producing changes in cloud cover with both warming and cooling results.

Much scientific attention is recently being directed to correlations between periodic changes in sunspot activity and climate change. Reasons for periodic changes that occur in the Sun's behavior, when they will occur, and their influences upon Earth's climate are not well understood, and current climate models cannot predict these factors. However, scientists are beginning to discern certain trends.

As first recognized in the 1800s, solar activity typically runs in roughly 11-year cycles, often varying between 9 and 14 years long. But sometimes periods of very low sunspot activity can stretch out for decades. During the 17th century, for instance, a 70-year-long period of little or no activity, known as the Maunder Minimum, corresponded closely with the LIA that extended into the 19th century. George Washington's famous winter at Valley Forge was associated with this LIA, as was Napoleon's bitter retreat from Moscow.[13]

Sunspot activity correlates with the strength of the solar wind, a plasma stream of charged particles from the Sun's upper atmosphere that interacts with all planets in our Solar System and defines the envelope border with interstellar space, called the "heliosphere." This border is a location where the wind's strength becomes insufficient to push back the wind of other stars—the boundary of the "heliopause," a shield of intersteller material that wards off a significant portion of cosmic rays originating from the surrounding galaxy. As our Sun's solar wind activity decreases, the heliosphere diminishes in strength, allowing more galactic cosmic rays to enter the inner part of our Solar System. Many scientists believe those penetrating cosmic rays cause atmospheric water vapor molecules to cluster into droplets, forming low-level clouds that produce cooling when sunspot activity is low.

Times of high solar activity appear to correspond with eight warming periods noted during the past 12,000 years, including the Medieval Warm Period and much of the recently past 20th century. It appears that the Sun's mood swings may be very consequential.[14]

Although the IPCC's 2007 AR4 report claimed that solar influence upon climate is "negligible," conclusions of a scientific study published in the journal *Physics Today* strongly take issue with that assessment. The authors, Nicola Scafetta and Bruce West, reviewed recorded data that the IPCC and many other climatologists had ignored as just "background noise," and they found that the "noise" perfectly matched solar activity over at least 4 centuries. They also found that the computer modeling by the IPCC and others was not producing accurate information because key solar flare and other activity data had not been entered. The study concluded the following: "If climate is sensitive to solar changes as the . . . findings suggest, the current anthropogenic contribution to global warming is significantly overestimated. We estimate that the Sun could account for as much as 69 percent of the increase in Earth's average temperature. Furthermore, if the Sun does cool off, as some solar forecasts predict will happen over the next few decades, that cooling could stabilize Earth's climate and avoid catastrophic consequences predicted in the IPCC report."[15]

The study of the Sun's activity leads some to anticipate colder, not warmer, temperatures in the future. Richard Mewald of Caltech observes that "In 2009, cosmic ray intensities have increased 19 percent beyond anything that we've seen in the past 50 years."[16]

Based upon current solar data, the Russian Pulkovo Observatory space research laboratory concludes that Earth has passed its latest warming cycle, and staff there predict that a fairly cold period will set in by 2012. Temperatures may drop much lower by 2041 and remain very cold for 50 to 60 years, or longer.[17]

Kenneth Tapping at Canada's National Research Council thinks we may be in for an even longer cold spell. He predicts that the Sun's unusually quiet current 11-year cycle might signal the beginning of a new Maunder Minimum cold period, which occurs every couple of centuries and can last a century or more.[18]

Solar activity peaked at the end of the 1990s, broke with a brief blip in 2002, and then slumped to almost none. This coincides with observed cooling, since 1999, which may well be continuing. There were only six sunspots during the entire year of 2008, the lowest number in 95 years. Yet as recently as 2006, NASA predicted that the upcoming solar cycle would be "a biggie."[19]

Scientists agree that the Sun's output is not constant, although it would have been considered heresy a couple of centuries ago to suggest this. The Sun has actually brightened about 30 percent during Earth's history, while interestingly and curiously enough, the Earth's average temperature has remained relatively constant.[20] The Sun may have been about 0.25 percent dimmer during the Maunder Minimum and other similar low-activity periods. A solar radiative energy reduction of about 0.1 percent measured against an average "solar constant," or watts of solar energy per square meter as a baseline measurement (about 1,367 W/m² at Earth's surface), has been observed to occur during fairly regular 11-year solar cycles.[21]

Solar minimum periods recorded over several decades since at least 1500 AD show positive correlations between times of greatest solar intensity and sunspot activity. In fact, these connections appear to be strong enough to enable sunspot frequencies to be used as a proxy for levels of solar brightness (or "irradiance"). Variations recorded by satellite measurements also demonstrate correlations between the solar cycles and weather influences. These observations contradict current climate models that have ignored solar influences thought to be too small to account for climate changes.

Some recent data indicates that variations in solar irradiance, spectral irradiance in particular, may be much more important than previously assumed. When focusing attention upon those short radiation wavelengths in the ultraviolet (UV) and extreme ultraviolet (EUV) thermal bands, the levels vary during 11-year cycles by more than ten times.[22]

Satellite data analyses conducted by Robert Lee at NASA's Langley Research Center have compared thermal radiation and solar-irradiance measurements from 1979 to 1989, which captured part of an 11-year solar cycle. During that period a 0.54°F–1.08°F cooling was recorded from 1979 to 1985, followed by a 0.36°F–0.54°F warming to 1989. The observations concluded that if solar forcing was the only cause of these temperature variations, the effects are five times greater than climate models predict. However, that larger response may have been influenced by a 1982 El Chichón volcano eruption, which could have produced some cooling effects in 1983 and 1984.[23]

Ongoing studies, such as the European Space Agency's Influence of Solar Activity Cycles on Earth's Climate project, are attempting to gain a better understanding of the complex nature of Sun-Earth weather and climate relationships. Yet it may be a long time before enough will be known to provide a serious basis for 21st-century climate forecasts. And as wise modelers recognize, a bad forecast is worse than no forecast at all.[24]

The Infamous Greenhouse Effect

GHGs have been getting a very bad rap in the media to the point that they are commonly accepted by many as something to avoid at all costs. Yet without them, it is estimated that our planet would be much colder, and life as we know it would never have existed.[25]

We can get a good sense of the greenhouse effect when we experience a dry, chilly desert at night in comparison with a humid, tropical area. Absent a desert cloud cover, the heat absorbed by the desert surface is radiated directly back to space in the form of infrared energy. In tropical locations, water molecules in the air overhead intercept ground heat and radiate it back toward the surface.[26]

At the present time, scientists don't really have a clear idea of how even the most prevalent GHG, water vapor, affects climate change. They do know, however, that water in the form of clouds has extremely important and complex influences upon ways greenhouse mechanisms work, producing both warming and cooling effects. While the ones we see from below tend to look gray, they would appear white from above if viewed from an airplane. Upper parts scatter about half of the incoming sunshine, which would otherwise warm the surface, back into space. Clouds absorb some of that radiation as well, but since the cloud tops are cooler than the ground, the overall heat loss is typically less. This creates a complicated exchange budget between the incoming sunlight in a visible spectrum and outgoing, invisible infrared thermal energy. In general, though, when everything is taken together, clouds—particularly the low ones—tend to be net coolers. Thin ones, however, have an overall warming effect. This presents large accounting problems for climate modelers, particularly since they don't know entirely how clouds form, what types will be created, or how expansive their cover will be at any given place or time.[27]

The vast majority of all greenhouse warming effects is caused by water vapor in the air (considered a gas) and water droplets in clouds, with minor contributions from CO_2 and methane. It is estimated that atmospheric water vapor may account for about 70 percent of this effect, compared with somewhere between 4.2 and 8.4 percent for CO_2, absorbing solar infrared over much of the same wavelength band range as CO_2 and even more. The thermal radiation emitted from the Earth's surface is mostly in the 7–30 micrometer wavelength range, while the radiation that most readily escapes back to space with least atmospheric absorption is between about 7 and 14 micrometers, accounting for about 70 percent of that which is lost.

Water vapor strongly absorbs in a range of about 4 to 17 micrometers, and CO_2 most strongly between about 13 and 19 micrometers.[28]

Since warming influences of GHGs have not proven to be as strong as theoretical climate models have predicted, some scientists attribute the discrepancy to underestimated levels of anthropogenic aerosols. Aerosols include atmospheric dust particles and sulfate droplets released from such human activities as fossil burning, forest clearing, and agriculture, in combination with natural sources, such as volcanos, sea spray, and land wind erosion. These elements block some incoming sunlight that would otherwise produce lower-level atmosphere and surface warming. Unlike CO_2, however, which becomes more globally distributed, aerosols tend not to travel nearly as far from their sources or to remain in the atmosphere as long.

The climate-forcing influences of aerosols are highly uncertain, partly because they rapidly fall out or are washed out of the atmosphere by rainfall in days or weeks. This does not allow them enough time to be mixed uniformly around the globe. For sulfate aerosols it is also very difficult to distinguish droplets from industrial versus biogenic sources, because key modeling parameters are not well understood.[29]

Unlike CO_2, which is sometimes associated with unwelcome warming but is popular with herbaceous plants, sulfate droplets cause cooling but are unwelcome in general. They are responsible for urban smog that contributes to respiratory health problems for people; in the 1970s and 1980s the acid rain that was believed to damage forests and cause acidification of lakes was attributed to this smog. Subsequently, a large, 10-year-long study concluded that the acid rain alarm had been exaggerated.

Greenhouse Bounties: Why Warm Is Cool

Global warming hysteria has gotten many people so heated up that they overlook the consequences of the opposite condition. And assuming that small CO_2 increases may come with the deal, as they have in the past, what's so bad about that? You might even consider the possibility that when Earth finishes warming its way out of the last cold period, the climate might slide down the temperature graph into another one, and it might possibly be a doozy. According to glacial and interglacial cycles over the past 400,000 years or so, be afraid . . . be very afraid (just kidding). And if anthropogenic CO_2 can really make a difference to help forestall or prevent that, let's maybe reconsider our interests.[30]

The United Nations' World Meteorological Organization released a December

2009 report claiming that the 10-year period from 2000–2009 was the warmest since records began in 1850. This assertion is rather comical in light of the fact that no one really knows with any real accuracy or certainty what the Earth's temperatures were even a few decades ago. While the WMO says the data is culled "from networks of land-based weather and climate stations, ships and buoys, as well as satellites," it might be reasonable to ask just how many satellites, ships, and buoys were measuring temperatures in 1850. And how many ground stations and records have existed or can be trusted? Those that currently exist are highly concentrated in the US and Europe, while few are located in Asia, Africa, and South America.[31]

Distributions and placements of the stations is another matter. Since these stations were first established 150 years ago, many have seen major urban development in the areas where they are located, and that has created heat islands. Are these the same stations used since 1850? Have some been added or dropped? Have record-keeping procedures and equipment standards remained constant? And how can old data be combined with later, more accurate records, particularly when global satellite instruments that offer fuller, more accurate readings were not available during about 80 percent of the period referenced?

Claims that the Earth is now warmer than at any other time in the past 1,000 years are readily disputable. A National Academy of Sciences review panel addressed this issue in 2006. It concluded that all that we can really be certain about is that the Earth was then warmer than it had been over the last 400 years. Considering that the LIA accounted for 250 of those years, that shouldn't be unduly alarming. History has demonstrated that a return to prolonged cooling would be a much more legitimate worry.

Yes, global warming—and cooling—is real, and is still going on to this day.

Now let's just imagine that our currently observed cooling trend is brief, and consider the alternative the next time someone nervously asks if you "believe" in global warming. As a student of history, your answer might be strongly affirmative and go something like this.

> Yes, I really believe in global warming. Evidence suggests that global warming is critical to keep people comfortable during day and night, preventing millions from freezing to death and starving. It provides long growing seasons and excellent plant conditions on large expanses of unfrozen land that allows essential

food to be grown for 8–9 billion people around the world. It enables many domestic and wildlife species to thrive that couldn't otherwise survive. And if this includes an upward temperature shift that causes some species from the tropics, where the greatest diversity exists, to extend to higher latitudes, that isn't necessarily a bad thing at all.

But that may not be what some of those people want to hear. You might not be invited to their cocktail parties again.

Section Two

Political Hijackers of Science

Chapter 4

FEVERISH CLIMATE CLAIMS

LARRY BELL

And then maurading bands of mosquitos will migrate to spread malaria and other plagues to northern lattitudes.

P romoting global warming alarmism has become an effective manipulating tactic to advance a variety of special-interest agendas that often have little to do with the environmental goals and social benefits espoused by responsible individuals and organizations. In 2006, for example, the Institute for Public Policy Research (IPPR), a think tank that actually supports CO$_2$ cuts, provided an analysis of the circumstances surrounding global warming debates that were occurring in the UK: "Climate change is most commonly constructed through the alarmist repertoire as awesome, terrible, immense, and beyond human control . . . It is typified by an inflated or extreme lexicon, incorporating an urgent tone and cinematic codes. It employs [a] quasi-religious register of death and doom, and it uses language of acceleration and irreversibility."[1]

The IPPR concluded that "alarmism might even become secretly thrilling"—effectively a form of what they referred to as "climate porn."

Mike Hume, director of the UK's Tyndall Centre for Climate Change Research and one of his country's top climate scientists, spoke out in late 2006 against mounting alarmism. He recognized that climate change is real and that humans contribute to it, but he took issue with such words as "catastrophic" and such claims as "climate change is worse than we thought," "[we are approaching an] irreversible tipping in the Earth's climate," and "[we are] at the point of no return." He noted that such ideas are planted as "unguided weapons with which forlornly to threaten society into behavioral change."

Recognizing that such language helps to advance climate science funding, he concluded, "We need to take a deep breath and pause. The language of catastrophe is not the language of science . . . Framing climate change as an issue which evokes fear and personal stress becomes a self-fulfilling prophecy. By 'sexing it up' we exacerbate, through psychological amplifiers, the very risks we are trying to ward off."[2]

Pounding Our Hot Buttons

During the steamy summer of 1988, Senator Al Gore's Committee on Science, Technology and Space hearings succeeded in putting man-made global warming at center stage in the national political arena. (Remember, however, that barely a decade earlier an alarm, based on the observed cooling trend during the 1960s and late 1970s, signaled the coming of a new Ice Age.) James Hansen's rather mild affirmation of that possibility was presented as persuasive and confident proof. This certainty was reinforced in a book titled *World on Fire: Saving an Endangered Earth*, written by Democrat and Senate Majority Leader George Mitchell and published in 1991. Senator Mitchell, the father of a prominent environmental activist, urged recognition of greenhouse warming as a global threat. By that time, the popular media in Europe and the United States had reached a common conclusion: They were declaring that "all scientists" agreed that warming was real and had catastrophic potential, and that rising atmospheric CO_2 levels released by burning fossils must be the cause.[3]

Since the late 1980s and early 1990s, we have been subjected to a barrage of global warming crisis alerts. Many such alerts find their origin in doomsday predictions repeatedly rendered by alarmist James Hansen and visually dramatized in Mr. Gore's print and film productions. These media present powerful statements and graphic images that leave lasting impressions of global warming devastation, present and future, which is represented to be based upon science. It's awesome to imagine a Manhattan under water, heartbreaking to see polar bears and penguins become extinct, and terrifying to think of horrible diseases that are spreading—all because of us.[4]

Others have gotten into the act, targeting impressionable young minds and sensitive big hearts with messages of fear and guilt. An example is the children's book *The North Pole Was Here*, authored by *New York Times* reporter Andrew Revkin. It warns children that some day it may be "easier to sail than stand on the North Pole in summer."[5] Of course, it's mostly their parents' fault because of the nasty CO_2 they produce driving the kids to school.

Many leading scientists (who don't work for oil companies) strongly disagree with these prognoses and the alleged science behind them. Let's consider some of their reasons.

Lower Tides of Despair

Although the UN IPCC is one of the biggest purveyors of climate change hysteria, the predictions in its own 2007 AR4 report "Summary for Policymakers" stating that sea levels will "probably" rise between 7.08 and 23.22 inches during the 21st century may at least relieve some angst regarding the mother of all scares. After all, that's about twenty times less than the 20- to 40-foot levels envisioned in the Academy Award–winning documentary *An Inconvenient Truth*.

The IPCC AR4 report confirmed that unlike the spectacular scenario depicted in the film, Antarctica's ice sheets will "remain too cold for surface melting," and the continent is "expected to gain [water] mass due to increased snowfall." It also states that no scientific consensus exists that Greenland's ice caps are melting enough to contribute to increased sea levels. While it acknowledges unknowns, including some observed variability and local changes in glaciers that could contribute to increased sea levels, it concludes that overall, "there is no consensus on their magnitude."

And what about the AR4's probable projection of the oceans rising anywhere from 7.08 inches to 23.22 inches in the 21st century? A study in the July 26, 2009, issue of *Nature Geoscience*, a top journal in the field, had concluded that the investigation "strengthens confidence with which one may interpret the IPCC results." The authors later retracted the report, titled "Constraints in Future Sea-Level Rise from Post Sea-Level Changes," after two other scientists pointed out technical research errors. One involved a miscalculation, and the other cited incomplete information about ice sheet melting, which caused the conclusions to be highly uncertain.[6] The researchers had used fossil coral data and temperature records derived from ice core measurements to reconstruct how the sea level has fluctuated with temperature since the peak of the last Ice Age and to project how it would rise with predicted warming over the next few decades.

According to a recent study conducted by US and Dutch scientists that appeared in the journal Nature Geoscience, previous estimates of ice melt rate losses in Greenland and West Antarctica may have been exaggerated as double the actual rate. The earlier projections apparently failed to account for rebounding changes in the Earth's crust following the last Ice Age, referred to as "glacial isostatic adjustment." Lead researcher Bert Vermeersen of Delft Technical University in the Netherlands described the phenomena as being similar to the way a mattress compressed by the weight of a sleeper recovers its shape when the person gets up. The total revised annual contributions of the combined ice melts to ocean rise would amount to only about 1.5 mm (0.1 inch), similar to a 1.8 mm (0.07 inch) annual rise in the early 1960s.[7]

Hendrik Tennekes, former director of research at the Netherlands Royal National Meteorological Institute, believes that the sea level has flattened since 2006. He also disputes claims that there has been any statistically significant warming of upper ocean surfaces since 2003, pointing out that Arctic Sea anomalies have actually decreased.[8]

Dr. Tennekes places much of the blame for poor sea level forecasting upon a failure to understand and include influences of natural events in models. He reported to the well-known climate science blog Climate Depot: "From my perspective it is not a little bit alarming that the current generation of climate models cannot simulate such fundamental phenomena as the Pacific Decadal Oscillation. I will not trust any climate model until it can accurately represent the PDO and other slow features of the world ocean circulation. Even then I would remain skeptical about the potential predictive skill of such a model many tens of years into the future."[9]

Nils-Axel Mörner is head of the Paleogeophysics and Geodynamics department at Stockholm University in Sweden; past president of the INQUA Commission on Sea Level Changes and Coastal Evolution; leader of the Maldives Sea Level Project; and one of the UN's "expert reviewers" of the IPCC's 2001 and 2007 reports. He agrees that concerns about rising sea levels are totally unfounded. His research in this area has taken him around the world, from Greenland to Antarctica and to most coastal regions.[10]

Dr. Mörner observes that of the twenty-two IPCC authors, none was a sea level specialist. He later said, "So all this talk that sea level is rising, this comes from the computer modeling, not from observations . . . The new level, which has been stable, has not changed in the last 35 years . . . But they [IPCC] need a rise, because if there is no rise, there is no death threat . . . If you want a grant for a research project in climatology, it is written into the document that there 'must' be a focus on global warming . . . That is really bad, because then you start asking for the answer you want to get."[11]

According to studies by the INQUA commission, ocean levels have even fallen in recent decades. The Indian Ocean, for example, was higher between 1900 and 1970 than it has been since.[12] The real sea change, it appears, has been in the way climatologists have predicted sea levels.

Science on Thin Ice

Much of the specter of global warming alarm centers upon Greenland and upon concerns that glaciers will cause disastrous sea level rise. A December 2005 BBC feature reported that two massive glaciers in eastern Greenland, Kangderlugssuaq and Helheim, were melting, with water "racing to the sea." It was predicted that continued recession of more than 2 miles per year would be catastrophic. That prognosis proved premature, however. Only 18 months later, and despite slightly warmer temperatures, the melting rate of both glaciers not only slowed down and stopped but also had actually reversed, and the glaciers began expanding in size. Landsat images revealed that by August 30, 2006, Helheim had advanced beyond its 1933 boundary.[13]

Even though Greenland has been experiencing a slight warming trend, satellite measurements show that the ice cap is accumulating snow growth at a rate of about 2.1 inches per year. Also consider that Greenland's temperatures over the past decade were no warmer than several others recorded during the 20th century; they only recently began to exceed those of the 1930s, and the 1980s and 1990s were colder than the previous 6 decades. Temperatures in the late 12th century in Greenland were considerably warmer than they have been in recent years.[14]

As reported by the Greenland glacier study lead author Ian Howat, in a February 8, 2007, *New York Times* interview: "Greenland was about as warm or warmer in the 1930s and 1940s, and many glaciers were smaller than they are now . . . Of course, we didn't know very much about how the glacier dynamics changed then, because we didn't have satellites to observe it. However, it does suggest that large variations in sheet dynamics can occur from natural variability." Further on in the interview he concluded, "Special care must be taken in how these and other mass-loss estimates are evaluated, particularly when extrapolating into the future, because short-term spikes could yield erroneous long-term trends."[15]

The International Arctic Research Center reported a 29 percent expansion of Arctic sea ice in 2008 over 2007's total. Alaska also experienced an unusually large amount of winter ice and snow during 2007–2008, followed by extremely cold temperatures in June, July, and August. "In June, I was surprised to see snow still at sea level in Prince William Sound," reported US Geological Survey (USGS) glaciologist Bruce Molnia. "On the Juneau Icefield, there was still 20 feet of new snow on the surface of the Taku Glacier in late July."[16]

Then, on March 31, 2010, scientists were once again surprised. According to the National Snow and Ice Data Center, Arctic sea ice reached the greatest expanse for that late date recorded since 1979, when satellite records commenced. The growth was largely attributed to cold weather and winds from the north over the Bering and Barents seas. So, what does this prove? Maybe very little—just about as little as you probably heard it reported in the news.

Snow Jobs

The IPCC has recently admitted that the assertion in its 2007 report that the Himalayan glaciers would likely melt by 2035 due to man-made global warming is false. That assertion had prompted great alarm across southern and eastern Asia, where glaciers feed the major rivers. Even though many glacier experts had considered such a prediction to be preposterous, the IPCC had kept it in its report. As it turned out, the prediction was traced to a speculative magazine article authored by an Indian glaciologist, Syed Hasnain, which had no supporting science behind it.

Mr. Hasnain works for a research company headed by IPCC's chairman, Rajendra Pachauri. IPCC author Marari Lai admitted to the *London Daily Mail*, "We thought that if we can highlight it, it will impact policymakers and politicians and encourage them to take concrete action."[17]

Other world climate alarm bells chimed when it was reported in the media that September 2007 satellite images revealed the Northwest Passage—a sea route between the UK and Asia across the top of the Canadian Arctic Circle—had opened for the first time in recorded history.[18] First, it should be pointed out that recorded history in this regard began only as recently as 1979, when satellite monitoring began. It should also be noted that the route froze again just a few months later (winter 2007–2008). In fact, the average Arctic sea ice extent for the month of December 2008 (4.84 million square miles) was actually 54,000 square miles greater than in December 2007; worldwide at that time, the average sea ice coverage was about the same as it had been in 1979.[19]

There is clear evidence that the Northwest Passage in reality has opened on previous occasions. The sea ice had been thinning ever since the end of the LIA (before the Industrial Revolution), and it had already warmed enough so that Eskimos first began fishing there for newly migrating cod in the 1920s.

In diary entries he wrote in 1903, sailor Roald Amundsen reported his experience on board a ship in those waters: "The Northwest Passage was done [had opened]. My boyhood dream—at the moment it was accomplished. A strange feeling welled up in my throat; I was somewhat over-strained and worn—it was weakness in me—but I felt tears in my eyes. Vessel in sight . . . Vessel in sight."[20]

During the early 1940s a Royal Canadian Mounted Police (RCMP) schooner assigned to Arctic patrol made regular trips through the Northwest Passage.[21] And in 2000 (that is to say, 7 years before the first-ever satellite records), another RCMP patrol vessel was renamed the *St. Roch II* and recreated the voyage, making the crossing in only three weeks. The crew reported seeing very little ice except for the occasional icebergs they passed.[22]

In February 2009, it was discovered that scientists have been underestimating the regrowth of Arctic sea ice by an area larger than the state of California (twice as large as New Zealand). The errors are attributed to faulty sensors on the ice.[23] And although the Arctic ice expanse was still slightly smaller in 2008 as compared with 1979, the Antarctic expanse was larger. The University of Illinois Arctic Climate Research Center posted an analysis in January 2009 concluding that global sea ice coverage in 2008 was nearly the same as satellites revealed in 1979.[24]

Research conducted by the Scripps Institution of Oceanography at the University of California–San Diego has turned up evidence that polar ice caps at least half as large as those we see now existed when Earth was at its warmest (72°F to 77°F), about 91 million years ago. That conclusion was based upon a study of tiny marine fossils, collected from the ocean floor, that contained a particular telltale isotope of oxygen molecules (d180). The study's coauthor, Richard Norris, observed: "Until now it was formerly believed no glaciers existed on the poles prior to the development of the Antarctic ice sheet about 33 million years ago . . . This study demonstrates that even the superwarm climates of the Cretaceous Thermal Maximum were not enough to prevent ice growth."[25]

To further support their conclusions, the research team pointed to evidence that sea levels fell between 82 and 131 feet during the period examined. This could be expected when that much water became landlocked in massive ice volumes.

As broadly advertised, it's true that famous glaciers at the peak of Mt. Kilimanjaro are indeed receding. Actually, they have been doing so since 1890, according to research by Kaser et al., published in the *International Journal of Climatology* (2004). By 1936, when Ernest Hemingway's *The Snows of Kilimanjaro* was released, the mountain had already lost more than half of its surface ice area over a period of 56 years. According to another report, published in *Geophysical Research Letters* (2006) by N. J. Kullen et al., this is being caused by a shift toward drier conditions, not by weather temperatures, that began around 1800.[26]

Global Warming "Spokesbears"

Are polar bears becoming global warming victims? Mr. Gore says they are, and that opinion, along with grief-evoking images, has been expressed by leading media programs and commentators. Even the DOI seems to believe this; it has recently added polar bears to the Endangered Species Act (ESA) listing. It must be true, right?

A January 20, 2008, global warming special hosted by Scott Pelley reported that polar bears "may be headed toward extinction," noting that researchers are finding them to be thinner and weaker, with less time to stock up on fat reserves because ice sheets are melting too fast. Mr. Pelley has strong convictions about global warming. He is the same reporter who once compared global warming skeptics to Holocaust deniers. Nick Lunn, the researcher featured in that special broadcast, somberly observed that the polar bear population in the Western Hudson Bay has declined during the last decade from about twelve hundred in the mid-1990s to about a thousand now. What wasn't mentioned is that the total population, estimated to be about five thousand in the 1970s, has increased to about twenty-five thousand today. And though it is true that the Western Hudson Bay population has been seeing some decline, other groups are stable and even increasing in number.

ABC's Sam Champion told *Good Morning America* audiences on February 8, 2008, that a 2-degree increase in global temperatures would make "polar bears struggle to survive." On November 6, 2007, NBC's *Today Show* cohost, Matt Lauer, said the bears "are facing an epic struggle for survival." Reporter Kerry Sanders warned, "If the Arctic ice continues to melt in the next 100 years, the US Wildlife Service says 'the only place you'll find a polar bear on Earth will be at the zoo.'" On a September 9, 2007, *Good Morning America* broadcast, Kate Snow called polar bears "the newest victims of global warming." The same segment featured Dr. Steven Amstrup, a USGS scientist, who stated that bears "could be absent from almost all their range by the middle of this century."[27]

It may be interesting to note that only 5 years earlier, a 2002 study by the same USGS had reported that the "[polar bear] populations may now be near historic highs."[28]

Dr. Mitchell Taylor, manager of wildlife research for the Government of the Canadian Territory of Nunavut, agreed with the US Geological Survey's 2002 assessment and recently reported that his organization's research shows that the Canadian polar bear population has increased about 25 percent during the past decade (from about twelve thousand to fifteen thousand).[29] Even Polar Bears International, a nonprofit organization that works to protect the animals, rates only five groups as "declining," another five as "stable," one as "increasing," and others as "data deficient" (impossible to measure) out of nineteen total world populations.[30]

We continue to see the polar bear represented as the "spokesanimal" for global warming threats. Al Gore's *An Inconvenient Truth* shows one apparently drowning because it is too tired from swimming in search of ice that we have caused to melt.

CBS reporter Daniel Sieberg, in an August 14, 2007, segment of the *Evening News*, echoed this presumption, explaining that, "Less ice also means the polar bears spend more time in the water, sometimes for so long they drown." An April 2006 *Time* magazine cover featured a bear seemingly "stranded" on melting ice. The Defenders of Wildlife website explains: "Loss of sea ice leads to higher energy requirements to locate prey and a shortage of food. This causes higher mortality rates among cubs and reduction in size among first-year adult males." Such claims appear to be supported by anecdotal evidence that four polar bears drowned while swimming in Alaska's Beaufort Sea, and that three polar bears attacked and ate others, allegedly due to hunger.[31] Some environmentalists also contend that human-induced global warming, which will cause most of the North Pole ice to melt in the next 50 years, will make it impossible for the bears to hunt seals, their preferred prey.

A problem with such reasoning—one that even Polar Bears International points out—is that swimming up to a hundred miles is not a big deal for the animals. The drowned bears that Gore referred to in his film turned out to be victims of a storm, not a lack of ice.

On March 28, 2008, Paul Milikin, a *National Geographic* photographer, stated on ABC's *Good Morning America*, "I realize what I need to do is try and tell these stories through *National Geographic* magazine by using animals, such as polar bears, to say that if we lose sea ice in the Arctic, and projections are to lose sea ice in the next twenty to fifty years, we ultimately are going to lose polar bears as well."

He went on to acknowledge how the photograph featured on *Time*'s cover in 2006, the seemingly "distressed" polar bear, came about: "It was just a moment where I was not thinking clearly. I was ten feet away, lying on my belly, and this bear is shaking water. And he was just . . . he took a lunge at me basically, but as [he] lunged up and was coming down on me, the ice broke and got away. And my first thought was, 'I know I have the shot,' so I was really excited that this shot would help tell the story that I want to tell about melting ice."[32]

Biologist Mitchell Taylor pointed out in his testimony to the US Fish and Wildlife Service (FWS) that modest warming may actually be beneficial to polar bears; it could both provide a better habitat for seals and dramatically boost the growth of blueberries, which the bears feed upon. In those cases where bear weights and numbers are declining, he thinks the cause is too many bears are competing for food, not Arctic warming.[33]

You might ask, what is the real basis for predicting these polar bear extinctions? Perhaps you may have guessed by now: It's those climate models that predict a dire, and warm, future.

A 2006 US DOI news release stated that it would consider further polar bear protection programs, and the agency acknowledged that "Alaska populations have not experienced a statistically significant decline, but Fish and Wildlife Service biologists are concerned that they may face such decline in the future."[34]

FWS then requested nine administrative reports from government agencies to bolster its case for listing the bears as an endangered species. All those reports were based upon climate models that shared common assumptions about sea ice levels during the 21st century—namely, that the area of the Arctic covered by sea ice in summer would decline by more than two-thirds, causing seal populations to decline. No ice, no seals; no seals, no bears; case closed.

Alaska's former governor Sarah Palin, along with many of the citizens she served, was and is not happy about the DOI's decision to add polar bears to the Endangered Species Act list. And this isn't because Alaskans don't like bears. In an October 2007 press release, Palin argued, "[Listing] a currently healthy species based entirely on highly speculative and uncertain climate and ice modeling and equally uncertain and speculative modeling of impacts on a species would be unprecedented. Listing polar bears under ESA could actually harm many of the existing and highly successful polar bear conservation measures."[35]

And why would anyone want to do that? Some suspicious minds wonder if maybe the main reason is oil drilling rather than bear welfare. As Ben Lieberman wrote in a January 25, 2008, Web memo for the Heritage Foundation, "The first victim of listing would be new oil and natural gas production throughout [Alaska] and its surrounding waters. It would put an end to any chances of opening up a small portion of the Arctic National Wildlife Refuge (ANWR), estimated to contain 10 billion barrels of oil—nearly 15 years' worth of current imports from Saudi Arabia."[36]

So now that polar bears are officially "endangered," the DOI, working through the Endangered Species Act, has been granted broad powers to work with other federal agencies to "solve the problem" by linking global warming threats to energy procurement and carbon emissions, two central agenda priorities under one legislative action. As Myron Ebell, director of global warming policy at the Competitive Enterprise Institute, postulates, "The larger goal is to compel regulatory controls on energy use that global warming alarmists have been unable to persuade Congress to enact."[37]

The polar bear issue illustrates how interest groups have used the pretense of a global warming crisis to advance other agendas. Still, if some polar bears gain from the deception, it's probably only fair. After all, consider all of the UN diplomats to whom we grant immunity, and they're certainly not an endangered population either.

Penguins: The Emperor Still Needs Warm Clothes

So, what about the overheated emperor penguins we've been told to worry about? Like polar bear cubs (but not necessarily the big, ferocious adults), they're cute too! Think about all those noble creatures we fell in love with in the big hit movie *March of the Penguins* as they battled to survive the coldest weather conditions on Earth. And now we're killing them by making the Earth too warm. It seems like we're always messing things up. Fortunately, however, it appears that the Antarctic climate has a changing mind of its own.[38]

Much of the media attention to climate change impacts upon penguin populations draws heavily upon press reports released by the World Wildlife Fund (WWF), which advocates large and immediate CO_2 emission restrictions. Those reports invariably emphasize connections between climate change and penguin declines, focusing upon carefully selected colonies that have experienced diminished populations during the past 10 to 20 years or so. Other colonies that show stable or expanding populations aren't deemed to be as interesting.

Antarctica is a huge place that exhibits a variety of climate fluctuations and trends at various temporal and spatial scales. The Antarctic Peninsula, which gets a lot of media attention for the study of periodic warming, comprises only about 2 percent of the continent; over the rest of the continent, temperature changes over the past 30 to 40 years have been slight or undetectable. And while sea ice extent may be declining off the peninsula, it has changed little, on average—and in some areas even has increased—around the continent in total.

Records show that overall, the continent of Antarctica has warmed about 1°F since 1957, yet average temperatures still remain about 50 degrees below zero. West Antarctica, which is most heavily influenced by atmospheric and ocean changes occurring thousands of miles to the north, is about 20 degrees warmer than East Antarctica and has warmed twice as fast. But temperature changes in the area rose up to five times more rapidly in the 1940s, and then they fell by the same amount after the warming effects of a major El Niño cycle were depleted.[39]

The 1997 El Niño was one of the most severe during the entire last century, and 1998 was an exceptionally warm year. Still, according to Australia's Commonwealth Scientific and Industrial Research Organisation, satellite measurements indicate that East Antarctica north of latitude 81° south gained up to 500 billion tons of ice over the last decade—one that Al Gore claimed to be the warmest in 100 years.[40]

Due to unique atmosphere-related weather influences, warming in Antarctica can actually bring more snowfall to the continent. Unlike conditions over most of the globe, where the stratosphere begins at an altitude of 8 to 10 miles above the Earth's surface, the stratosphere over Antarctica begins at an altitude of about 5 miles, or roughly 25,000 feet above sea level. As airstreams over the flat ocean encounter the rougher landmass, they are slowed, and they have nowhere to go but up. In doing so, the air becomes compressed between the surface and the stratosphere (a phenomenon called "convergence"). This forms shallow-height clouds that both reflect the Sun's energy up toward space (net cooling) and cause precipitation. Ocean warming produces more humid air currents (more clouds and snow).

There is no clear connection between Antarctica's climate and average surface temperatures elsewhere around the globe, and certainly none that can be linked to human influences. But count on it to remain very cold.

The only long-term emperor penguin studies have taken place in East Antarctica: at Terre Adélie, on the Mawson Coast, and on the Prince Olav Coast/Riiser-Larsen Peninsula. Although their numbers have dwindled around the Antarctic Peninsula near Palmer Station, on Anvers Island, the Terre Adélie population has tripled since the 1950s at Marguerite Bay, about 400 kilometers to the south. Nevertheless, the population at Terre Adélie, which experienced a significant decline in the 1970s, had begun to stabilize until recently, and it then declined again. Similarly, emperor colonies at Taylor Glacier and Auster, along the Mawson Coast, seemed to be stable while monitored from 1988 to 1999, but the Prince Olav Coast/Riiser-Larsen Peninsula populations recently declined in 2000.

Conditions at Palmer Station are warming, and therefore the area is readily accessible for observation. Researchers are witnessing a large proliferation of southern fur seals and elephant seals that were present during the 1990s only as small colonies. One population formerly of six seals now numbers about five thousand. Such species that prefer open water, which was limited to the northern and eastern parts of the peninsula where the ocean didn't freeze in winter, are expanding their ranges. As the "polar" ecosystem has shifted southward, so have the emperor penguins migrated from Terre Adélie. While they seem to like lots of ice, they don't like too much of it; its greater expanse makes it too strenuous to reach open water for foraging. David Ainley of H. T. Harvey & Associates, who studies these penguins in the southern Ross Sea area, observes, "As ice breaks up, there should be more habitat, and we should see more penguins."[41]

About 25 percent of all emperor penguins worldwide are believed to live near the Ross Sea, an area of Antarctica subject to changing climate patterns. Researchers have not yet found evidence to suggest either an overall increase or a decrease in the emperor population between 1983 and 2005.

To sum up the data, local and regional climate variations, which have always occurred along with fluctuations in aquatic food abundance, impact various penguin species and colonies differently. Some are expanding their ranges, some groups are declining in numbers while others are growing, and most appear to be doing pretty well. Because of their remote habitat, which makes them so difficult to observe, a lot remains to be known about many aquatic mammals and birds, including emperor penguin populations. Satellite imaging is used, yet many studies have concluded that data remains insufficient for broad analysis of impacts, such as any related to climate change.

Coral Catastrophes: Taking Claims with a Pinch of Salt

Such organizations as WWF and the Pew Charitable Trusts have raised the issue of global warming and CO_2 impacts upon the bleaching (killing) of coral reefs as a key environmental concern. Such influences are not to be taken lightly, because ocean reefs, like the world's rain forests, are vital habitats for wide varieties of life and thus deserve protection. But as Dr. Gary Sharp, a marine biologist who is the scientific director of the Center for Climate/Ocean Resources Study in Salinas, California, points out, "We need to look closely at what is most likely to affect the reefs, and what is not."[42] (According to its website, the center is linked with the International Oceanographic Data & Information Exchange of the Intergovernmental Oceanographic Commission of UNESCO.) Dr. Sharp cautions about being too alarmed regarding influences of anthropogenic greenhouse emissions for several reasons.

He observes that conjectures that global warming will kill reefs are based upon predictions that sea temperatures may increase about 3.6°F over the next hundred years and that rising CO_2 levels are making oceans more acidic. Yet coral reefs currently exist in waters with temperature gradients of 10.8°F–12.6°F, so all reefs aren't likely to die even if that increase were to occur. It's also not very probable that such an increase will happen. The Earth's ocean circulation pattern maintains a relatively narrow temperature boundary according to natural cycles, and it would be extremely unusual for sea surface temperatures in the open ocean to change that much.

The oceans appear to now be heading into one of their periodic cooling phases in accordance with a typical 55-to-70-year dipolar warm/cool pattern. Whether ocean waters warm or cool depends upon where you happen to be within these large-scale processes. The current trend is ongoing and is expected to dominate global circulation between 2008 and 2012. The effect of this cycle can be witnessed in recent long, cold winters with near-record low temperatures caused by highly mobile polar cold fronts measured as cold high-pressure regions in various places. This cold phase may be expected to continue for about 20 to 25 years before a transition into another epoch of generally warmer, remedial climate.

And what about claims made by the Pew Charitable Trust that CO_2 from burning fossils is "acidifying" the oceans? This alarm is primarily based upon a June 2006 release of data from a NOAA study showing that the water sampled from our oceans had an average pH of approximately 8.175 (0.025 units), which had declined from 8.2; this indicates the water had become more acidic over the last 15 years. However, recent studies also show that the pH difference was twelve times that miniscule change (8.5 units) at the time of the last glaciation period, and the reefs thrived under that falling pH. It would require a drop forty-seven times more than that recorded by NOAA to reach a pH level of 7—the point when acid/alkaline neutrality would occur and the coral would die. That would not only require that oceans absorb billions more tons of CO_2 than mankind is ever going to emit; it would also require that its buffering agents—carbonate, nitrate, and other radicals that minimize ocean acidity by accepting and expelling hydrogen ions—disappear. In fact, CO_2 is a fundamental building block necessary for coral to exist.

Pandemic Pestilence: The Political Variety

What is it, exactly, that we are supposed to be alarmed about regarding global warming? It seems that Mr. Gore's predicted 20- to 40-foot ocean rise isn't very credible, even to the IPCC, so Palm Beach property owners can relax. Polar bears can carry on their normal business of merrily multiplying, except for the invasions of privacy posed by polar paparazzi. Penguins are moving south, a trend paralleling that of snowbirds on this continent. And bleached coral reefs aren't either likely or sexy enough to compete with bleached blondes for popular centerfold attention.

Okay, let's try examining the threat of global warming causing really nasty tropical diseases to spread, just as *An Inconvenient Truth* dramatically warns. That should warrant some fear. Well, maybe not. At least Paul Reiter, a medical entomologist and professor at the Pasteur Institute in Paris, doesn't think so. He is one of the scientists featured in the film *The Greatest Global Warming Swindle*, produced by WAG-TV in Great Britain in response to the Gore movie. Dr. Reiter was also a contributory author of the IPCC's 2001 report who resigned because he regarded the processes to be driven by agenda rather than science. He later threatened to sue the IPCC if they didn't remove his name from the report he didn't wish to be associated with.[43]

Professor Reiter's career has been devoted primarily to studying such mosquito-borne diseases as malaria, dengue, yellow fever, and West Nile virus, among others. He takes special issue with any notion that global warming is spreading such illnesses by extending the carriers to formerly colder locales where they didn't previously exist. In reference to statements in *An Inconvenient Truth* that the African cities of Nairobi and Harare were founded above the mosquito line to avoid malaria, and that now the mosquitoes are moving to those higher altitudes, Dr. Reiter comments, "Gore is completely wrong here—malaria has been documented at an altitude of 8,200 feet—Nairobi and Harare are at altitudes of about 4,920 feet. The new altitudes of malaria are lower than those recorded 100 years ago. None of the 30 so-called new diseases Gore references are attributable to global warming. None."[44]

Although few people seem to realize it, malaria was once rampant throughout cold parts of Europe, the US, and Canada, extending into the 20th century. It was one of the major causes of troop morbidity during the Russian/Finnish War of the 1940s, and an earlier massive epidemic in the 1920s went up through Siberia and into Archangel on the White Sea near the Arctic Circle. Still, many continue to regard malaria and dengue as top climate change dangers—far more dangerous than sea level rise.

Dr. Reiter submitted written testimony to the British House of Lords Select Committee on Economic Affairs on March 31, 2005. His testimony included the following critique of the chapter written by Working Group II—much of which was devoted to mosquito-borne diseases, principally malaria—for the IPCC's Second Assessment Report:

> The scientific literature on mosquito-borne diseases is voluminous, yet the text references in the chapter were restricted to a handful of articles, many of them relatively obscure, and nearly all suggesting an increase in prevalence of disease in a warmer

climate. The paucity of information was hardly surprising: Not one of the lead authors had ever written a research paper on the subject! Moreover, two of the authors, both physicians, had spent their entire careers as environmental activists. One of these activists has published "professional" articles as an "expert" on 32 subjects, ranging from mercury poisoning to land mines, globalization to allergies, and West Nile virus to AIDS.[45]

Hurricane Hullabaloo

Despite large modeling uncertainties with undemonstrated reliability even over short forecast periods, the IPCC's "Climate Change 2007" AR4 report "Summary for Policymakers" predicts (with greater than 66 percent confidence) that the next century will experience an increase in droughts, tropical cyclones, and extreme high tides. Yet as John Christy, a professor of atmospheric science at the University of Alabama, points out in an October 20, 2000, article published in *NASA Science*, "The fact that different computer models often produce different forecasts doesn't offer much reassurance. For example, one model predicted that the Southeastern US would become more jungle-like in the next century, while another model predicted the same region would become a dried-out savanna."[46]

An event preceding the release of the 2007 AR4 summary report offers reasons to be even less confident about some of the IPCC's conclusions. It occurred following the summer of 2004, a year when a deadly storm season brought five devastating hurricanes that made landfall in Florida. The terrible destruction made headlines throughout the world, and many conjectured the hurricanes were linked to global warming.

Opportunities to capitalize on the unusual and terrifying hurricane pattern to validate man-made global warming threats were not lost on some IPCC officials, who rapidly responded. In October 2004, the IPCC's Kevin Trenberth participated in a press conference that announced, "Experts warn global warming likely to continue spurring more outbreaks of intense activity." But there was a serious problem. The IPCC studies released in 1995 and 2001 had found no evidence of a global warming–hurricane link, and there was no new analysis to suggest otherwise.

Christopher Landsea, an expert on this subject at the Atlantic Oceanographic and Meteorological Laboratory, was astounded and perplexed when he was informed that the press conference was to take place. As a contributing author to both of the previous reports and an invited author for the 2007 AR4 report, he believed there must be some huge mistake. He had not done any work to substantiate the claim. Nobody had. There were no studies that revealed an upward trend of hurricane frequency or intensity. Not in the Atlantic basin or in any other basin.[47]

Landsea wrote to top IPCC officials, imploring, "What scientific, refereed publications substantiate these pronouncements? What studies being alluded to have shown a connection between observed warming trends on Earth and long-term trends of tropical cyclone activity?" Receiving no replies, he then requested the IPCC leadership's assurance that the 2007 report would present true science, saying, "[Dr. Trenberth] seems to have come to a conclusion that global warming has altered hurricane activity, and has already stated so. This does not reflect consensus within the hurricane research community . . . Thus, I would like assurance that what will be included in the IPCC report will reflect the best available information consensus within the scientific community most expert on the specific topic."[48]

After the assurance didn't come, he resigned from the 2007 AR4 report activities and issued an open letter presenting his reasons. And while the IPCC press conference proclaiming that global warming caused hurricanes received tumultuous responses in the world press, Mother Nature didn't pay much attention. Hurricane seasons since then have returned to average patterns noted historically over the past 150 years.

Feverish Concerns, Cold Sweats

Potentially scary global warming predictions originate from other sources besides the IPCC. For example, a really good one came from the US Pentagon, a place that has to worry about a lot of frightening scenarios. This one concerns a hypothesis that global warming could cause parts of the world to become colder, a problem for some who like it hot.

It seems that the Pentagon, which had been studying possible national security issues associated with climate change for many years, contracted with a US think tank called Global Business Network to research potential global warming consequences. The resulting research report titled "An Abrupt Climate Change Scenario and Its Implications for United States National Security," which was released in October 2003, produced more than most Pentagon officials expected.

Andrew Marshall, director of the Pentagon's Office of Net Assessment (which is responsible for identifying long-term threats to the United States), was not pleased with then-President George W. Bush's lack of anxiety regarding global warming. Through a decision to bypass the White House, he presented the summary information and voiced his concerns to *Fortune* magazine, which published an article on the subject on February 9, 2004. In that article, Mr. Marshall explained how melting at the North and South Poles, and from glaciers around the world, presented an impending global weather disaster.[49]

Briefly summarized, the theory entails the following scenario, which was prominently featured in *An Inconvenient Truth*—both the documentary and the book—in the discussion involving "thermohaline convection."

The Gulf Stream, or "North Atlantic thermohaline conveyor," is a roughly figure eight–shaped stream of water that transfers heat from south of the equator as it flows over the ocean surface toward the north and warms northern parts of America and Western Europe. It is a primary force in driving the world's weather patterns. After the Gulf Stream transfers heat to the air through convection and cools down, it drops to the bottom of the ocean and returns as an underwater river that flows back toward the equator, warms again, rises to the surface, and returns north again, like a huge thermal conveyor.

The motor that drives the conveyor to keep the water moving is purported by the theory to be located in the north, where the ocean's salt density causes the Gulf Stream to drop, pulling warm water up from the south. But if the poles were to melt, large amounts of added fresh water might excessively dilute the Atlantic Ocean's salt density, causing the Gulf Stream not to drop as far, and also (in theory) causing it to slow down. This would cause less warmth to be transferred to the North Atlantic region, affecting the climate-heat balance-driven weather patterns. Northern parts of Western Europe would be particularly affected due to prevailing winds that move heat in that direction, possibly producing another interglacial cold spell like the LIA.

This scenario is extremely unlikely to happen for several reasons. First of all, the Gulf Stream disruption theory is based upon different circumstances that occurred about 12,500 years ago during the Younger Dryas episode, when a giant ice dam burst in North America, causing two enormous lakes to drain rapidly into the sea. The previous Ice Age had created an ice sheet up to 9,000 feet thick over large northern regions of Europe and North America. For example, the Laurentide Ice Sheet extended over all of the Great Lakes, west into Iowa, and south into Indiana and Ohio. When the ice melted, more than 100,000 cubic kilometers of freshwater were rapidly discharged into the sea, and the Gulf Stream really was overwhelmed. This can be compared with freshwater injections from recent Greenland ice melts amounting to only a few hundred kilometers per year, which show signs of stabilizing, at least currently. Since the trillions of tons of ice that existed prior to our interglacial period melted more than 10,000 years ago, there simply isn't enough left to trigger a repeat performance.[50]

There is also no evidence that recent warming is slowing the Gulf Stream, and the thermohaline conveyor is actually observed to be producing increased flow rates of deep Atlantic currents. Thermohaline circulation is now believed to be primarily a wind-driven system energized by the Earth's spin and lunar tides, rather than by Gulf Stream salinity differences and sea temperatures.

Global circulation models based upon real-world data also don't indicate any danger. A team of researchers at the Lamont-Doherty Earth Observatory ran several versions of the Gulf Stream Collapse Theory on a global climate model at NASA's GISS and found no evidence of a "tipping point" that would produce a Gulf Stream shutdown.[51]

While the National Research Council's Committee on Abrupt Climate Change previously warned about "large abrupt climate changes" of "as much as 10°C (50°F) in 10 years," which were claimed to be "not only possible but likely in the future,"[52] the Lamont-Doherty team found no basis for such dramatic thresholds in their model runs. Instead, they concluded that the Atlantic conveyor "decreases linearly with the volume of freshwater added through the St. Lawrence" and that it does so "without any threshold effects."[53]

Another team, at the UK's Hadley Centre for Climate Change, used a different model to test the same hypothesis regarding a meltwater shutdown of the ocean's circulation, and they found just the opposite: "Accompanying the freshening trend, the [thermohaline circulation] unexpectedly shows an upward trend, rather than a downward trend." This agrees with real-world evidence that deep ocean currents are becoming stronger with increased warming and precipitation.[54]

Rain Forest Rebuttal

An ultimately embarrassing assertion in the IPCC's 2007 AR4 report was that 40 percent of the Amazon rain forest in South America is endangered by global warming.

Those findings were based upon numbers taken from a non-peer-reviewed paper written by a freelance green activist journalist and published by the WWF. The paper warned that "up to 40 percent of the Amazon forests could react drastically to even a slight reduction of precipitation . . . It is more probable that forests will be replaced by ecosystems . . . such as tropical savannas." The disaster would be triggered, according to the IPCC's assessment, by a slight drop in the rainfall rates expected for a warming world.

The original claim was based upon a WWF study, "Global Review of Forest Fires," written "to secure essential policy reform at national and international levels to provide a legislative and economic base for controlling harmful anthropogenic forest fires." The 40 percent figure was taken from a letter published in the journal *Nature*, which related to harmful logging activities.[55]

Although the global warming–rain forest endangerment connection has been debunked by serious scientists, the IPCC has yet to retract or amend the claim. NASA-funded analyses of satellite imagery over past decades indicate that in fact the rain forests are remarkably resilient to droughts. Even during a 100-year dry-season peak in 2007, the jungles appeared basically unaffected. Arindam Samanta of Boston University, lead author of a recent study based on satellite data from NASA's Moderate Resolution Imaging Spectroradiometer, or MODIS, remarked, "We found no big differences in the greenness level of these forests between drought and non-drought years." Sangram Ganguly, author of another study at the NASA-affiliated Bay Area Environmental Research Institute, added, "Our results certainly do not indicate such extreme sensitivity to reductions in rainfall."[56]

Following Earth's Runaway Twin

One of the best ways to cause man-made greenhouse warming theory believers' knees to tremble is to assert that the world is at the cusp of a "tipping point." As the Worldwatch Institute's "State of the World 2009" report defines that term, it is when "climate change begins to feed on itself and becomes essentially irreversible for centuries into the future."[57] A "really-bad-case" scenario suggests that this can lead to conditions similar to those on our "sister planet," Venus.

As reported by Mark Bullock at the Laboratory for Atmospheric and Space Physics at University of Colorado–Boulder, in a 1999 *Scientific American* article, "Since Venus and Earth have a number of similarities, there are implications here for our own future."[58] Venus is Earth's twin in the sense that it's made up of a similar composition, and it is believed to once have had a similar atmosphere. But when it comes to current climate, it couldn't be much more different. Venus is the hottest planet in the solar system, with an average temperature of more than 400 and a surface pressure nearly one hundred times greater than Earth's. And while both planets have clouds, those on Venus contain sulfuric acid and CO_2. Venus is slightly smaller than Earth, is closer to the Sun, and has no plate tectonics. Its continents simply tip up every 500 million years or so like the lid on a boiling pot and slide down into a molten core, spewing huge amounts of heat into the atmosphere as they do so. That is a real tipping point!

At some point in Venus's past, its global magnetosphere shut down. Without this force field the Sun's solar wind was able to reach the planet and tear away at its atmosphere, stripping away the lighter atoms. The lightest atom is hydrogen, a constituent of water, which is a major component of Earth's atmosphere (and GHG).[59]

Another really big difference between the two planets—one that accounts for substantially different climate features—is that Venus doesn't rapidly rotate on its axis, creating short day/night cycles as Earth does. In fact, a Venusian day is slightly longer than a Venusian year. This means that the same surface area is exposed to radiant solar heat without relief for very long periods of time. And according to our best reports, there are no sunbathing humans to enjoy these conditions or thus contribute to greenhouse emissions. So don't sweat sibling relationships!

Also, according to MIT scientist Richard Lindzen, "There is no physical basis for suggesting 'tipping points' . . . especially given that the impact of each added amount of CO_2 [in the atmosphere] is less than the impact of its predecessor (i.e., we have diminishing returns)."[60]

Convenient Illusions

Al Gore has represented himself as a learned authority on the mechanisms and threats of a global warning crisis. And if drama trumps real facts in his pronouncements, doubts regarding his convictions may be unwarranted. Still, as someone who frequently quotes a wise observation by Mark Twain, a person he greatly admires, Mr. Gore might carefully consider that advice: "It ain't what you don't know that gets you in trouble. It's what you know for sure that just ain't so."

Another reported "hero" Gore has credited as an important influence is his former Harvard professor Dr. Roger Revelle, a distinguished oceanographer. Dr. Revelle, however, has expressly disagreed with frightening global warming scenarios that Mr.

Gore has promulgated, saying, "Evidence of global warming does not justify drastic measures so far, unless they were justified by reasons having nothing to do with the climate change issue."[61]

Gore obviously wasn't very happy about having his previously touted authority challenge the urgency and rationale of his mission. He countered by accusing his former professor of having become senile when he made those remarks shortly before his fatal heart attack in 1992. Not a very nice way to treat a hero.

Dr. Revelle was not alone in his strong disagreement with factually impaired "Gore lore." Yet most informed scientists who know better are reluctant to publicly speak out on the matter. Such reticence may be attributable to a widespread "emperor's clothes" syndrome associated with multiple causes. Some might be hesitant to say anything that would reflect poorly upon the sanctity of the IPCC, the UN-sanctioned tribunal of truth endowed with the Nobel Prize distinction it shares with fellow Nobel laureate Al Gore. Many may also recognize that contradicting alarmist statements are not helpful in gaining public support essential to sustain an exploding climate science industry.[62]

However, more and more concerned people are speaking out to correct scientifically unsupportable and misleading statements. For example, a judge in London's High Court ruled in October 2007 that the film *An Inconvenient Truth* can be shown only in secondary schools if accompanied by guidance notes for teachers to balance Mr. Gore's "one-sided" views.[63] In comments regarding his ruling, Sir Michael Burton pointed out that the "apocalyptical vision" presented in the film was politically partisan, and not an impartial analysis of the science of climate change: "It is built around the charismatic presence of the ex-vice president Al Gore, whose crusade is to persuade the world of the dangers of climate change caused by global warming . . . It is now common ground that it is not simply a science film—although it is clear that it is based substantially on scientific research and opinion—but it is [clearly] a political film."[64]

John Coleman, founder of the Weather Channel in 1982, expressed strong opinions about Gore's promotions of warming hysteria and his cap-and-trade agenda at an International Conference on Climate Change that was held in New York March 2–4, 2008. The event was sponsored by the Heartland Institute and was attended by more than two hundred scientists from several countries. Coleman told the audience his strategy for exposing what he called "the fraud of global warming": "[I] have a feeling this is the opening. If the lawyers will take the case—sue the people who sell carbon credits. That includes Al Gore. That lawsuit would get so much publicity, so much media attention. And as the experts went to the [media] stand to testify, I feel that could become the vehicle to finally put some light on the fraud of global warming."[65]

Lord Christopher Monckton, a policy adviser to former prime minister Margaret Thatcher who also participated at the New York conference, agreed with Coleman that the courts are a good avenue through which to show real climate science. He also expressed a belief that science will eventually prevail, and that the "scare" of global warming will go away. Anthony Watts, another of the conference speakers, commented, "I was surprised to learn that Al Gore had been offered an opportunity to address this conference, and his usual $200,000 speaking fee and expenses were met, but he declined. I also know that invitations went out to NASA GISS principal scientists Dr. James Hansen and Dr. Gavin Schmidt weeks ago as evidenced by their write-up of the issue on their blog, RealClimate.org, a week or so ago."[66]

It's a shame that Mr. Gore was unable to attend the conference when the weather was nice and warm. It would have been so much better for his message than the timing of a global warming speech he presented in the same city in January 2004, one of the coldest days ever recorded in New York. But then, you can never be certain about the weather.

Chapter 5

UN POLITICAL SCIENCE LESSONS

International experts agree that US capitalism is causing global climate peril.

LARRY BELL

A s I first mentioned in the introduction, most of what we hear daily about global warming—the really scary stuff that gets media headline coverage, wins Academy Awards, and earns Nobel Prizes—originates from reports issued by a United Nations–sponsored corporation, the Intergovernmental Panel on Climate Change. Given the IPCC's tremendous influence in shaping international public opinions, economic policies, environmental and energy legislation, and the political landscapes that determine huge science budget allocations, its background and workings warrant special attention.[1]

The IPCC's genesis is linked in large measure to some converging forces and events that occurred in the US and Europe during the late 1980s. Following the phenomenal growth in environmental movements that began about a decade earlier, green parties in Europe and private special-interest groups in the US gained even greater momentum under a global warming banner. Well-organized lobbying campaigns, backed by large budgets and voting blocs, appealed to the interests of prominent political figures, and leading captains of the media were enlisted in the call for action.[2] Fund-raisers and pundits recognized that "saving the planet" sells well, and what sells even better is the underlying message "pay now or fry."

Global warm-mongering got a boost in 1997 when Washington, DC, group, Ozone Action sent a "Scientists' Statement on Global Climactic Disruption" to then-President Clinton, which they claimed had been signed by 2,611 scientists from the US and abroad. The document was offered to endorse "conclusive" evidence of man-made global warming.[3] But according to Citizens for a Sound Economy, a group that opposed climate alarmism, only about 10 percent of those signers had experience in fields associated with climate science. Others included two landscape architects, ten psychologists, a traditionally trained Chinese doctor, and a gynecologist.[4]

The UN has sponsored and organized a variety of environmental programs that led up to the IPCC's creation and activities. One, termed the Montreal Protocol on Substances That Deplete the Ozone Layer, responded to concerns that human activities were responsible for causing an ozone hole in the stratosphere over Antarctica. The source of the problem was attributed to releases of chlorofluorocarbons (CFCs) used as refrigerants, aerosol propellants, and cleaning solvents. The treaty, which took effect January 1, 1989, has since undergone seven revisions: 1990 (London); 1991 (Nairobi); 1992 (Copenhagen); 1993 (Bangkok); 1995 (Vienna), 1997 (Montreal); and 1999 (Beijing). By September 2007, about two hundred countries agreed to eliminate CFC use by 2020; developing nations were given until 2030. Some critics have argued that richer countries can afford CFC substitutes whereas poorer ones that cannot are realizing increased death rates from food-borne illnesses.

In 1988, the UN turned most of its attention to human GHG emissions when members of two of its organizations—the World Meteorological Organization (WMO) and the United Nations Environment Programme (UNEP)—were assigned to establish the IPCC. The IPCC panel is composed of representatives appointed by governments and is led by government "scientists" who meet about annually and whose role is to control the organization's structure and procedures. While the governments are encouraged to appoint people with appropriate expertise, in practice this may be the exception rather than the rule. Many are primarily bureaucrats, and few have credentials as climate scientists.[5]

Roy Spencer, in his book *The Great Global Warming Blunder*, reports that former IPCC chairman and chief environmental scientist in the Clinton-Gore administration Robert Watson (1997-2002) made it his priority to regulate CO_2 before much of any climate modeling had ever occurred. This intent was expressed to Dr. Spencer and his colleague John Christy soon after Watson had acted as a key 1987 Montreal Protocol negotiator for CFC regulations.

Why did the UN establish the IPCC? Was it to objectively study and determine whether there really was a climate change crisis? Did they wish to explore which ones among a known variety of climate forcings were dominant? Were they curious as to what extent human activities played into the mix? The answer to those questions is, not very likely.

Or rather, had the UN already determined that recently observed climate change was dangerous and that human releases of CO_2 through excessive population growth, industry, and free-market capitalist consumption in developed countries was responsible? And did the UN wish to gain the lead role in straightening everything out through global regulation and resource redistribution? Let's explore these possibilities.

Working the System

First, what the public doesn't generally realize is that the IPCC doesn't actually carry out any original climate research, nor does it even continuously monitor climate-related data. Instead, it simply issues assessments based primarily upon other independent peer-reviewed and published scientific and technical literature. At least, that is what the panel is supposed to do. Yet some of the most influential conclusions that are summarized in its reports have been neither based upon truly independent research nor properly vetted through accepted peer-review processes.[6]

Most of the IPCC's actual work is conducted by separate "working groups" and a "task force" that generally produce quite thorough and objective lengthy technical reports. These individuals are selected on the basis of their special expertise to address designated topics. It should be assumed that most take these responsibilities very seriously. Yet in the interest of international parity, and not in the interest of science, each of the working groups has two cochairs: one from a developing country, and one from the developed world. As might be imagined, this does not reflect a balance of the most qualified expertise.

What each of the working group's reviewers learns goes into a report. If they aren't sure what they have learned about an issue, or they can't agree, they vote among themselves regarding what they think they are most sure about, and their levels of confidence. Some voting members may have little or no real experience in dealing with the particular subjects; they are there to ensure international representation. From the vantage point of political correctness, this process may be fair; scientific correctness, however, is an entirely different matter.

You may have seen references to a "network of thousands of international scientists" involved with IPCC studies. One such source was *Time* magazine's statement that "thousands of scientists from around the world contribute to IPCC reports," as represented by official US government organizations such as the Department of Energy's Pacific Northwest National Laboratory.[7]

How can that many experts be wrong? For starters, let's begin with that wildly exaggerated number of experts. Dr. Vincent Gray reports a far different circumstance based on his firsthand experience as a reviewer for the IPCC's 2007 AR4 report "Summary for Policymakers": "Forget any illusion of hundreds of experts diligently poring over the report and providing extensive feedback to the editing teams. The true picture is closer to 65 reviewers for any one chapter, with about half not commenting on any other chapter and one quarter commenting on just one other."[8]

Unfortunately, very few people ever read those full reports. What happens to those big compilations is that they go through international bureaucratic reviews, where political appointees dissect them line by line to glean the best stuff in support of what IPCC wanted to say in the first place. These cherry-picked items are then assembled and spun into highly condensed reports calibrated to get prime-time and front-page attention.[9]

Political summary editing processes usually progress through a series of drafts that become increasingly media worthy. For example, the original text of an April 2000 Third Assessment Report (TAR) draft stated, "There has been a discernible human influence on global climate."[10] This was followed by an October version that concluded, "It is likely that increasing concentrations of anthropogenic greenhouse gases have contributed significantly to the observed warming over the past 50 years."[11] In the final official summary, the language was toughened up even more: "Most of the observed warming over the past 50 years is likely to have been due to the increase in greenhouse gas contributions."[12]

When the UN Environment Programme's spokesman Tim Higham was asked by *New Scientist* about the scientific background for this change, his answer was honest: "There was no new science, but the scientists wanted to present a clear and strong message to policymakers."[13]

Summary revisions also play down or totally ignore findings that appointed IPCC bureaucrats don't want the public to consider. An earlier TAR draft stated, "In many developing countries, net economic gains are projected for mean temperature increases up to roughly 2°C (36°F). Mixed or neutral net effects are projected in developed countries for temperature increases in the approximate range of 2°C–3°C (36°F–38°F), and net losses for larger temperature increases."[14] Because any mention of net benefits from even moderate global warming would have been unacceptable, the statement in the final summary was changed to "An increase in global mean temperature of up to a few degrees C would produce a mixture of economic gains and losses in developed countries, with economic losses for larger temperature increases." As Bjorn Lomborg points out in his book *The Skeptical Environmentalist*, this "political decision stopped IPCC from looking at the total cost-benefit of global warming and made it focus instead on how to curb further greenhouse gas emissions."[15]

Any scientific objectivity behind IPCC summary reports is illusory. Referring to bureaucratic influence, Keith Shine, a leading IPCC author, described the editing process as follows: "We produce a draft, and then the policymakers go through it line by line and change the way it's presented . . . They don't change the data, but the way it's presented. It is peculiar that they have the final say in what goes into a scientist's report."[16]

And how objective are the scientific editors who participate? Recently deceased Stephen Schneider, a prominent man-made warming theory proponent, served as a lead author of the IPCC Working Group I (1994–1996) and Working Group II (1997–2001) reports. He was also lead author for the IPCC "Guidance Paper on Uncertainties" and coauthor of the "Key Vulnerabilities Cross-Cutting Theme" parts for the 2007 AR4 report. The Stanford University professor obviously became a global warming convert sometime after he had written *The Genesis Strategy* (published in 1976), which addressed global cooling risks. In a 1989 *Discover* magazine interview, he candidly expresses a professional-versus-personal conflict between the side of a scientist concerned with seeking truth and the side concerned with being a citizen who must take an interest in political efficacy.

> On the one hand, as scientists we are ethically bound to the scientific method. On the other hand, we are not just scientists, but human beings as well. And like most people, we'd like to see

the world a better place, which in this context translates into our working to reduce the risk of potentially disastrous climatic change. To do that we need to get some broad-based support, to capture the public's imagination. That, of course, entails getting loads of media coverage. So we have to offer up scary scenarios, make simplified, dramatic statements, and make little mention of any doubts we might have.[17]

In other words, trust not what we tell you, but believe that we have your best interests in mind because our personal intentions are ethical. Accept what we tell you for that reason. If we have to exaggerate the truth and frighten you to get your attention, it's for a righteous cause.

The Confidence Game

To lend scientific authority, IPCC summary reports must above all sound confident. Global forecasts tell us within a comically precise decimal point range that this or that is "virtually certain," "very likely," or "likely" to occur within such and such a time. If we should happen to remember that past predictions have been wrong or significantly revised, the IPCC reassures us that climate models are better now. They are confident about that, and we should be too!

Which might lead us to ask, better than what? If these models are still wrong, how wrong must they be to qualify as totally misleading and useless?

Climate models contain huge uncertainty factors that are broadly recognized by IPCC scientists. They don't (can't) incorporate important unknown and poorly understood variables and relationships, and the parameters can be adjusted ("tuned") to fit almost any climate, including one with no warming or one that cools. Despite the fact that no model has yet successfully predicted any future climate sequence, IPCC summaries confidently present "projections" looking forward hundreds of years based upon creative storylines and untested theories. Those theories are primarily directed to anthropogenic greenhouse forcing factors and warming consequences. Other possible causes and effects are virtually ignored. Yet, although the IPCC has provided an abundance of information about atmospheric GHG concentrations and changes, no evidence of past or future harmful effects, or relationships to "unusual" weather, has yet been produced.[18]

Science researcher Roy Spencer observes that "what scientists claim to know about man-made global warming is based as much upon faith as it is upon knowledge." He regards probabilistic language applied in IPCC summary reports as misleading and inappropriate, stating that "its use is a pseudoscientific way of conveying the level of faith a scientist has in his/her beliefs."[19]

Chapter 8 of the 2000 IPCC TAR report, titled "Model Evaluation," contains this confession: "We fully recognize that many of the evaluation statements we make contain a degree of subjective scientific perception and may contain much 'community' or 'personal' knowledge. For example, the very choice of model variables and model processes that are investigated are often based upon the subjective judgment and experience of the modeling community."[20]

In that same report, the IPCC further admits, "In climate research and modeling, we should recognize that we are dealing with a coupled non-linear chaotic system, and therefore that the long-term prediction of future climate states is not possible."[21] Here, the IPCC openly acknowledges that its models are not accurate. Yet it obviously needs to apply them to justify its ever-growing budget and influence. Without unreliable data from the models, the IPCC might be out of business.

Politics: The Ultimate Scientific Authority

As confirmed by evidence exposed in the purloined CRU e-mail files, scientists with contrary views regarding anthropogenic greenhouse warming or the efficacy of present-day climate models aren't likely to be prominently represented in IPCC processes or summary reports. Prior to release, drafts are circulated to "expert reviewers" throughout the world for comment, and unwelcome statements are deleted. Statements that are not consistent with the views of designated main authors stand little chance of being seriously considered. The first 1990 report, which was particularly influential as the basis for negotiating the United Nations' FCCC (the Kyoto Protocol), included the following statement: "Whilst every attempt was made by the lead authors to incorporate their comments, in some cases those formed a minority opinion which could not be reconciled with the larger consensus."[22]

In the IPCC's 1995 Second Assessment Report (SAR), the crucial Chapter 8 of the final draft denied any evidence connecting observed climate changes to anthropogenic greenhouse causes (the "fingerprint" factor). In fact, Figure 8.10b of that report showed the pattern correlation of measured observations and climate models actually decreasing during a major surface warming surge between 1916 and 1940. The consulting scientists approved the draft, along with the full report, in December 1995.[23] Its conclusions, based upon reviews of 130 peer-reviewed science studies, were these:

- "None of the studies cited above has shown clear evidence that we can attribute the observed [climate] changes to the specific cause of increases in greenhouse gases."
- "While some of the pattern-based studies discussed here have claimed detection of a significant climate change, no study to date has positively attributed all or part [of the climate change observed] to [man-made] causes. Nor has any study quantified the magnitude of a greenhouse gas effect in the observed data—an issue of primary relevance to policy makers."
- "Any claims of positive detection and attribution of significant climate change are likely to remain controversial until uncertainties in the total natural variability of the climate system are reduced."
- "While none of these studies has specifically considered the attribution issue, they often draw some attribution conclusions, for which there is little justification."
- "When will an anthropogenic effect on climate be identified? It is not surprising that the best answer to this question is, 'We do not know.'"[24]

This all was to change. Sir John Houghton, chairman of Working Group I, received a letter from the US State Department dated November 15, 1995, and signed by then–Acting Deputy Assistant Secretary Day Olin Mount. He reported to Undersecretary of State for Global Affairs Timothy Wirth, a former senator (D-CO), close political ally of then-Vice President Gore and ardent believer in man-made global warming. The letter said, "It is essential that the chapters not be finalized prior to the completion of the discussions at the IPCC Working Group I Plenary in Madrid, and that chapter authors be prevailed upon to modify their text in an appropriate manner following the discussion in Madrid."[25]

The following year, Mount was appointed by President Bill Clinton to the prestigious position of Ambassador to Iceland. Wirth was appointed to head the United Nations Foundation. Both knew on which side their toast was buttered.

The Madrid Plenary, which took place in November, was a political meeting involving appointed representatives from ninety-six nations and fourteen nongovernmental organizations (NGOs). Participants went over the "accepted" Chapter 8 text, line by line. That chapter, which should have governed the entire IPCC report, was then substantially rewritten to advance a global warming campaign being waged by the UN, the NGOs, and the White House.

In May 1996, after the report was released, the Chapter 8 conclusions were startlingly different from the scientists' accepted version. The Chapter 8 lead author, Ben Santer, from the US government's Lawrence Livermore National Laboratory, had excised denials of any scientific evidence of man-made warming, replacing them with statements asserting just the opposite: "The body of statistical evidence in Chapter 8, when examined in the context of our physical understanding of the climate system, now points to a discernible human influence on the global climate."[26]

Mr. Santer's changes appeared to be based primarily upon two unpublished papers he himself had submitted, which had not been peer-reviewed at the time. However, a published paper he coauthored at about the same time contradicted his Chapter 8 IPCC report insertions. That paper concludes that different estimates of three natural climate variability influences are inconsistent, and until that question is resolved, "it will be hard to say, with confidence, that an anthropogenic climate signal has or has not been detected." That, in fact, is very much in line with the original Chapter 8 science conclusions.[27]

But that's not what most people remember. The "discernible human influence" insertion, which reversed the entire IPCC climate science report, purportedly ended all debate on this matter, providing an official foundation for the UN-sponsored Kyoto Protocol to follow in 1997.[28]

The revision epitomizes the reality of political intrusions into science. The *Wall Street Journal* condemned the 1995 SAR revision in a July 1996 editorial, "Coverup in the Greenhouse."[29] The journal *Nature*, which unlike the *Wall Street Journal* tended to favor a Kyoto Protocol rebuffed the IPCC for rewriting Chapter 8 to "ensure that it conformed" with political correctness. Former National Academy of Sciences president Dr. Frederick Seitz detailed his objections to the illegitimate rewrite in a *Wall Street Journal* article titled "A Major Deception on Global Warming" on June 12, 1996.[30]

Challenging Processes

The IPCC's activities concentrate on tasks assigned by the WMO's Executive Council and the UNEP's Governing Council resolutions and decisions, along with priorities that support the UN Framework Convention on Climate Change process guidelines. Prominent critics have called into question both those activities and those priorities. As noted by Dr. Fred Singer in the foreword of this book, one of these critics is Dr. Seitz, who publicly denounced the SAR report, stating, "I have never witnessed a more disturbing corruption of the peer-review process than the events that led to this IPCC report."[31]

Referring to the third report (TAR), Sir John Maddox, a former editor of the journal *Nature*, observed, "The IPCC is monolithic and complacent, and it is conceivable that they are exaggerating the speed of [climate] change."[32]

The UK House of Lords' "Scientific and Economic Analysis Report" on the IPCC for the G-8 Summit, July 2005, stated, "We have some concerns about the objectivity of the IPCC process, with some of its emissions scenarios and summary documentation apparently influenced by political considerations."[33]

A study conducted by the National Center for Policy Analysis, a nonprofit, nonpartisan policy research organization, determined that the IPCC's 2007 AR4 report clearly violated 60 of 127 principles associated with sound forecasting methods, and only really followed 17 of those. As reported by H. Sterling Burnett, author of the *Washington Times* story that reported the study, "A good example of a principle clearly violated is 'Make sure forecasts are independent of politics' . . . Politics shapes the IPCC from beginning to end. Legislators, policymakers and/or diplomatic appointees select (or approve) the scientists—at least the lead scientists— who make up the IPCC. In addition, the summary and the final draft of the IPCC's Fourth Assessment Report was written in collaboration with political appointees and [is] subject to their approval."[34]

Commenting upon observations by Kesten Green and J. Scott Armstrong, who conducted the IPCC audit, Burnett said, "Sadly, Mr. Green and Mr. Armstrong found no evidence that the IPCC was even aware of the vast literature on scientific forecasting methods, much less applied the principles."[35]

Edward J. Wegman, a George Mason University professor who chaired the panel of audit investigators, concluded that based upon the IPCC's flawed statistical analyses and procedures, the idea that the planet is experiencing unprecedented warming "cannot be supported." He warned that policy makers should take this into account before enacting laws to counter global warming that would have severe economic consequences.[36]

Some of the East Anglia CRU e-mails confirm pressures to provide clear and politically compelling IPCC report conclusions, whether or not they were supportable by solid science. Keith Briffa commented in one exchange, "I know there is pressure to present a nice tidy story as regards apparent unprecedented warming in a thousand years or more." In another he stated, "In reality the situation is not quite so simple" (based upon tree ring research involving the illegitimate hockey stick charts he coproduced with Michael Mann).[37]

In September 2000, Fillipo Giorgi of the International Centre for Theoretical Physics in Trieste, Italy, wrote an e-mail stating that he felt pressure to cite model simulations that hadn't yet been peer-reviewed. He worried that this demonstrated an unacceptable relaxation of scientific standards in which the IPCC rules "have been softened to the point that in this way the IPCC is not any more an assessment of published science which is not its proclaimed goal." He added: "At this point there are very little rules and almost anything goes. I think this will set a dangerous precedent."[38]

Roger Pielke, a University of Colorado political science professor, believes that many IPCC participants want to compel action instead of "just summarize science."[39] Andrew Weaver, a senior Canadian climate scientist at the University of Victoria, agrees that IPCC leadership has allowed the panel to advocate for action on global warming rather than serve as a neutral science advisory body.

In a January 2010 interview with the Canwest News Service, Weaver echoed published sentiments of other top climate scientists in the US and Europe: "There's been some dangerous crossing of the line. Some might argue we need a change in some of the upper leadership of the IPCC, who are perceived as becoming advocates. I think that is a very legitimate question."[40]

Weaver specifically urged that IPCC's chairman, Rajendra Pachauri, should resign and that other officials should cease being "overly enthusiastic" in pushing policy changes. Even the activist organization Greenpeace has joined a push for Pachauri's ousting to benefit IPCC credibility. Greenpeace director John Sauven argued that "we need someone held in high regard who has extremely good judgment and is seen by the global public as someone on their side."[41]

The InterAcademy Council, an Amsterdam-based association of the world's leading academic national science academies, agreed that a "fundamental reform" of IPCC's management structure is needed. In a report released on August 30, 2010 following a review of IPCC practices and methodologies leading to their 2007 report, the Council found two types of errors. Its chairman, Harold T. Shapiro, stated that, "One is the kind where they place high confidence in something where there is little evidence. The other is the kind where you make a statement . . . with no substantive value." The Council also found the IPCC guilty of making a fraudulent claim that the Himalayan glaciers will be gone by 2035, stating that, "IPCC was not paying close enough attention to what reviewers said about this example."[42]

There are also those who point to some apparent conflicts of interest on the part of the IPCC's chairman. Since Dr. Pachauri took control of the Tata Energy Research Institute (TERI) in the 1980s, that large Indian company has vastly extended its interests in virtually every kind of renewable and sustainable energy technology. For example, its Tata Group has invested $1.5 billion in a huge wind farm project. Another project, cofinanced by the UK Department of Environment, Food and Rural Affairs and the German Insurance firm Munich Re, is studying how India's insurance industry, including Tata, can benefit from exploiting the supposed risks of exposure to climate change.[43]

Some believe that Pachauri's obstinate refusal to quit despite the heavy weight of condemnation by even his own panel members may be having an effect upon his mental stability. Responding to critics in a *Financial Times* interview, he characterized global warming skeptics as "people who say that asbestos is as good as talcum powder." He also expressed hope that such people would "apply it to their faces every day."[44]

Ross McKitrick, who challenged and exposed the now-infamous hockey stick temperature data, believes that the IPCC's scientific failings and its willingness to cross the line into advocacy will eventually percolate into the public policy arena. He claims, "The halo has come off of the IPCC. At the time of the 2007 report, there were very few politicians willing to question statements from the IPCC. Now, as this plays out, people will start to be embarrassed to cite the IPCC."[45]

The Big Heist: Political Hijacking of Science

In essence, then, we've seen that the IPCC, the primary source of much of what we hear about global warming, is not a scientific body. It is a UN-sponsored political advocacy mouthpiece for its own special interests. It does not conduct science; it conducts politics. It performs or supports no original research. Rather, it invites and appoints people who do research, along with others who don't, to review reports that agree with fixed views and agendas—and to ignore or even block findings that do not.

The global warming rubric has served as an ideal platform to enable the UN to advance large philosophical visions, wealth distribution agendas, and world governance goals under a banner of global environmentalism. Dangerous climate change and attributing its cause to human activities serve as pretenses for a much broader global environmentalism doctrine aimed at defeating capitalism and free market choices.

If this sounds a bit like conspiratorial paranoia, let's review the words spoken by then-President Jacques Chirac of France in a 2000 speech supporting a key Western European Kyoto Protocol objective: "For the first time, humanity is instituting a genuine instrument of global governance, one that should find a place within the World Environmental Organization which France and the European Union would like to see established."[46]

IPCC Working Group II "Summary for Policymakers" reports go far beyond science, offering prescriptions for a better, more equitable distribution of wealth and resources. They explicitly point out that due to environmental scarcity, cars and trains should be restricted to lower, more efficient top speeds; sails should be emphasized for ships to save fuel; biomass should become the primary fuel source; and bicycle use should be encouraged. Regionalized (smaller) economies should be created to reduce transportation demand; lifestyles should be reoriented away from consumption; and sharing resources should be emphasized, such as through co-ownership. Citizens should be encouraged to pursue free time over wealth, to choose quality rather than quantity, and to "increase freedom while containing consumption." People should resist indoctrination by the media to want things that shape their values and identities. The media should direct our paths toward a more sustainable world, raising awareness among media professionals of the need for GHG mitigation and the role of the media in shaping lifestyles and aspirations to encourage a wider cultural shift.[47]

Irresponsible claims within IPCC summary reports have led to legal ones in the form of junk lawsuits. In one, the plaintiffs asked defendant utility plants to reduce their CO_2 emissions throughout a wide area of the US. The New York Federal Appellate Court ruled in September 2009 that this regulation-by-judge could go forward even though the EPA is considering such regulations as well.

In a second case, the plaintiffs alleged that global warming caused by the CO_2 emissions released by fossil fuel–burning utility companies increased the ferocity of Hurricane Katrina. The class action suit seeks payment for all storm area damages, and the Federal Appellate Court in New Orleans ruled that the case can go forward.

An Alaskan Indian tribe filed a suit in San Francisco alleging that its village will be destroyed by rising sea levels as glaciers melt due to global warming. The tribe is seeking reimbursement costs from energy and power company defendants because of its need to relocate. In this instance the trial court dismissed the case.[48]

Finally, some US federal and state legislators are beginning to combat the IPCC's scientific abuses. Senator John Barrasso (R-WY) has called for Rajendra Pachauri to resign, stating that "new scandals" emerge "every day" about the "so-called facts" in the panel's reports and that "the integrity of the data and the integrity of the science [have] been compromised . . . The scientific data behind these policies must be independently verified."[49]

Unsurprisingly, Senator Inhofe, the ranking member of the Senate Committee on Environment and Public Works, is joining Senator Barrasso in calling for an investigation of the IPCC. Senator Inhofe has been a strong and vocal critic of climate fearmongering, calling man-made global warming "the greatest hoax ever perpetrated on the American people." Prior to the Climategate scandal, he released a committee report titled "More Than 700 International Scientists Dissent Over Man-made Global Warming Claims—Scientists Continue to Debunk 'Consensus' in 2008 and 2009."[50]

Representative Blaine Luetkemeyer (R-MO) has introduced a House bill that would cut US funding for the IPCC. He characterized the organization as one "which is nothing more than a group of UN bureaucrats that supports man-made claims on global warming that many scientists disagree with."[51]

Texas authorities have announced that the state is taking legal action against the EPA's efforts to curb GHG emissions under the Clean Air Act. In its filing, the state argued that the EPA based its decision on IPCC data.

According to the Associated Press, Virginia attorney general Kenneth T. Cuccinelli has asked the EPA to delay final consideration of the endangerment finding regarding CO_2 emissions so that "newly available information" can be reviewed.[52]

In total, what has the IPCC's review of climate change science reports determined? It has concluded that policy makers rather than the free markets should determine our economic desires and lifestyles. Since global warming—the basis for this justification—has no boundaries, the UN would be the logical world seat of governance. There, politicians from around the world can jointly determine what is proper and fair for all of us. And they received a Nobel prize for this?

Chapter 6

CONTRAILS OVER COPENHAGEN

Earth's last chance before the next last chance.

T he Copenhagen Summit of 2009 was billed as "the Earth's last chance."
The real agenda, however, was to pressure the US and other industrialized
countries to pay retributions to less fortunate nations for excessive energy
consumption. This was not the first time that an international forum gathered to
promote the cause of global warming. The buildup to this ultimately hapless event
began more than 20 years earlier.

A period of global cooling that ended in the 1970s was followed by a warming surge. Losing no time, the UN, through its WMO and UNEP, not only had established by 1988 that the warming was due to a "greenhouse effect" but also, even more remarkably, had already determined that human activities were substantially to blame. They pronounced that immediate and drastic reductions were needed to stabilize conditions. That ominous conclusion, in turn, provided the rationale for the UN to sponsor the huge Conference on Environment and Development (UNCED), or Earth Summit, in Rio de Janeiro in June 1992, where participating countries began to negotiate international agreements for stabilizing "dangerous" anthropogenic GHGs (principally CO_2) at 1990 levels. The original deadline for accomplishing this was 2000, and 154 nations agreed to sign on.

Yet no scientific data existed to serve as a sound basis for either those danger assertions or the UN's motivation to establish its Framework Convention on Climate Change in 1992, which stated that "human activities have been substantially increasing the atmospheric concentrations of greenhouse gases, that these increases enhance the natural greenhouse effect, and that this will result on average in the additional warming of the Earth's surface and atmosphere and may adversely affect natural ecosystems and mankind."[1]

No, there was no scientific evidence to back up those statements or to justify the Kyoto Protocol, which the FCCC spawned to cap CO_2 emissions in developed countries while giving China and India a pass. There wasn't any evidence to support those assumptions in February 2005 when the agreement went into force—and there still isn't today.

The Road from Rio: Politics in the Fast Lane

Heads of state from dozens of countries that were concerned that global warming was a real and dangerous threat to mankind attended the Earth Summit. The event, chaired by billionaire Canadian businessman Maurice Strong, attracted an estimated forty thousand participants. Mr. Strong had previously served as secretary general for a 1972 UN Conference on the Human Environment, and in 1992, he was executive director of UNEP. He later became a key person in bringing together the thousands of international bureaucrats, diplomats, and politicians who participated in the Kyoto Protocol deliberations.

Mr. Strong has an interesting and active background. He and his wife, Hanne, an occultist, had earlier established a global headquarters in San Luis Valley,

Colorado, for the New Age movement called "Baca," after a mystic informed them it "would become the center for a new planetary order which would evolve from the economic collapse and environmental catastrophes that would sweep the globe in the years to come." Together, the Strongs created the Manitou Foundation, which brought together devotees of diverse religious sects, both traditional and mystical. Actress Shirley MacLaine's astrologer told her to move there, and she did.[2]

The Strongs' Baca Grande ranch sat on one of the North American continent's largest freshwater aquifers, from which Mr. Strong intended to pipe water to the desert Southwest. The plan was abandoned due to protests from environmental groups. Strong ended up with a $1.2 million settlement from the local water company, yet retained rights to the water.

A 2005 inquiry into the corrupt UN "Oil-for-Food" program revealed that nearly $1 million was funneled into a Strong-owned family company account by Iraq Foreign Minister Tariq Aziz through a North Korean contact. His purpose was to persuade the UN to grant Saddam Hussein's government certain exemptions from an export ban. Since Kyoto, Strong had acted as a personal intermediary for UN Secretary General Kofi Annan for various missions, including contacts with North Korea's communist regime. He had also maintained close friendships with top Chinese government leaders going back in time to the Cultural Revolution under Mao Tse-tung. After his role in the scandal was revealed 8 years later, he took up residence in a penthouse flat of a building occupied by UN agencies in the Chinese capital.[3]

Strong was a major contributor to a 1987 Brundtland Commission report titled "Our Common Future," which had been sponsored by the UN's World Commission on Environment and Development. The WCED is broadly credited with igniting the "green movement" and popularizing the term "sustainable environment." Its purpose was to address growing concern "about the accelerating deterioration of the human environment and natural resources and the consequences of that deterioration for human and social development."

It is no secret where Strong placed most of the blame for that deterioration. He has complained that "the United States is clearly the greatest risk to the world's ecological health." Furthermore, he clearly stated in the UNCED August 28, 1991, report: "It is clear that current lifestyles and consumption patterns of the affluent middle class . . . involving high meat intake, consumption of large amounts of frozen and convenience foods, ownership of motor vehicles, small electric appliances, home and work place air-conditioning, and suburban housing are not sustainable . . . A shift is necessary toward lifestyles less geared to environmentally damaging consumption patterns."[4]

Strong wrote the introduction to *Beyond Interdependence: The Meshing of the World's Economy and the Earth's Ecology*, which was published in 1992 by the Trilateral Commission, a private organization founded by David Rockefeller, chairman of the UN Council on Human Relations in 1973. In that introduction, Strong boasts, "This book couldn't appear at a better time, with the preparation for the Earth Summit moving into gear . . . it will help guide decisions that will literally determine the fate of the Earth . . . Rio will have the political capacity to produce the basic changes needed in our international economic agendas and in our institutions of governance."[5]

And Rio later attempted to accomplish just that. Chairman Strong made it quite clear to the Rio audience that he was an environmentalist at all costs: "We may get to the point where the only way of saving the world will be for industrial civilization to collapse." This was a Strong beginning in that direction for certain.

Timothy Wirth, then serving as undersecretary of state for global affairs in the Clinton-Gore administration, seconded Strong's statement. He left no doubt regarding his indifference toward protecting scientific integrity, which became evident later in the 1995 SAR rewrite events: "We have got to ride the global warming issue. Even if the theory of global warming is wrong, we will be doing the right thing in terms of economic policy and environmental policy."[6]

Also speaking at the Rio conference, Deputy Assistant of State Richard Benedick, who was then head of the policy divisions of the US State Department, agreed: "A global warming treaty must be implemented even if there is no scientific evidence to back the [enhanced] greenhouse effect."[7] Doesn't that pretty much say it all with regard to agenda?

Wealth of Nations: An Unfair Advantage

The UN's central Kyoto Protocol theme, codified through its Rio meeting agenda framework, revolved around a "common but differentiated responsibilities" rationale that has remained eternally clear and constant. In Rio, all the parties were in agreement about the following:

- "The largest share of historical and current global emissions of greenhouse gases has originated in developed countries."
- "Per capita emissions in developing countries are relatively low [this was before China and India changed that picture]."

- "The share of global emissions originating in developing countries will grow to meet their social and development needs."

The treaty that was negotiated in Kyoto, Japan, in December 1997 opened for signature on March 16, 1998, and went into effect on February 16, 2005, following ratification by Russia on November 16, 2004. As discussed later, Russia's decision to sign on had nothing to do with climate issues. As of April 2008, a total of 178 countries and other governmental entities had signed on and ratified its terms. Actual compliance, however, has fallen far short of that number.

The agreement placed virtually all responsibility for GHG reductions upon "Annex I" (industrialized countries), particularly those among them listed as "Annex II" (developed countries)—a subset made up of members of the UN-sponsored Organization for Economic Cooperation and Development established in 1960. The Annex I signatories agreed to (1) reduce GHG emissions (particularly CO_2) to targets below their respective 1990 levels by 2012 when the Kyoto Treaty expires; (2) purchase emission credits from other nations; and (3) invest in sanctioned conservation measures. Annex II ratifiers are required to pay costs to assist developing (exempt) countries in reducing emissions. The US and Australia, both prospective Annex II members, have refrained from ratifying the agreement.[8]

Kyoto Protocol: Annex I and Annex II Categories
Industrialized and Developed Countries

°Australia, *Austria, Belarus, Belgium, Bulgaria, *Canada, Croatia, Czech Republic, *Denmark, Estonia, *Finland, *France,*Germany, *Greece, Hungary, *Iceland, *Ireland, *Italy, *Japan, Latvia, Liechtenstein, Lithuania,

*Luxembourg, Monaco, *Netherlands, *New Zealand, *Norway, Poland, *Portugal, Romania, Russian Federation, Slovakia, Slovenia, *Spain, *Sweden, *Switzerland, Turkey, Ukraine, *United Kingdom, °United States,

and separately, the *European Union

Annex I Industrialized Countries
*Annex II Developed Countries (Ratifying)
°Annex II Developed Countries (Non-Ratifying)

Although it sounds very official, the Kyoto Protocol agreement terms were drafted and approved by a global warming alliance involving NGOs appointed by functionaries of the United Nations. Neither the UN nor its NGO appointees actually control any people or territories, or are headed by publicly elected representatives. NGOs are much more prominent in Europe than they are in this country. For example, the Climate Action Network in Europe is a group of more than 365 NGOs funded by the European Commission along with the Dutch and Belgian governments; the Climate Action Network in the United States consists of about forty NGOs. Still, such organizations collectively managed to mobilize nearly twenty thousand attendees who traveled to Rio for the Earth Summit from all over the world. Most of them actually attended a parallel "cheerleaders" conference (an NGO forum held nearby), and only about twenty-four hundred attended the actual summit as delegates.[9]

The Kyoto Protocol built upon the success of another UN-sponsored agreement, the Montreal Protocol of 1989, which focused world attention on reducing manufactured ozone-depleting chemicals ("CFCs"), which were posited as causing an "ozone hole" over Antarctica that had led to higher incidents of skin cancer.[10] Since that scare, there now appears to be a trend of recovery in the ozone layer, and the hole may soon close more rapidly than reduced CFC levels would produce. Some research indicates that this reversal may be caused, or at least assisted by, shifts in atmospheric wind patterns.[11]

Green parties in Western European nations have expanded greatly since the 1970s, and they have become an important force within fragile government political coalitions. Accordingly, the participation of thousands of environmental activists at Rio captured great political attention in the UK. Primary themes continue to be that cheap energy is the root cause of technological abundance that has created modern "throw-away" societies, and that the answer is to turn away from fossils, replacing them with cleaner solar and wind alternatives. Organic farming is also emphasized to avoid evils posed by artificial chemicals. Paul Ehrlich, a prominent environmental scientist at Stanford University and author of the best-selling book *The Population Bomb* (1968), clearly espouses these views, and he attributes many of the world's problems to "too many rich people."[12]

The late Aaron Wildavsky, a professor of political science at the University of California–Berkeley, identified a close connection between the proclamation that global warming is the mother of all environmental scares and the ultimate goals of some green coalition activists: advocacy. He said, "Warming (and warming alone), through its primary antidote of withdrawing carbon from production and consumption, is capable of realizing the environmentalist's dream of an egalitarian society based on rejection of economic growth in favor of smaller populations eating lower on the food chain, consuming a lot less, and sharing a much lower level of resources more equally."[13]

Fossils and their CO_2 emission progeny then become important targets, due to their central connections to industrial growth, transportation, and modern life in general. This thinking also serves the interests of the United Nations. Applying a convenient greenhouse theory, the global warming scare provides an ideal way to expand influence and power through an ability to impose de facto rationing of scarce and vital resources.[14]

Of course, this is intended for the public good. As the FCCC's Article 2 states, the objective is to "achieve stabilization of GHG concentrations in the atmosphere at a level that would prevent dangerous anthropogenic interference with the climate system." Yet nowhere in either the FCCC or the Kyoto Protocol is it ever clarified what GHG levels are "dangerous," either to humans or to the ecosystems, or how the danger claim is truly justifiable.[15]

The US Senate Sends a Message: No Way!

The US Senate recognized that proposed Kyoto Protocol regulations would bring disastrous consequences to America's economy and took action to kill that threat. In a rare spirit of solidarity, the Senate unanimously passed (95-0) the bipartisan Byrd-Hagle US Senate Resolution (S Res 98), which made it clear that the United States would not be a signatory to any agreement that "would result in serious harm to the economy of the United States." The Senate was particularly antagonistic toward any agreement that didn't include binding targets and timetables for both developing and industrialized nations.

Then-President Bill Clinton, no stranger to political pragmatism, immediately got the message and never submitted a US approval request for congressional ratification. You can bet that his vice president, who had participated in Kyoto Protocol negotiations on behalf of Clinton's administration in 1997, wasn't one bit happy about these developments.

Al Gore was gearing up for his ultimately unsuccessful run for the presidency in 2000, featuring environmental priorities as a big pitch point. Then, as now, he promoted global warming as a threat to humanity, hawking cap-and-trade legislation as the road to salvation. The US Senate rebuff of Kyoto, along with Gore's own administration's unwillingness to pursue ratification, was an obvious and embarrassing setback. Yet in subsequent speeches, Gore never seems to clarify those real circumstances during his global publicity forays, suggesting instead that Kyoto was "Bushwacked." Perhaps he counts on the likelihood that his audiences are too young to know differently, too old and senile to remember, or just too indifferent to have been paying attention. In any case, the political tide—if not the polar seas—had truly risen, and for a time had turned against him.

On June 11, 2001, a few months after taking office, President George W. Bush commented publicly regarding his views of the Kyoto Protocol, calling it "fatally flawed in fundamental ways." He reported that his cabinet-level Working Group on Global Warming had "asked the highly respected National Academy of Sciences to provide us with the most up-to-date information [on] what is known about and what is not known about the science of climate change."[16] He then summarized the conclusions of that working group:

- "First, we know the surface temperature of the Earth is warming. It has risen by 0.6°C [1.08°F] over the past 100 years. There was a warming trend from the 1890s to the 1940s; cooling from the 1940s to the 1970s; and then sharply rising temperatures from the 1970s to today."

- "There is a natural greenhouse effect that contributes to warming . . . Concentrations of greenhouse gases, especially CO_2, have increased substantially since the beginning of the Industrial Revolution. And the NAS indicates that the increase is due in large part to human activity."

- "Yet the Academy's report tells us that we do not know how much effect natural fluctuations in climate may have had on warming. We do not know how much our climate could or will change in the future. We do not know how fast change will occur, or even how some of our actions could impact it. For example, our useful efforts to reduce sulfur emissions may have actually increased warming because sulfate particles reflect sunlight, bouncing it back into space. And, finally no one can say with any certainty what constitutes a dangerous level of warming, and therefore what level must be avoided. The policy challenge is to act in a serious and sensible way, given the limits of our knowledge."[17]

From the beginning, prominent US scientists and economists have opposed the Kyoto Protocol provisions. Some of those critics are from Al Gore's alma mater; a strongly critical review article titled "Problems with the Protocol," for instance, was published in the November/December 2002 issue of *Harvard Magazine*. Common observations were that the Kyoto Protocol was economically inefficient, nonobjective, inequitable, and ineffective. One of the major failures cited is the exclusion of China, "the largest future source of CO_2 emissions" (and now the current largest source). Critics also argued that the agreement gave Europeans a massive advantage over other countries in reducing CO_2 emissions below 1990 levels.[18]

The 2008 completion date mandated by the Protocol was recognized to present major problems for the US. Economists argued that the typical lifetime of a power plant is approximately 30 years, and the average US automobile is on the road for about 11 years. Changing the energy economy too rapidly by retiring equipment would be economically unproductive.

Other disagreements with the protocol argued against the postulated environmental advantages that would result from GHG restrictions. For example, it awards credit for planting forests to sequester carbon but does so in a way that provides economic incentives to destroy wetlands, potentially creating net excess CO_2 releases. It also doesn't set long-term goals for reduction in atmospheric CO_2 concentrations. Many believe that the real effects upon climate change would be virtually nonexistent in any case, because an estimated 2 to 3 percent emission reduction by 2050 would be well within the margin of error, not to mention being trivial compared with natural sequestration by the marine and terrestrial biosphere.

European Agendas: Hot Air and Smoke Screens

The terms and conditions put forth in the Kyoto Protocol have been strongly influenced and advocated by Western European governments that have been greatly displeased with the United States' unwillingness to buy in. They have argued that the American refusal to ratify the protocol gives this country an unfair economic advantage in competition with other industrialized countries and is unreasonable because of the high US GHG emission levels as compared with theirs. Considering their own lack of any real progress toward meeting those emission reduction targets, one might wonder why they persist in championing those elusive and terrifically costly goals. Many contentious disagreements are rooted in a political history and socialist philosophy that differ from ours in notable ways.[19]

One important difference between the US and many Western European countries is the way political systems are structured and operate. Unlike this country's two-party system with winner-take-all elections, European governments are most typically coalitions where minority parties, such as "greens," can wield important and deciding leverage regardless of who wins. This gives minority groups with special agendas real, often determinate power in the political arena.

Europe's strongly socialist leanings saddle its populations with high tax burdens essential to support large welfare programs that stunt economic investment and profitability essential for competition in global markets. In contrast, US emphasis upon economic growth through lower taxes, high productivity, and strong employment levels is designed to support consumer purchase power. It is only reasonable, at least from a Western European political perspective, to want to saddle the US with the high energy costs associated with Protocol compliance that will help level the field of international commerce.[20]

Selecting 1990 as the base year from which Kyoto emission reductions are to be measured suspiciously favors several European countries at the expense of US interests, placing most of the economic burdens upon American industries, consumers, and taxpayers. This would occur regardless of whether any climate benefits were realistically achievable or not.

While US emissions today are higher than they were in 1990, the emissions in some European nations are actually lower. By the time the Kyoto Protocol was negotiated, German and British GHG emissions were both already about 9 percent below 1990 levels. The reunification of Germany has led to the elimination of many East German industries that were huge polluters, lowering their emission levels below the 1990 benchmark date. And the discovery of large natural gas fields in the North Sea enabled Prime Minister Margaret Thatcher to break up the British Coal Union in the 1980s and move the energy system to gas, phasing out large segments of its coal industry. Yet, although Prime Minister Tony Blair later proposed to reduce CO_2 emissions 60 percent by 2050, British CO_2 emissions have actually increased more than 3 percent since 1997.[21]

The Kyoto Protocol provides a good excuse for European governments to levy even higher taxes on oil for consumers in the laudable cause of saving the planet—taxes that are already several times the actual cost of each barrel. Neither current lack of compliance nor prospects for even higher taxes, however, appears to have substantially dampened general Kyoto popularity in Britain, particularly not in segments of its scientific community.[22] For example, the Royal Society (the UK and Commonwealth's national academy of science) recently wrote an open letter to the US oil company ExxonMobil demanding that it stop funding global warming skeptics. The letter particularly mentions the negative effects of such skepticism on the implementation of Kyoto Protocol CO_2 emission reductions.[23]

Miraculous Conversion: Russia Gets Religion

The Kyoto Protocol was stalled between 1997 and 2005 for lack of sufficient signatories. Both the US and Australia had refused to ratify, for somewhat different reasons. The US objected to the unwarranted destructive economic impacts and to the compliance exemptions extended to China and India. Australia primarily objected to a condition that linked GHG emission reduction targets to per capita population ratios, which penalized them as an industrial country with relatively few people. Russia had been another holdout, and the Europeans badly needed them to get on board.

Originally, Russian president Vladimir Putin had announced on December 2, 2003, that his country would not ratify the protocol for reasons similar to those stated by President George W. Bush and prominent scientists in the United States. Putin observed that the treaty was "scientifically flawed" and that "even 100 percent compliance with the Kyoto Protocol won't reverse climate change."[24]

The Russian Academy of Sciences presented scientific arguments against signing Kyoto in a statement issued on July 1, 2005. It noted that the world's temperatures do not follow CO_2 levels. Instead, the academy observed a much closer correlation between world temperatures and solar activity than with CO_2 levels. The Russian scientists had determined that sea levels were not rising faster with warming; rather, they had been increasing steadily about 6 inches per century since the Little Ice Age ended in about 1850. They discounted one of the most significant danger claims about global warming—that tropical diseases would spread—noting that malaria is a disease encouraged by sunlit pools of water where mosquitoes can breed, not by climate warmth. They also pointed out the lack of a correlation between global warming and extreme weather, which a British government scientific delegation admitted it could find no evidence to support.[25]

What, then, ultimately caused Putin and the Russian Duma to change their position and ratify the protocol? It is widely speculated that Europeans were instrumental in getting Russia admitted to the World Trade Organization (WTO) and thus categorized as a developing country rather than a developed one in applying the protocol's regulations. Russia also received an opportunity to sell to European countries billions of dollars' worth of its former Soviet-era emission credits associated with former dirty industries that had been casualties of economic meltdown. This would also help Europe meet Kyoto's first-phase requirements without actually cutting emissions or energy use.

Europe's 1990 CO_2 emissions of 4,245 million tons fell to 4,123 million tons in 2002 due to reductions in burning coal in both Britain and former East Germany. Yet Kyoto Protocol requirements stipulated further European Union (EU) cutbacks, to 3,906 million tons before 2012. A December 2003 UN report predicted that the EU would miss that reduction target by even more than that amount, namely, by dropping an additional 311 million tons. Since Russia's 1990 emissions were 2,405 million tons and had fallen by 2001 to 1,614 million tons, they could sell up to 800 million tons of credits to the Europeans at an "auction" price. This would be cheaper for Europe than shutting down fossil-fired power plants or removing trucks from its vital transportation infrastructure by escalating already high diesel fuel taxes.

Incidentally, the United States would not be given comparable breaks such as those accorded to the Europeans and Russians. First, unlike European and former Soviet countries that were treated as separate emission credit–trading entities, the US was treated as a single nation (no credit exchanging between states to meet quotas). Second, the US emissions in 1990 were not inflated to high target allowance levels as was the case in Germany, Britain, and Russia, making compliance much more difficult to achieve.[26]

Protocol Progress: Detours along the Road

Since early 2005, many key signatory countries have found that their CO_2 emissions are increasing rather than diminishing. Problems in meeting targets have become clear to many—some of whom realized this probability before the Kyoto Protocol was even enacted.

Canada, which ratified the treaty on December 17, 2002, had agreed to reduce emissions to 6 percent below 1990 levels between 2008 and 2012. The country was influenced by numerous polls indicating high levels of public support (about 70 percent approval). By 2003, Canada's federal government had already claimed to have spent or committed $3.7 billion on climate change programs. Yet by 2004, its

CO_2 emission levels had risen to 27 percent above 1990 levels (compared with an increase by 16 percent in the US during that time). On April 25, 2006, Canadian environment minister Rona Ambrose announced that the country would have no chance of meeting its targets.[27]

By May 31, 2002, all fifteen then-members of the EU had deposited ratification paperwork at the UN, accounting for about 22 percent of global greenhouse emissions at the time. This called for a cut, on average, to about 8 percent below 1990 levels. In response, the EU created an emissions trading system that introduced reduction targets in six key industries: energy, steel, cement, glass, brick making, and paper/cardboard. It also imposed fines on member nations that failed to meet obligations. There was some criticism among other developed nations that the EU's target level was unfair because it enabled reductions in East Germany to cover nearly the entire 15 percent goal. On June 28, 2006, the German government then announced that it would exempt its coal industry from compliance.[28]

Between 1990 and 2004, greenhouse emissions reported by the UN had increased in more countries than had experienced reductions. Included were Greece (+27 percent), Ireland (+23 percent), Japan (+6.5 percent), and Portugal (+41 percent). As of 2005, Japan was nearly 8 percent above its 1990 levels and considered seeking to purchase emission rights from Russia. Attempting to meet its obligation any other way might have reversed its decade-long recovery from an economic recession, thrusting the nation back into a full-scale depression.[29]

Why have these increases occurred? A key reason is because fossils continue to be the lifeblood of industry and commerce, and alternative sources have not significantly offset growing net energy demands.

In the meantime, China has overtaken all other countries as the world's largest CO_2 emitter. Exemptions of China and India were granted on the rationale that even large developing countries have not historically contributed as much to atmospheric CO_2 levels as have developed, industrialized nations; that emission levels should be calculated on a per-capita population basis; and that stringent restrictions will handicap economic development critical for those nations' social well-being. At a June 2005 G8 meeting, Indian prime minister Manmohan Singh repeated the argument that per-capita emission rates are but a tiny fraction of those in the developed world. Adopting the Kyoto principle of "common but differentiated responsibility," India agrees that the major responsibility of curbing emissions rests with those developed countries that have accumulated emissions over a long period of time.[30]

By 2005, China and India, both experiencing rapid industrial and economic growth, were making up for that lost time. China's huge economy had been expanding more than 8 percent per year, and India's more than 5 percent—compared with about 3 to 4 percent annual US growth and lagging economies and high unemployment in the EU.[31]

Neither China nor India welcomed restrictions that would limit their progress. As Lu Xuedu, deputy director of China's Office of Global Environmental Affairs, pointed out, "You cannot tell people who are struggling to earn enough to eat that they need to reduce their emissions."[32]

A gloom regarding Kyoto Protocol progress descended even before Russia's ratification carried it into full force in February 2005. During the tenth Conference of Parties that was held in Buenos Aries only a few months earlier, science writer Ron Bailey believed it was already hopeless.

> The Kyoto Protocol is dead—there will be no further global treaties that set binding limits on the emissions of greenhouse gases after Kyoto runs out in 2012 . . . The conventional wisdom, that it's the United States against the rest of the world in climate change diplomacy, has been turned on its head. Instead, it turns out that it is the Europeans who are isolated. China, India, and most of the rest of the developing countries have joined forces with the United States to completely reject the idea of future binding greenhouse gas emission limits.[33]

Italian environment minister Altero Matteoli had stated in Buenos Aires, "The first phase of the protocol ends in 2012; after that it would be unthinkable to go ahead without the United States, China, and India . . . Seeing as these countries do not wish to talk about binding agreements, we must proceed with voluntary accords, bilateral pacts, and commercial partnerships."[34]

It had also become clear after the Kyoto Protocol was officially enacted that a second phase of the treaty beyond 2012 would require even more aggressive steps over and above the original 5.3 percent cut (from 1990 levels) to stabilize atmospheric CO_2 concentrations. For the most part, global industrial economies were growing, most particularly in much of the Third World. Yet it was already apparent by 2005 that most industrialized members would not even meet those first-phase emissions reduction targets—not by a long shot. European businesses and their customers were already experiencing rising energy and production costs that resulted from attempts at compliance. Power outages were also beginning to occur, and many bureaucrats were feeling heat of an unnatural kind.

Hot Economic Disputes: Stern Warnings

The global warming crisis has been promulgated as not only what I call a "warma-ggedon" in human terms, but one with epic economic consequences as well. This prophetic view gained a great deal of traction, particularly in the UK, thanks to a government-sponsored "study" that produced the politically intended alarmist results.

In July 2005, then-Chancellor Gordon Brown of the UK (later prime minister, and strong global warming theory advocate) asked Sir Nicholas Stern, a former World Bank vice president, to lead a major review on the nature of economic challenges associated with climate change. The seven-hundred-page report, the "Stern Review on the Economics of Climate Change" (hereafter referred to as the Stern Review) was released on October 14, 2006, and gave Brown just what he seemed to want—something that would really attract public attention to the matter. The report also got its author a lot of attention. As British environmental secretary David Miliband observed, "Nick Stern is now an international rock star in the climate change world."[35]

The Stern Review was not inhibited by facts or caution in presenting its conclusions. It warned that inaction on climate change will result in a depressed UK economy worse than the Great Depression of the 1930s, and that the financial cost would be higher than that depression combined with the subsequent two world wars. In human terms, resulting droughts and flooding would displace 200 million people from their homes, creating the largest migration in history. Natural disasters would also result in the extinction of up to 40 percent of the world's known species. To avert this tragedy we would collectively need to spend 1 percent of global gross domestic product (GDP), which was equated with about half of what the World Bank estimates would be the cost of a full-blown flu pandemic.[36]

The grim, urgent news made headlines around the world. As summed up by the *New York Times,* "[It] predicted apocalyptic effects from climate change, including droughts, flooding, famine, skyrocketing malaria rates, and the extinction of many animal species. This will happen during the current generation if changes are not made soon."[37]

From an economic standpoint, that news was mixed. The bad news was that the overall costs and risks from climate change are equivalent to losing at least 5 percent of global GDP now and forever, and possibly up to 20 percent. But alternatively, strong action to combat these losses will cost only about 1 percent of the GDP—a real bargain!

As Upton Sinclair once observed, "It's hard to get a man to understand something when his job depends upon not understanding it." Sir Nicholas did his job superbly, a fact that has been recognized by climate authorities more knowledgeable about the subject than he. But many other authors of academic papers characterize his report as a "political document," often applying such terms as "preposterous," "incompetent," "deeply flawed," and "neither balanced nor credible" to the report's conclusions.[38] Among the variety of criticisms that have been levied against the Stern Review are these:

- "The report fails to present an accurate picture of scientific understanding of science change issues and massively exaggerates prospective impacts of global warming that are tilted toward unwarranted alarm." (Stern's background is economics, not science.)
- "Dangers from climate change and benefits of action are vastly inflated. As several peer-reviewed papers point out, the Stern Review does not present new data, or even a new model. There is no way to justify conclusions outside the normal range. Damages are counted several times and sometimes arbitrarily increased eightfold or more according to new and conjectured cost strategies that have never been peer-reviewed."
- "Costs of actions are vastly underestimated; implausibly, costs of renewable fuels are projected to drop sixfold by 2050; and costs of action beyond 2050 are not included, although they will continue to escalate far into the 23rd century."[39]

Mike Hume, a professor in the School of Environmental Sciences at the University of East Anglia, commented that the "Stern Review is not the last word of scientists and economists, it's the last word of civil servants."[40]

But then, who can really blame them? As Sir John Houghton, lead author on the first three IPCC "Summary for Policymakers" reports, wrote in his book, *Global Warming: The Complete Briefing* (published in 1994), "Unless we announce disasters, no one will listen."

Warm Remedies: Comparing Pains and Gains

For the sake of examination, let's make three assumptions: (1) that dangerous levels of global warming are likely to occur; (2) that human CO_2 emissions are responsible for global warming: and (3) that Kyoto emission reduction countermeasures are strictly adhered to by all ratifying countries. Now let's ask the follow-on question: How much difference will it make if those assumptions are true? Scientific studies indicate that the benefits would be negligible and probably too small to even measure. Even if all developed, industrialized nations that signed the Kyoto Protocol were able to not only reduce their overall emissions by 20 percent below what they would otherwise have been between 2008 and 2012, but also stick to those reductions until 2050, the estimated temperature-lowering benefit would be only about 0.1°F. Then, by 2100, it would still be only about 0.3 degrees lower. This would only postpone the projected temperature increase of 4.7 degrees by 5 years—to 2105 rather than by 2100.[41]

Even those tiny delays are extremely unrealistic. First, most of those signatory nations are not coming close to meeting their reduction targets presently, and it would become even more difficult for them to do so as populations and industrial production levels continue to grow. Second, as countries that can't reach their reduction targets through cutbacks turn to purchases of excess emission rights from Russia and other countries, actual reductions are largely fictitious. Effective net outcomes will probably be very tiny indeed. And if no other treaty replaces Kyoto after 2012, the total effect will be to postpone global temperature increases about a week or less by 2100. These estimates, based upon IPCC's models, are why a November 6, 2004, editorial in the *Washington Post* refers to Kyoto as a "mostly symbolic treaty."

Computer models that estimate cost/benefit correlations between CO_2 cuts and climate changes have been around since the early 1990s. Most are quite similar, and they have a couple of big problems in common. One is that even current models can't begin to accurately predict temperature changes associated with added or reduced atmospheric CO_2 concentrations, because there are many other forcing influences and interactions that are poorly understood. A second is that benefits of higher temperatures, which can also be very significant, don't fit into the preconceived policy strategies. Still, let's continue with the economic projections anyway.

It has been estimated that for full Kyoto Protocol implementation (including US participation), the total cost over the coming century would be more than $5 trillion, and for this investment any influences upon climate would be tiny at best and highly speculative altogether. The US would bear most of this cost, about four times as much as Europe—not a very good deal for us. That money can otherwise be spent on lots of other things that have measurable consequences, such as education, public health services, roads, Social Security benefits, tax relief, and yes, even foreign aid to underdeveloped and developing nations.[42]

The scheme would, however, be a good deal for the Russians, who might sell their old Soviet-era emissions credits to the US and Europe at a high price, nearly $3 trillion. That's a lot of money for hot air, and much of that burden would fall on the backs of American taxpayers. Politicians, be afraid—be very afraid—of the repercussions. All this for a theoretical and highly unlikely lowering effect on global temperature of about 0.7°F by 2100. This assumes, of course, that the cooling trend we are currently experiencing doesn't accomplish this, and do so very naturally.

Contentions in Copenhagen

The Copenhagen Summit of December 2009 got off to a chilly start, but that was only the beginning. Not even the GHG emissions spewed by more than 1,200 limousines and 140 private jets that delivered 110 heads of state and other distinguished participants seemed adequate to comfortably warm the political atmosphere. Called "the Earth's last chance," this fifteenth United Nations FCCC gathering ultimately proved to be a real, not a mythic, disaster for the fifteen thousand attendees and their global warming boosters.

Some inauspicious events leading up to the meeting may have contributed to that disaster. The CRU scandal had been exposed on global media outlets just weeks before. A December defeat of Australian prime minister Kevin Rudd's proposed cap-and-trade legislation as a job-killing bill was undoubtedly another disappointment.

While developing countries called for a demand that the rich ones commit many billions of dollars to them and accept sharper emission cuts, US and European representatives stated that their nations were willing to provide their "fair share," amounting to $10 billion per year from 2010 to 2012. This, according to Sudan's UN ambassador Lumumba Stanislaus Di-Aping, would not be nearly adequate: "[It] would not buy developing countries' citizens enough coffins."[43]

George Soros agreed. During a press conference at the Copenhagen talks, he said that the $10 billion proposal is "not sufficient," and that the gaps between what developing countries want and what developed countries are willing to give "could actually wreck the conference." Instead, he suggested moving $100 billion from the International Monetary Fund (IMF), which is being used for financial systems that have been bitten by a global economic downturn, to help countries mitigate and adapt to climate change.

Discussions were temporarily interrupted as representatives of several undeveloped countries walked out of the meetings and angry riots broke out in the streets over the social injustice of such paltry penance. Secretary of State Hillary Clinton then came to the rescue, offering to up the ante with a $100 billion annual contribution from the United States and our more prosperous friends to the "poorest and most vulnerable [nations] among us" by 2020. She said that the money would come from "a wide variety of sources, public and private, bilateral and multilateral, including alternative sources of finance." Where it would actually come from no one knew, including Hillary and her boss.

Judging from the tumultuous standing ovation following a speech by Venezuelan president Hugo Chavez, there was general agreement regarding where to lay blame for the world's social, economic, and climate problems.

- "If the climate was a bank, [the West] would have already saved it."
- "The destructive model of capitalism is eradicating life."
- "Our revolution seeks to help all people . . . Socialism, the other ghost that is probably wandering around this room, that's the way to save the planet; capitalism is the road to hell . . . Let's fight against capitalism and make it obey us."[44]

It is possible that an almighty force signaled approval of Chavez's vision by dumping 4 inches of snow on the Copenhagen delegation there to fight global warming. Denmark's maritime climate and winters are warmer than those of its Scandinavian neighbors. According to Henning Gisseloe, an official at Denmark's Meteorological Institute, there was "a good chance of a white Christmas." This hadn't occurred in 14 years and has happened only seven times during the last century.[45] But with all that hot air at the podium, most of the attendees may not have noticed the blizzard outside.

China offered merely to reduce its "carbon intensity per unit of production."

Given that country's rate of growth, total emissions will nevertheless double over the next decade under even the most optimistic scenario.[46]

Nevertheless, China did add to the dialogue by introducing the topic of population control, one of the real agenda items hidden beneath the UN's movement to stop global warming. The topic was introduced in Copenhagen by Chinese delegate Zhao Baige: "Population and climate change are intertwined, but the population issue has remained a blind spot when countries discuss ways to mitigate climate change and slow down global warming." She did not mention, however, that her country faces what some have called a looming demographic crisis resulting from "family planning practices," with an aging population, a reduced workforce, and a severe nationwide gender imbalance from sex-selective abortions.[47]

Some delegates, such as Diane Francis, who authored a broadly circulated December 8 opinion article in the Canadian newspaper *National Post*, expressed her belief that imposing China's one-child policy on all nations is just what is needed. This would reduce the current world population of 6.5 billion to 3.5 billion by 2075. And just prior to the summit, Britain's Optimum Population Trust launched a carbon-offset scheme. Participants who attended would be able to offset the 1.1 tons of carbon emissions spewed into the atmosphere from their trans-Atlantic flights by donating $7 to a family planning program. Apparently, no benefits were offered to those who traveled by bicycle or sailboat, the preferred travel modes recommended by the UN's IPCC.[48]

One week prior to the summit, Jairam Ramesh told India's Parliament that the country would plan to reduce the ratio of pollution to production by 20 to 25 percent compared with 2005 levels, but like China, they would not accept a legally binding emissions reduction target. India currently ranks fifth in the world in CO_2 emissions, accounting for 4.7 percent of the total.[49]

President Obama arrived near the end of the meetings and confirmed that global warming is real and the time for talking is over. Then, after talking with leaders from China and India and announcing a "breakthrough" in understanding, he returned to Washington into a raging record-breaking snowstorm that covered most of the Eastern Seaboard. So, on second thought, maybe that effort to stop global warming achieved some temporary influence after all.

Where does the road from Copenhagen lead? The next stop is a 2010 climate summit that will take place in Mexico City. It is, once again, the Earth's only chance.

A Different Copenhagen Consensus

In 2004, Bjorn Lomborg, then-director of the Danish government's Environmental Assessment Institute, conducted a project cosponsored by his government and the *Economist* newspaper. The project, called the Copenhagen Consensus, invited some very smart people to indicate where best to put resources to solve the world's most urgent challenges, based upon "rational prioritization." The first panel involved top-level economists, including four Nobel laureates who were asked to suggest the best solutions for a series of problems. For example, with global warming, the solution might be CO_2 taxes or the Kyoto Protocol; for malnutrition, it might be agricultural research; and for malaria, it might be mosquito nets. The experts were not just asked which solutions would be desirable; they were also required to determine the dollar values and costs. They estimated benefits of Kyoto for each of the positive impacts upon agriculture, forestry, fisheries, water supply, human damage, etc., and they estimated costs through losses of production. In the case of malaria solutions, the beneficial aspects would be measured in terms of the assigned value of fewer dead, fewer sick, fewer work absences, more robust populations with respect to other diseases, and increased production. Malaria intervention costs would be equated to dollars spent to purchase, distribute, and use mosquito nets.

The study asked the experts to prepare a summary global priority list of challenges and opportunities divided into "very good," "good," and "fair" categories according to the relative amount of benefit for each dollar spent. "Bad" opportunities—those that would cost more than their value—were also listed. Some of the top priorities the experts listed correspond with primary risk factors that have been identified by the World Health Organization. Preventing HIV/AIDS turned out to be best. Each dollar spent on condoms and information was estimated to produce about 40 dollars' worth of social good (fewer dead, fewer sick, less social disruption, etc.), with $27 billion saving 28 million lives over the coming years.[50]

The panel placed climate change opportunities at the bottom of the list under the "bad" category. Of these bad opportunities, Kyoto ranked second to the last, just below an "optimal carbon tax ($25–$300)." In other words, Kyoto would end up doing very little good for the world relative to costs.

The Copenhagen Consensus study then invited eighty college students from all over the world to assess top global priorities through a 5-day workshop discussion.

This group included representatives from the arts, physical sciences, and social sciences, with an equal number of young men and women and with 70 percent from developing countries. After meeting with world-class experts on each of the major challenge and opportunity categories, the students arrived at conclusions that were very similar to those of the first group. Malnutrition and communicable diseases ranked as top priorities, and climate change was next to last.

It didn't end there. In 2006, the project was conducted again, this time involving a wide range of UN ambassadors in the poll. In addition to participants from the three largest countries—China, India, and the United States—representatives of nations as diverse as Angola, Australia, and Azerbaijan participated, along with Canada, Chile, Egypt, Iraq, Mexico, Nigeria, Poland, Somalia, South Korea, Tanzania, Vietnam, Zimbabwe, and many others. This political group was considered to be more difficult to pin down to firm conclusions because they tended to prefer treating all issues as equal priorities—wanting to solve everything with unlimited financing. But they ultimately did make choices. And those choices closely matched those arrived at by the other groups of 2004. Communicable diseases, clean drinking water, and malnutrition ranked highest. Again, climate change dragged along near the bottom.[51]

Climate Change: Politics of Planetary Peril

If the results of the Copenhagen Consensus seem surprising, why is that? Is it true that most people's priorities don't include a global warming fix? If so, then why is global warming considered to be such a big deal? Is it because we are being told over and over that we are facing a climate change crisis, but find it difficult sometimes to remember what it is that is so frightening—except that it must be something really, really bad? Didn't it have something to do with New York City becoming New York Atlantis . . . and exhausted, drowning polar bears . . . and, oh yeah, the hurricanes?

It is difficult to imagine a time in recent history when so much political hype has swirled around so little substance. Is it logical to wager trillions of dollars based upon flawed science practices and suspect agendas?

Consider, for example, the momentum of Kyoto and Copenhagen. Was the UN's Framework Convention on Climate Change seriously motivated by concern about global warming causing rising oceans due to anthropogenic GHGs, only about a decade after scientific conjectures about a coming Ice Age? Did IPCC summary reports have solid scientific bases on which to support their conclusions, or were their assertions based upon admittedly unreliable climate models that global warming would continue to present global threats throughout the century unless CO_2 emissions were dramatically reduced? Were Kyoto Protocol emission-cutting terms, based upon IPCC conclusions, significantly influenced by particular economic interests of European Union members, along with China and India? Did Russia have a religious epiphany concerning Kyoto ratification that reversed its skepticism about global warming importance, which coincided with Europe's invitation to join the World Trade Organization and market Soviet-era emission credits? And is there a logical basis for the US, or any country, to subject citizens to the economic burdens that Kyoto compliance would impose, when any climate benefits would be immeasurably small?

Who will pay the ultimate costs of fighting the unnecessary and unwanted war against climate change? You will. Your children and grandchildren will. People who can least afford them will. And these costs won't be cheap. Yale University economist William Nordhaus, who is probably the best authority on this subject, estimates that the first phase of Kyoto would cost about $716 billion, with the US, if participating, bearing two-thirds of the global burden. [52] We can be very certain about one thing however: That's only the beginning.

Carbon Demonization Scams

Chapter 7

CAP-AND-TAX DAISY CHAIN

Follow the money.

LARRY BELL

Cap-and-trade legislation, a major Obama-Biden administration priority, has no defensible purpose without a supporting global warming crisis rationale. It also makes no sense from an economic standpoint. It will place onerous cost burdens upon energy consumers, continue to drive businesses overseas, and offer no real climate or environmental benefits whatsoever. The same consequences apply in the event that CO_2 emissions come to be regulated by the EPA through the auspices of the Clean Air Act. Such action would serve as a carbon-rationing precedent that paves the way for cap-and-trade to follow.

Government restrictions upon carbon emissions are being promoted on the basis of three errant and deceptive premises: (1) that they will help to protect our planet from dangerous climate change and pollution; (2) that they are needed to wean the United States and the world away from excessive energy consumption; and (3) that they will incentivize energy technology and conservation innovations that will lead to independence from foreign oil.

The initial premise is wrong on two accounts. First, there is no real evidence of any human-caused climate crisis. Second, there is no real evidence that any attempts to reduce atmospheric CO_2 emissions would have any significant climate influence. Simply because the EPA, parroted by media propaganda, condemns CO_2 as a "pollutant," that does not make it so. Such a declaration only misleads people and confuses this natural and essential molecule with real pollutants that truly should be restricted.

The second premise, that carbon restrictions are necessary for energy consumption control, follows the ideological agendas of the UN and its IPCC. Specifically targeted at the US and other affluent industrial countries, the restrictions are intended to artificially drive up energy costs to levels that curtail consumption-based capitalism. The burdens of this zero-sum-gain strategy will fall heaviest upon population segments that can least afford them.

The third premise, that carbon penalties attached to fossil-fueled utilities will incentivize alternative technology innovations, is misleading in several respects. Heavily financed promotions fail to inform the public of the limited-capacity potentials afforded by "renewable" energy sources, most particularly in regard to the urgent time frames required to substantially offset demands. Unfounded technology promises provide excuses for expanding government control and spending, unwarranted mandates, subsidies, and profit-taking fortunes for those who play the system. Free markets built upon delivery of competitive values are compromised when government is empowered to pick the winners and losers through policies that reward promises over performance. We, the taxpayers and captive consumers, cover the costs.

Carbon Cap-Trap

In case you're not very familiar with the way cap-and-trade works, here is a very basic description. It enables fossil fuel–dependent corporations to promote themselves as being "carbon neutral" by purchasing "carbon offsets" from other entities in the form of emissions reductions elsewhere, or by claiming that they are achieving CO_2 absorption by planting trees to offset their "carbon footprints." You might liken the concept to the sale of indulgences by medieval churches through divine authority. A more contemporary illustration would be to imagine that someone in prison offers to pay for some of your "good behavior" credits, literally as a "get-out-of-jail ticket." The central question would be, how much do you think it would really reduce crime? As former Clinton-Gore administration employee Joseph Romm characterized the legislative ploy, "The vast majority of offsets are, at some level, just rip-offsets."[1]

Unlike futures markets that can be defended as a means to secure long-term investments essential to help stabilize volatile energy and food prices, trading of carbon credits involves creation of a market that arbitrarily prices a fictitious commodity that has no value whatsoever.[2] Such a market can exist only as long as fear of global warming crises can be perpetuated by special interest agendas. It requires that government legislation be enacted to ration emissions at compliance levels that give carbon a trade value, albeit a negative one, so that allowances can be sold by those who don't need them to others who have run out of forgiveness coupons. Energy and product consumers transform the negative carbon commodity into positive cash benefits for both sides through higher prices.[3]

Then there is the matter of continued expansion of government legislative interference in free market operations. How might this impact volatility? Uncertainties and rumors about government policy changes have major market impacts, so just think about the added volatility a new derivative carbon bureaucracy could create. When that market tanks, who will bail out the losers? Any guesses?

Before cap-and-trade legislation is enacted, consider some important lessons from the Kyoto Protocol.

1. Most of the signatories have not found it possible to comply, even though the 1990 benchmark date gave the EU every advantage.
2. Trading conditions between corporations would be no different from Russia peddling its old Soviet-era credits to other countries—with no net reductions.
3. Assuming that full compliance was achieved, which is extremely unlikely, the climate change impacts would be too small to measure. And even the most optimistic CO_2 reduction goals are founded upon highly speculative assumptions that climate change is unnatural, that man-made GHGs are

a principal cause, and that consequences of continued warming (if that happens) are worse than the alternative—a colder world. History suggests otherwise.

It may be interesting to note that the United States has indeed made real progress in energy economies, along with emissions reductions as a by-product. Based upon the amount of energy used to produce a dollar value in output, this country reduced energy intensity by 20 percent over the period from 1992 to 2004, compared to only 11.5 percent in the EU under a mandatory approach. This has also enabled economic growth, which averaged more than 3 percent annually between 1992 and 2005 as compared with about 1 percent in the EU.[4]

The federal Energy Information Administration (EIA) reported in May 2010 that GHGs fell 7 percent during 2009, the largest-ever percentage and absolute decline since the EIA began tracking such data in 1949. In fact, the US carbon footprint has shrunk in three of the last four years. The 2009 decline was particularly dramatic and was attributed to a severe economic downturn. It took a 3.3 percent drop in per capita GDP and a 4.8 percent decline in overall energy consumption (9 percent in industry) to produce most of this circumstance. Expanded switching by electric utilities from more carbon-heavy coal to natural gas is also believed to have had some influence. Yet it should always be recognized that economic health and energy use are tightly linked, as well as that oil, coal, and other fossils continue to make up about 83 percent of America's energy mix. Cap-and-trade and/or EPA-imposed restrictions on carbon will have costly economic and social consequences.[5]

Big Deals

Some companies would definitely benefit from cap-and-trade, a policy that was supported by one of the strongest corporate US boosters of the Kyoto Protocol. Enron, a major natural gas distributor, recognized that the approach would kill coal-fired electricity production and provide its energy traders opportunities to capitalize on big trading commissions. An internal Enron memorandum initiated by its head, Kenneth Lay, stated that Kyoto would "do more to promote Enron's business than almost any other regulatory initiative outside the restructuring [of] the energy and natural gas industries in Europe and the United States."[6]

Enron had a major influence on events that led up to proposed cap-and-trade legislation in the United States. So did Al Gore and some other people and organizations that collaborated with them.

Back in the 1990s, Enron was diversifying its energy business to emphasize natural gas. The company had already owned the largest natural gas pipeline that existed outside Russia, a colossal interstate network. Natural gas was having difficulties competing with coal, and the company needed help in Washington to tip the playing field. Hype about a global warming crisis advanced by then-Senator Gore's 1988 congressional hearings on the topic provided a dream opportunity, and Enron hired Gore's star witness, James Hansen, as a consultant. They also began direct discussions with Senator Gore.[7]

Some Democrats in Congress were already aggressively pursuing development of green legislation models. Senators John Heinz (R-PA) and Timothy Wirth had previously cosponsored "Project 88" to provide a pathway for converting environmental issues into business opportunities. Media-fueled alarm about acid rain provided a basis for legislation to create markets for buying and selling excess sulfur dioxide (SO_2) and nitrogen dioxide emission credits, and Project 88 became the Clean Air Act of 1990. Enron was a big SO_2 market cap-and-trade player.

So Enron and others wondered, why not do the same thing with CO_2? Because natural gas is a lower CO_2 emitter than coal is, that development would certainly be a profitability game changer. But there was a problem. CO_2 wasn't a pollutant. At least it wasn't considered to be then, and the EPA had no authority to regulate it.

After Senator Wirth became undersecretary of state for global affairs in the Clinton-Gore administration, he began working closely with Enron's boss, Lay, to lobby Congress to grant the EPA authority to control CO_2. Between 1994 and 1996, the Enron Foundation contributed nearly $1 million to the Nature Conservancy, and together with the Pew Center and the Heinz Foundation, they engaged in an energetic and successful global warming fear campaign that included attacks on scientific dissenters.[8] Yes, that is the exact same Heinz Foundation, headed by Teresa Heinz Kerry, that gave a $250,000 award to James Hansen, who then publicly supported her husband in his failed presidential bid.

A September 1, 1998, letter from Enron CEO Lay to President Clinton requested that he "moderate the political aspects" of the climate discussion by appointing a "Blue Ribbon Commission." The intent of the proposed commission, which was billed as an "educational effort," was clear: to trash disbelievers and cut off debate on the matter. Lay had direct contact earlier with the White House when he met with Clinton and Gore on August 4, 1997, to prepare a strategy for the upcoming Kyoto conference that December. Kyoto was the first step toward creating a carbon market that Enron desperately wanted Congress to support.[9]

Carbon Brokers: Pros and Cons

Cap-and-trade pressure on US legislators extends beyond our borders and also involves state government proponents. The International Carbon Action Partnership (ICAP), established in October 2007, operates as an "open forum" comprised of state, regional, and international authorities and governments that have pursued or are actively pursuing mandatory cap-and-trade systems. Members include the EU, Australia, New Zealand, and Norway, along with several US state governments and the Canadian provinces of British Columbia and Manitoba. ICAP's organizing purposes are to enable members to learn from one another how to create a consistent regulatory framework across national borders and how to develop future linked markets.[10]

Several entities have become well positioned to capitalize upon those markets. Al Gore's Generation Investment Management LLP, for example, is a London-based firm established in 2004 that invests money from institutions and wealthy investors that are "going green." GIM plans to purchase CO_2 offsets as soon as federal government regulations are passed to mandate cap-and-trade. Gore's cofounding partners in the venture are former chief of Goldman Sachs Asset Management (GSAM) David Blood, along with Mark Ferguson and Peter Harris, also of Goldman Sachs. Bloomberg reported in March 2008 that the investment fund had hit its hard cap of $5 billion and had been turning away investors.[11] Now many of those investors may be running away after suffering big losses due to shifting political winds in Washington, DC.[12]

Another organization with friends in very high places is the Chicago Climate Exchange (CCX), which was created in 2003 as a "voluntary pilot agency" and aspires to be the New York Stock Exchange for carbon-emission trading. The CCX was initiated in 2000 with support from a $347,000 grant to Northwestern University's Kellogg Graduate School of Management from the Chicago-based Joyce Foundation for a study to test the viability of a future carbon-credit market. This transaction occurred when a young community organizer, Barack Obama, served on the Joyce Foundation's board of directors, along with his mentor and present White House adviser, Valerie Jarrett. A current CCX board member is none other than Al Gore's longtime pal and Rio de Janeiro Earth Summit leader Maurice Strong. Another is Stuart Eizenstat, who led the US delegation to Kyoto.

The Joyce Foundation has a history of funding liberal causes. For example, it has been a big financial supporter of legal scholarship to demonstrate that the Second Amendment of the US Constitution doesn't protect individual gun ownership, and it has made contributions to the Center for American Progress and George Soros's Tide Foundation. Total Joyce Foundation start-up contributions for CCX were about $1.1 million, and its president, Paula DiPerna, later left the organization to become executive vice president of CCX.

CCX was cofounded by Richard Sandor, a former research professor at Kellogg when they received the Joyce grant, and former Goldman Sachs CEO Hank Paulson. Sandor has received 8 million shares of CCX stock, which are now estimated to be worth about $260 million even before a national cap-and-trade system is in place. GSAM is the biggest CCX shareholder (about 18 percent), and Al Gore's GIM—with his three Goldman Sachs cofounders—is fifth largest (about 10 percent). Mr. Sandor has projected that CCX will become a $10 trillion company by 2050 with passage of cap-and-trade legislation. That would certainly afford a very lucrative investment payback.[13]

Goldman Sachs is also heavily invested in the Obama presidency. According to figures released by the Federal Election Commission to the Center for Responsive Politics, Goldman's political action committee and its individual contributors were the campaign's second largest donors ($994,795).[14]

So far, however, CCX has a long way to go before delivering on investor expectations. Trading commenced at $1 per cubic metric ton of carbon in January 2008, reaching a $7 per metric ton peak in May of that year. The market (along with GIM's investment value) then plummeted to $0.10 in October 2009. The early May 2008 speculators lost 98.6 percent of their investment.[15]

The actual operating system for CCX trading has been provided by deposed former Fannie Mae head Franklin Raines, who originally purchased the unpatented technology rights developed by the late Carlin Bartells. Raines, who received $90 million in salary and bonuses over 5 years, had became an expert in bundling worthless real estate mortgages that led to the near collapse of the US economy. This serves as an indispensible talent for bundling worthless air credits. Fortuitously, a patent was issued for the technology on November 7, 2006, the day after Democrats swept the congressional elections.

CCX member organizations include, among other companies, the Ford Motor Company, Amtrak, DuPont, Dow Corning, American Electric Power, International Paper, Motorola, and Waste Management, along with the states of Illinois and New

Mexico, seven cities, and a number of universities. As planned, these members would "purchase" carbon offsets on the CCX trading exchange and make contributions to or investments in organizations that provide "alternative" or "renewable" energy.[16]

Almost from its inception, CCX has had a strong connection with the Atlanta-based Intercontinental Exchange, Inc. (ICE), whose subsidiary is the International Petroleum Exchange (IPE), the world's largest petroleum futures options market. In May 2010, ICE agreed to purchase the CCX and its parent company, Climate Exchange, along with two of its other exchanges (Chicago Climate Futures and European Climate Exchange), for $603 million. While this amount is lower than the more than $1 billion ICE reportedly paid for the New York Board of Trade in 2007, it still represents a healthy valuation of fifty-eight times earnings.[17]

ICEcapades

During a May 8, 2006, Senate Democratic Policy meeting, Senator Carl Levin (D-MI) stated that futures speculation trading on ICE had been a driver for adding $20–$25 to the price of every barrel of oil, causing hardship to industry, households, and underdeveloped nations.[18] Senator Levin's website reported that in 2007, his Subcommittee on Investigations released a report titled "Excessive Speculation in the Natural Gas Market," which found that a single hedge fund named Amarath, trading through ICE, had dominated the natural gas market during the spring and summer of 2006. The report concluded that an "Enron Loophole Act" had enabled unregulated trading, which increased hedging costs that increased winter gas purchases of the Municipal Gas Authority of Georgia by $18 million alone. Levin's subcommittee reported: "Amarath's massive trades turned the natural gas market into a giant electronic casino, where all natural gas buyers and sellers were forced to bet either with or against Amarath. American businesses and consumers were socked with higher prices for natural gas last winter as a result. We cannot afford to let large energy traders continue to play speculation and manipulation games with US energy prices and supplies. It's way past time to close the Enron loophole and put the cop back on the beat in all US energy markets."[19]

Richard Sandor—the cofounder and chairman of CCX, now chairman of the Climate Exchange, and ICE board of director since 2002—is considered to be one of the fathers of derivatives and futures. He concocted weather futures, earthquake futures, Ginnie Mae futures, and others. He has also served as a director on the board of the London International Financial Futures and Options Exchange, the largest trading market in London.[20]

On September 7, 2004, ICE released an announcement with this headline: "CCX and IPE Sign Corporation and Licensing Agreement for EU Emissions Trading Scheme/Chicago Climate Exchange Sales and Marketing Subsidiary to Be Based in Amsterdam." That arrangement created the European Carbon Exchange (ECX) as a CCX wholly owned subsidiary. According to Sandor, "This agreement positions CCX as a global leader in emissions trading, and complements IPE's leadership in the European energy markets." Carbon offsets have now been trading on ECX since 2005.[21]

As a result, arrangements are already in place and waiting for the US Congress to create a lucrative and consumer-costly carbon-trading market in the United States. Investment advocates are ecstatic about the windfall profit prospects. Sandor predicts that CO_2 will become the largest commodity traded in the world market as governments curtail emissions of GHGs "that scientists say accelerate global warming."[22]

It's a Small World After All

ShoreBank, a small Chicago bank that nearly went bankrupt from subprime mortgage fiascos during the depths of the recession, was saved by $35 million in taxpayer TARP bailout money, along with additional financial assistance from powerful friends. Included were the Joyce Foundation, some big Wall Street firms such as Goldman Sachs, and influential private partners. It is now heavily invested in a variety of green businesses, including solar panel manufacturing. CCX has designated ShoreBank as its "banking arm" and holds a big shareholder stake.[23]

Probably coincidentally, one ShoreBank cofounder, Jan Piercy, was a Wellesley College roommate of Hillary Clinton, and she and former president Bill Clinton are small investors. A former ShoreBank vice chairman, Bob Nash, was the deputy campaign manager for Hillary's presidential bid. Another cofounder, Mary Houghton, was a friend of President Obama's mother who had worked for Treasury Secretary Tim Geithner's father at the Ford Foundation. Howard Stanback, a ShoreBank board member, formerly served as chairman of the Woods Foundation where Barack Obama and terrorist Bill Ayres were board members. Stanback had been previously employed by New Kenwood, Inc., a real estate development company co-owned by Tony Rezko (who had arranged a great deal with our President on a home purchase). ShoreBank's director, Adele Simmons, is a close friend of Valerie

Jarrett, and now-deposed Obama-Biden administration green czar Van Jones serves as their green projects marketing director.[24]

ShoreBank, its partners, and its investors will benefit handsomely if cap-and-trade legislation is passed. Assuming that an estimated $10 trillion passes through CCX accounts each year, the bank might earn close to $40 billion in interest charges. Al Gore could rake in many billions during the first year alone, as would GIM, Goldman Sachs, and the Joyce Foundation. And even if this money doesn't materialize, think of all the many reminiscences that can be shared among longtime friends at ShoreBank reunions!

Climate Legislation: Changing the Labels

Cap-and-trade recently acquired a more lofty-sounding new name to counteract toxic cap-and-tax derisions. Proponents began referring to it as the "Climate and Energy Bill," or simply the "Climate Bill." Cosponsors were senators John Kerry, Joe Lieberman (I-CT), and Lindsey Graham (R-SC). Senator Kerry explained that the original term should be dropped because "we're talking about setting a target for the reduction of pollution, which is why we don't call it cap-and-trade anymore. It's a pollution reduction target with a private investment incentive for companies to be able to invest in deciding how they want to meet the pollution reduction target."[23]

Although the authors claimed that the proposed legislation didn't include a cap-and-trade system, critics argued that the language allowed for such mechanisms within power generation and manufacturing sectors. As Senator Inhofe commented, "The one thing all of the versions [introduced in recent years] have in common is that they are cap-and-trade."[24]

Then, just when we might have thought cap-and-trade legislation labels couldn't get more disinguous, senators Kerry and Lieberman upstaged their earlier moniker with a newly proposed "American Power Act." A more appropriate description might be "American power grab." In reality, it has little to do with developing our nation's vast domestic fossil energy resources. Rather, it emphasizes ways to mitigate their alleged effects upon climate and expand government bureaucracy by creating at least sixty expensive new agencies and projects.[25]

Introduced in May 2010, the American Power Act includes a $7 billion annual "linked fee" to be added to gasoline prices to "improve US transportation and efficiency." The way it works is to have producers and importers of gasoline and jet fuel buy non-tradable carbon allowances pegged to a fixed price established by trading auction prices. So, is this actually referred to as a linked fee or tax? Of course not! But you probably won't recognize any difference when you pay the added costs at the gas pump. In addition, $2 billion has been allocated per year for researching and developing effective carbon capture and sequestration methods—kind of like creating a GITMO for dangerous carbon terrorist provocateurs. In addition, there's a new multibillion-dollar revenue stream for agriculture through a carbon-offset program. Should someone inform the sponsors that tilling soil releases deadly CO_2 . . . not to mention the increased flatulence hazards associated with livestock?

Recognizing that bill enactment will send costs soaring, the legislation will "provide assistance to those Americans who may be disproportionately affected by potential increases in energy prices." Do you suppose they are referring to taxpayers?

The frenetic efforts of Democrats to pass ObamaCare have drained the will of many of their congressional minions to fall on their political spears in another controversial war. The original Climate and Energy Bill has been plagued by delays caused in part by repeated rewrites attempting to keep green groups and key industry players on board during a time of growing reelection anxiety. Cap-and-tax, by any name, also competes for attention with other front-and-center Obama-Biden administration priorities, most particularly immigration reform. Another reform— namely, reckless spending—demands even greater attention.

Corporate Carbon-Capping Collaborators

Many might be surprised to learn of large corporations that would ordinarily be assumed to be on the economic losing end of GHG emission regulation actually supporting it. Why would that be? Granted, we should assume that their leaders, stockholders, and employees care about environmental stewardship regardless of whether or not they subscribe to the CO_2 demonization hype. But what about responding to the fiduciary bottom line? How does that factor in? Let's consider some possible examples.

Many of these organizations are members of the US Climate Action Partnership (USCAP), a lobbying organization with more than thirty large corporate and nonprofit members that are pushing hard for federal cap-and-trade legislation. Participants include Alcoa; major automobile, electrical, and chemical companies; and oil corporations.[26]

Alcoa, an early USCAP participant, has implemented successful energy conservation programs, driven by good business planning, which have also reduced GHG emissions through expanded use of recycled materials. This is because aluminum produced from recycled metal requires only about 5 percent as much energy to manufacture as the energy required to produce primary aluminum, and nearly 70 percent of all aluminum ever produced is still in use today.

Perhaps Alcoa might have originally hoped to be able to receive emission credits for GHGs they are "not" emitting through their normal and laudable profit-seeking activity by pushing the time reference baseline back to 1990 (as Kyoto did). In short, the company would have been eligible for windfall trading profits on top of profits it has already realized through efficient business practices since 1990. This would enable other companies that exceed their allotments to purchase Alcoa's credits without expensive fixes. And even if they didn't succeed, USCAP membership would give them a seat at the negotiating table. If so, can we really blame them? Yet at the same time, how, exactly, will this reduce total GHH emissions, much less really influence climate for the better?

After it merged with Cinergy, Duke Energy joined USCAP in May 2005. Cinergy was a company that, much like Alcoa, had accomplished 97 percent emission reductions as a result of implementing major efficiency improvements in its overwhelmingly coal-fired electric generating stations. Its $1.94 million investment in efficiency upgrades reduced CO_2 emissions by 349,882 tons, at a cost of $1.11 per ton. If early action credits provided by Phase I of the Climate Stewardship Act (originally proposed in 2003 by senators John McCain (R-AZ) and Joe Lieberman (I-CT); a new version was introduced in 2005) were applied—valuing the credits at $15/ton in 2010 and $45/ton in 2025—Cinergy might reap windfall profits between 1,263 and 3,990 percent. Not a bad investment.[27]

DuPont invested $50 million in the late 1990s to reduce nitrous oxide (N_2O) emissions from its production of adipic acid, a chemical used to produce nylon. N_2O is a gas with roughly 310 times the greenhouse warming potential of CO_2. By 2000, DuPont had reduced these emissions by 63 percent over a 1990 base year (56.2 million metric tons on a CO_2-equivalent basis). Assuming that DuPont was awarded a tradable allocation of 90 percent of its 1990 emissions at an average market price of $10/metric ton, its reductions by 2000 would yield more than 900 percent return on investment. DuPont sold the nylon business to Invest in 2004, terminating its ownership of related emission credits, but DuPont has since eliminated emissions from a refrigerant with even greater greenhouse warming potential as an unintended by-product of another process change that might compensate for that lost opportunity.[28]

It is very clear that some companies would richly benefit from laws and regulations that drive up the price of carbon and that mandate or subsidize wind and solar power. For example, General Electric would gain expanded markets in such areas as manufacture of wind turbines, solar panels, electricity grid modernization, nuclear reactors, natural gas turbines, and other energy production projects representing hundreds of billions of dollars in worldwide sales in coming years.

Carbon caps would also help GE market "greener" products through its eco-imagination line of appliances as energy costs escalate. The company spent $7.6 million to lobby for favorable legislation during the second quarter of 2009 alone. Again, GE's energy conservation innovations and profitability are very good things for everyone and are all accomplishable in free market competition based upon merit, and at lower costs to consumers and taxpayers.[29]

PG&E's interests as a significant hydroelectric and nuclear company would be similar to GE's. They would benefit as alternative energy (including nuclear) sources become more cost competitive with skyrocketing fossil-fuel energy prices. Yet those escalating costs will occur in any case. GHG legislation will only make them higher, with disproportionately heavy burdens falling upon those who can least afford them.

How would automotive companies benefit from cap-and-trade? Higher fuel costs will motivate many people to purchase new, more efficient cars and trucks. So again, that's a good thing, which an increasingly cash-strapped and conservation-minded public will do in any case. A good case can be made for government corporate average fuel economy, or CAFE for short, standards aimed at boosting vehicle mileage efficiency without artificially raising fuel costs based on a bogus climate crisis platform. But bucking Obama-Biden administration agendas is not an option so long as the government continues to assert unprecedented control over their businesses.

The former British Petroleum was a USCAP member, but it has recently dropped out after losing many incentives. BP has been spending millions of dollars in television ads featuring ordinary-looking folks wondering why the energy industry hasn't thought about switching to cleaner natural sources "because they work." But apparently these ads haven't been working very well for Europe's second largest fully publicly traded company's bottom line. In February 2008, BP's new CEO mentioned that the oil giant might off-load part or all of its Green Business Unit, valued at between $5–$7 billion, and drop its "Beyond Petroleum" slogan, which was based primarily upon portfolio investments rather than actual business activities. Environmental critics have long been arguing that this had been nothing more than a marketing gimmick anyway.[30]

The London-based company has a history of very large environmental PR problems to overcome. One was an oil spill attributed to poor pipeline maintenance that leaked more than 200,000 gallons of crude oil onto the Arctic tundra at BP's Prudhoe Bay, Alaska, oil field and led to a partial shutdown. Another was a refinery explosion at its Texas City, Texas, refinery that killed fifteen workers and injured at least 170, also blamed upon cost-cutting-related maintenance and safety deficiencies. Most recently, the massive offshore oil spill disaster in the Gulf of Mexico, beginning in late April 2010, put the entire oil drilling industry in economic jeopardy. The company was forced to continue cost-cutting measures, primarily through restructuring, to close its business gap with rivals Royal Dutch Shell and ExxonMobil.[31]

Conoco Phillips and heavy equipment maker Caterpillar joined BP in announcing in February 2010 that they won't renew their USCAP memberships. This may be a continuing trend as more and more companies recognize that diminishing public alarm about global warming, coupled with growing concern about energy costs, makes carbon-capping legislation less likely. This skepticism is growing at a time when climate science scandal revelations are becoming routine and Republicans are expected to gain seats in Congress. Although the Obama administration worked hard to persuade industry groups to back cap-and-trade initiatives after the Democrats' big 2008 wins, the political value of seats at the government negotiating table appears to have depreciated. Still, according to Whitney Stanco, a policy analyst for Concept Capital, "The saying in Washington is that if you're not at the table, you're on the menu."[32]

Winston Churchill advocated a similar political survival strategy. He described an appeaser as "one who feeds a crocodile, hoping it will eat him last."

BP and Conoco Phillips spokespeople maintain that the companies will continue to support legislation to reduce greenhouse emissions; they'll just be working outside USCAP's umbrella. Caterpillar prudently maintains that it will continue to promote green technologies, although it is unlikely to abandon its large coal industry equipment business interests anytime soon. Still, these decisions to withdraw from USCAP may reflect the beginning of a broader corporate climate change.[33]

ExxonMobil has encountered enormous criticism and pressure for not jumping on the climate crisis bandwagon early enough and shifting its business emphasis toward alternative energy. During a May 2008 annual meeting, the company's chairman and CEO, Rex Tillerson, defeated a shareholder effort led by some of founder John D. Rockefeller's descendants to force the issue through four non-binding proxy resolutions. One called for taking away one of his job titles to split the company's leadership. Another, which also failed, urged that more attention be directed to studying effects of global warming and development of renewable energy technologies.[34]

At a press conference following the meeting, Mr. Tillerson was asked about the global warming issue and replied, "My view is that climate change policy is so important to the world that to not have a debate on it is irresponsible. We don't know everything about it. Nobody has figured this out. We have to understand that climate change policy, whatever it turns out to be, is going to hurt some people. But let's at least have an open debate about it, so everybody knows what the facts are."[35]

It might be noted that while ExxonMobil hadn't tended to publicize its actions to advance that understanding until quite recently, it has donated at least $100 million to Stanford University's Global Climate and Energy Project. The company also provides funds to support the National Academy of Sciences.[36]

Carbon-Capping Costs

Enactment of cap-and-trade (aka climate and energy) legislation urged by the Obama administration will have costly consequences. At the time of this writing, the latest definitive rendition of this initiative was presented in the American Clean Energy and Security Act of 2009 (aka the Waxman-Markey Bill), which narrowly gained approval in the House of Representatives on June 27, 2009, by a vote of 219 to 212.

In June 2009, the CBO released its analysis that Waxman-Markey would cost citizens only $175 per household annually. This was based upon a CBO study that projected a CO_2 emission price of $28 per ton in 2020. Included were escalating projected allowance revenues of $119.7 billion, $129.7 billion, $136 billion, $145.6 billion, and $152.9 billion for the years 2015–2019 as CO_2 caps become more stringent. However, the allowance costs don't really add up, because they do not account for such economic costs as decreases in GDP that will result from the caps. In short, it was only an accounting analysis, not an economic analysis—a fact reported in the CBO report's footnote.

A study by the Heritage Foundation's Center for Data Analysis (CDA) estimates that Waxman-Markey climate change legislation would cost $161 billion (2009 dollars) annually by 2020. For a family of four, this translates into $1,870. The CDA also found that for all years cited, the average GDP loss would be about $393 billion . . . more than double the 2020 hit to family incomes. By 2035 (the last year analyzed by the CDA), annual GDP losses, adjusted for inflation, would be $6,790 per family . . . and that is before they paid their $4,600 share of carbon taxes.

A study by the National Association of Manufacturers projects that CO_2 emission caps—similar to 63 percent of the cuts called for by 2020 by Senate advocates—would reduce US GDP by up to $269 billion and result in the loss of 850,000 jobs by 2014. The CDA estimated that such restrictions would produce total cumulative GDP losses of up to $4.8 trillion and annual employment losses of more than 500,000 jobs by 2030.

Still, whatever the United States does, it's going to be exceedingly difficult to keep up with Europe in the carbon combat crusade. The influential Environmental Audit Committee of the British Parliament advocated that every adult be required to use a "carbon ration card" when he or she pays for petrol, airline tickets, and household energy. Those who exceed their designated entitlements would then have to pay for what are called "top-up credits" from others who haven't used up all of their allowances. The amount charged would be handled through a "specialist company."

As Member of Parliament Tim Yeo, a Tory and a leading promoter of the plan, stated, "We found that personal carbon trading has real potential to engage the population in the fight against climate change and to achieve significant emission reductions in a progressive way."[37]

Therein lies an opportunity for the Brits to rewrite a famous statement presented by Winston Churchill regarding a different war to now say: "Seldom have so many done so much for so little."[38]

Caps, Crooks, and Cops in the EU

Experiences across Western Europe prove that huge cap-and-tax profits, combined with vast operational complexities, present enticing temptations for fraud. Europol, the European criminal intelligence agency, reported that emission trading system fraud resulted in about €5 billion in lost revenues during 2009, as carbon traders schemed to avoid paying Europe's value added tax (VAT) and pocket the difference. The agency estimated that as much as 90 percent of Europe's carbon trades involved fraudulent activity. Oscar Reyes, of a watchdog group called Carbon Trade Watch, observed that "carbon markets are highly susceptible to fraud, given their complexity and the fact that it's not always clear what is being traded."[39]

Twenty-five people were recently arrested in raids by British and German authorities as part of a crackdown on carbon credit VAT avoidance. Raids on eighty-one offices and homes nabbed thirteen people in England and eight in Scotland. German officials raided 230 locations, including the headquarters of Deutsche Bank in Frankfurt and the offices of RWE, one of Europe's largest energy firms. Maybe there's a lesson in this for Congress: Don't count on big business enterprises built on hot air to share windfall profits with taxpayers.

Endangerment: End Run of Congress

But who needs the US Congress to protect the planet from CO_2 emissions? The Obama-Biden administration has warned that it can accomplish the same goal by applying the EPA's recent CO_2 Endangerment Finding under the Clean Air Act if Congress doesn't act. Now Lisa Jackson, the EPA administrator who seemed perfectly willing to implement the ruling, is discovering that the EPA may need to contend with congressional warnings about doing so after all, following an outcry from some Democratic members along with state regulators.

Eight Senate Democrats wrote to Jackson expressing concerns about potential economic and energy impacts of the policy, and dozens of state regulators argued that they didn't have adequate staffs to handle the expected influx of new permits. Industry officials joined the resistance movement, pointing out that the new regulations will be overly burdensome to many energy-intensive sectors, such as steel production and cement kilns that rely upon coal-fired energy.[40] Senator Lisa Murkowski (R-AK) filed a "resolution of disapproval" regarding the EPA's abuse of authority and prospective impacts upon the nation's economy. Senator Jay Rockefeller (D-WV) introduced a bill that would put a 2-year freeze on the EPA's ability to regulate greenhouse GHGs from power plants.[41]

Bowing to pressure, Jackson agreed to delay subjecting large greenhouse GHG emitters, such as power plants and crude oil refineries, to new regulations until 2011. She also agreed to raise the threshold for using the Clean Air Act to regulate

CO_2 emissions, stating, "I expect the threshold for permitting will be substantially higher than the 25,000-ton limit that the EPA originally proposed."[42]

Now, the EPA is once again proceeding with GHG regulation plans. Beginning July of 2011, permits issued for all new facilities with greenhouse gas emissions of at least 100,000 tons per year and modifications to existing businesses that will increase emissions by at least 75,000 tons per year must demonstrate use of best available technology to minimize GHGs. How, exactly, that technology is defined remains unclear, and that uncertainty discourages essential investment.[43]

Led by the US Chamber of Commerce, several states and large businesses are launching dozens of legal challenges to block the EPA power grab. Yet these cases are still in their preliminary stages and are unlikely to bring about any relief before the regulations are enacted, if ever.

Senator Inhofe reported that "Lisa Jackson, Obama's EPA administrator, admitted to me publicly that the EPA based its action today (issuing the findings) in good measure on the findings of the UN's Intergovernmental Panel on Climate Change, or IPCC. She told me that the EPA accepted those findings without any serious independent analysis to see if they were true."[44]

On June 10, 2010, the US Senate voted 53–47 against banning the EPA from regulating carbon without the consent of Congress. Senator Rockefeller (WV) sided with the losing GOP voters, along with his fellow Democrats Mary Landrieu (LA), Evan Bayh (IN), Mark Pryor (AR), Ben Nelson (NE), and Blanche Lincoln (AR).

While some companies would get very rich through implementation of cap-and-trade or EPA endangerment rules, millions of businesses and families would pay dearly. More than thirty states depend upon coal for 35 to 98 percent of their electricity. All rely upon oil and natural gas. As recognized by the US Chamber of Commerce, an organization that is vocal on such matters, such regulations will have burdensome impacts upon energy costs; will ship needed jobs overseas; and will shackle living standards and civil rights for most American citizens.

Chapter 8

CLIMATE AS RELIGION

LARRY BELL

*Vapors rise as / Fever settles on an acid sea / Neptune's bones
dissolve / Snow glides from the mountain / Ice fathers floods for
a season / A hard rain comes quickly / Then dirt is parched*
                                                    —Al Gore

lobal warming has become a religious mantra, a call to action in a
crusade against larger evils we have perpetrated against nature, a punishment for our sins. Author Michael Crichton articulated the essence of that
creed in a 2003 speech that draws a parallel with the Judeo-Christian belief system:
"There's an initial Eden, a paradise, a state of grace and unity with Nature; there's

a fall from grace into a state of pollution as a result from eating from the tree of knowledge; and as a result of our actions, there is a judgment day coming for all of us. We are energy sinners, doomed to die, unless we seek salvation, which is now called sustainability. Sustainability is salvation in the church of the environment. Just as organic food is its communion, that pesticide-free wafer that the right people with the right beliefs imbibe."[1]

Michael Crichton was not arguing against the importance of living more environmentally responsible lives that apply resources in more sustainable ways. He was talking about doing this with intelligence that is less clouded by emotion, which can impair judgment.

The temple of global warming is built upon religious rather than scientific foundations. Climate change is not Mother Nature's punishment for our human audacity to multiply and survive, any more than a tornado that destroys a church is God's retribution for belonging to the "wrong" denomination. Get over it! It's not all about us! Climate change is the way nature balances itself, moves heat around, and produces motivations for species to evolve. CO_2 is a small but nonetheless important part of that system. Without it, life would not exist at all. No polar bears, no penguins, no coral reefs—and certainly no rain forests that directly breathe in lots of the stuff. Don't call it "pollution."[2] At least show it a little respect!

Fear Merchants

Religion plays an important, if not central, role in most of our lives, whether we subscribe to a particular orthodoxy or not. It guides us to believe that we are all parts of something much larger than ourselves. It provides lessons that encourage us to live cleaner, use resources more responsibly, and be nicer to all of nature's creatures. Perhaps it's really okay if we need to be a bit frightened about the consequences of things we're doing wrong to motivate us to do better. But don't we expect something different from science? Isn't it supposed to tell us real facts about what it doesn't know as well as teach us what it has actually learned? When "science" emulates religion, it oversteps its bounds, and we can no longer trust it. And in the case of global warming, science has overstepped its bounds. Nobel Physics laureate Ivar Giaever calls global warming "a new religion."[3]

Many global warming zealots apparently envision life in Earth's distant past as an Eden with idyllic conditions. Those were the good old days before industrialization and modern technology wrecked everything. Yet realities going back a hundred years and more reveal a different picture: one displaying widespread poverty, starvation, disease, and hardship. Yes, and throughout human history, people have had to adapt to climate changes—some long, some severe, and often unpredictable. They have blamed themselves for bad seasons, believing they had invoked the displeasure of the gods through a large variety of offenses. High priests of doom told them so, extracting oaths of fealty and offerings of penance for promised interventions on their behalf. In this regard, at least for some, it seems little has changed.

Media networks, politicians, and other headline grabbers readily buy into doomsday pronouncements, offering them up as packaged sound bite–sized news flashes, and competition for audiences and advertising revenues is fierce. Unfortunately, many voices we have previously trusted have become too busy, biased, or indifferent to check the data. Or sometimes they may be disinclined to do so because the "facts" are just too juicy to pass up when facing a ratings war.

Global warming has been effectively marketed as newsworthy because it provides really exciting visuals: icebergs calving, polar bears exhausted from swimming, and such. Endless authorities will back these images up with speculations regarding just how bad things are likely to get. Included are wild projections of climate futures based upon unproven theories and computer models, along with speculative estimates of past temperatures that are to be accepted as articles of faith.

More from Gore

Al Gore and other perhaps less divinely inspired modern-day Noahs continue to speak out about an imminent threat of floods posed by rising ocean levels resulting from melting ocean and glacier ice. The "Goracle" carried on his prophetic ministry at the Copenhagen conference, declaring an impending Arctic disaster. Citing new research undertaken at the US Navy's Naval Postgraduate School in Monterey, California, Mr. Gore told attendees, "These figures are fresh. Some of the models suggest to Dr. [Wieslaw] Maslowski that there is a 75 percent chance the entire north polar ice cap, during the summer months, could be completely ice-free within five to seven years . . . It is hard to capture the astonishment that the experts in the science of ice felt when they saw this."[4]

Scientists were astonished by Gore's statements. One was none other than Dr. Maslowski himself, who responded, "It's unclear to me how the figure was arrived at

. . . I would never try to estimate likelihood at anything as exact as this." Mr. Gore's office later admitted that the 75 percent figure was one used by Dr. Maslowski as a "ballpark figure" several years ago in a conversation with Mr. Gore.

Predictions of Arctic ice collapse are not new, ranging from warnings in 2008 that the "North Pole may be ice-free for the first time this summer" and "the entire polar ice cap will disappear this summer." Much of this was based upon satellite data provided by the National Snow and Ice Data Center showing that Arctic ice was rapidly disappearing back toward a low 2007 level. Yet the August 2008 ice coverage was approximately 10 percent greater than it had been the same month in 2007. Fast-paced freezing in November 2007 followed the rapid rate of melting observed during September and October. NASA's Earth Observatory images reveal that some 58,000 square miles of ice formed for 10 days in late October and early November, a new record. Nevertheless, the extent of sea ice recorded in November was still well shy of the median observed over a 25-year period between 1979 and 2003.[5]

According to NASA Marshall Space Flight Center data, global sea ice expanses in January 2009 approximately equaled those in 1979, and Arctic ice realized a substantial recovery. Bill Chapman, a researcher at the University of Illinois Arctic Center, reported that this was due in part to colder temperatures and also because wind patterns were weaker. Strong winds can slow ice formation and force ice into warmer waters where it will melt.[6]

In November 2009, the average rate of Arctic sea ice growth slightly exceeded the 1979–2000 average growth rate for the month, although at month's end, some regions, including the Barents Sea and Hudson Bay, had less ice cover than normal. Both Hudson Bay and the Barents Sea experienced a slow freeze-up during fall 2009, reportedly caused by different and very complex interactions among the sea ice, the atmosphere, and the ocean.[7]

Religious history is replete with stories of floods, from Noah to Gilgamesh. But melting and freezing patterns are far too complex and regional to be predicted by models. In addition, accurate satellite records only recently became available, and those changes have not been in lockstep with either global temperature or CO_2 concentration trends.

Knee-jerk responses to alarmist forecasts make for great media, but they do so at the expense of good science. If claims that continuous Greenland melting accelerations were correct, even at previously measured advancing rates it would take thousands of years to significantly affect sea levels. And a study presented in the July 2008 issue of the journal *Science* notes that Greenland's melt rate may actually be decreasing when viewed over a long timescale. This research, led by Dr. Roderick S. W. van de Wal of the Institute for Marine and Atmospheric Research in Utrecht, is based upon 17 years of satellite measurements. It concludes that speedups in melting rates are strictly short-term, transient phenomena, occurring primarily during summer months.[8]

Global Warming and Traffic

As noted in earlier chapters, Dr. James Hansen, a high priest of the climate change religion, continues to produce much media flood fodder. You will most likely see his name attached to any widely circulated headline reports of Greenland ice melting at alarming rates and of sea-level rise predictions that make IPCC's seem extremely comforting by comparison. Hansen also continues to stay very busy with television and magazine interviews and public lectures outside his official NASA duties, obviously unfettered by constraints imposed by any government officials on his free speech. An April 14, 2008, *Newsweek* lead cover article, "Who's the Greenest of Them All?" (referring to presidential candidates), quotes him as having observed, "Anything beyond 350 parts per million of carbon dioxide threatens widespread global melting and rise of sea levels. We are at 385 and counting."[9]

Hansen continues to be convinced that a climate crisis is upon us, warning that warming during the summer of 2009 has pushed the climate system toward tipping points that will lead to irreversible and catastrophic effects. He had previously gained headline media coverage when he declared that October 2008 was the warmest on record for that month. NASA later corrected that record after Hansen was caught fudging the numbers. NOAA's registration of 63 snowfall records and 115 lowest-ever temperatures for October ranked 2008 as only the 70th warmest in 114 years. As Christopher Booker wrote in the UK's *Daily Telegraph*, "The reason for the freak figures [presented by Hansen] was that scores of temperature records from Russia and elsewhere weren't based upon October records at all. Figures from the previous month had been carried over for two months running."[10]

Some recent e-mail messages obtained by Christopher Horner, a senior fellow at the Competitive Enterprise Institute, through the Freedom of Information Act call into question the reliability of climate data applied by NASA's GISS, which Hansen heads. Even some top NASA scientists apparently considered the climate dataset produced by GISS to be inferior to data maintained by the University of East Anglia's CRU. In fact, they often depended upon CRU data. The GISS data was also regarded to be inferior to that provided by the National Climatic Data Center's Global Historical Climatology Network, whose information had been given directly to a reporter from *USA Today* in August 2007 but was never published.[11]

Hansen's past predictions haven't all proven to be divinely inspired. During an interview in 2001, he was asked to predict how global warming would affect the scene outside his New York City GISS office building 20 years hence. Gazing out of his upper-level window onto the area below, he said, "Well, there will be more traffic." Then he went on to say, "The West Side Highway [which runs along the Hudson River] will be underwater. And there will be tape across the windows across the street because of high winds. And the same birds won't be there. The trees in the median strip will change." Then he added, "There will be more police cars." When asked why, he explained, "Well, you know what happens to crime when the heat goes up."[12] At least he was right about the traffic.

Skeptical Judgments

The climate change believers have launched what amounts to an aggressive jihad against those who have differing opinions. Results of that climate war have brought great injustice to individuals who disagree, have hampered sensible dialogue and debate, and have produced government policies guided by emotion and fear rather than by balanced reasoning and sound judgments.

One tactic used to defame those who don't subscribe to global warming crisis hysteria is to associate disbelievers with those who have turned their backs on true villainy. For example, when television commentator Scott Pelley was asked in a March 23, 2006, CBS PublicEye blog post why he didn't interview anyone who didn't agree that global warming is a threat, he compared scientists who are skeptical about human-caused catastrophic climate change to Holocaust deniers: "If I do an interview with [Holocaust survivor] Elie Wiesel, am I required as a journalist to find a Holocaust denier?"[13]

David Roberts, a regular contributor to Grist, a prominent environmental news and commentary blog site, carried the denier Holocaust theme even farther. Referring to the "denial industry," he stated that we should have "war crime trials for these bastards—some sort of climate Nuremberg."[14]

An Australian columnist agrees with Roberts, proposing that climate change denial should be outlawed: "David Irving is under arrest in Australia for Holocaust denial. Perhaps there is a case for making climate change denial an offence—it is a crime against humanity after all."[15]

IPCC's top scientist and chairman, Rajendra Pachauri, goes beyond the Holocaust to compare the views of global warming deniers with those of Hitler himself. Referring to the well-known global warming skeptic Bjorn Lomborg, Pachauri stated, "Where is the difference between Lomborg's view on humans and Hitler's? You cannot treat people like cattle."[16]

With regard to IPCC's scientific objectivity, that pretty much says it all.

Eco-Evangelism

In the church of climate change, most or all unfortunate events that occur on our planet are attributed to human causation. Eco-elitist crusaders argue that economic growth, promulgated by large corporate interests, is the enemy of the environment. They overlook the fact that global economic progress yields technological innovations and prosperity essential to support more resourceful, cleaner, and healthier lifestyles. A return to the small, self-sufficient, agrarian communal societies of our ancestors is no longer practical or desirable, either for us or for the ecosystems we depend upon.

Environmental evangelism has been a unifying influence in a wide variety of other non-climate-related initiatives with mixed cost-benefit results.[17] Do you remember the huge amount of attention during the 1970s and 1980s that surrounded the issue of acid rain damage to lakes and forests, which was attributed to industrial SO_2 emissions from Midwestern utilities?[18] And did you ever hear about the results of a more-than-half-a-billion-dollar, 10-year-long National Acid Precipitation Assessment Program study that was initiated in 1980 to research the matter?[19] Probably not.

As it turned out, those fears of widespread damage proved to be largely unfounded, since only one species of tree at a high elevation suffered any notable effect, and acidity in lakes was traced to natural causes. The scientists reported that they had "turned up no smoking gun"; that the problem was far more complicated than had been thought; that other factors combine to harm trees; and that sorting out cause and effect is difficult and in some cases impossible. As Robert Bruck, a North Carolina State University plant pathologist who worked on the project, observed, "If you're environmentally oriented, you're going to find things to be concerned about; if you're one who finds no reason to get excited, you'll find much to support that, too."[20] Is this beginning to sound familiar?

Although the Reagan-Bush administration refused to sponsor any acid rain legislation before the results were in, a regulatory groundwork had already been established within the EPA, with many new careers in the balance. So, although the acid rain threat had been demonstrably overblown, pressures upon the George H. W. Bush administration added costly SO_2 emission restrictions within new Clean Air Act regulations. The IPCC, along with other scientific organizations, now recognize SO_2 as a gas that counteracts atmospheric greenhouse warming effects—though few on either side of the global warming debate are likely to argue that this is a worthwhile benefit to be encouraged.[21]

Knee-jerk environmental legislation likewise poses unforeseen political and other hazards. An example is a cap-and-trade regulatory mechanism proposed under the Clean Air Act of 2005 by the George W. Bush administration to reduce sources of mercury pollution 29 percent by 2010, ramping up to 79 percent by 2018. Mercury is universally recognized to be a highly toxic health hazard, and although the reduction cost to the electricity industry (principally transferred to consumers) is estimated to be $2 billion or more, general public support appears to be strong. Yet even though such regulations have not previously existed, some environmental groups are critical, demanding that such cuts are not nearly enough, arguing that the "weak" plan is a conspiracy to hurt our nation's children.[22]

In February 2008, the United States Court of Appeals for the District of Columbia Circuit Court ruled that the EPA-endorsed "Clean Air Mercury Rule" was invalid because a cap-and-trade program would enable power plants that fail to meet emission targets to buy credits from plants that did, rather than having to install their own mercury emission controls. Seventeen states argued that the cap-and-trade approach would endanger children living near power plants that couldn't comply by "doing it legally." If this were the case, why would cap-and-trade legislation for CO_2 emission allowances be any different? That certainly appears to be a problem in most countries that signed on to Kyoto Protocol emission targets.[23]

Another ironic twist and turn in the mercury regulation saga revolves around new US government legislation that will phase out use of traditional incandescent bulbs in 2012, replacing them with more energy-efficient compact fluorescent lighting (CFL) that contains mercury. Many argue that the resulting environmental and health costs will cancel out the benefits realized through energy conservation.

While advocates argue that the mercury content in a single CFL bulb is relatively low, comparable to that in watch batteries and tilt thermostats, a difference is that these items don't tend to shatter when accidentally dropped. Critics argue that as federal legislation continues to push CFLs into home use, exposures will add up over time, with increased risks to the health of babies, children, pregnant women, the elderly, and those in poor health.

Disposal of spent bulbs will present large cleanup costs, and those that end up in landfills will leak mercury into the air and groundwater. A spokesman for General Electric, a major CFL producer, admitted that even a little mercury in each bulb will add up to a big problem when sales really expand. Huge amounts of mercury will also enter the global environment from factories in China and other nations where pollution control regulations are much more lax or nonexistent.[24]

Conscience of an Environmentalist

Environmentalists are almost universally motivated by love and reverence toward nature, vital concerns about our impacts upon planet Earth and its ecosystems, and a strong sense of responsibility regarding the legacy we leave for generations who will follow. These basic priorities are not founded upon specific scientific theories or beliefs; rather, they are founded upon shared values that fundamentally define and guide our most evolved human qualities. Included are our abilities to reason objectively, to create innovative solutions that make things better, and to learn from mistakes that occur even when we mean well.[25]

There can be no doubt that environmental issues have captured mainstream public consciousness, and so they should. Just look at the recent explosion of protective legislative initiatives, government- and corporate-sponsored climate research funding, and tax-supported investments in green energy technologies. People of all backgrounds, including scientists, politicians, and regular folks, are passionate about such matters. Those passions have yielded urgent and beneficial changes along with some very costly lessons.

The beginning of the popular "environmental movement" is conventionally associated with a virtual tsunami of reaction to Rachel Carson's *Silent Spring* after it first appeared in 1962. Endorsed by Supreme Court Justice William O. Douglas, the book spent several weeks on the *New York Times* best-seller list and inspired widespread public concerns regarding human impacts upon the environment. Most

particularly, it called attention to a thinning of the eggshells of certain bird species that threatened their existence, along with the toxic problems throughout the
food chain that resulted from indiscriminate crop spraying of the pesticide DDT.
Although now scientifically challenged, this claim is clearly credited with a prohibi-
tion against DDT use in the United States since 1972, and a similar ban in Europe.[26]

Because of threatened European trade restrictions against countries that used
DDT, African nations terminated use of the effective mosquito pesticide for malaria
control. Since that time, death rates from the disease have increased dramatically.
The US Centers for Disease Control estimates that between 155,000 and 310,000
people have died each year based upon 1997–2002 data tabulated at forty-one African sites. The vast majority of these victims are desperately poor, including large
numbers of young children and the elderly, who are especially vulnerable.[27] Arguably, there would have been millions fewer deaths if African nations had continued
to use DDT. How does anyone compute an environmental cost-benefit assessment
that factors in the intrinsic value of those lives?[28]

The malaria-DDT paradox presents an ironic connection to recent claims by
some that global warming is causing mosquito populations to expand into formerly cooler latitudes, with the potential of producing malaria epidemics in various
parts of the world. Although many highly informed scientists strongly dispute any
such influence, it again brings pesticide issues to the center stage of environmental
debate.

Assuming that an important goal of environmental policies is to help underdeveloped and developing nations gain the health advantages developed nations
enjoy, perhaps a good way is to assist in lifting them out of poverty and pollution
through modernization. Yet "environmentalists" continue to block plans to construct hydropower dams in Africa and India that can provide clean energy needed
to refrigerate and safely preserve food. Obstructionists who enjoy those essentials
cite overriding ecological concerns.[29]

Paul Ehrlich's The Population Bomb, published in 1968, was one of several books
that spread doom-and-gloom predictions attributed to human pressures on the
environment. It projected that worldwide crises in food supply and natural resource
availability would lead to major famines and economic failures by 1990. Ehrlich's
predictions were based upon the premise that while agricultural production was
growing linearly, population was expanding at a much faster and unsustainable geo-
metric rate. What he failed to consider is that as developing countries modernize,

birth rates tend to fall, and agricultural output increases even faster using less farm-land. The United States is a prime example.[30]

John Holdren, the Obama-Biden administration's science and technology czar, has been ordained as another high priest of climate calamity. Holdren was an early protégé of Ehrlich and coauthored a book with him in 1977 titled *Ecoscience: Population, Resources, Environment*, which explored measures a government might take to limit population growth if a population crisis is to occur. The book defended the constitutionality of compulsory abortion and sterilization, a topic reopened at the Copenhagen climate change meeting in 2009. In 1986, Holdren declared that global warming could cause the deaths of 1 billion people by 2020.

Mr. Holden also holds several other influential White House positions: assistant to the president for science and technology, director of the White House Office of Science and Technology Policy, and cochair of the President's Council of Advisors on Science and Technology. Fortunately, during his confirmation hearings, Holdren stated that the government should not determine the optimum US population, and he now believes that the figure of 1 billion deaths by 2020 is "unlikely."[31] We can breathe a collective sigh of relief!

Holdren is a strong advocate of cap-and-trade as a means to control energy consumption, and he supported this strategy long before Al Gore got windy on wind. In a paper released in 1995, Holdren explained his model for sustainable development as one in which "humans are included as just one species and not treated specially."[32] Another Holdren sustainability tenant is to launch "a massive campaign to restore a high-quality environment in North America and to de-develop the United States"; to achieve this end, he believes that "resources and energy must be diverted from frivolous and wasteful uses in overdeveloped countries to filling the genuine needs of underdeveloped countries."[33]

Does any of this sound familiar? As if it could have come from the United Nations and its IPCC, for example? Or maybe the Karl Marx doctrine? Is it what we would expect the nation's highest appointed science and technology adviser to advocate? Is this where eco-evangelism has driven us? Has our ship of state drifted to a foreign port, or is this still the United States of America?

Chapter 9

GETTING A REAL GRIP ON "GREEN" ENERGY

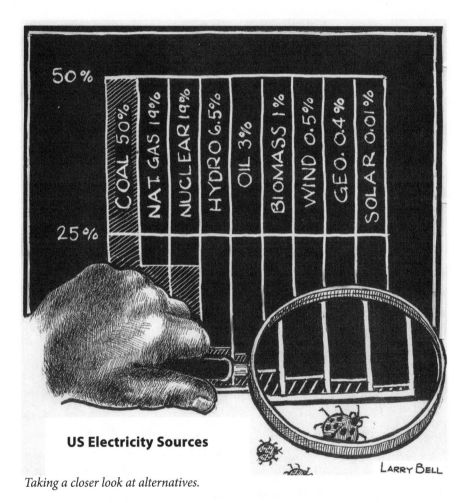

US Electricity Sources

Taking a closer look at alternatives.

The United States is facing energy challenges that can only get worse. It is clear that we must develop and exploit all reasonable alternatives and also practice rational conservation measures as we observe that global demand increases, readily accessible oil and gas deposits dwindle, competition for world supply accelerates, and costs rise. Equally important is a need to curb regulatory obstruction of vital and time-critical energy initiatives based on unwarranted assertions of moral and scientific authority. All these priorities demand trustworthy public information and leadership. Therein lie the greatest obstacles of all.

In response to man-made global warming and foreign oil dependence alarms, many companies are rushing to "green up" their investment portfolios, advertising images, and lobbying campaigns. And they are realizing great successes, cheered on by a hopeful, grateful public and its representatives. After all, who can resist the tantalizing allure of cleaner, perpetually sustainable, unlimited new supplies of power and fuel that will provide independence from unreliable, often unfriendly foreign sources?

Many are beginning to realize that most green expectations are oversold and color-blind. Increasing numbers of skeptics and critics are challenging the actual benefits and consequences of various energy choices. Included are growing numbers of taxpayers, consumers, and more than a few environmental groups.[1]

Alternative (aka "green") energy initiatives are receiving rapidly expanding levels of arguably well-justified encouragement and support through a variety of federal, state, and local incentive programs. Many tens of billions of dollars have already been provided through such mechanisms as subsidies, production credits, accelerated depreciation tax credits, and public funding for research. As of February 2008, twenty-five states plus the District of Columbia have instituted mandatory renewable portfolio standards (RPSs) that set timetables for increasing percentages of legislated green power production.[2] It may be interesting to note, however, that the majority of government-owned utilities in these states have successfully lobbied for reprieves from the costly, often unrealistic requirements.[3]

A federal Energy Policy Act of 2005 authorized by the US Congress mandates a biofuel RPS phase-in starting at 4 billion gallons in 2006 and reaching 7.5 billion gallons by 2012.[4] In December 2007, the US House of Representatives passed another RPS requiring all investor-owned utilities (but not municipal systems and rural cooperatives) to obtain 2.75 percent of their power from renewable sources by 2010 and 15 percent by 2020. The Senate version rejected any RPS provision that would transfer wealth from already distressed electricity customers to a heavily subsidized wind power industry.

Consumers generally have no idea how expensive green power actually is, because so much of the cost is passed on through taxpayer subsidies and preferential treatment that drives conventional power prices higher. Even with that invisible support, it still costs more than most utility customers are willing to pay voluntarily. When public polls are taken asking people if they would pay more for alternatives that are "better for the environment," the results are usually overwhelmingly positive. Yet, when they are asked to actually sign up and pay more, their euphoria immediately disappears.

In addition to currently uncompetitive costs relative to coal, natural gas, and nuclear for electricity, and oil for transportation, a major and long-term green energy industry problem is its very limited practical expansion capacity. Consider that alternatives presently account for only about 6 percent of the total US electrical power production (half of that from hydropower). Wind power (about 0.5 percent of total electricity—less than 0.01 percent of total energy) is the only alternative with a prospect for significant growth, and it has a very long way to go in replacing dependence upon fossils (about 72 percent of total electricity—75 percent of total energy), and nuclear (about 19 percent of total electricity—11.5 percent of total energy). Hydropower (about 6.5 percent of total electricity—0.33 percent of total energy) has little expansion capacity. Solar, which currently provides only about 0.01 percent of total US electricity—even much less of total energy—isn't a contender for a significant share of the commercial market on the basis of either cost or capacity. Geothermal (less than 0.5 percent of total electricity—negligible total energy) is even more restricted, both economically and geographically, in terms of expansion.

In reality, renewable energy development has a long way to go before it can even begin to significantly offset increasing demands, much less play dominant supply roles. All combined, these alternatives currently provide only about 6 percent of US total energy, with the vast majority of that amount split between hydropower and such biofuels as ethanol and wood.

It is essential to our national and global future that development and utilization of alternative energy sources and technologies continue and grow. This includes improvement and expansion of nuclear power, along with innovations to produce cleaner energy from coal and other fossil sources for which there is presently no practical substitute.

It is also vital that the public be made much better informed about the comparative advantages and disadvantages of all alternatives, and that public policy decisions at all government levels be more fully guided by the facts. Currently, this is not happening. Performance benefits of unproven options, such as cellulosic ethanol, have been asserted but not demonstrated. Expansion capacities of various alternative energy options have been wildly exaggerated by promoters, leading many in the general public to believe that abundant replacements for fossil sources are available, but are being neglected by the energy utilities in response to "big oil" interests.

It is not useful to either overestimate those capacities or underestimate their costs and limitations. Both errors are prevalent in media and marketing hype that tells us what we would really like to believe, namely, that there are simple, Earth-friendly, sustainable answers that can make energy problems go away. Unfortunately, this is not the case. It is difficult to comprehend how miniscule the potential capacities of these so-called renewable sources are relative to the colossal amounts of energy we will continue to require.

The term "green energy" has become meaningless because the environmental consequences of all alternatives have been ignored by some and aggressively attacked by others. Some fossil-dependent energy resources have been mischaracterized as renewable and nonpolluting. Upon closer examination of those green options, many will appear decidedly "browner" than advertised, and they will not present a major supply-side solution to our energy challenges.[5]

Biofuels: Field of Dreams

Can we grow our way out of an energy deficit? Federal legislation with such titles as the Renewable Fuels Act (2005) and the Biofuels Security Act (2006) are both misleading with regard to ethanol, the primary biofuel. First, it really isn't renewable when you consider that nearly as much fossil fuel–generated energy is required to produce it as it actually yields. Alternatively, if all the energy used to plant, fertilize, harvest, and process the biofuel came from the ethanol produced, it would displace a gasoline consumption equivalent to only about 3.5 percent. This is about the same amount that the Natural Resources Defense Council (NRDC) estimates might be saved by inflating tires properly.[6]

Regarding energy security, biofuels suffer from some very serious reliability and capacity limitations. Corn crops, the plant stock for US ethanol, are vulnerable to periodic drought conditions. On average, a crop yield decline of nearly one-third occurs about 1 year out of 20 due to insufficient rainfall. And even during good years, the total offset on gasoline consumption will be very small, regardless of any mandates established by federal and state governments.

Ethanol refiners (actually wood alcohol "distillers") cite energy independence as a compelling argument for the massive subsidies they receive. Imported oil continues to provide about 60 percent of all petroleum fuel we use, and exposes the United States to large economic risks and massive trade imbalances that ethanol will not alleviate.[7]

But if we were to produce enough ethanol to replace gasoline altogether, it would require that about 71 percent of all US farmland be dedicated for energy crops.[8] By way of illustration, let's just think about distilling all of our present US corn production into that 180-proof grain alcohol—ethanol. That would only displace, at most, about 14 percent of the gasoline we currently guzzle. In 2007, ethanol consumed approximately one-fourth of all US corn production. In 2008, that amount grew to about one-third, and the percent will continue to rise. The 2007 amount was estimated to have offset US gasoline consumption by 3.5 percent while corn costs had doubled over a 2-year period.[9]

Assuming that it is possible for the United States to produce a mandated 36 billion gallons of ethanol by 2022, it won't really make a big difference. That would replace only about 1.5 billion barrels per day (bbl/d) of oil, amounting to only about 7 percent of our needs; that is, providing we hold consumption to current levels.[10]

Because US farmland is scarce and expensive, each additional acre of corn used to produce ethanol is one less that is available for other crops such as soybeans and wheat, which have seen price increases of more than 240 percent since 2006. This, in turn, produces a ripple effect that raises the costs of meat, milk, eggs, and other foods with international export consequences. Since US farmers provide about 70 percent of all global corn exports, even small diversions for ethanol production have produced high inflation levels in America and food riots abroad.[11]

Two professors at the University of Minnesota's Center for International Food and Agricultural Policy, C. Ford Runge and Benjamin Senauer, estimate that filling a 25-gallon tank of an SUV with pure ethanol requires more than 450 pounds of corn. That would be enough calories to feed one person for a year.[12]

Ethanol also competes with people and livestock for water—lots and lots of water. It requires about 4 gallons of water to produce 1 gallon of the alcohol fuel, in addition to other water that production plants typically recycle. Many Corn Belt regions where the production facilities are sited, particularly in the Midwest and the Great Plains, are beginning to experience significant water supply problems. Beef and dairy cattle feed lots located near the plants to take advantage of the co-product distillers' grain for livestock feed, add to local water demands, as do agricultural irrigation and urban expansion.

About one-half of all ethanol plants use municipal water for some or all production, and the rest sink their own wells. In many areas, the aquifers that supply the water are being depleted faster than they can recharge, a situation that is occurring in the Chicago-Milwaukee region, for example. By definition, this is an unsustainable condition that may, quite possibly, prove to be the Achilles heel of future corn-based ethanol programs nationwide.[13] Applying Minnesota's water consumption averages to national ethanol production estimates, water consumption will have increased 254 percent by volume between 1998 and 2008. Lack of adequate water is already curtailing some requests for new ethanol plant permits. An example is a planned Lincoln-Pipestone Rural Water System application that couldn't meet a 350-million-gallons-per-year water requirement needed for a proposed 100-million-gallons-per-year ethanol plant.[14]

Ethanol production is also being linked to water pollution. US farmers, who planted more corn in 2007 than at any time since World War II, are tilling more and more land that is not well suited for intensive agriculture, exacerbating erosion and pesticide runoff that are infiltrating groundwater and aquifers. Rather than rotating corn planting with soybeans to replace soil nitrogen, many farmers are planting corn year after year and adding large amounts of nitrogen fertilizer. On average, about 30 pounds/acre of each 140 pounds/acre of nitrogen fertilizer leaches away and runs off into creeks, lakes, and aquifers. Some winds up in drinking water, posing special health problems for children and pregnant women. More runoff occurs when corn isn't rotated with other crops because the soil develops more clumps, which results in the need for more tilling and hence becomes looser, which can result in more erosion.[15]

Then there is the issue of emissions. Even though ethanol fuel may produce marginally less CO_2 than does gasoline, it nevertheless releases large quantities of nitrogen oxide (smog) that causes respiratory disease. This can add to an already large problem in many urban areas, such as Los Angeles and throughout the Northeast.[16] Thus, living near ethanol plants can be unpleasant. More than two hundred such plants, located in a swath extending from Nebraska and Kansas east into Ohio, emit thousands of tons of CO_2 and various pollutants. As Frank O'Donnell, president of Clean Air Watch, observed, "I think word is getting out that ethanol refineries can be a heck of a problem if you live near them. You're taking areas that are generally not seeing a lot of pollution now and darkening the skies."[17]

What about ethanol's prospective benefits to reduce global warming? After all, Al Gore often mentions with pride how, as vice president, he cast a tie-breaking Senate vote August 4, 1994, that mandated use of ethanol. It guaranteed ethanol and other renewable fuels a 15 percent share of the lucrative fuel oxygenate market in 1995, with that amount increasing to 30 percent in following years.[18] Mr. Gore also joined the venture capital group Kleiner Perkins Caufield & Byers (in November 2007), whose key partner, venture capitalist John Doerr, is pushing for expanded biofuel use. Yet there is growing evidence that biofuels may actually release more CO_2 emissions than conventional petroleum-based gasoline does. As reported in the journal *Science*, "Corn-based ethanol . . . instead of producing a 20 percent savings, nearly doubles greenhouse emissions over 30 years . . . Biofuels from switchgrass, if grown on US corn lands, increase emissions by 50 percent." This is because biofuel markets encourage farmers to level forests and convert wilderness areas into farmland, which would otherwise serve as CO_2 sinks.[19]

Still another problem with ethanol is that it isn't very efficient as an energy source as compared with petroleum. For one thing, since its energy density is about one-third less than that of gasoline, more must be burned to produce the same amount of power. It is also more energy intensive to produce. On average, an oil company burns energy equivalent to about 1 gallon of oil to process 20 gallons of gasoline, while ethanol yields versus energy requirements are only slightly positive at best. It takes burning almost a gallon of ethanol to produce 1 gallon of ethanol (subject to debate even on that small gain). Sugarcane ethanol processing in Brazil is only about one-third as energy intensive as corn ethanol processing, but the fuel is virtually barred from US import by a $0.54/gallon tariff applied to protect American markets. Since large amounts of fossils are consumed to irrigate, fertilize, harvest, and process corn ethanol, it serves as little more than a way to recycle oil and natural gas into a different fuel form, offering no real advantages and some major liabilities.

Ethanol transportation imposes additional energy costs. Unlike oil and natural gas, it can't be moved through existing pipelines because it readily absorbs water and various impurities. Instead, it must be transported by truck or rail, either of which is much more expensive. Ethanol produced from plant cellulose rather than corn is advertised as a promising alternative to avoid competition with food crops, but it has yet to be demonstrated as a viable commercial option. It would also impose even vastly larger transportation requirements in addition to the processing complexities and difficulties. Replacing 50 percent of current gasoline consumption using cellulosic ethanol would require about 13 percent of all US land, along with enormous environmental and economic costs.[20]

And what about the costs to the consumer? Who comes out ahead on the deal? You may have guessed by now that we're being hosed at the pump along with the fuel.

During 2006, US taxpayers provided subsidies, courtesy of our government, that totaled about $7 billion for 4.9 billion gallons of ethanol ($1.45/gallon of ethanol and $2.21/gallon of gasoline replaced).[21] Because producing that gallon of ethanol cost $0.38 more than making gasoline with the same quantity of energy, that amounted to $1.12 extra profit. Of the total, $2.5 billion came from subsidies of $0.51/gallon paid out of taxes as a blender's credit, and $0.9 billion was paid out of tax money for corn subsidies. In addition, consumers paid $3.6 billion extra at the pump. Compared with subsidies paid to the oil industry based upon amount of energy produced, ethanol subsidies are more than fifty times higher.[22]

The conglomerate Archer Daniels Midland Company (ADM) has done well since it first began pushing ethanol in the 1970s. A decade later, ADM was producing 175 million gallons/year; the business has now grown to produce more than 1 billion gallons/year, supported by more than two hundred different tax breaks and subsidies worth at least $5.5 billion/year.[23] Since 2000, ADM has contributed about $3.7 million to state and federal politicians. For more than a decade, nearly half (or more) of the company's profits have come from products the US government has either subsidized or protected.[24]

So just how green is ethanol? Its production requires tremendous amounts of fossils, water, and agricultural land that would be more productive if used to grow food crops. At best, ethanol could replace but a small percentage of fossil-fuel demands, and then it could only be cost competitive through high tax–supported subsidies.

Power Lunches: They're Not Free After All

So, maybe ethanol alcohol isn't the big energy solution that many thought it was brewed up to be. What about all that free wind and Sun power that's unlimited and clean? Also, there's power from water flow, from Earth's heat, and from simple hydrogen molecules—all very natural sources. Why aren't we taking fuller advantage of them? Has anyone really thought about that? The answer is yes.

WIND ENERGY: A NATURAL LONG-TERM INVESTMENT

Wind power—in contrast to ethanol, for example—actually provides some net energy advantages, although not nearly as much or as cheaply as we might imagine. Still, given the facts that energy costs will continue to rise as fossil-fuel resources become scarcer, we will need every source that can offer real contributions. It is vital to begin expanding infrastructures now for future needs, and to begin to amortize investment costs on a long-term basis. Currently, virtually all these up-front costs are being borne by taxpayers, through subsidies and other development incentives, and by consumers, through higher electricity bills. Yet there is a precedent for this. Large hydropower programs were built on public funding too.

Advocates of green energy have grossly exaggerated the capacity of wind power to make a major impact on US electrical needs. Greenpeace is off the charts in this regard, claiming that "wind could supply more than three times the total amount of electricity produced in the United States." Any euphoric fantasy that an unlimited, free, and clean alternative to carbon-cursed fossil-fuel sources is blowing by and we're giving it scant notice is exceedingly naive and misguided.[25]

A major point of public confusion regarding wind power potential lies in a failure to differentiate maximum total capacities, typically presented as megawatts (MW), with actual predicted kilowatt-hours (kWh) that are determined by annual average wind conditions at a particular site. Wind is intermittent and velocities constantly change. Unfortunately, wind isn't always available, especially when it is needed most—such as during hot summer days when demands for air-conditioning are highest. For this reason, a backup power system (usually a gas turbine system) or electrical supplies from other power grid sources must carry the load. Even when wind is available, the highly fluctuating intensity requires that the power grid balance the supply on a second-by-second basis, adding complexities and costs to the total network. The backup supplies, called "spinning reserves," add significant operational costs that are passed on to customers.[26]

Output volatility due to wind's intermittent nature varies greatly according to location and time of year. In 2006, wind farms in California, a major wind state, produced power at only about 10 percent of their rated capacity. Texas, one of the most promising wind energy states, produced at about 17 percent capacity. In early 2007, the Electric Reliability Council of Texas, an independent state operator, determined that only about 8.7 percent of installed wind capability could be counted on as dependable capacity during peak demand periods.[27]

The dependable capacity of any electrical system is referred to as the "base load" capacity: the minimum amount of proven, consistent, around-the-clock, rain-or-shine power that utilities must supply to meet customer demands. Here, wind and sunshine have big disadvantages.

Taking these volatility reductions into account, consider a May 2007 prediction made by the American Council on Renewable Energy that it is "technically feasible to increase wind capacity to supply 20 percent of this nation's electricity by 2030," providing 340 gigawatts (GW), or 340,000 MW, by that time. What exactly does that mean in terms of real, available kWh-generating output? Actually, it means very little if merely a minor percentage of that technical feasibility actually provides electricity when needed.[28]

By the end of 2006, wind energy provided about 0.5 percent of US electricity, with 11.6 GW of installed capacity. The industry has set a new target of producing 100 GW by 2020, which is suggested to compare with the capacity of about a hundred nuclear plants. A reality check indicates a different picture. Unlike for nuclear plants, which produce reliable power levels continuously, it is necessary to factor in a big discounted equivalency factor for wind. To be extremely generous, let's assume that the actual average output would be 30 percent of total installed capacity. In that optimistic case, the real output would be equivalent to less than 5 percent of the country's electricity, and more realistically, about half that amount.[29]

A major limitation of individual wind farms is that they simply don't produce power on the massive scales needed in large cities and industrial areas where space is at a premium and land is prohibitively expensive. Another limitation is that places where wind conditions are most ideal are often remote from areas where demands are highest, requiring large investments for power transmission lines and land right-of-way use.[30]

Sites with suitable wind conditions for power production are geographically limited. From an energy-generation point of view, the best ones are typically along mountain ridges and coastal areas. Unfortunately, these same types of locations are also prized for scenic views and are overflown by bird and bat species that become turbine blade casualties. And even though national environmental organizations such as Greenpeace and the Sierra Club have become wind power advocates in their war against fossils, others who live in proposed wind farm locations have launched strong opposition to turbines. Those areas include the Green Mountains of Vermont, the Adirondacks in northern New York, the Chesapeake Bay off the Atlantic coast between Maryland and Virginia, Cape Cod in Massachusetts, and the ridges of northern Appalachia. Local residents have filed successful protests. They don't want their own backyards cluttered with towering turbines that would interfere with the spirit-soothing views they paid a lot of money to enjoy.

Yet what true "environmentalist" could possibly object to nonpolluting wind power that will help save our planet from the dreaded CO_2 scourge? Well, for one, there was Robert F. Kennedy Jr., nephew of a popular president and prominent lawyer for the NRDC, who fought against a proposed 130-turbine offshore development called "Cape Wind" in Nantucket Sound. Another uncle, the late Senator Ted Kennedy (D-MA), along with Senate colleague and fellow Massachusetts resident John Kerry, didn't want Cape Wind disturbing his vistas either. Senator Kerry explained his reasons this way: "I've always said that I think Senator Kennedy has raised very legitimate issues with respect to the siting process and with respect to location. I've also suggested that it's my opinion there may be even better locations for it. I've sat with Jim Gordon [president of Cape Wind], I've sat with other folks, I've met with Coast Guard people, I've tried to do due diligence on it, and I'm not sure there aren't both windier and, you know, more accessible areas."[31]

Yes, areas not off his front beach. And there are others besides members of the New England elite class who don't want to live near wind turbines either. Take Texans, for example.

In early 2007, owners of the famous King Ranch, one of the world's largest, lobbied the Texas Legislature to pass a law to regulate wind turbine development.[32] They were seeking a bill requiring companies to obtain state permits based upon studies to determine whether the noise from turbines "interferes with the property rights of nearby landowners." This was prompted after the King Ranch president, Jack Hunt, heard that managers of a neighboring Kenedy Ranch were going to allow 240 wind turbines to be installed on that property. He charged that the smaller ranch (only 400,000 acres) was "sacrificing the long-term value of a rare resource for short-term revenue," and that the turbine siting was "a horrific location." Some folks, even those with lots of surrounding space, just don't want to live near wind farms. Period!

Mortality impacts upon migratory bird populations and endangered bat species continue to rally anti–wind farm activists who have blocked developments with lawsuits. Studies have shown that as many as forty-four thousand birds, including golden and bald eagles, have been killed by turbines in the Altamont Pass east of San Francisco over 2 decades.[33] One reason appears to be that prey animals tend to take shelter at the turbines and multiply, serving as attractive bait for raptors.

In May 2006, Superior Renewable Energy received approval to build the nation's largest offshore wind farm, with five hundred 400-foot-tall turbines off the coast of Padre Island, Texas. That site is right in the middle of the path that an estimated two-thirds of all birds in eastern and central North America follow as they migrate. One plan that has been considered to help protect birds that are forced to fly low during bad weather is to use technology that turns off the blades at those times. It's not easy to prevent all environmental risks.

And what about wind farm influences upon whales? Yes, you read this right! On June 25, 2010, environmental groups filed a legal challenge to block the planned Massachusetts offshore Nantucket Sound project because it will endanger migratory birds and whales. Are they possibly underestimating whale intelligence?

There are also costs and risks for those who ultimately pay for wind energy projects, namely, taxpayers and customers. Without large public subsidies and other incentives, the industry would not be solvent. More than half of all potential return on investment for companies that install and operate the systems comes from federal, state, and local tax benefits. During 2006, federal tax incentives alone were about $2.75 billion.

Special public incentives for wind energy development come in a variety of forms. A primary break involves tax avoidance mechanisms afforded through production tax credits (PTCs), accelerated depreciation, and reduced or forgiven property and sales taxes.

The federal PTC program, which began in 1992 with a 1.5¢ per kWh subsidy for wind power owners, increases at the rate of inflation (now about 3¢ per kWh). These credits are directly deductible from federal income taxes and are particularly valuable to large companies that have lots of profits in other areas. The PTC program is also attractive for small wind farm developers as a way to sell their projects to larger companies for the tax benefits they provide.[34]

Federal accelerated depreciation offers a subsidy that enables wind farm investors to take a generous double-declining 5-year depreciation tax shelter. The investors can deduct 40 percent of capital investments the first year, and 24 percent the second, and can continue until all deductions are complete before the end of the fifth year. This is a tremendous advantage that allows generators of this energy to give money back to shareholders rapidly; conventional electricity plant developers, by comparison, must use 20-year depreciations. Some states that "conform" their corporate income tax programs to the federal system allow otherwise taxable income to carry through to the wind farm developers' state income tax returns as well.

Some federal and state programs afford green energy providers guaranteed markets at premium sales prices. States that have legislated mandatory RPSs require electric utility companies to purchase designated amounts of energy from wind, solar, and biofuel providers, typically at higher-than-conventional costs that are passed on to their customers. Some states require or encourage electric utilities to offer "green program" advertising ("greenwashing") to ask customers to voluntarily sign up for higher-priced, more "environmentally responsible" electricity. Since subscription levels tend to be low, the extra costs are distributed among all customers and hidden in invoices. There is strong lobbying by the renewable energy industry to have RPSs legislated by the federal government.[35]

Federal and state government agencies are mandating that purchases of the electricity they use come from renewable sources at related premium prices. Several state and local governments enable wind energy developers to reduce or eliminate property taxes. Some states authorize utilities to charge special public benefit taxes to customers who pay money to wind farm operators. And some states provide industrial development bonds that enable wind farms to be financed by state-backed loans that have lower-than-commercial interest rates.

Although wind may never be a big power player in the United States, and certainly is less of a force than represented by enthusiasts, one fact is clear: So long as fossil-fuel costs are manipulated by government, emission regulations continue to rise, energy demands increase, and generous subsidies flow, wind industry forecasts will be at least gusty.

Much to the chagrin of DOE officials and other advocates, a report from Spain discredited the idea that wind power is a job creator, an idea touted by the Obama-Biden administration. US officials banded with trade lobbyists to minimize the exposed facts. The study, released by researchers at King Juan Carlos University, concluded that every "green job" created by the wind industry killed off 2.2 jobs elsewhere in the Spanish economy.[36]

Research director Gabriel Calzada Alvarez didn't fundamentally object to wind power. He did, however, find that when a government artificially props up the industry with subsidies, higher electrical costs (31 percent) and tax hikes (5 percent), along with government debt, follow. Every green job created was estimated to cost $800,000 per year to create, and 90 percent of those green jobs were temporary.

Alvarez specifically presented lessons for the United States. He warned of potential "self-inflicted economic wounds" and forecasted that this country could lose 6.6 million jobs if it followed Spain's example.

A few months after the study was released, researchers at the Danish Center for Politiske Studier reached similar conclusions about underwriting wind power based on their country's experience: "It is fair to assess that no wind energy would exist if it had to compete on market terms."[37]

Both of the reports have been pointedly ignored by the Obama-Biden administration, which has declared an agenda—with $2.3 billion to be allocated in tax credits— to create seventeen thousand "high-quality green jobs." President Obama has said, "Building a robust clean energy sector is how we will create the jobs of the future."[38]

Then, in response to a release of the reports and a critical *Washington Post* column by George Will, bureaucrats at the Energy Department, left-wing activists, and trade lobbyists went into defensive mode. E-mail files, obtained by Christopher Horner at the Competitive Enterprise Institute, reveal concerted damage control efforts. Their strategy was to hide facts, discredit foreign academic sources, and concoct their own white paper as a rebuttal.

One such e-mail, sent by Elizabeth Salerno of the American Wind Energy Association (AWEA) to Suzanne Tegan of the DOE's National Renewable Energy Laboratory, illustrates how the industry lobby and a US taxpayer-funded government entity can collaborate. It states, "It's critical we respond (to the Spanish report). This thing won't die and it's doing a good job of undermining our green job message. If we put together a call with CAP [the Center for American Progress], can UCS [Union of Concerned Scientists] participate on a comprehensive response?"[39]

Tegan then called for a telephone meeting the next day to draft a response. In an e-mail follow-up, she wrote: "We are working with AWEA (who is working with UCS and others) to put out a response to this report, which is methodologically unsound and states that the renewable energy policy in Spain (and therefore the US) is a waste of money and actually costs jobs rather than creates jobs. The report actually addresses the Obama administration's ideas and policies." Tegan urged nine people on her recipient list to look over the report and provide comments she could pass up her chain of command. She referred to lobbyists at AWAE and CAP as "colleagues."

CAP is a far-left organization funded by George Soros and led by John Podesta. According to logs, Podesta visited the White House thirty-one times over 2 months in the fall of 2009, the only period for which records are available. In an e-mail to the *Investor's Business Daily*, which provided this information, Horner commented:

> The least revelatory aspect of this was the hollowness of the Obama administration's claims to have driven lobbyists from the executive branch. Providing an inside role for politically favored industries in developing official administration statements falls even further from the rhetoric. Worse, with direct communications with ideological activists like CAP and UCS undoubtedly the anticipated and regular subject of FOIA [Freedom of Information Act] requests, we also see how the Obama administration employed an industry lobby to channel the influence of such groups into the administration's inner workings to circumvent the expected pathway for security.[40]

Horner also noted that DOE officials have since misled Congress on such matters.

The wind industry spent $5 million on lobbying in 2009, up from $1.7 million the previous year. It currently is reported to have thirty-six lobbyists, up from two in 2004.

Does the industry create jobs? In all fairness, yes. For example, a new wind farm in West Texas created twenty-eight hundred jobs. Unfortunately, twenty-four hundred of those were in China, with just four hundred temporary positions in the United States.[41]

SOLAR POWER: REMOTE POSSIBILITIES

Like wind, solar power is a natural, free source of energy—provided, of course, that public subsidies and customers of high-price electricity cover the large costs. Solar power is also very versatile. It can provide thermal energy to heat water and electricity to power spacecraft above Earth's atmosphere as well as small handheld devices.

It can also produce utility-grade electricity for those who live in a desert and have a habit of going to bed very early without their television on. But don't count on solar power to deliver us any distance along the road to energy independence. Not even during the industry's sunniest seasons.

This is likely to come as a very unwelcome observation to many people. When the trade association for the nuclear power industry asked a thousand Americans in 2007 about what energy source they thought would be used most in 15 years, the winner was the Sun, the choice selected by 27 percent of those polled.[42] Yet it will be truly remarkable if solar power accounts for more than even 1 percent in the coming decades. It currently provides only about 6 percent of the US electricity that is derived just from renewable sources.

Nationwide solar power expansion is severely constrained by both geography and the power source's fundamentally intermittent nature. High capital cost is also a factor, but let's assume that increasing fossil-fuel prices and technological advancements cure those problems over time—as well they might—and that regions are favored with clear skies over much of the year and that rain, dust, and snow accumulations don't interfere. And even under the best conditions, there is a recurring cyclical problem. It is called "night."

Thanks almost entirely to a variety of federal and state subsidies the solar industry is witnessing growth, up about 43 percent during 2007. This added 110 MW of new capacity, but onto a very small previous base. At least eight large-scale solar power projects are reported to be under development, comparable to adding six 500 MW coal-fired plants.[43]

The solar power industry really has two very different types of segments: One markets photovoltaic panel units to private and commercial customers, and another provides utility-scale electricity from central power stations. Each segment is realizing progressive technology developments that lower costs and improve efficiencies.

Panel-type units (typically bolted to roofs) that convert sunlight directly into electricity continue to be very expensive relative to power benefits. A small, 4 kW home installation costs about $34,000 before government rebates and tax breaks. Solar energy conversion efficiencies range from an average of about 16 percent to as high as 22 percent in direct sunlight. But, like wind, power is intermittent; often, it isn't available when you need it or in the amounts required. A lot depends upon both location and the orientation of the roof or other structure the system is mounted to. An advantage of solar over wind is that peak power occurs at midday, which is, correspondingly, a peak demand period.

World markets for silicon, a key ingredient of solar cells, have contributed to the high costs of photovoltaic panel systems. Some newer technology markets are replacing the panels with thin-film photovoltaic sheets that are less expensive, but presently, these are only about half as efficient.[44] Accordingly, they require more space and are mostly geared for large commercial business applications. Traditional photovoltaic cell systems now constitute about 90 percent of the market.

Utility-scale concentrating solar power (CSP) systems, which use lenses or mirrors that track the Sun to focus radiation on thermal collectors or photovoltaic cells to produce electricity, are another alternative. They can range in size from as small as 10 kW to more than 100 MW. Because they require direct sunlight (not diffuse light), their use is limited to Sun Belt locations. CSP systems that use lenses to concentrate light onto photocells are much more efficient and require less surface area than standard photovoltaic panel approaches do. Solar thermal CSP systems reflect sunlight energy onto receiver units that contain a heat transfer fluid or molten nitrate salt to drive power turbine generators. Overall, solar-electric conversion efficiencies are relatively low, ranging from about 13 to 25 percent.

Energy storage continues to be a big problem for CSP, just as it is for wind. Installations can operate only as part of a larger system network that provides backups such as fossil-fuel generation or connections to a nuclear-powered grid. New plants in sparsely populated desert locations also impose power transmission infrastructure development costs, oftentimes as much as $1.5 million per mile.

As with all energy options, some environmentalists don't like CSP stations either. One complaint is that they take up too much desert land, thus displacing certain animal and reptile species. A mirrored CSP installation may require between 5 and 15 acres per MW, compared, for example, with an equivalent gas-fired generation requirement that can be as little as $\frac{1}{25}$ of an acre.[45]

During 1993 congressional hearings, the Sierra Club and the Wilderness Society testified in favor of preserving areas within California's Mojave Desert from commercial development, including solar and recreational uses. The president of the Wilderness Society explained why:

> The California desert contains some of the most wild and beautiful landscapes in America, but these lands are being continually

degraded. The fragile desert soils, scarce water, unique ecosystems, irreplaceable archaeological sites, and spectacular scenic beauty are receiving too little protection in the face of a variety of development pressures. The opportunity to experience what remains of the frontier quality of the region is rapidly disappearing as development spreads. The public has lost much of this priceless heritage already; it is time to save the best of what remains as a lasting gift to future generations.[46]

Based on that argument, another environmentalist even argued that a nuclear option might be preferable: "From the standpoint of scenic pollution and destruction of wilderness, there are distinct advantages to the hard energy option . . . A nuclear plant modifies a relatively small area compared to a large-scale solar installation."[47]

And then there's the problem with pollution from photovoltaic solar panels. Can this be true? Haven't we been told that solar power is clean? Sure, but making those collectors isn't, because they are manufactured using highly toxic heavy metals, gases, and solvents. Some of the materials are carcinogenic. Some of the gases are lethal, and some are explosive. Not all factories that produce photovoltaic panels incorporate scrubbers to protect against accidental releases, but workers in those plants must be strictly protected. Fires in such facilities can be particularly hazardous. After solar panels are decommissioned following about 20 to 30 years of useful life, they are supposed to be disposed of in special toxic dumps rather than sent to waste incinerators where the heavy metals (such as cadmium and lead-based solder) can vaporize into the atmosphere. Or, if dumped into landfills, the arsenic and lead can leach into the soils and water tables.[48]

New designs are lower in toxicity and are required to pass DOE tests to reduce these hazards. Still, large photovoltaic farms capable of producing 1,000 MW per year would cover 50 square miles or more of land, and their production would yield substantial quantities of toxic waste that present costly and difficult disposal challenges.

Solar power continues to require subsidies to be competitive even in desert locations where clear skies prevail. The United States Air Force is taking advantage of these incentives to support development of the largest North American solar plant to provide electricity for the Nellis Air Force Base located outside Las Vegas. The power facility covers 140 acres of the Nevada desert with a massive photovoltaic array of silicon cells that rotate to track the Sun. The facility is capable of producing 15 MW of power, enough to provide about 30 percent of Nellis's requirements, where 12,000 people work and 7,215 residents live. The Air Force expects to save $1 million per year in power costs, thanks to multimillion-dollar federal and state financial subsidies and incentives. "Without those, prices wouldn't be competitive," according to Daniel Tomlinson, editor of a solar newsletter for Navigant Consulting. David Edwards, a market analyst of green power with ThinkEquity Partners of San Francisco, agrees: "The price of solar is coming down, but today those subsidies are important."[49]

The Nellis project was developed through a complex arrangement between the Air Force and three financial partners. The Air Force will not pay any of the construction costs, but essentially guarantees the market. Private investors will pay more than $100 million in capital costs and receive substantial federal tax subsidies. For example, MMA Renewable Ventures and its investors enjoy a 30 percent tax credit, have the benefit of accelerated capital depreciation schedules, and sell solar energy credits generated by the project to NV Energy, which must obtain 20 percent of its power from renewable sources by 2015.

So there you have it. Our country's Air Force (that is, the US government) is saving about $1 million a year because that same US government is providing many tens of millions of dollars in tax incentives, in combination with generous contributions in the form of higher electricity prices charged to Nevada customers. Just think of all that money the government is saving us! Caution: Don't attempt this stunt at home.

HYDROPOWER: FEW DAM PROSPECTS

Hydropower is an important and sustainable source of energy that many environmentalists don't want to claim as an alternative. Although it produces nearly half of all US renewable electricity—about equal to biomass—its impact upon fish and aquatic ecosystems earns it enmity.

Expansion of hydroelectric capacity is not a major option in this country because most primary sites are already being exploited or are off-limits for environmental reasons. Dams currently provide about two-thirds of all electricity in the Pacific Northwest region and are dominant sources in Idaho and Washington.

Although hydropower produces no pollutant emissions per se, dam construction and operations can have significant ecological repercussions. As they swim downstream toward the ocean, many young salmon in the Northwest are killed by turbine blades, and adult fish attempting to swim upstream to reproduce are blocked by dams. After salmon populations were dramatically reduced in the Northwest Columbia Basin, fish channels and side channels were built to help alleviate this problem. Also, because water in the dams tends to be colder and oxygen-poor at the bottom as compared with the surface, rapid releases of dam water can kill fish and damage wildlife vegetation food sources downstream.

Pressure from mainstream environmentalists persuaded the Bush-Quayle administration to drop incentives to promote hydro development in the Energy Policy Act of 1992, and both the Sierra Club and Trout Unlimited criticized the Clinton-Gore administration that followed for including it as a global warming prevention strategy.

Trout Unlimited is also lobbying to remove four major dams that have been constructed at enormous cost on the Columbia River, due to alarming trout casualties. Farmers who have come to depend upon the dams for water irrigation oppose the opposers. Other groups attribute the salmon losses to overfishing by indigenous Indian residents (the US government purchased a half million dollars' worth of nets for their use) and consumption of fingerlings by a large colony of terns from a nearby island bird sanctuary created by the United States Army Corps of Engineers. Trout Unlimited also wants to eliminate the bird sanctuary, a proposal that is opposed by the Audubon Society.

As further evidence of hydropower's recent politically incorrect status, it was dropped from renewable category statistical listings in the 1995 edition of the *Electric Power Annual,* published by the US Energy Information Administration. Environmental lobbying even prompted the US Export-Import Bank to deny funding for China's 18,000 MW Three Gorges Project when Friends of the Earth and other groups expressed concerns about water quality, endangered species, and population resettlement impacts.[50]

Then there's the possibility of harnessing wave and tidal energy. Those should be limitless sources, right? After all, oceans are really big, and all you need to move water around is a Sun-Moon system, and we have one of those.

But some of the technologies do use turbine blades, presenting potential dangers to fish and aquatic mammals. Tidal power generators, mostly in experimental and prototype testing stages, draw energy from underwater currents. One type uses the oscillating motion of water flowing past hydroplane fins to drive motor generators, while another operates with propeller blades like an underwater wind turbine. Sea-Gen, a system being tested in Northern Ireland, uses sets of rotor turbines rated at about 1 MW.[51]

One big limitation of tidal power is that it occurs only twice per day, and neither of these times coincides with peak power demand periods. Another constraint is that practical locations are limited to places where high-amplitude tides exist, including river and fjord estuaries in the former USSR, Canada, Korea, and the UK. Also problematic are relatively low output capacities, high maintenance costs due to corrosion of mechanical parts, and expenses of transmitting power from offshore installations to end users.

Harnessing power from wave motion may eventually yield more energy than from tides. New technologies are being developed involving generators that can either be coupled to floating devices or turned by air displaced by waves. The amount of power produced is determined by wave height, speed, wavelength, and water density at a given location and time, and wind conditions are also influential. Northern and southern temperature zones offer the best wave power locations, with prevailing westerly winds in winter blowing strongest to produce a "fully developed sea." Prospective placements include shoreline, offshore, and deepwater applications. Power conversion methods include hydraulic rams, elastomeric hose pumps, pump-to-shore systems, and hydroelectric or air turbines. Despite being innovative and interesting, potential capacities from tides and waves to be sufficient to seriously offset dependencies upon other energy sources are extremely doubtful.

GEOTHERMAL ENERGY: REGIONAL REALITIES

Geothermal energy seems too good to be true, and unfortunately for most parts of the United States, it probably is. Think of all that heat, pure energy, directly under all of our feet—enough to provide countless times more power than we will ever need. But accessing it is where the big problem arises.

Geothermal options fall into two general categories: conventional and unconventional. The conventional option is hydrothermal, which taps into hot water and steam reservoirs that exist only in certain regions of the country. The most economically feasible hydrothermal resources are principally located west of the Rocky Mountains, and only California, Hawaii, Nevada, and Utah currently have operating power plants. The majority of thermal springs and other surface manifestations of underlying geothermal resources are also located in the West, including Montana,

North Dakota, and Wyoming.[52] Some lower-temperature resources also exist in central Texas. In total, more than twenty hydrothermal power plants (the only utility-scale geothermal facilities) produce less than 0.5 percent of all US electricity.[53]

More than 90 percent of all installed US geothermal capacity is generated in California and Nevada, with about half produced at the Geysers in northern California. While that energy is very clean with regard to emissions, it is not technically renewable because the heat content of reservoirs gradually declines over years of production, often playing out to unusable temperatures in 50 years or less. Power output at the Geysers, for example, dropped about 40 percent between 1990 and 2000, due in large part to reduced reservoir volume.[54]

As is the case with all energy options, geothermal is not immune from environmental critics. Because most of the usable reservoirs are located in remote, scenic wilderness areas, construction of plants, access roads, power lines, and other infrastructure is perceived as a blighting intrusion on nature. Geothermal power also consumes large amounts of water, which can impact aquatic ecosystems and wildlife habitats. Wastewater released from plants can potentially contaminate surface and groundwater as well. For these reasons, many prospective sites are restricted from development.[55]

According to a lawsuit filed against two proposed power plants in the US District Court for the Eastern District of California, the developments would introduce "highly toxic acids" into geothermal wells in the state's Medicine Lake Highlands, turning the lands into "an ugly, noisy, stinking wasteland." The lawsuit asserted that groundwater pollution would pose a threat to trout and other wildlife; that the plants would require excavating 750,000-gallon toxic waste sumps; and that trucks and drilling equipment would break the normal solitude of the area. Construction would include unsightly 150-foot-high drilling rigs, nine-story power plants on 15-acre pads, seven-story cooling towers capped by steam plumes, crisscrossing roads, high-tension transmission lines, and pipelines.[56]

Unconventional geothermal installations, should they come into existence, aren't likely to be popular with many environmental groups either. They include (1) enhanced geothermal systems (EGSs) that create new reservoirs using oil and gas industry technology, and (2) geopressured and geothermal operations that either drill or take advantage of abandoned oil and gas "wells of opportunity" to assess and exploit deep reservoir resources.

EGSs are proposed to produce energy from geothermal resources that are otherwise not economical due to lack of water and/or ground permeability. This involves pumping cold water or water containing acids or other chemicals into ground cracks that are too small to allow geothermal fluids to flow, causing fractures that enlarge them to productive sizes. An enthusiastic report published by MIT estimates that this approach could produce 100 GW of US power by 2050. Total US electrical power consumption is currently about 3,300 GW.[57]

A study by Jeremy Griggs at Louisiana State University of geopressured geothermal aquifer potential points out some limitations. A big impediment is development scale, particularly where commercial aquifers are likely to be in excess of 10 square miles, causing small-acreage landowners to derail project opportunities. He concluded that medium-term development prospects will depend upon sustainability of high natural gas prices; application and acceptance of new technologies; and diversification of conventional exploration/production companies and electric utility companies to accept the opportunities. The long-term likelihood of large-scale geopressured aquifer development was predicted to be low.[58]

HYDROGEN ECONOMY: AN OXYMORON

Imagine the wonderment of a new energy economy based upon vehicles and industries fueled by hydrogen with no emissions other than water. Wouldn't that move us away from fossil-fuel dependence toward a blissfully clean environment? Regrettably, only in your dreams! Conserving energy through hydrogen use is the logical equivalent of converting processed petroleum back into crude oil in order to stretch oil reserves and avoid pollutants.

In reality, hydrogen is not characterized by anyone with a background in physics or chemical engineering as an energy source at all. Instead, it is defined as an energy "carrier"—a way to convert energy produced from another source for storage and use in a different form. This always imposes energy penalties along with other costs that may sometimes be justified, but should not be ignored. A free lunch it definitely is not.

Although hydrogen is popularly associated with renewable fuels, most of the commercial hydrogen in use today is produced as a by-product of fossil-fuel sources, primarily natural gas. Producing that steam requires energy. It also consumes natural gas, a nonrenewable fossil-fuel resource.

Producing hydrogen through water electrolysis is possible but extremely energy intensive, with a large net energy loss. If that electricity source is wind, the power required must be subtracted from competing electricity uses. If the wind farm is part of a utility grid, then natural gas consumed for the spinning reserve also constitutes a cost. If the electricity comes from solar power, the penalty of water consumption in arid desert power plant locations becomes a major environmental and practical impediment.[59]

In addition to requiring more energy to create than it yields, hydrogen also imposes other energy penalties associated with compression, liquefaction, transportation, bulk storage, and transfer to end-use destinations. These problems primarily relate to the fact that hydrogen gas is the smallest molecule that exists in nature, making it difficult to contain so that it doesn't leak out. Unlike natural gas, it can't be transported through pipelines.

Hydrogen does not compress easily, requiring energy to increase pressure sufficiently to compensate for a low energy/volume density. Compressing it into small containers for transport requires strong and heavy tanks, which adds equipment costs. Liquid hydrogen imposes even more costs for liquefaction and tank insulation to prevent the gas from boiling away.

Although hydrogen has a good energy density based upon weight, it has a poor energy density relative to storage volume. To illustrate, a gallon of liquid gasoline weighing 0.9 pounds actually contains about 50 percent more hydrogen than a gallon of liquid hydrogen weighing 0.6 pounds. This means that a fuel tank for a hydrogen-fueled car will be much larger and heavier than a fuel tank for a car that runs on gasoline, unless the driving range on a tank is reduced substantially.

If hydrogen for automotive use is produced from natural gas, it would make more sense to use the original fuel directly. One reason is for safety. Hydrogen is highly combustible and will burn in concentrations as low as 4 percent in air. It explodes upon ignition when mixed with air, a fact well recognized by rocket scientists and some poorly supervised high school chemistry students.

Hydrogen does offer important energy conservation benefits in certain applications. A prime example is for combined heat and power fuel cell operations that recycle the heat product back into a power system or use it for other purposes, such as air-conditioning. Hydrogen technologies and applications are most certain to have expanding roles in our energy future on Earth and in space. But short of some revolutionary and unforeseeable breakthrough, they will not present a supply-side solution to our energy challenges.

Nuclear Power: Elephant in the Closet

Nuclear energy must certainly qualify as the world's least appreciated and understood power source. Although it provides some of or all the electricity used by more than 1 billion people, and nearly 20 percent of the US supply, it is virtually invisible even to nearby consumers who don't realize it is in their backyards. Few are aware that there are 104 nuclear power plants distributed throughout many regions of this country, which enjoy cleaner air due to their presence.

Nuclear power plants are environmentally benign and reliable. They occupy very little land area, produce only water vapor emissions, and require no major transportation infrastructure. They are extremely safe, presenting no explosion or radiation contamination risks, which tend to worry many people most. And in stark contrast to so-called renewable or sustainable options, as well as fossil-fuel sources, nuclear power expansion and longevity capacities are vast.

Nuclear safety and waste hazards primarily arise from regional, national, and geopolitical issues rather than intrinsically technological problems. In general, unreasonable and misguided policies are often driven by opposition to nuclear power based upon unwarranted fear associated with the Chernobyl and Three Mile Island incidents, which are now readily preventable. Licensing and construction of vital power plants and waste storage accommodations are being delayed at a time when other countries are greatly benefiting from developing these facilities. The United States, once a leader in nuclear technology development, has fallen behind, both in science and in infrastructure. This circumstance, resulting from counterproductive opposition, a misinformed public, and bad policy decisions, is causing excessive use of precious fossil-fuel resources and economic burdens that we and future generations can little afford.

The DOE's EIA estimates that US electricity demands will increase by about 45 percent by 2030, requiring at least 350,000 MW of new capacity.[60] Given that "renewable" sources such as wind, solar, geothermal, and hydro afford extremely limited expansion potential, the only other non-fossil-fuel alternative is nuclear. Very fortunately, this option offers large and lasting growth possibilities. The Nuclear Energy Institute proposes to expand the nuclear share of US electricity production to 50 percent by 2050.[61] The World Nuclear Association, the World Energy Council, and the International Atomic Energy Agency believe that uranium resources are adequate to meet global power demands for thousands of years.

Uranium is abundant in the United States and in many other parts of the world, and no other known source can compare in terms of energy density.[62] One ton of ore can yield about 4 to 6 pounds of yellowcake uranium, enough to produce a single pellet of low-enriched uranium oxide weighing 0.24 ounces (about 7 grams—slightly less than the weight of three pennies). That one small pellet contains the same energy as:

- 1,780 pounds of coal
- 149 gallons of oil[63]
- 157 gallons of regular gasoline[64]
- 17,000 cubic feet of natural gas

Consider this density in terms of power plant land requirements for various options based upon 1,000 MW of installed capacity:

- According to the AWEA, 1,000 MW of wind farm capacity requires about 60,000 acres (94 square miles); other agencies more than double that estimate (intermittent power).[65]
- Producing 1,000 MW from solar power will require photovoltaic arrays covering more than 50 square miles (also intermittent power).[66]
- An equivalent 1,000 MW of energy from biofuel alcohol could require about 6,200 square miles of cornfields; about 9,000 square miles of rapeseed fields for bio-oil; or burning of about 12,000 square miles of wood biomass.
- A 1,000 MW nuclear plant requires about ⅓ to ½ of a square mile.[67]

Nuclear energy is finally gaining political traction from some global warming/carbon-trading cadres who were previously staunch opponents. For example, Patrick Moore, a cofounder of Greenpeace who rose to prominence in the 1960s for his strong stand against nuclear testing, told the House Government Reform Subcommittee on Energy and Resources in April 2005, "Nuclear energy is the only non-greenhouse-gas-emitting power source that can effectively replace fossils and satisfy global demand for energy."[68]

Nuclear plant operators are poised to reap billions of dollars in windfall profits if carbon cap-and-trade legislation is enacted. Those who stand to gain most include the Exelon Corp.; FPL Group Inc.; Constellation Energy Group; Entergy Corp.; FirstEnergy Corp.; NRG Energy, Inc.; and Public Service Enterprise Group Inc. They will gain in two ways. First, they won't have to purchase emission allowances, giving them an advantage over fossil fuel–dependent companies. Cap-and-trade will also push wholesale electricity prices higher in deregulated markets, as coal- and natural gas–burning utilities jack up charges to their customers, making nuclear energy even more competitive.[69]

Yet, notwithstanding its appealing features for dreaded GHG avoidance and windfall cap-and-trade profits that will raise energy costs to promote conservation, nuclear power continues to have powerful environmental opponents. The Sierra Club, for example, remains strictly antinuclear, although its position has vacillated over time. During the 1960s, when the group was lobbying against big hydroelectric projects it believed were damaging California wilderness areas, its slogan was "Atoms, not Dams." In 1970, its board voted in favor of nuclear plants, such as one in Diablo Canyon, and issued a "crisis report" requesting that irrigation districts build and manage a nuclear plant for the city of San Francisco rather than another planned hydropower dam. Then, 5 years later, the board reversed its policy, began to oppose nuclear plants, and lobbied to shut down the Diablo Canyon plant.[70]

While the United States has refrained from reprocessing spent fuels, some other countries are combining the plutonium oxide that is chemically separated from spent fuels with plutonium from warheads to create a low-enriched (about 4.5 percent) power reactor fuel referred to as "MOX." Europeans have been doing this for more than 20 years, reducing stockpiled weapons-grade plutonium in the process. World stockpiles of nuclear warhead plutonium, now estimated to be about 260 metric tons, offer the potential to provide 1 year's worth of global uranium needs for electricity. MOX will eventually be produced from plutonium and highly enriched uranium obtained from dismantled weapons at the DOE's Savanna River site in South Carolina. Yet antinuclear groups oppose the manufacturing and use of MOX, even though it converts war materials into energy for essential and peaceful uses. Turning weapons stockpiles into low-enriched and proliferation-resistant fuel would seem to be a purpose that everyone might support.

Many Americans tend to be quite unaware of just how much our nation depends upon nuclear power and of the industry's long, impressive safety record throughout the world. This ignorance, based heavily upon widely circulated media misconceptions and strident opposition campaigns, thwarts progress in addressing vital energy priorities. Informed education is key to progress.

Other countries, including France and Finland, educate children about nuclear power from early years so they grow up to have realistic perspectives. It took France only 2 decades to switch over 80 percent of its electricity generation to nuclear, and now many of that nation's informed young people have grown up to become leaders in nuclear power technology development. The world's most advanced experimental thermonuclear fusion reactor is under construction in Cadarache, France, and the country—with fifty-nine nuclear plants already—is the largest net exporter of electrical power. The French reprocess spent fuels and are developing a deep underground radioactive waste repository at Meuse/Haute Marne. The DOE has purchased MOX fuel fabrication services from France to convert plutonium from dismantled bombs to electrical plant fuel, as have other countries.[71]

Isn't it unfortunate that our nation, which pioneered the science and technology to harness atomic power for war, must now turn to another country for the technology to convert those weapons into fuel for peaceful use? How politically correct is that?

NUCLEAR WASTE STORAGE—NOT IN MY MOUNTAIN!

After more than $10 billion spent so far in developing the national Yucca Mountain nuclear waste repository that Nevada once advocated, the project has now been canceled by the Obama-Biden administration thanks to strong political opposition from the state and environmental lobbies. But this has not always been the case.[72] Back in the 1970s, Nevada legislators actually authored a bid to create a national waste repository within the nuclear test site in order to create thousands of jobs. This would help the state recover from a loss of federal money following the termination of nuclear device tests and related employee layoffs. By the 1980s, they didn't need or want it anymore.

A rapidly expanding gambling industry created about five hundred thousand new jobs, along with Nevada representatives with louder voices and national clout. In 2007, Harry Reid rose to the position of Senate majority leader and became a powerful project opponent, stating, "It is abundantly clear that there is no such thing as 'sound science' at Yucca Mountain."[73]

State of Nevada representatives, along with various anti-repository groups, accused the project of fraud, asserting that some United States Geological Survey scientists had suggested in e-mail exchanges that they had fabricated research data. A US attorney dismissed the charges in 2006, ruling that the brouhaha had resulted from a misunderstanding.[74]

Still, Nevada needs nuclear power. Las Vegas and its millions of neon lights have depended for decades upon hydroelectricity from the Colorado River. Now a prolonged drought, which may continue, is creating electrical shortages as well as shrinking the city's water supply and economic future.[75]

It's somewhat bewildering to ponder why the Obama-Biden administration would announce that the government would guarantee more than $8 billion in loans needed to build the first two US nuclear power plants in nearly 3 decades at nearly the same time it announced it would drop plans to proceed with the Yucca Mountain waste repository and consider what it believes are "better options."[76]

Termination of the repository will predictably hobble efforts to build "a new generation of safe, clean nuclear power plants" as presented in the president's first State of the Union address. Without a permanent solution for nuclear waste storage, several states, including California, won't let new plants be built. And as Michael Morris, chief executive of American Electric Power, contends, "There has to be a reaction" to the closing because Yucca is the only site that has been vetted and deemed capable of storing waste from the nation's 104 operating reactors.[77]

Nuclear electrical power expansion is a necessity—not an option. While nuclear power is not typically characterized as an alternative energy source, in reality it is the only alternative other than fossils that offers substantial expansion potential. The Nuclear Regulatory Commission anticipates that more than thirty reactor projects will finally be seeking licensing permits. Following a lengthy approval process, each will require about 4 to 5 years to build, at a cost of between $6 billion and $10 billion per reactor.[78]

Although these plants produce only water vapor emissions, radioactive waste containment and releases due to accidents or terrorism are issues of public concern. Safety records at nuclear facilities have been excellent, however, and technology advancements are further reducing risks and any potential consequences. Waste problems could be reduced by recycling spent materials using breeder reactors, but this approach was outlawed during the Carter-Mondale administration due to concerns about proliferation of weapons-grade fuel that might get into enemy hands. Given that there are much more efficient and terrorist-accesible ways to obtain bomb materials from maverick foreign government sources, there is little current basis for such prohibitions.

Alternative Futures

It is essential to our national and global future that development and utilization of all alternative energy options continue. This includes improvement and expansion of nuclear power and innovations to produce cleaner energy from coal and other fossil-fuel sources for which there is no practical substitute.

It is also vital that the public be much better informed about the comparative advantages and disadvantages of all alternatives, and that public policy decisions be more fully guided by the facts. Performance benefits of unproven options such as cellulosic ethanol have been claimed but not demonstrated. Expansion limitations of other options have been obfuscated, leading many to believe that abundant replacements for fossil-fuel sources are available but neglected by the energy industry. Green energy has become a meaningless term because the environmental consequences of most alternatives have been ignored and misrepresented in marketing campaigns and in the media. Fossil-dependent fuels have been mischaracterized as "sustainable." Examples are ethanol, which requires fuel for farming and processing, and hydrogen, derived from natural gas.

Proposed carbon-emission cap-and-trade legislation predicated on global warming hysteria and the demonization of CO_2 will solve nothing. It will only constrain new power plant development, making energy more expensive. Although resulting shortages and price escalations may eventually promote support for much-needed nuclear power expansion, permitting and development of those vital plant infrastructures must begin immediately to keep the lights burning.

But if any green will be realized through carbon trading, it will primarily move from pockets of consumers—through paying increased power, fuel processing, and product costs—to the bank accounts of hedge fund speculators and subsidy recipients. Let our current ethanol experiences be a lesson.[79]

Section Four

Retaking America's Future

Chapter 10
REENERGIZING FREE ENTERPRISE

Bureaucracy protecting the planet from carbon hoofprints.   Larry Bell

America's energy progress has been held hostage to political and legal pressures applied by groups its citizens did not elect to represent the future best interests of their children and grandchildren. Vilification of CO_2 as a pollutant, burning fossils as a climate cooker, and oil dependence as a security threat offers means to justify many ends. All provide the rationale to promote carbon-off-set-trading bonanzas, to subsidize alternative-energy pricing advantages, to advance ideological social-engineering agendas, to validate political and governmental power grabs, and to serve global wealth distribution agendas. These motives are championed beneath banners whose slogans promise salvation from environmental guilt, essentials for resource conservation, energy independence, and most recently, creation of green jobs by legislative fiat.

Global warming supporters seem to be loudest in their assault on the use of fossils, which ironically will necessarily be our most important source of energy for the foreseeable future. Let's examine how the climate change lobby has acted to keep this key to our energy security buried.

Coal: That Ol' Black Magic

Al Gore calls for a bold new energy policy. All US electricity will soon be provided by wind, solar, and other renewable sources, and reliance upon fossils will end. But beyond the superheated greenhouse atmosphere of Planet Gore, real-world circumstances are likely to be dramatically different. Nuclear power, conspicuously absent in Gore's vision, is the only serious non-fossil contender to add electricity capacity, and coal, the implicitly denigrated fossil, represents the only practical hope to reduce oil and natural gas dependence for liquid fuel.[1]

Despite our enormous dependence upon coal for electricity, heating, and important by-products, coal industries have been unfairly characterized as "dirty businesses." Global warming alarmism is now fueling a heightened wave of environmental activism that is blocking new developments, particularly for electricity generation. Many proposed coal-fired plants are being canceled by states from coast to coast as stringent CO_2 emission restrictions deny permits, produce legal challenges, and make construction and operational costs prohibitively high.

Coal is the largest source of worldwide electrical power generation, and coke from coal processing is a vital component in the reduction of iron ore. We are fortunate in the US to have relatively abundant reserves: an estimated 250-year supply, compared with perhaps only a few decades for oil and natural gas. The US Geological Survey projects that US reserves contain about 1.7 trillion tons of identified deposits; many geologists believe that future discoveries may more than double that amount. Not all is readily recoverable, however, due to technology limitations, high access costs, and environmental restrictions. Total recoverable reserves are estimated to be about 472 billion tons, but because current mining technologies leave substantial amounts in place, near-term recoverable assets are estimated to be about 262 billion tons. This may be more than one-fourth of the world's total recoverable supply.[2]

Uncontrolled coal burning releases many substances that none of us want in our environment, including sulfur and a variety of heavy metals such as arsenic and lead. And there is no question that surface mining has had destructive impacts upon site land areas, has polluted waters, and has destroyed natural habitats. These are very real and serious issues that the coal industry must address. This has begun to happen. Relatively simple and inexpensive "clean coal" technologies are available to remove most of the SO_2, smoke-producing oxides of nitrogen oxide (including nitric oxide, nitrogen dioxide, and nitrous oxide), and particulate emissions from the coal-burning process is accomplished through chemical washing, gasification, and special treatments of flue gases before they are emitted. Processes to capture, transport, and store CO_2 are much more costly and, arguably, irrelevant.

Just how clean is clean coal? It can be washed and gasified to burn quite cleanly, with most offensive residual particulates captured in the incineration venting process. CO_2, which is much more difficult to collect and contain, has come to be vilified as a polluting coal-burning by-product solely on the basis of dubiously claimed climate influences.

The clean coal technology field is moving rapidly toward gasification, which breaks coal down into its basic chemical components rather than burning it directly. Modern gasifiers expose the coal to hot steam and carefully controlled amounts of air or oxygen under high temperatures and pressures. This breaks the carbon molecules apart through chemical reactions that produce carbon monoxide, hydrogen, and other gaseous compounds that burn cleanly. Hydrogen gas, in fact, has been used to drive electricity-generating turbines, with enhanced fuel-efficiency outputs of up to 60 percent.

With regard to environmental damage from mining, the largest problem has been associated with open-pit excavation, which accounts for about 60 percent of total US recovery. This method is primarily used in western regions where near-surface deposits can be up to a hundred feet thick; underground mining, which presents greater risks to human safety, is mostly applied east of the Mississippi in the Appalachian states. The April 5, 2010, explosion in the Upper Big Branch mine in Montcoal, West Virginia, which killed twenty-five workers, serves as a tragic example.

Open-pit operations are now typically required to post bonds for each acre of surface mined, and later to restore the soils as nearly as possible to original contours with native vegetation and trees. More than 2 million acres of coal land have been restored in this manner over the past 2 decades.[3]

Regardless of growing opposition by the Sierra Club and other activist combatants beating global warming war drums, the demand for coal can only increase. US utilities currently burn more than 9 billion tons annually in more than six hundred plants, and coal's share of electricity generation is projected to grow about 60 percent over the next 2 decades. While the Sierra Club alone continues to spend many millions of dollars in legal actions to block coal-fired plants, the nation has no other significant power growth option other than nuclear. Utilities certainly know this. The vast majority of the American public will ultimately learn this also, and hopefully in time to prevent disruptive shortages.[4]

"Clean coal" plants that convert coal into a combustible gas for utility generation are now being blocked and canceled. For example, a hearing judge at the Minnesota Public Utilities Commission urged commissioners to reject a plan for the Northern States Power Company, a unit of Xcel Energy, Inc., to purchase 8 percent of its energy from a coal gasification plant proposed by Excelsior Energy Inc. He concluded that it wouldn't be good for customers because it would cost an extra $472 million in 2011 dollars to make the plant capable of capturing about 30 percent of its CO_2 emissions, plus another $635 million to build a pipeline to carry the CO_2 to the nearest available deep geological storage in Alberta, Canada. This would inflate the cost of power by $50 per megawatt hour, making it twice as costly as older, exempted plants.[5]

Potential federal carbon-emission cap-and-trade legislation has added to coal development miseries by discouraging investment financing. Citigroup Inc., JP Morgan Chase & Co., and Morgan Stanley all report that uncertainties about what these prospective regulations will mandate present big risks that are forcing conservative bank strategies. Under new "Carbon Principles," the banks are requiring companies applying for coal-fired plant financing to show that they've first looked at "energy efficiency" and "renewable energy options" and found them to be insufficient. They also demand evidence that proposed plants are being designed to capture and eventually store CO_2 emissions, while still charging high enough electricity rates to pay for extra emission allowances needed to cover CO_2-capping penalties.[6]

In July 2007, Citigroup downgraded coal mining company stocks, noting that "prophesies of a new wave of coal-fired generation have vaporized." Steve Leer, CEO of Arch Coal, Inc., said that some of the power plants they had expected to build "may get stalled due to uncertainty over climate concerns."[7]

In January 2008, the DOE announced a $648 million federal plan to restructure its FutureGen project aimed at demonstrating cutting-edge carbon capture and storage (CCS) technology at multiple commercial-scale, integrated gasification combined cycle (IGCC) clean coal power plants. Its goal is to at least double the amount of CO_2 sequestered over a previous technology approach announced in 2003. This was the largest amount requested for the DOE's coal program in more than 25 years. Under the plan, the DOE's investment will provide funding only for the CCS power plant component—not the entire construction—beginning as plants are commissioned between 2015 and 2016, subject to site environmental impact statement approvals.[8]

Acting upon a US Supreme Court ruling issued in 2007 that required the EPA to regulate CO_2 emissions under the Clean Air Act, a Georgia state court ruled in 2008 that a planned 1,200 MW coal plant could not be built until emission standards are met. Bruce Nilles, a Sierra Club lawyer, was elated: "This will further accelerate the beginning of the end of the coal push." Mr. Nilles also lauded the denial of a permit for a planned coal-fired plant in Kansas, stating, "In 2008 we will really begin to act on stopping the majority of these plants."[9]

Wall Street remains cautious regarding any assumptions that advanced clean coal technologies will meet yet-to-be determined CO_2 cap emission allowances, and it is nervous about the extent to which the federal government (that is, we taxpayers) will be willing to pay the differences. Wall Street is, after all, in business to make money, not to keep our lights on and businesses open.

During the recent $32 billion private equity purchase of TXU Corp., the buyers decided to eliminate eight of eleven planned coal-fired plants in Texas following aggressive environmental lobbying by actor Robert Redford and others. Reversals have also occurred in Florida, North Carolina, Oregon, and other states; nearly two dozen projects have been canceled since 2006. Some projects perished because permits were denied and others because court challenges deterred investor financing.

Coal has powerful opponents in the US Congress as well. Senate Majority Leader Harry Reid, who has worked hard to derail nuclear development and construction of the Yucca Mountain waste repository in Nevada, has also fought against the creation of three proposed coal-fired plants in his state. Since Nevada doesn't have hydropower, this raises concerns among others about just how Nevada will meet its future electricity requirements—particularly at night and when the wind isn't blowing. As Doug Fischer, a utilities analyst with the investment firm AG Edwards, observed, coal opponents, including Reid, could "put us in a bind where we're not going to have the energy we need."[10]

Coal-to-Liquid: Wringing Out Diesel and Jet Fuel

Coal offers the potential to substantially reduce dependence upon domestic and foreign oil for automotive and aviation fuel. This isn't a new idea, and the technology to do so is well proven. Petroleum poor, Germany fueled its Nazi World War II war machine primarily on coal-derived diesel. South Africa generates about 40 percent of its automotive fuel from coal and natural gas, using processes it developed to meet energy needs during its isolation under apartheid.[11]

Coal-to-liquid synthetic fuel development also has a long history in the US. It began when Congress passed a Synthetic Liquid Fuels Act in 1944 that authorized $30 million to study the construction and operation of demonstration plants to produce liquid fuels from oil shale, agricultural and forestry products, and other substances. Soon afterward, some members of Congress and administration officials urged that the oil industry be encouraged to construct a coal-to-liquid demonstration plant, but without success. Oil executives resisted, arguing that synthetic fuels would not be competitive with crude oil.

Undaunted, the US Bureau of Mines proceeded with an initiative of its own. With assistance from some captured German scientists, the agency contracted with the Bechtel Corporation to convert a synthetic ammonia plant into a coal hydrogenation facility. By 1949, the fully operational plant was processing lignite into 200 bbl/d of diesel fuel. It later used bituminous coal as the feedstock. Then, between 1949 and 1953, the demonstration plant produced 1.5 million gallons of 78-octane unleaded coal-derived gasoline.[12]

In 1948, the US depended upon foreign oil imports for more than half of all its domestic needs. By the mid-1950s, America's energy sights had shifted toward the giant oil fields of the Middle East. National political interests followed, driving large deals with Persian oil sheiks. During that same period, the US Carbide and Carbon Chemical Company (later renamed Union Carbide) built and operated the first private US coal hydrogenation plant at Institute, West Virginia, and began to process 300 tons of coal daily into a variety of chemicals. But US interest in synthetic fuels was already fading. In 1953, a Republican-led House Appropriations Committee killed funding for synthetic fuel plants, claiming that the product prices were too high. It was widely believed that this decision resulted from pressures by oil companies that didn't want competition from coal or other alternatives. In any case, the US Bureau of Mines' operation in Missouri went back to processing ammonia for military uses.[13]

Price has been a major stumbling block for coal-to-liquid development ever since the 1980s, when costs for crude oil stabilized at low levels. This situation may now be rapidly changing. In 2005, Energy Secretary Samuel W. Bodman contacted the National Coal Council, a federal advisory committee, requesting that it draft a report detailing the role coal can play in the near future. In its response, the council found that "application of coal-to-liquids technologies would move the United States toward greater energy security and relieve cost and supply pressures on transportation fuels by producing 2.6 MM bbl/d [2.6 million barrels per day] of liquids. These steps would enhance US oil supply by 10 percent and utilize an additional 475 million tons of coal per year."[14]

According to a June 5, 2006, *MoneyWeek* report, "Breakeven for a coal-to-liquids plant in the US would be in the range of $39–44 a barrel, assuming no tax incentives," a lot lower than we are likely to see again. Yet obtaining financing for large projects remains a major obstacle due in large part to uncertainties regarding prospective CO_2 emission–capping legislation.[15]

Proposals to convert coal to liquid fuel for automotive use have powerful congressional opponents because they compete with biofuel lobbies and proponents. In February 2007, House Republicans moved to recommit a biofuels research bill back to committee, with instructions to include coal synfuels as an "alternative fuel." The motion failed to carry; voting went along party lines. Then in March, Senator Inhofe tried to amend a Senate bill that was calling for implementation of recommendations presented in the 9-11 Commission by attaching billions of dollars for liquid coal in the name of national security. Senator Lieberman used his power as the 9-11 bill sponsor to prevent Senator Inhofe from introducing the amendment. A key argument was that liquid fuel from coal would not reduce CO_2 over emission levels produced by petroleum.[16] So global warming trumped energy priorities once again.

The Dirty Side of the Liquid Fuel Debate

America, characterized by some as the "Saudi Arabia of coal," enjoys an enviable opportunity to fully utilize this natural benefit for liquid fuel as well as electrical power. Yet powerful environmental organizations such as the Natural Resources Defense Council oppose all coal development programs, including conversion to liquid fuels. The NRDC states, "Relying on liquid coal as an alternative fuel could nearly double global warming pollution per gallon of transportation fuels and increase the devastating effects of coal mining felt by communities and ecosystems stretching from Appalachia to the Rocky Mountains."[17]

Given that no energy alternative is immune from strong environmental impact criticisms, and that such objections can be directed to most all human activities, let's put that argument aside for consideration elsewhere. Let's also take the "global warming pollution" argument at face value and assume that CO_2 is really dreadful stuff. In that case, how does liquid coal actually compare with other fuels?

The NRDC asserts that coal is a "carbon-intensive fuel, containing almost double the amount of carbon per unit of energy compared to natural gas and 20 percent more than petroleum." It argues that liquid coal use actually produces two different CO_2 streams: one from the plant that produces it and the other from engine exhaust. The NRDC acknowledges that vehicle CO_2 emissions are comparable for liquid coal and other transportation fuels and that those produced from liquid coal processing plants are much higher than those that refine crude oil into gasoline and diesel. It then estimates that if 90 percent of the CO_2 from liquid plants is captured, instead of released into the atmosphere, "wheel-to-wheel emissions from coal-derived liquid fuels would [still] be 8 percent higher than for petroleum."[18]

And the NRDC's solution? A *Securing America* report jointly published by the NRDC and the Institute for the Analysis of Global Security found that "a combination of more efficient cars, trucks, and planes; biofuels; and smart growth transportation options can cut oil dependence by more than 3 million bbl/d in 10 years and achieve cuts of more than 11 million bbl/d by 2025."[19]

Okay. So we don't really need that oil after all? The Idaho National Laboratory conducted a study of environmental aspects of coal-to-liquid technology in connection with Baard Energy's Ohio River Clean Fuels project under development in Wellsville, Ohio, that produced conclusions different from those presented by NRDC. The results showed that coal-to-liquid fuels would yield 46 percent fewer emissions of CO_2 and other GHGs than conventional low-sulfur diesel transportation fuels when a 30 percent biomass co-feed, CSS, and a combined cycle cogeneration process was used. All emission reductions were measured on a wheels-to-wheels basis using a testing model developed at the Argonne National Laboratory. The study also found that the coal-derived fuel was virtually sulfur free, contained 20 percent less nitrogen oxide than did standard diesel, and reduced both particulate and volatile organic compound emissions by close to 20 percent.[20]

The NRDC seems to have no real problems concerning CO_2 and other emissions associated with the biofuels, which it and many other environmental activist groups advocate. However, using the same logic it applies to coal-derived fuels, that isn't quite fair. Consider the refineries that process the crude oil into diesel to fuel the tractors that plant and harvest the corn. They release CO_2, sulfur, and particulate emissions. And the plants that produce the fertilizer . . . what about them? Then there is the issue of the emissions from the natural gas or other fuels that create the heat to process the corn into alcohol. That should count. And recall that lots of water and power are needed for crop irrigation and processing—those are resources too—not to mention the damage caused to the land and ecosystems from the farming . . . all those trees lost that could be absorbing climate-killing CO_2. Where's the justice?

The US is lagging behind in the area of vital coal-to-liquid fuel development, due to environmental obstructionism. Still, there is hope that the US private sector can begin to make some progress against strong currents of bureaucratic resistance and perils of uncertain carbon-emission legislation. DKRW Advanced Fuels and Arch Coal, Inc., plan to begin construction on a coal-to-liquid plant in Wyoming using technologies licensed by General Electric and ExxonMobil. Product costs are estimated to be about $67–$82/barrel based upon the experiences of Sasol, a South African coal, oil, and chemicals firm. That range depends upon the costs of water and coal for the water- and power-intensive process. Unfortunately, there is no free energy lunch anywhere.

Ironically, China, the world's largest atmospheric coal-fired polluter, is becoming the leading implementer of cleaner advanced coal-to-liquid fuel technologies that will advance progress toward oil conservation. Unlike the US, Australia, and India, all of which are interested in coal but constrained by environmental lobbies, China is building the world's largest coal-derived plant complex in the grasslands of Inner Mongolia. The plant, which is being developed through an agreement with Sasol, will annually convert about 3.5 million tons of coal into 1 million tons of oil products, such as diesel fuel for automobiles. This amounts to about 20,000 bbl/d, compared with the estimated 7.2 million bbl/d of oil that China currently consumes.[21]

This level of production is tiny compared with China's demands, but it is only the beginning. Inner Mongolia—twice as large as France, Germany, and England combined—contains China's biggest coalfield, and the region may be able to yield 50 million tons of liquid fuel per year by 2020. This equates to about 286,000 barrels, about 4 percent of China's needs based upon present consumption. The state-owned Shenhua Group that, along with Sasol, oversees the project is also conducting feasibility studies for two more coal-to-liquid plants in the Shaanxi and Ningxia provinces.

China realizes that its future energy security demands reduced dependence upon foreign oil imports, just as ours does, and is prepared to invest accordingly. In 2003, China imported about 100 million tons of oil, and booming economic and industrial expansion, along with growth in private automobile ownership, is creating rapidly expanding demand pressures. While coal-to-liquid processing has long been too expensive to be price competitive with standard crude oil, this condition is changing. The Chinese will also market sulfur extracted from the process to offset costs, as well as hydrogen, another by-product, for fuel cell power applications.

Chinese and South African partners will be in positions to provide advanced coal-to-liquid technologies to other nations, rich and poor alike, willing to forgo presently cheaper crude for enhanced, longer-term energy security. Similar technologies can also be used to produce liquid fuels from natural gas, which is even more economical than coal processing is. Sasol is now switching its liquid fuel feedstock to natural gas in its South African plant. The process will also compete with evolving technology to extract oil from tar sands, which is being expanded in Canada and now accounts for about one-quarter of that country's automotive fuel.[22]

Any predictions that coal-to-liquid technologies will offer a substantial solution to US oil and natural gas dependence would be premature and speculative. Likewise, these technologies may ultimately not even prove to be the best use of valuable coal resources. Advancements in battery design, for example, may enable clean coal to be used more directly and efficiently for power to recharge greatly improved electric vehicles. The free market, not government, will decide. Or will it?

Increasingly, federal and state governments are determining which alternatives will prevail. Some receive tax-supported subsidies and consumer cost-burdening mandates, while others are penalized by regulatory disincentives that inhibit investment and competitive profitability. Decisions that will have critical impacts upon future energy security are being predicated on enormously theoretical climate models and unsupportable alarmist premises. Alternatives with broadly recognized capacity limitations gain favor in the balance.

Coal isn't going to win any beauty pageants based upon sex appeal. It isn't photogenic like wind turbines filmed against azure blue skies, mirrored sunbeam reflections on large solar panels, and verdant corn farmlands. Instead, picture decapitated hills; huge, black rock piles; monstrous earth-chomping equipment, Caterpillar vehicles; and grimy-looking workers who have nothing better to do with their lives than keep your computer and household appliances powered up. Not very glamorous at all.

Now picture your home dark and cold. Imagine that you're not going to work today because businesses are closed (but you couldn't have gotten there anyway because your car's fuel tank is empty and public transit schedules are sporadic). Hope that tomorrow will be windy and sunny; that corn-fueled food prices will drop; and that global warming is real and doesn't bypass your neighborhood. Isn't that dirty coal beginning to look a lot better?

Oil and Gas: Natural Realities

The US is experiencing a two-part strategic and practical dilemma regarding oil and natural gas development. On one hand, it is irresponsible not to conserve use of dwindling global supplies that may be substantially depleted before children attending kindergarten today reach typical retirement ages. It is unthinkable to bankrupt vital resources for future generations. On the other hand, it is foolish and perilous not to begin developing US reserves now. This is necessary to ensure that fuel will be available to sustain families, commerce, and our larger economy decades hence.

Conflicting priorities regarding near-term energy sufficiency, long-term sustainability, environmental issues, and fossils versus alternatives are producing raging disputes over oil and natural gas drilling initiatives. Current federal and state government environmental policies make large natural reserves in ANWR, the Rocky Mountain basins, the Outer Continental Shelf (OCS) of the East and West coasts, and the eastern Gulf of Mexico off-limits or severely restricted.

If we can't drill our way out of a looming energy crisis, we also can't wish our way out with sunshine collectors, moonshine alcohol, or blowhard-style wind power projections. While US politicians dither about global warming dangers posed by fossil-fuel use, other nations are forging strategic energy alliances to corner global supplies.

Regulations: Drilling in Troubled Waters

Since offshore drilling is particularly challenging and expensive, it demands long lead times and large long-term investments before products and industry profits materialize a decade or more later. Opponents argue that this delayed condition is a good reason not to drill, because benefits won't occur rapidly enough. As Senator Richard Durbin (D-IL) declared, "We can't drill our way to lower prices."[23]

About 85 percent of America's OCS, a region where big oil and gas discoveries have been occurring, is currently off-limits to drilling. In June 2008, then-President George W. Bush urged a Democrat-controlled US Congress to lift a ban that would open up twelve restricted OCS areas, including two off Alaska, two off the Pacific coast, three in the Gulf of Mexico, and three along the Atlantic coast—all subject to approval by coastal state legislators. This plan responded to a public outcry about alarmingly high gasoline prices at that time. The following September, Congress allowed some restrictive legislation to lapse, opening up 8.3 million acres in central and eastern Gulf of Mexico areas. President Obama indefinitely postponed that plan soon after assuming office in February 2009.

If some influential Democratic Senate and House members have their way, much of the OCS will be permanently off-limits to drilling. On February 21, 2006, California senators Barbara Boxer and Dianne Feinstein (both D-CA) joined with Congresswoman Lois Capps (D-CA) in sponsoring a California Ocean and Coastal Protection Act that would "provide permanent protection for the California coast from future drilling and from efforts to assess and inventory oil and gas reserves off the coastline."[24]

Democratic coastal state resistance to offshore drilling immediately stiffened and expanded following the disastrous April 20, 2010, BP Deepwater Horizon rig explosion and oil spill in the Gulf of Mexico. About three weeks later, on May 13, Democratic senators Maria Cantwell and Patty Murray from Washington, along with senators Ron Wyden and Jeff Merkley from Oregon, joined with senators Boxer and Feinstein to extend the offshore ban to include their states. Their proposal would amend the Outer Continental Shelf Lands Act. Senator Cantwell explained, "We must act to safeguard our precious coastal waters and our dangerous addiction to fossils . . . It is simply unacceptable to risk irreparable harm to our coastal communities, economies and ecosystems just to feed our addictions with a short-term fix—especially when new technologies are emerging that give us real alternatives."[25]

Let's hope those new, emerging alternatives arrive soon. California crude oil currently accounts for only about 37 percent of what the state consumes: roughly 44 million gallons of gasoline and 10 million gallons of diesel every day. The state's crude oil production has decreased 23 percent since 1996. Beginning in 1994, its refineries received more imported oil from other states than was produced from California reserves.[26]

Public commitment to protecting coastal waters and shores from all possible drilling calamity risks is a rational necessity. Yet also consider increased risks associated with protectionist legislative policies that drive drilling operations many miles farther out and thousands of feet deeper to add hazards, complexities, and costs. A similar technical failure to the Deepwater Horizon event occurring in closer-in, shallower waters would have been a much quicker and easier fix, with greatly contained impact. It would also have been much less likely to occur in the first place.

Since 1992, American oil companies have drilled more than twenty-one hundred wells in the Gulf of Mexico at depths greater than a thousand feet. These were extremely expensive to construct, each typically costing $100 million or more, and often they haven't been successful. But sometimes the oil companies did get very lucky. In September 2006, for example, Chevron, Devon Energy, and Norway's Statoil ASA announced that their Jack No. 2 deepwater well in the Gulf of Mexico might have opened up access to 15 billion barrels of oil, enough to boost US strategic reserves by 50 percent. The find is located in a region called the "lower tertiary trend" about 270 miles southwest of New Orleans.

Shell, in partnership with BP and Chevron, is building and deploying a huge oil drilling platform, known as "Perdido," in the Gulf of Mexico, which was originally set for production in 2010. Perdido is expected to yield more than 100,000 bbl/d of crude. The rig is nearly as tall as the Eiffel Tower, and is secured to the seabed by moorings spanning an area the size of downtown Houston—an enormous investment.[27]

It is located in deep water 8 miles north of a maritime boundary defined by a Jimmy Carter–era treaty dividing the gulf for purposes of resource development by the US, Mexico, and Cuba. While the Shell partnership believes the oil to be pooled on the US side, Mexico claims that Perdido will siphon oil from its side. And although Mexico would like to join the group, its state-owned oil company, Pemex, is forbidden by law from participating with foreign partners in developing its crude.

Ironically, while our oil companies are prohibited from drilling next to the

US, we drill close to Mexico and turn a blind eye when other nations drill next to us. Cuba's state-run company, Cubapetroleo, has forged an agreement with China's Sinopec to explore for oil on its half of the Florida Strait using Chinese equipment and operational services. The USGS estimates that the North Cuban Basin contains about 4.6 billion barrels of oil.[28]

American oil companies are being forced to make spectacular investments to go farther and deeper offshore because of off-limit drilling restrictions in more accessible coastal reserves. At the same time, some congressional leaders continue to blame the companies, rather than their own actions, for escalating gasoline prices.

Deepwater Horizon: An Unwasted Crisis

Did the Deepwater Horizon disaster provide a rallying event to assert stranglehold control over drilling by opposing environmental bureaucrats and lobbies? Let's review some developments.

Following the event, Interior Secretary Ken Salazar convened a group of seven experts identified by the National Academy of Engineers to prepare a situation assessment with recommendations. The panel later protested that Salazar altered their report after it was signed, misrepresenting two key recommendations:[29]

- The original report called for a "temporary pause in all current drilling operations for a sufficient length of time" to perform additional safety tests for the thirty-three exploratory deepwater wells already working in the Gulf of Mexico, whereas the altered version urged "an immediate halt to drilling operations on the thirty-three permitted wells, not including the relief wells currently being drilled by BP, that are currently being drilled using floating rigs in the Gulf of Mexico. Drilling operations should cease as soon as safely practicable for a 6-month period."
- The version the experts signed recommended a 6-month moratorium on permits for new exploratory wells in water deeper than 1,000 feet. The altered version recommended a 6-month moratorium on "new wells being drilled using floating rigs." This included rigs in water deeper than 500 feet, covering more of them.

Objecting to the revisions, the panelists argued that the 6-month moratorium on deepwater drilling would make operations less safe, sending technical experts to foreign locations along with the rigs that will relocate.

President Obama then appointed a seven-person commission to determine what caused the oil spill and to take steps to make offshore drilling safer. Unlike the technically distinguished presidential Rogers Commission convened to investigate the NASA space shuttle *Challenger* tragedy, the offshore drilling commission had no appointees with appropriate engineering or petroleum industry backgrounds. In fact, most of them don't favor drilling at all.[30]

- Commission cochair Senator Bob Graham (D-FL) has fought drilling off the Florida coast throughout his career.
- Cochair William Reilly headed the EPA under President George H. W. Bush, but is best known as a former president and chairman of the World Wildlife Fund, one of the largest and most aggressive environmental lobbies.
- Member Donald Boesch, a University of Maryland biological oceanographer and strong opponent of drilling off the Virginia coast, has previously argued that "the impacts of the oil and gas extraction industry . . . on the Gulf Coast wetlands represent an environmental catastrophe of massive and underappreciated proportions."
- Member Terry Garcia, an executive vice president of the National Geographic Society, directed coastal programs during the Clinton-Gore administration with particular emphasis on "recovery of endangered species, habitat conservation planning, and Clean Water Act implementation."
- Member Fran Ulmer, chancellor of the University of Alaska–Anchorage, is also a member of both the Aspen Institute's Commission on Arctic Climate Change and the Union of Concerned Scientists board, which opposes nuclear power and more offshore drilling, favoring government policies "that reduce vehicle miles traveled" (i.e., driving cars).
- Member Frances Beinecke, president of the Natural Resources Defense Council, has called for bans on offshore and Arctic drilling on at least five occasions since the Deepwater Horizon accident. She has stated, "We can blame BP for the disaster, and we should. We can blame lack of government oversight for the disaster, and we should. But in the end, we must place blame where it originated: Americans' addiction to oil."

- Harvard's Cherry A. Murray has a professional background in physics and optics, not petroleum engineering, modern drilling techniques, or rig safety, although she has served as dean of the Harvard School of Engineering and Applied Sciences.

Federal US District Court Judge Martin L. C. Feldman temporarily overturned the Obama-Biden administration's 6-month moratorium on deepwater drilling on June 22, 2010. His twenty-two-page ruling in response to a lawsuit filed by Hornbeck Offshore Services, LLC, made it clear that even presidents aren't empowered to impose an "edict" that isn't justified by science or safety. Feldman's findings expressed "uneasiness" over the administration's claim that its safety report, which recommended the ban, had been "peer reviewed" by experts, because they had since publicly disavowed the ban. The opinion found "no evidence" that Mr. Salazar "balanced the concern for environmental safety" with existing policy and "no suggestion" that he considered any alternatives. The judge listed environmental groups that had joined the administration's defense against the suit. One was the NRDC, headed by drilling commission member Frances Beinecke.[31]

Ken Salazar promptly responded to Judge Feldman's ruling with a revised ban and a federal legal challenge. This time, instead of banning drilling deeper than 500 feet, he banned all drilling by floating rigs (the only equipment that drills in deep water). He also set a firmer November 30th moratorium deadline.

Twenty-two of this country's total thirty-three deepwater rigs are located near already-economically ravaged Louisiana. Pending lease sales have also been canceled off the Virginia and western Gulf of Mexico coasts, along with a drilling program in Alaska's Chukchi and Beaufort seas that had been scheduled to begin in June 2010. While of more than 50,000 US offshore wells the Deepwater Horizon represents the first significant accident, the ultimate future of offshore drilling will inevitably be influenced by the political party dominance results of the 2010 and 2012 national elections.

The International Association of Drilling Contractors estimates that moratorium delays costs as much as $330 million per month in direct wages, not counting lost businesses for servicing the rigs.[32]

According to the Louisiana Mid-Continent Oil & Gas Association, each idled deepwater rig can eradicate 1,420 jobs, with salaries averaging $1,804 per week. In the meantime, many of the rig owners are likely to relocate their platforms to more politically reliable foreign regions, including Brazil, China, and the North Sea sites. Some may never return. Diamond Offshore has announced plans to relocate one of its rigs to Egypt and another to the Republic of the Congo. Scotland's Stena Drilling is shifting one to Canada.[33] Many of the deepwater rigs idled by the moratorium are likely to be acquired by Petrobras for Brazil's offshore fields. The company plans to drill at depths up to 14,000 feet. In August 2009, the US Export-Import Bank issued a "preliminary commitment" to loan Petrobras $2 billion. George Soros will benefit from his $900 million investment in the oil giant.[33]

It might be noted that in June 2010, that very same US Export-Import Bank (Ex-Im, for short) denied loan guarantees to Reliance Power Ltd., an Indian utility that is building a coal-fired plant near Sasan, India. The deal would have enabled Bucyrus International Inc., based in Milwaukee, Wisconsin, to export about $600 million in mining equipment over three years. Although the Reliance-Bucyrus project met all Ex-Im qualifying criteria, including tougher CO_2 standards imposed by the Obama White House, the bank caved under pressure from the Treasury and State departments. Obama-appointed Ex-Im chairman Fred Hochberg explained, "President Obama has made clear his administration's commitment to transition away from high-carbon investments and toward a cleaner-energy future."[34]

A May 2010 NBC News/Wall Street Journal poll revealed that overall public support for offshore drilling remained strong, even while BP's damaged well continued to gush huge amounts of crude into coastal areas. Six out of every ten respondents replied that they backed more drilling off the US coast (34 percent "strongly supported" the idea), and another 26 percent agreed "somewhat." More than half (53 percent) agreed with the statement "The potential benefits to the economy outweigh the potential harm to the environment." Gulf state respondents (63 percent) were most inclined to support additional offshore drilling and rigs.[35]

A legitimate concern cited against offshore drilling is that it leaks oil pollutants into ocean ecosystems, even under safe operational conditions. Yet putting this issue into perspective, a recent National Academy of Sciences study estimates that of the 260,000 metric tons of oil seepage that is thought to occur in waters off North America each year, about 63 percent of that amount escapes naturally from formations below the seafloor. Activities associated with oil and gas exploration, on average, are estimated to be about 3,000 metric tons, less than 1 percent. The rest comes from petroleum tanker transportation and releases from cars, boats, and other sources.[36]

ANWR: Turmoil in the Tundra

Particularly intense controversy exists over whether or not to lift a 30-year government moratorium that prevents drilling in the Arctic National Wildlife Refuge area, which the US Department of Interior estimates to contain between 9 and 16 billion barrels of recoverable oil; the DOE estimates this figure to be about 10.6 billion barrels (potentially producing 876,000 bbl/d). John Cogan, an industry attorney at McDermott Will & Emery in Houston, believes there may even be much more—possibly as much as the 16 billion barrels suggested by the Interior Department—because the DOE based its recovery estimate on outdated methods.

While top Alaskan government officials strongly favor such drilling, environmental lobbies aggressively oppose it. Alaska has had little luck opening up restricted federal lands (65 percent of the state) to oil and natural gas development. Efforts to release ANWR for drilling have been stymied for more than a decade.

On May 13, 2008, Senator Chuck Schumer (D-NY) rose on the Senate floor to demand that arms sales to Saudi Arabia cease unless the kingdom "increases its oil production by one million barrels per day." Interestingly, this is nearly the same amount that might be flowing from ANWR if President Clinton hadn't vetoed drilling there in 1995. Yet senator Schumer doesn't support drilling in ANWR, or anywhere else in the US.

Alaska's then-governor Sarah Palin was and still is incensed that drilling in ANWR is being prevented at a time when the state and nation are facing energy shortages and skyrocketing economic impacts: "It's a very nonsensical position that we are in right now, as we send the president and Secretary [of Energy Sam] Bodman overseas to ask Saudis to ramp up the production of oil so that hungry markets in America can be fed, when your sister state in Alaska has those resources . . . But these lands are locked up by Congress and we are not allowed to drill."[37]

While various polls show that the majority of Alaskans and other Americans still favor expanded drilling on government-controlled lands and waters, opponents of ANWR drilling are particularly vocal, raising the specter of despoiling a vast wilderness and wildlife. In reality, the actual operations would be confined to a tiny fraction of the 1.4-million-acre reserve—namely, a 2,000-acre plot of land smaller than the footprint of the Los Angeles LAX airport.

Alaska has a strong vested interest in maintaining a pristine natural environment, because tourism is the state's largest private-sector employer, accounting for one out of eight jobs and growing. Still former governor Palin doesn't buy the notion that ANWR drilling is going to have any significant impact upon the region's wildlife: "There are magnificent caribou and wolves and bears and porcupines and birds all through Alaska. You can see them thriving today as you could in the 1960s, before pipelines were built. Talk about coexistence; we've got grizzlies roaming on the pipelines and caribou migrations passing beneath them."[38]

And what about polar bears? The governor has some opinions about them, too: "We have been coexisting with bears for decades to no detrimental effect; our bear population is thriving . . . This [Endangered Species Act] listing is nothing but interference from outsiders who insist on keeping Alaska from developing."[39]

Alaska has other, larger oil and natural gas resources that could begin producing even faster than a drilling operation in ANWR. The Chukchi Sea area has a large number of exploration bids for offshore development, and a privately funded, new $30 billion natural gas pipeline project has been approved. The pipeline will be the largest private construction project in North American history, consisting of a gas treatment plant on the North Slope of the state and approximately 2,000 miles of pipe connecting to Alberta, Canada. If required, an additional 1,500-mile-long extension will deliver natural gas from Alberta to Chicago.

Trading Oil for Carbon

In April 2010, a little over a year after assuming office, President Obama appeared in the press to have undergone a miraculous energy policy conversion by announcing that "in order to sustain economic growth and produce jobs, and keep our businesses competitive, we are going to need to harness traditional sources of fuel." Accordingly, he proposed a plan to expand oil and natural gas exploration in the Atlantic, the eastern Gulf of Mexico, and Alaska.

Did this apparent departure from the traditional opposition of his very liberal base signal a "drill baby drill" epiphany? Was it, in fact, a real agenda change at all, or was it possibly just a cap-and-trade bargaining strategy? Let's review some of the circumstances a bit more closely.

Public anger over high 2008 gasoline prices prompted the Bush White House and Congress to lift a long-standing ban on offshore drilling and approve a 5-year plan to open a significant portion of the OCS, including a lease to begin drilling off the Virginia coast that was to be bid out in 2011. Interior Secretary Ken Salazar later postponed the deal until 2012. An assumption held by many is that this would provide more time for activist environmental groups to fight implementation in courts.

A new moratorium was also placed upon those aspects of the Bush plan that would have allowed leasing along the North Atlantic and Pacific coasts. Accordingly, the big news was that President Obama vowed to support development of leased areas off of Alaska's North Slope, referring to a $2.6 billion lease sale in the Chukchi Sea that had already been signed in 2008. He also proposed to "study" drilling along the South Atlantic coast. (These plans are now on hold pending his oil spill commission's conclusions.)

Not highlighted was the president's plan to cancel five other Alaskan leases, which include two in Chukchi, a location with an estimated 77 billion gallons of oil.

The Obama-Biden administration would now allow drilling along a strip in the eastern Gulf of Mexico, 125 miles off the coast of Florida, but there's a big catch: This will require congressional approval, and ten coastal state Democrats have recently declared opposition to offshore drilling. Such resistance can present a real obstacle.

Suspicions abound in some circles that President Obama's proposal has the net effect of leveraging about 13 billion barrels of oil and 41 trillion cubic feet of gas controlled by his administration and party through locked-up leases as a trade barter for Republican support of his Comprehensive Energy and Climate Bill (aka, the newly proposed Power Bill, or cap-and-trade). Speaking at a solar panel fabrication plant in Fremont, California, on May 26, Obama used the strategically staged opportunity to say, "Climate change poses a threat to our way of life. In fact we're already beginning to see its profound and costly impact . . . And the spill in the Gulf, which is heartbreaking, only underscores the necessity of seeking alternative fuel sources."[40]

In a June 3, 2010, speech at Pittsburgh's Carnegie Mellon University, the president further stated, "I will make the case for a clean-energy future wherever I can, and I will work with anyone from either party to get this done . . . The next generation will not be held hostage to energy sources from the last century."

Again, on June 15, the president devoted a major portion of an Oval Office speech regarding the spill to pitch comprehensive energy reform legislation as a means to end US dependence on fossil fuels and foreign oil and to create a clean-energy future: "For decades we have known the days of cheap and easily accessible oil were numbered . . . For decades, we have failed to act with the sense of urgency this challenge requires . . . We cannot consign our children to this future."

As Daniel Weiss of the Center for American Progress observed, "The oil disaster adds a new urgency and a new opportunity for connecting with the public . . . The administration was going to do it anyway, but that gives it a new way to talk about it."[41]

But successful bargaining with coastal state Democratic congressional leaders to gain Republican support for energy/climate legislation now appears to be unlikely, as attacks on offshore drilling escalate in the aftermath of the BP oil spill disaster off the Louisiana coast.

Recognizing a problem, bill cosponsors senators Kerry and Lieberman have shifted legislation emphasis away from previous drilling advocacy. In late 2009, Kerry had called for a bill that included "additional onshore and offshore oil and gas exploration." In May 2010, he confessed to *Investor's Business Daily* that changes had to be made to win votes in the wake of the oil spill. Those changes include a provision that will let any coastal state ban drilling otherwise permitted by a neighboring state within 75 miles of its coastline if a mandatory study indicates that an accident could harm that impacted state's economy or environment.

Although it is reported that Senator Kerry and President Obama had previously discussed drilling leniency to woo Republicans, it mostly just turned off Democrats. Accordingly, there was little or nothing to barter for cap-and-trade provisions embodied in the proposed legislation. In any case, that's one trade that should be capped without question.[42]

Oil Prices: Politics and Prognoses

President Obama, along with some members of Congress, has declared war on Big Oil. The proposed 2011 White House budget will kill $4 billion in long-established accelerated depreciation allowances and other incentives for oil and gas drilling. Senator Robert Menendez (D-NJ) has introduced a bill that would remove another $20 billion in industry tax breaks. The Independent Petroleum Association maintains that these tax increases will fall disproportionately on small drilling companies, potentially reducing annual oil and gas production by 20 to 40 percent. This despite EIA estimates that fossil fuels will still account for 79 percent of US energy demand in 2030, regardless how many tax incentives are hurled at biofuels, wind and solar. As a result, energy prices will soar, and vital investments and supplies will dwindle.[43]

World competition for oil is becoming more and more aggressive as developing countries such as China and India continue to increase consumption through industrial growth and economic prosperity. According to the DOE's EIA, global demand is expected to increase by 60 percent over the next 2 decades, while demand in developing countries may grow by 115 percent during this period, due in part to increasing automobile ownership. The US currently imports about 70 percent of the oil it consumes (roughly 13 million bbl/d), and these imports are expected to increase to an estimated 17.7 million bbl/d within the next 2 decades.[43]

Today, the US consumes more than one-fourth of the world's oil and crude oil imports, amounting to about $700 billion each year and constituting about a quarter of the nation's balance-of-trade deficit. More than two-thirds of this consumption is in the transportation sector, where energy demands are growing rapidly. Continuously increasing crude oil prices with major impacts upon gasoline costs for consumers are likely to impact driving habits and promote purchases of more efficient vehicles that will moderate consumption rates, but total influences are highly conjectural. Historic consumption levels have been driven by high per-capita ownership of automobiles, large vehicles, private versus public transportation preferences, and relatively low gasoline costs compared with most other countries. Still, US consumers, on average, probably spend a smaller fraction of their incomes on gasoline now than in previous decades.

According to Bureau of Transportation statistics, the US now has about 251 million registered motor vehicles (6.6 million motorcycles and 135 million passenger cars); more than 8,000 commercial aircraft and 224,000 general aviation aircraft; and 12.7 million recreational boats.[44] Some argue that supply shortages and high fuel prices are just the medicine our country needs to curb an "addiction to oil" through forced efficiencies and development of "sustainable alternatives." That philosophy would be more compelling if transitioning to those actively touted nonfossil alternatives offered any real potential to replace oil and natural gas dependence. But they don't. Biofuels are little more than an energy breakeven at best: Hydrogen is a big energy loser, and wind, solar, and geothermal power options have extremely limited growth prospects.

Here again, global warming alarmists, carbon-trading lobbies, alternative energy hypesters, and environmental activist groups wield powerful influences over policies that will determine America's energy future. Arguments that short oil supplies will hasten a transition to biofuels as a solution to transportation needs ignore the unreality of the alleged energy benefits those biofuels afford, and their broader economic impacts upon energy, food, and business costs. These burdens will fall most heavily upon the segments of the population that can least afford them. The result will be more, rather than less, dependence upon unreliable foreign oil supplies, while simultaneously weakening US economic capacity to invest in vital new energy technology development.

Important Democrat leaders appear to support the idea that high energy prices are useful to drive conservation and to hasten investment in a transition to nonfossil alternatives. Speaking as a then-senator and a presidential candidate, Barack Obama stated that he had hoped the rise in gas prices would have been a "gradual adjustment" (not an avoidable adjustment) so that Americans could adapt to the reality of four-dollar gasoline. That adjustment is pretty tough on independent truckers who must pay $1,500 to fill up their tanks and school districts that are forced to eliminate bus stops—and even entire routes.

Even though the Democrat-controlled Congress passed the Energy Independence Act of 2007, the party majority remains steadfastly opposed to drilling in areas that contain enormous amounts of oil and natural gas. As a result of large political uncertainties regarding future legislation, nervous oil markets are driving pump prices even higher. Oil futures traders, anticipating tightened supplies, are upping their bids, a condition that will be exacerbated if cap-and-trade legislation is enacted. Since drilling prohibitions and carbon cap-and-trade advocacy tend to have strongest support among Democratic Party representatives, the outcomes of upcoming presidential and congressional elections will continue to have important and enduring consequences upon domestic oil and gas development and expenses.

Speculators pay close attention to world markets. As China has increased annual petroleum use by 920 million barrels over a 5-year period, the institutional investors (or "index speculators") upped their demand for petroleum futures by 848 million barrels over the same period. Buying sizable "long" positions, they have been betting that oil prices, regardless of how high they may seem, will continue to rise. Because of an "Enron loophole" allowed in federal trading regulations, the investors have been able to circumvent typical speculative limits. The resultant lopsided betting has propelled prices upward.

After 2007, when crude oil prices rocketed to about $70 per barrel, lawmakers threatened to close the loophole by regulating electronic trading, and they gave the Federal Trade Commission more authority to guard against market manipulation. Trading experts are asking that special attention be directed to pension funds, endowments, and other institutional investors who have been big players, pouring billions of dollars into a variety of commodities—oil is but one of them—with dramatic price-hiking results. Other notable examples are corn, soybeans, wheat, and rice.

But demand-based speculation forces aren't the only causes of the nervous oil markets that drive up prices. Uncertainties about the steadiness of the supply sources are important too; consider the potential political turmoil in Nigeria or production problems in an unstable Mexico. As John Felmy, chief economist for the American Petroleum Institute, has observed, "If oil prices really were so much higher than supply-and-demand forces would suggest, then holders of crude oil would be unable to find buyers, and inventories would build—but that's not happening." As least, not so long as China's large needs and deep pockets continue to expand.[45]

We Shale Overcome?

What if there was a domestic source of oil that could support all of America's needs for the next 400 years or so? Well, maybe there is. In that case, everyone would be really excited, right? No, probably not. At least that's the current situation.

On July 22, 2008, then-President Bush announced that he wanted to remove all barriers to extracting oil from enormous shale formations located in a swath of federally owned land encompassing parts of Colorado, Wyoming, and Utah. This followed a 15–14 vote by the Senate Appropriations Committee that would have ended a 1-year moratorium on enacting rules for oil shale development on federal lands. Senator Salazar, a Democrat and leading opponent of oil shale development, had inserted the moratorium into an omnibus spending bill in December 2007. He then successfully proposed the new May 2008 bill to extend it for another year.[46]

Extension of the moratorium was a big setback for Royal Dutch Shell and other oil companies that had already invested many, many millions of dollars in shale oil development research since the passage of the Energy Policy Act of 2005. That legislation established the original framework for commercial leasing of federal oil shale lands, similar to provisions for on-land and offshore drilling arrangements. Extension of the moratorium came at a time when Senator Salazar and his fellow Democratic colleagues had been blasting Big Oil for not reinvesting enough of their profits in developing new sources of oil, when in 2007 the oil shale project represented Shell's largest R&D expenditure. And in addition to forbidding the DOI from leasing federal shale lands, Democratic legislators also threatened to block imports of oil from Canadian tar sand reserves because it was considered to be too environmentally "dirty."

Just how big is that US oil shale reserve? It's really, really big. Estimates range from an equivalent of 800 billion barrels of crude up to possibly 2 trillion barrels. The 800 billion estimate equals about three times the amount of all Saudi Arabia's oil—in fact, more than Saudi Arabia, Iran, Russia, Venezuela, Iraq, and Mexico oil reserves combined. One trillion barrels of crude equals all the oil the world has used since it was first discovered in Titusville, Pennsylvania, in 1859. When developed, the Green River Formation would provide oil shale comparable to the extent of the energy potential of Alberta's tar sands reserves. Together, the US and Canada would have the world's largest oil supply.[47]

Why hasn't that huge resource been developed before now? The several reasons warrant some discussion. The first is cost.

While oil from shale is similar to crude, it is much more complex and expensive to extract, and it also requires quality upgrading prior to being used as refinery feedstock. The oil is contained in sedimentary rock that contains solid bituminous materials, called "kerogen," that are released as petroleum-like liquids when heated. The kerogen was formed by a natural process that also created crude, but under conditions with less heat and pressure. The shale contains enough oil to actually burn, and some countries use it directly for fuel.

Oil shale has seen limited development worldwide because many countries lack large amounts, and those that do tend to rely upon cheaper crude. These circumstances have inhibited technology advancement, although Estonia, China, and Brazil have quite well-established oil shale industries. High oil prices during the 1970s and 1980s stimulated US interest and technology investment, which waned after those prices fell.

Old oil extraction practices that involved mining the shale and processing it on the surface are now being replaced by in situ methods that leave the shale rocks in place underground. Shell's process places electric heaters in deep vertical holes dug into the shale to gradually raise its temperature over a 2-to-3-year period. At about 600°F–700°F, the oil separates and is gathered in collection wells within the extraction zone.[48]

Shell's current plan uses ground-freezing technology to establish an underground barrier (a "freeze wall") around the extraction zone perimeter, using pumped refrigeration fluid to block groundwater from entering and to keep hydrocarbons from leaving. This remains unproven at a commercial scale but is regarded by the DOE to be promising. These processes are energy and water intensive, yet Shell believes that as fuel prices continue to rise, shale oil processing will be competitive.

Water use in the Green River Formation region within the Colorado River drainage basin is a major oil shale concern. Each barrel of oil will require about 3 barrels of water. Senator Orrin Hatch (R-UT), a strong oil shale proponent, compares this requirement with ethanol processing: "Let's compare it to ethanol. Corn needs about 1,000 barrels of water for the energy equivalent of a barrel of oil. That's a crazy amount of water, but it's worked out alright so far because corn is grown in rainy areas, for the most part. But if you want to increase the amount of ethanol, you're going to have to go to irrigation, and then there will be major water limits on how much we can afford to grow."[49]

Senator Hatch observed that even though water is a lot scarcer in western Colorado than in Iowa, the oil companies would recycle much of the water they would use. And in regard to other environmental impacts, he said, "Let's talk about land use and wildlife habitat. One acre of corn produces the equivalent of 5 to 7 barrels of oil. One acre of oil shale produces 100,000 to 1 million barrels . . . That's 1 million barrels that we would not be importing from Russia and the Middle East. People are going to go berserk when they find out that all along the way we had the capacity, within our own borders, to alleviate our dependency in an environmentally friendly way."[50]

American Processing Picture: Crude, Unrefined

The US faces a dangerous lack of adequate oil refinery capacity. The last facility to be constructed was the Ashland Refinery, near Garyville, Louisiana, completed in 1976. Fewer than half of the number of plants that existed in 1981 still remain, down from 324 to 149. Disruptions of production due to maintenance, accidents, and natural disasters at one or more of the plants can create supply shortfalls and price hikes with regional and national impacts.[51]

Although demand for refined products—transportation fuels in particular—continues to rise steadily, refineries are high on the list of least-wanted industries in many locales. In California, where ten plants representing 20 percent of that state's refining capacity were closed between 1985 and 1995, it is unlikely that more will be built due to concerns about smog, truck traffic carrying hazardous materials, and potential leaks in the event of earthquakes.

Despite a reduction in plant numbers, refinery capacity has managed to keep up with the national demand so far through expansion of existing facilities. This has also been less expensive than building new plants due to stringent environmental restrictions. Now, even that approach to bring capacities more in line with growing demands is being challenged.

The NRDC asked a federal judge to stop a $3.8-billion expansion of a Whiting, Indiana, refinery owned by BP because it will discharge more CO_2 than it has been approved for. The NRDC has been actively working to block virtually all attempts to create more energy from fossils, using the Clean Air Act as a weapon. Another example is a proposed refinery in Arizona that has now been blocked for more than 10 years.

The National Center for Policy Analysis estimates that nearly 25 percent of all capital investment that went into refineries during the 1990s was used to comply with environmental regulations. Between 1992 and 2001 this amounted to more than $100 billion in costs to bring refineries into compliance with environmental rules.

As with restrictions on drilling, regulatory constraints on refinery development and expansion will predictably increase our energy dependence upon foreign sources. Huge plants now under construction in India, Asia, and the Middle East, which will produce tanker loads of gasoline, diesel, and jet fuel, will most likely meet the demand for refined oil products in the US and other countries. By 2012, India's refining capacity is projected to double to about 4.8 million bbl/d through $70 billion in investment. And they won't be worrying about CO_2 emission lawsuits.

The Political Environment: Time for a Climate Change

Unless and until better options are available, there is no alternative but to develop and optimize real resource possibilities. This must involve exploring and developing untapped domestic fossil-fuel reserves; improving and applying clean coal and coal-to-liquid fuel technologies; exploiting opportunities to benefit from vast US oil shale deposits; upgrading and expanding refinery infrastructures; and becoming a world leader in the development and beneficiary of safe nuclear power opportunities.

These priorities do not in any way preclude the importance of developing solar power, geothermal power, and hydropower for electricity, or biofuels for automotive applications. And they are certainly no substitute for essential conservation practices that will stretch all energy resources. Yes, of course, energy conservation is essential, but it is quite a different matter to think that we can conserve our way to future prosperity without also expanding the supply side. Energy fuels the economic and technological progress needed to advance conservation goals we all share. These economies are essential to lower our energy consumption rates, our living costs, and the impacts on our environment.

America is blessed with a great abundance of resources. Key among these are the advantages afforded by a free market system and a proactive, entrepreneurial spirit that enables innovation to flourish. These time-proven strengths are now under assault. The radical environmentalism that grew out of movements during the 1960s gained new purpose and traction through apocalyptic climate visions in the late 1980s, and it has grown exponentially since. As a result, obstructionist groups have increasingly gained license to shut down vital energy initiatives that are recognized and supported by the general public.[52]

Chief villains on the environmental opposition "hit" parade, listed in order of both vitriolic reaction and the amount we depend upon them for total US electricity, are coal, nuclear, and hydropower. Coal is also the primary target that carbon cap-and-trade promoters have in their sights. Global warming GHG hysteria has been fixated upon coal-burning CO_2 emissions as "pollution" that threatens the natural world, whereas nature regards CO_2 as a fundamental part of all carbon-based life. The real fossil combustion pollutants, sulfur and various particulates, can be more readily removed, while CO_2 sequestration is more costly—and also nonsensical—particularly if the Earth continues to cool as scheduled.[53]

If Americans are concerned about costly energy now, they should realize that we haven't seen anything yet. Strategies to address these problems through shortage-forced conservation measures and CO_2 footprint–reducing miracle cures aren't going to be popular for very long. Such approaches will simply be unsustainable, along with the alternatives that have captured media prominence.

Another sobering reality is that energy production will probably never be entirely risk free. For example, there is no guarantee that, rare as they are, future oil spills won't occur. If we don't drill at home, more oil is certain to arrive by tankers and barges, with even greater accidental spillage threats nearer to our shores. Meanwhile, other countries less careful than we are will continue to exploit oil and gas resources in nearby waters. Such risks are very real and serious, and the costs of doing business must include ample allowances for prevention and cleanup. Those responsibilities come along with the benefits of the diverse energy resources we most fortunately enjoy.

Chapter 11
DEMANDING TRUTH AND ACCOUNTABILITY

LARRY BELL

Climate models reveal dramatic warming trends since the Industrial Revolution.

We have been grossly deceived regarding purported scientific evidence of a man-made climate crisis. Anyone who claims to know what climate changes will occur a year, a decade, or even longer ahead is either a fraud or a fool. Speculations are a different matter, and variant theories abound. That's what moves science forward and helps keep it honest through authentic discourse and objective examination.

The corruption of science that was publicly exposed through the release of purloined CRU e-mails came as no surprise to many who have witnessed these travesties or dared to challenge the claims. Timothy Ball, a former climatology professor at the University of Winnipeg, received death threats for presenting his beliefs. As he puts it, "CO_2 was never a problem, and all the machinations and deceptions exposed by these files prove that it was the greatest deception in history, but nobody is laughing." He adds that he has "watched climate science hijacked and corrupted by this small group of scientists . . . Surely this is the death knell for the CRU, the IPCC, Kyoto and Copenhagen, and the carbon credits shell game."[1]

Has the importance of the CRU scandal been overblown? This isn't simply a matter involving a few random researchers who lost their professional compasses and made some inconsequential mistakes. Rather, it involves several of the most influential representatives of a climate science community that has received more than $30 billion from US taxpayers over the past 20 years . . . and one that guides many trillions of dollars in policy decisions. These are key people who have

- controlled central processes and findings of the UN's IPCC climate science reviews and leading publications in that field;
- issued alarming predictions that have dominated world headlines;
- mobilized and presided over international climate change crisis summits attended by thousands upon thousands of delegates;
- provided the rationale for draconian environmental and energy regulations that significantly impact local, regional, national, and global economies;
- dictated moral imperatives to justify massive transfers of wealth and power between population segments and nations, and between citizens and their governments;
- established the basis for government agencies rather than competitive free market processes to pick energy and technology winners and losers; and
- afforded a good cover story for blatant and unproductive cap-and-trade profiteering.

Is this all connected to a diabolical, centrally organized conspiracy? Probably not. More likely, it reflects a confluence of separate agendas that are well served by, if not totally dependent upon, a man-made global warming premise in general and demonization of carbon in particular. The vast majority of the proponents should be assumed to be very good, honorable, and sincere people who believe in their causes and the scientific claims that support them. The same goes for competent and dedicated scientists on all sides of climate debates who are deserving of public trust and support.

Silent Hearings in the Senate

Senator Inhofe, an outspoken critic of global warming disaster theories, has worked very hard to bring solid science into the debate. As ranking member of the Senate Committee on Environment and Public Works, he has convened hearings to question authorities on the matter with scant media interest. This number of "skeptics" now exceeds six hundred fifty, including Japanese chemist Kiminori Itoh, who calls global warming alarmism the "worst scientific scandal." Dr. Itoh is one of many who formerly worked with IPCC and have since come to oppose the UN's positions. His group is growing rapidly, far outnumbering the fifty-two UN scientists who authored IPCC's 2007 AR-4 "Summary for Policymakers" report.[2]

Senator Inhofe is demanding an investigation of scientific improprieties revealed in the CRU e-mails, calling the affair a wake-up call for America. "The notion that these scientists tried to declare the science settled for personal reasons is disgraceful," says Inhofe. "They were purposefully misrepresenting the facts. They tried to make America believe, and it worked, for a time. Even my grandkids came home filled with this stuff, saying that 'anthropogenic gases cause global warming'! I reminded them that these things go in cycles. We've had warming, then cooling, then warming and cooling again. I'm delighted that people are discovering that the science has been cooked for a long period of time."[3]

Senator Inhofe noted that the CRU data used in the IPCC's 2007 summary was subsequently used by the EPA in preparing its guidelines on carbon emissions, connections that are very worrisome for the American taxpayer: "There are tremendous economic ramifications to what these guys were trying to do . . . The IPCC for years has been costing the government so much money, and now, wasted time in trying to pass faulty legislation based on bad data."[4]

Hans von Storch, the former editor of *Climate Research*, said on November 23,

2009, that the behavior outlined in the hacked CRU e-mails went too far, and that the East Anglia researchers "violated a fundamental principle of science" (by refusing to share data): "They built a group to do gate-keeping, which is totally unacceptable." Von Storch is now a professor at the University of Hamburg's Meteorological Institute.[5] Lord Monckton, at Britain's Science and Public Policy Institute, went even farther in his condemnation, saying that these researchers "are not merely bad scientists—they are crooks. And crooks who have perpetrated their crimes at the expense of British and US taxpayers."[6]

Unsustainable Energy Claims

Arguably the most serious public deception perpetrated by the war against climate change is the notion that cleaner, sustainable energy options are available in sufficient abundance to replace dependence upon dwindling fossils that currently provide about 85 percent of all US energy. Regrettably, this is broadly recognized not to be the case at all, and this circumstance, not global warming, presents epic challenges. Ironically, many of the same groups that champion environmental and human causes are inhibiting progress toward vital solutions.

Perhaps the least publicly understood aspect of various carbon-free "sustainable" energy alternatives such as wind, solar, and geothermal power are their anemic capacities to contribute in significant ways to achieving higher levels of independence from foreign sources as world demands and prices continue to escalate. Pervasive green advertising, which suggests that sustainable fuel and power are virtually unlimited, is extremely misleading in this regard and does the public great disservice. Such pretense obfuscates the importance of exploring and exploiting untapped fossil fields, including oil shale deposits; strengthening production infrastructures; and greatly expanding nuclear potentials that have no near-term substitutes at any costs. Even as those other alternatives become more market competitive by virtue of technology and processing economies, government incentives, and rising oil prices, the prospects for real growth or environmental benefits fall far short of popular illusions.

There is much we can learn from European experiences. The EU, which like the US relies heavily upon fossils and imported oil, has found little salvation through its enormous investments in renewable alternatives. This realization is now causing pain accompanied by second thoughts as members witness their economies threatened by rampant fuel hikes and menacing power shortages. A contributing factor can be attributed to an emphasis upon unsuccessful CO_2 emission–reduction efforts that have also failed to fill large energy gaps. As a result, the European Commission has concluded that nuclear power offers the only clean-energy solution that can avert a rapidly approaching crisis. This, despite the commission's own polls indicating that although France, the UK, the Czech Republic, Poland, and a handful of other European states are strongly pro-nuclear, only about 20 percent of Europe's total citizenry support its use since Chernobyl.[7]

Yet even formerly antinuclear Italy now plans to begin building nuclear plants within 5 years. The Italians seem to have become weary of paying the highest electricity prices in Europe.

Massive European subsidies for expensive wind, solar, and hydropower projects have delivered poor investment/return ratios, and the food-versus-fuel debate has deflated the biofuels bubble. Loud public protests have influenced the Scottish Parliament to deny permission to develop a huge Isle of Lewis wind farm, and other proposals have drawn similar opposition because of the large land tracts required. Offshore wind farms have proven to be extremely costly to build and maintain. Still, other than nuclear power, the EU regards wind to be its most viable nonfossil alternative hope.

Europe, like America, sits upon vast quantities of coal that are becoming appreciated more and more. Yet Germany's recently announced plans for a new generation of coal-fired power plants have hit a wall of environmental resistance over carbon emissions that have already caused some proposals to be canceled. This has built a stronger case for more nuclear development in Germany, reversing previous intentions to phase nuclear out. France and Britain have hatched a joint plan to construct a new generation of nuclear power stations and export technology around the world, yet EU leadership remains bogged down in trying to win a public debate over its energy future. As Czech prime minister Mirek Topolanek recently warned, "We must do more than talk about nuclear energy. It is really five minutes to midnight."[8]

The energy security alarm clock is ticking for America, too, and nuclear development is an inevitable priority. Vital aspects of long-overdue infrastructure expansion are necessary in order to (1) reassert technological science and plant construction; (2) ensure leadership; (3) establish an active spent fuel reprocessing program; and (4) provide safe, effective storage for radioactive waste products.

The Energy Independence Myth

Political slogans that offer visions of an energy-independent America powered and fueled by abundant sunshine, wind, and corn aren't likely to come to fruition.

Never mind that CO_2 reduction efforts applying alternative energy in EU countries have accomplished nothing, and that the level of CO_2 emissions between the years 2000 and 2004 grew 2.1 percent, compared with 1.3 percent for the US. Forget that global temperatures haven't risen since 1998 despite higher CO_2 emissions worldwide; that the 2008 Antarctic summer ice melt was the smallest on record; and that cooling is expected to continue at least through 2015. But don't forget that hot or cold, flood or drought, energy, not climate, is a global problem that won't go away.[9]

The terms "energy independence" and "energy security" should be recognized to mean very different things. Energy independence is an empty but appealing political slogan. It offers a fantasy illusion of an autonomous America, powered and fueled by limitless sunjuice, friendly breezes, and amber waves of grain that sever our reliance upon dirty smokestacks and greedy tyrants, both foreign and domestic. Forget it! It's not going to happen.

Energy security, however, is an urgent goal that should be taken very seriously. That goal is to secure sustainable supplies of energy to ensure an uninterrupted high quality of life for the citizens of this country, and to advance continuing social and economic progress for generations to come as members of a larger world community. This does not imply subscribing to a "new world order" or abandoning independent national interests. It does imply that we must realize that globalized markets, including energy, are an unavoidable reality and an indispensable necessity.[10]

America's future prosperity will hinge upon its ability to produce and exchange value in an oil-fueled world market, which includes countries that don't like us. Oil is the new currency that defines bargaining power, both for those who provide it and for those who can afford the price. The quest for that currency is producing some very disturbing alliances among large emerging consumer nations and unsavory adversarial regimes. They draw upon huge national budgets, share technologies and operational costs, and function with environmental impunity in our coastal waters.[11]

Oil-hungry China has been putting together oil and gas deals with Argentina, Brazil, Cuba, Peru, Ecuador, and most troubling, Venezuela—the fourth-largest US oil supplier. A series of agreements will enable Chinese companies to explore for new resources and set up refineries in that South American country, which currently is headed by an anti-American dictator. A similar circumstance is developing in Cuban waters in the Gulf of Mexico near Florida. China's continued penetration into the Western Hemisphere, including ambitious efforts to secure agreements with Canada, will have profound economic and political implications for America's future energy security.

India's booming economy, which has been growing at a remarkable rate of 8 percent per year throughout the past decade, is driving escalating competition with other countries for oil imports. Presently, 70 percent of India's energy needs are supplied by domestic coal reserves and only 30 percent by oil, 70 percent of which is imported. At current growth rates, the IEA predicts that India will continue to increase energy consumption by at least 3.6 percent annually, causing it to double by 2025 when the nation will import more than 90 percent of its petroleum supply.[12]

Looking to the West, India is working to pursue relationships with Venezuela, which the Indian petroleum minister has referred to as "our arrowhead in Latin America" that can be used to open up other South American markets. Closer relationships between India and Venezuela will run counter to US attempts to isolate the regime of Hugo Chavez. Venezuela, the fifth-largest exporter of oil worldwide, is seeking to diversify its markets in order to reduce dependence upon the US, which buys more than 60 percent of its crude.

Russia's economy, like that of China and India, has been growing at an amazing rate. In 2007, its real GDP rose by more than 8 percent, surpassing the growth rates in all other G8 countries and marking the seventh consecutive year of economic expansion. Most of that growth has been driven by energy exports due to aggressive oil production and high world oil prices. The country has been meeting more than half of its domestic energy needs from enormous natural gas reserves, while energy consumed from oil has actually decreased from 27 percent in 1992 to about 19 percent currently. According to IMF and World Bank estimates, Russia's oil and gas sector generated more than 60 percent of its export revenues in 2007.[13]

Russia is actively pursuing cooperative energy deals with other countries, including China, Cuba, and Venezuela. In 2008, the Kremlin dispatched Deputy Prime Minister Igor Sechin to negotiate a bilateral China-Russia agreement involving crude oil trade, joint development of new deposits, construction of oil and gas pipelines, and development of refining and chemical production facilities. Both countries have agreed to build an Eastern Siberia–Pacific oil pipeline to China, along with a $10 billion pipeline to transport natural gas to China from eastern and western regions of Siberia.[14]

Energy Minister Sergey Shmatko announced in August 2008 that Russian oil companies have "sufficiently promising prospects" to develop cooperation with Cuban partners for joint oil prospecting in the Gulf of Mexico. He further commented, "I think that working groups will soon be set up as part of an agreement signed by the Russian Energy Ministry and the Cuban Ministry of Basic Industry at the commission session to examine the issue." Russia may provide assistance in overhauling Cuba's oil production infrastructure, sharing oil transportation technologies, helping repair Cuba's crude oil storage facilities, and inspecting pipelines.[15]

Shmatko further indicated that the Venezuelan state-owned petroleum company Petróleos de Venezuela will also be involved in Russo-Cuban oil processing cooperation, seeing as Venezuela is Cuba's strategic partner. Given China's and India's interest too, it looks as though the Gulf of Mexico off America's coast is going to be a very popular place for drilling—with everyone except US Congress Democrats.

As other countries continue to exploit readily accessible oil and natural gas reservoirs, including some in North America's coastal waters, US companies are being constrained by regulations that preclude similar opportunities. Accordingly, costs associated with finding and developing US resources are rising sharply; they nearly doubled between 2004 and 2006. These high costs are motivating American companies to limit capacities through a "just-in-time" production strategy similar to approaches used in manufacturing, power generation, and consumer goods. This involves cutting back on operations of oil wells and platforms that aren't essential to meet immediate demands in order to avoid unnecessary expenses.[16]

If the US really wants to make progress toward energy independence, why not begin by opening up offshore access to domestic supplies before state-owned national companies controlled by Cuba, China, and Mexico siphon off the shared reservoirs?

It is safe to bet that days of cheap oil are over without requiring any help from added government fuel taxes, price-hiking alternative fuel incentives, and carbon-emission cap-and-trade shenanigans. Growing global competition for dwindling supplies will guarantee that happens. Continued federal restrictions upon domestic drilling will also maintain petroleum and natural gas prices at high levels for American consumers relative to world levels, placing US exploration companies at even greater cost disadvantages when up against large state-owned operations. Consequently, we will be forced to increase imports, becoming more, not less, dependent on foreign sources. Some, such as China, Cuba, and Mexico, may be willing to sell us some of what they obtain from our own offshore Gulf Coast regions as US companies experience continued depletion of their legacy fields.[17]

California Dreaming: A Wake-Up Call

In December 2009, Governor Arnold Schwarzenegger (R-CA) released a report based upon a California Energy Commission study predicting that global warming would cause San Francisco Bay waters to cover Fisherman's Wharf and Treasure Island by 2100. This somber forecast adds to a sea of rising debt the entire state is already experiencing in part due to its recent GHG emissions legislation.

A law passed by the governor and legislative Democrats in 2006 (AB32) mandates that GHGs be reduced to 1990 levels (about 25 percent) by 2020. While the state continues to lose industries, jobs, and people, its top executive hasn't relented, stating, "We must be prepared if climate change continues to worsen."[18]

A 2009 study undertaken by economists at California State University at Sacramento estimated that AB32 implementation costs "could easily exceed $100 billion" and that the program would raise the cost of living by $7,857 per household annually by 2020. The California Small Business Roundtable commissioned the research.

Opponents of AB32 have submitted eight hundred thousand signatures (nearly double the number needed), seeking to suspend the law in a November 2010 ballot. If approved, AB32 would not be reinstated until California has four consecutive quarters when the unemployment rate is 5.5 percent or less.

Among noted critics of the AB32 suspension initiative is a small company called Serious Materials, a California building materials manufacturer and the only window producer to receive tax credits through the Obama-Biden administration's "cash for caulkers" stimulus package. Perhaps coincidentally, the company's director is married to Cathy Zoi, the administration's assistant secretary of energy efficiency and renewable energy, who controls $16.8 billion in stimulus funds. Zoi (formerly the CEO of Al Gore's ACP) and her husband hold 120,000 shares in Serious Materials, along with stock options. The two are also reported to hold a substantial interest in the Swiss firm Landis+Gyr, which makes "smart meters," a central component of the administration's "smart grid" plans.[19]

State Assemblyman Chuck DeVore (R-Irvine) and others are questioning the alleged science behind such economically damaging decisions, particularly in light of the CRU e-mail revelations. He observed, "Combined with the $21 billion deficit we're facing in the coming year, this shows we ought to be focusing our attention on more mundane things—like living within our means." Then he added, "To use this all-encompassing rubric of climate change as a power grab to usurp property rights is something we shouldn't be doing."[20]

While California focuses upon windmills, solar panels, and electric cars, vast offshore oil resources go undeveloped and nuclear power is ignored. Consequently, the energy-starved state's economic future is bleak. A 2009 Milken Institute study shows a recent loss of nearly four hundred thousand manufacturing jobs. Other, well-intentioned environmental policies have caused more than 450,000 acres of previously fertile agriculture land in the San Joaquin Valley to be turned into desert through water diversion aimed at saving an obscure species of tiny delta smelt fish. Farmers in that area that once fed the world now line up at food pantries. Valley-wide unemployment averaging 17 percent has soared upward to 40 percent in some small towns.

The regulatory environment in California has turned the dreams of good lives into nightmares for many who are leaving in hordes, taking much of the state's tax base with them. About 2.14 million fled to other states between 2005 and 2007, while only about 1.44 million moved in. Meanwhile, the state's debt rises at a rate of about $25 million per day.

Texas benefits from California's population and business migrations; the state has realized 70 percent of all new US job growth since 2008. The state also leads all others in the number of Fortune 500 companies headquartered there (sixty-four, compared with fifty-six in New York and fifty-one in California). Much of this prosperity can be attributed to an emphasis in Texas on laissez-faire markets and individual responsibility, which contrasts with California's reliance upon central planning, tax-supported energy subsidies, and social entitlement programs. At the same time, Texas is also becoming a leader in wind power development, applying an "all-of-the-above" energy policy and no personal state income tax.

Bad Science—Sponsored by Us

Who paid for that goofy science speculation that Governor Schwarzenegger's scary global warming, oceans rising, engulfed land, emission control–urgent report was based on? We did, of course, along with additional contributions from generous California taxpayers to cover about $150,000 in presentation costs. After all, through our federal and state governments, we pay for most science, good and bad, which is entrusted to agencies and their minions to distribute, administer, or conduct.

To suggest that science research trickles down from government would be a gross understatement. Actually, it cascades from mountains on high, presided over by people whom we generally assume to be knowledgeable and objective. Often, we might assume wrong. This occurs when a particularly orthodox view becomes inculcated into government leadership and surrogate organization power structures . . . Yes, exactly like man-made global warming, for example. Then follow the rivers, streams, and creeks as those influences spread.

Agencies get funding appropriations based upon how important they are, or more accurately, how important we are persuaded to think they are. In the case of environmental issues, they are a lot more important if they appear to address (certainly not waste) a crisis. Climate change, a topic offering an opportunity to regulate something really dangerous, like natural air, is just too wonderful to pass up.

Who populates these agencies? People with correct orthodox credentials, of course. It helps a lot if they have published books or articles that favor and advance those views, or at least associate with influential organizations that do. Let's call that the "orthodox mainstream." Then again, most of those books and articles wouldn't have been published at all if the authors didn't have good science credentials, right? They would need to have undertaken research that was published in respected journals.

Farther downriver, the universities that support learned research and hire scientists to conduct it depend upon money from federal and state government agencies (again, from us). To compete for that money they must address topics that are recognized by the orthodox mainstream as being very important. Only then can they hire and produce people who write successful proposals to support staff to do the research to prepare the papers that get published in the respected journals.

But what if those learned people's papers can't get published in the respected journals because they contradict views of influential orthodox mainstream gatekeepers who attack their merit—as with, for example, the exact circumstances exposed in the CRU e-mail communications. In this case, those scientists wouldn't win grants and contracts (from tax and tuition money we supply) to gain tenure and promotions at leading universities and research laboratories, or to gain credentials to get hired by the agencies and surrogate organizations that distribute the funding. Others who play the game by rules of politics are likely to fare much better.

Where is responsible journalism, the "fourth branch of government," in all this? All too often its mainstream is very far downstream from real facts. Besides, sensationalism sells much better than scholarship does, and it earns invitations to alarmist briefings high up in the mountains of power whence all waters flow.

Green Envy

"Saving the planet" makes for a great cover story to conceal power and wealth redistribution agendas that have no such laudable purposes. This was witnessed at the 2009 Copenhagen Summit, and is also evident on the US national scene. As Czech president and economist Vaclav Klaus has observed, environmentalism has become a banner name under which governments are given license to seize commanding heights of economies and societies. Another name for this—dare we say it aloud?—is socialism, and manipulated science is its servant.

In the 1970s and early 1980s, Third World countries, by force of numbers, and European socialist green parties, through powers of aggressiveness, seized control of the UN and began calling for a New International Economic Order (NIEO). The NIEO's central goals were unambiguous: namely, to transfer unfair wealth from the industrialized West to their majority; to establish global socialism; and to obtain postcolonial reparations for perceived past misdeeds. That dream lives on in the spirit and actions of the IPCC, the Kyoto Protocol, the Copenhagen Summit, and the hearts and minds of those who have perpetuated the crusade—and will continue to do so.

One such voice is Maurice Strong, then-executive director of the UN's Environment Programme, who expressed an even stronger NIEO view in his opening speech at the UN-sponsored Rio Earth Summit in 1992: "We may get to the point where the only way of saving the world will be for industrial civilization to collapse. Isn't it our responsibility to bring this about?" Mr. Strong coauthored a book titled *Earth Charter* with Mikhail Gorbachev in 1992. The former president of the Soviet Union recognized the importance of using climate alarmism to advance socialistic Marxist objectives, stating in 1996, "The threat of environmental crisis will be the international disaster key to unlock the New World Order." This may have seemed like the last hope for that agenda following the USSR's economic and political collapse in 1991. Yet, even today, Gorbachev continues to call for a kind of *perestroika* or "restructuring" of societies around the world, starting with the US; he argues that the economic crisis since 2007 demonstrates that our economic policy model is failing and must be replaced.

Former US senator Timothy Wirth agreed with Maurice Strong about the urgency of using climate crisis as a means to force social and economic change, even if there was no science to support it. The senator, who had been arranging prayer breakfasts, came to head the National Religious Partnership for the Environment. Later, as undersecretary of state for global issues, he addressed the Rio Earth Summit audience, saying: "We have got to ride the global warming issue. Even if the theory of global warming is wrong, we will be doing the right thing in terms of economic policy and environmental policy."[21]

The call to "stop man-made global warming" has served as a central rallying theme in socialist warfare against US free market capitalism in Europe as well as in Third World countries. While the big guns may appear to be aimed at a CO_2 enemy, the real target is likely to be our economy and world dominance.

The 2000 Lisbon Declaration—supported by a group of "civil society organizations," including EU institutions, the World Bank, and the UN Council of Europe, among other government, private, and corporate entities—asserted that the EU would "leapfrog" the US in productivity and output by 2010, yet by 2005, it was apparent that this forecast was misguided. Rather than surpassing the US in its share of world output, the EU was losing ground at an increasing rate.[22]

The EU's contributions to world GDP have fallen from about 36 percent in 1969 to roughly 27 percent today. While that is slightly higher than the US percentage of the world's $47.9 trillion output, it should be recognized that the EU has about 80 million more people than this country does. In a few years, economic power of both the US and the EU is likely to be eclipsed by that of Asia thanks to booming economic developments in China and India. Yet the US can be expected to remain a world GDP leader for decades to come, provided we avoid self-inflicted carbon penalties and bring runaway government spending and largesse under control.

European green parties with major influences over UN climate-based agendas are really angry at the US for not adopting legally binding Kyoto-type GHG emission restrictions. They also advocate massive wealth transfers from developed countries (primarily the US) to the Third World to combat alleged global warming impacts. Not surprisingly, the so-called Group of 77 developing countries is pushing this idea, insisting that it won't accept tokenism. Secretary of State Hillary Clinton's 2009 Copenhagen promise to raise an annual $100 billion contribution for this purpose signifies that the Obama-Biden administration acknowledges US climate transgressions and intends to make amends. The big question is whether China will continue to lend us the necessary money.

Meanwhile, as the US government proceeds on a colossal borrowing and spending binge, added impacts of cap-and-trade legislation upon economic recovery and growth warrant true alarm. And if this isn't frightening enough, think about new mechanisms that have been put in place to accomplish carbon regulations even without congressional consent.[23]

On the very first day of the 2009 Copenhagen Summit, the EPA claimed authority to regulate carbon emissions by declaring them an "endangerment" to public health. Given the broad and intrusive influence this ruling establishes over every aspect of our economic life, it represents an epic circumvention of constitutionally established legislative responsibilities. If the timing of this announcement was intended to impress less democratic world audiences in Copenhagen, there is little evidence of success. Hugo Chavez didn't appear to notice—and got most of the applause.

Restoring the Republic

The US has recently been witnessing sweeping governance changes that are rapidly shifting power from the private sector and state governments to federal elected and appointed officials, regulatory agencies, and politically favored special interest lobbies. While this trend is not altogether new, its acceleration and outreach are unparalleled at any other period since the end of World War II. Setting aside the nationalization of much of the banking and automotive industries within the period of a single year, along with aggressive efforts to do the same with medical and insurance providers, consider looming prospects for climate-based energy legislation. To help put this into perspective, let's review dossiers of some nonelected people who even have power to end-run constitutional roles of the US Senate and Congress. They are called "czars," and probably for valid reasons.

Global warming energy czar Carol Browner was formally appointed as the Obama administration's director of the White House Office of Energy and Climate Change Policy. The president has outlined these goals in her job description: "to create jobs, achieve energy security, and combat climate change, which requires integration among different agencies; cooperation between federal, state, and local governments; and partnerships with the private sector."[24] These duties involve key aspects of three different cabinet-level departments: the EPA, the Energy Department, and the Interior Department. Ms. Browner has stated that "we face an environmental, a public health, and an economic challenge in global warming unlike anything we have faced so far."[25]

Insiders believe that Ms. Browner probably has more actual power than does either the head of the EPA or the secretary of energy, both Senate-confirmed positions. She also served as a lead negotiator with the automobile industries regarding emission levels, and reportedly told them "to put nothing in writing." Some may argue that her intent was to encourage the spokespeople to speak freely.

Heritage Foundation director B. Kenneth Simon and Matthew Spalding of the foundation's Center for American Studies both believe that Browner's activities appear to "be beyond congressional legislative intent" and seem to "circumvent the authority of the EPA administrator."[26]

Carol Browner formerly ran the EPA, and she also served on the board of John Podesta's Center for American Progress, which he cofounded with Al Gore and George Soros. Podesta also cochaired President Obama's transition team.

The Socialist International, an umbrella organization for many of the world's social-democratic parties, including Britain's Labour Party, listed Ms. Browner as a member with distinction. She was also noted as a leader of its Commission for a Sustainable World Society, which advocates "global governance," believing that wealthy nations must shrink their economies to address global warming. Browner's name and profile were removed from the organization's website in January 2009.

International climate czar (or "Special Envoy for Climate Change") Todd Stern served as former assistant to the president and as staff secretary in the Clinton-Gore administration. Acting as the administration's chief climate negotiator from 1993–1998. He is now a principal adviser on international climate policy issues and strategies.[27] Stern, like Browner, was associated with the Center for American Progress; as a senior fellow there, he focused upon climate change. He has been a strong supporter of the Kyoto Protocol and a US cap-and-trade policy. As a top aide to President Clinton, he helped to negotiate the Kyoto and Buenos Aires climate pacts, both of which were unanimously rejected in principle by the US Congress. Stern places a great deal of blame for global warming on US businesses.

Science and technology czar John Holdren, a point man in the White House for climate change, is revealed in hacked CRU e-mall correspondence as a staunch defender of debunked research by Michael "Hockey Stick" Mann. At that time, Holdren was working at the Woods Hole Research Center in Massachusetts, an independent environmental policy organization—not to be confused with the prestigious Woods Hole Oceanographic Institute. In a letter sent on November 23, 2009, Holdren defended his earlier e-mail correspondence: "I'm happy to stand by my contributions to this exchange. I think anyone who reads about what I wrote in its entirety will find it a serious and balanced treatment of the questions of 'burden of proof' in situations where science germane to public policy is in dispute."[28]

In the book *Ecoscience: Population, Resources, Environment,* which he coauthored with *Population Bomb* author Paul Ehrlich, Holdren wrote that families "contribute to general social deterioration by overproducing children" and "can be required by law to exercise reproductive responsibility." Page 943 of the book suggests the creation of a "Planetary Regime to act as an international superagency for population, resources, and environment." The coauthors envisioned that "such a Planetary Regime could control the development, administration, conservation, and distribution of *all* natural resources, renewable and nonrenewable, at least insofar as international implications exist" (emphasis in original). That regime "might be given responsibility for determining the optimum population for the world and for each region and for arbitrating [the] various countries' shares within regional limits." Possible methods of population control the authors discussed are "sterilizing women after their second or third child" and adding "a sterilant to drinking water or staple foods."[29]

EPA administrator Lisa Jackson isn't actually a czar, but she looks like a good candidate. Her agency ignored and quashed internal research that contradicted the scientific validity of a CO_2 endangerment finding. Ms. Jackson then announced in December 2009 that an EPA "tailoring rule" would follow that would set a GHG emissions threshold of 25,000 tons per year for regulators under the Clean Air Act. As a result, any new construction or modifications that would affect GHG emissions would require an application for permits that include "best available technology." The tailoring rule GHG threshold would affect between 1 million and 4 million construction facilities across the country. "This is certainly not an ending," Ms. Jackson said. "We will continue to work under the Clean Air Act."[30]

Secretary of Energy Steven Chu doesn't like to consider all energy options . . .

not even the one that provides half of our current US electricity. He has repeatedly said, "Coal is my worst nightmare." Why does he dislike coal? Fly ash! He claims that fly ash from coal burning is a hundred times more radioactive than radiation emitted by nuclear plants, which really amounts to one hundred times nothing. Plus, most fly ash from coal-fired plants is readily recovered and recycled as a primary ingredient in concrete, stucco, and other products to greatly increase their strength. Mr. Chu also appears to have nighttime hallucinations about global warming, having warned, "Climate change . . . will cause enormous resource wars, over water, arable land, and massive population displacements. We're talking about . . . hundreds of millions to billions of people being flooded out, permanently."[31]

Is climate change now a big Department of Labor consideration? And if so, why? The first answer is probably yes. The second appears to come straight out of the IPCC/Marx/Kyoto lesson plan. Hilda Solis, the Obama-Biden administration's labor secretary, stated her conviction that "I am fighting for environmental justice."[32]

Nancy Sutley, chairwoman of the President's Council on Environmental Quality, explained during her Senate confirmation hearing that no agency would be left out of the choir: "[Climate change] is an issue that will affect the entire federal government; almost no agency is untouched by climate change."[33]

We can continue to debate human impacts upon global temperatures, but there is one anthropogenic influence that we cannot escape: The dangerous political climate we are witnessing today is entirely one of our making, and it urgently needs to change.

Healthy Skepticism

Whom can we trust? We rely upon information from respected government, scientific, and media sources that we assume to be authoritative and objective. It is disconcerting when we discover that they have deceived us about important matters. Misrepresentation regarding the existence and causes of, and the urgent interventions against, a climate crisis rank among the greatest deceptions of all.

Here are some real facts that we can be confident about:

1. There is no scientific evidence that any climate crisis exists other than the hardships periodically imposed upon affected regions as a result of naturally occurring changes. The next, now overdue Ice Age will present a big

crisis, but no one can predict when that will happen. Enjoy these warm times of ecological and human bounty.

2. Over the past several glacial and interglacial climate fluctuations, atmospheric CO_2 concentrations have generally increased after, not before, temperatures have risen. This is because warming oceans release CO_2, and colder oceans absorb it. There doesn't appear to be much, if any, correlation between CO_2 contributions from human activities and temperature fluctuations. Yup, temperatures have fallen many times when CO_2 levels have continued to rise, just as they are now.

3. Climate models cannot predict climate change events or consequences, although the scary warnings we constantly hear are based upon them. Many climate forcing mechanisms remain poorly understood, and all interact in interdependent and complex ways. Most scientists who create and apply climate models know this and will freely admit it. Claims by IPCC officials that confidence in such models is increasing are misleading. Accurate forecasting over years, much less decadal or multidecadal periods, has never been demonstrated.

4. Most of the "greenhouse effect" predicted in climate models suggests that warming should be greatest at mid-range to high atmospheric elevations in the tropics, yet balloon and satellite observations show cooling there. Water vapor is by far a more important GHG than is CO_2, yet even together, their climate contributions are likely to be much smaller than current models suggest.

5. More scientific attention is now being directed to the effects of solar activity upon climate. A low level of activity appears to match the prolonged period of cooling that occurred during the Little Ice Age, while an active Sun in the 1930s and again near the end of the last century corresponds with observed warming. The current solar cycle is the longest low-activity event witnessed in more than a century. This suggests that the cooling observed since about 1998 may continue for some time.

6. Multidecadal cycles in the ocean correlate quite closely with solar cycles and global temperatures. The Pacific Ocean began to cool in the late 1990s, and the Atlantic began to cool from its peak in 2004. Warmer oceans from the 1930s to the 1950s, and again from the 1980s to the early 2000s, caused diminished summer Arctic ice extent. Antarctic ice has actually

been increasing at a record pace within the span of satellite monitoring history. Although Arctic ice has been thinning at a rate of about 3 percent per decade, Antarctic ice, which is twenty times more expansive, has been growing at 1 percent per decade. So, while the 2007 summer Arctic ice melt was the biggest on record, the 2008 Antarctic ice melt was the smallest.[34] Melting ocean ice doesn't cause sea levels to rise anymore than do melting ice cubes in a drink cause that level to rise in a glass. (Of course, when you take a sip, it changes everything, so if you try this experiment, try not to cheat.)

You, the Jury

The corruption of science exposed in the CRU e-mails is finally putting man-made warming alarmism on trial in the "court of public scrutiny." Imagine that one after another the crisis claimants are called to testify. You, a member of the jury, must determine if their legitimacy warrants trust.

First on the stand is Al Gore. He presents a lengthy PowerPoint presentation, complete with melting ice caps, drowning polar bears, rising sea levels, marauding hurricanes, and all. He ends with an impassioned pitch for cap-and-trade legislation as humankind's best chance of salvation from sins we have wrought upon our planet.

Perhaps on cross-examination we discover that most of those "inconvenient facts" don't hold up. We can forgive him. After all, scientists disagree on many points. Let's further acknowledge that it is really okay that he has accumulated a large fortune promoting green products he has financial interests in and that he plans to make a bundle more marketing carbon offsets. It can be argued that these actions only demonstrate true conviction in his cause. Let's forget that the annual utility budget for his twenty-room Nashville home and pool house would pay for a new Toyota Prius. Let's give him some credit for bravery in purchasing a new $8.875 million ocean-view home in Montecito, California—from which he can keep watch to warn us of a dangerously rising sea level and such. And we might cut him some slack for apparently confusing the Earth with the Sun in asserting that the temperature of our planet's core is "several million degrees." Even Nobel laureates can't be expected to be right all the time. But maybe his science is not entirely settled after all.

Next to testify is Dr. James Hansen, the father of global warming hysteria and

Mr. Gore's science adviser. He continues to be celebrated in mainstream media as a top climate expert. Never mind that his doomsday predictions over the past 3 decades have never materialized, that he is linked to conspiratorial CRU e-mail correspondence, and that his claim of record-high 2008 temperatures was proven to be hot air. In fairness, his warning that world temperatures are balancing at a "tipping point" is proving correct, but not because of dangerous CO_2. Once again, temperatures have been tipping downward since 1998, while atmospheric CO_2 concentrations have risen.

In this scenario, we might assume that testimony offered by key participants in the CRU e-mail climate science debauchery follows. As potential subjects of legal indictments, perhaps some may have been advised by their attorneys to remain silent. Likewise, we might assume that the IPCC, which used CRU data, responds only with a brief written statement. Essentially, it reaffirms its conclusion that global warming presents a continuing threat; that the IPCC is even more confident in its predictive climate models; that we, the industrialized nations, are responsible for a looming crisis; and that $100 billion in reparations to other, less developed countries for our excesses won't be nearly enough.[35]

Then, perhaps, we might hear testimony from a few of the six hundred fifty scientists who expressed "contrary" views in a 2008 US Senate minority report prepared by Senator Inhofe.[36] For example:

- Ivar Giaever, Nobel Prize winner for physics: "I am a skeptic. Global warming has become a new religion."
- UN IPCC Japanese scientist Kiminori Itoh, award-winning environmental physical chemist: "[Warming fears are the] worst scientific scandal in history . . . When people come to know what the truth is, they will feel deceived by science and scientists."
- Indian geologist Arun Ahluwalia, board member of the UN-supported International Year of Planet Earth: "The IPCC has actually become a closed circuit; it doesn't have open minds . . . I am really amazed that the Nobel Peace Prize has been given on scientifically incorrect conclusions by people who are not geologists."
- Finnish scientist, chemical engineer, and former Greenpeace member Jarl Ahlbeck: "So far, real measurements give no ground for concern about a catastrophic future warming."
- Norwegian Space Center senior adviser solar physicist Pål Brekke: "Anyone

who claims that the debate is over and the conclusions are firm has a fundamentally unscientific approach."

- Institute of Geophysics, National Autonomous University of Mexico researcher Victor Manuel Velasco Herrera: "The models and forecasts of the UN IPCC are incorrect because they . . . are based [only] on mathematical models and presented results at scenarios that do not include, for example, solar activity."

- New Zealand professor Geoffrey Duffy, Department of Chemical and Materials Engineering, University of Auckland: "Even doubling or tripling the amount of carbon dioxide will virtually have little impact, as water vapor and water condensed on particles as clouds dominate the worldwide scene and always will."

- Russian geographer and Antarctic ice-core researcher Andrei Kapitsa: "The Kyoto theorists have put the cart before the horse. It is global warming that triggers higher levels of carbon dioxide in the atmosphere, not the other way around . . . A large number of critical documents submitted to the 1995 UN conference in Madrid vanished without a trace. As a result, the discussion was one-sided and heavily biased, and the UN declared global warming to be a scientific fact."

- Stanley Goldberg, US government atmospheric scientist at the Hurricane Research Division of NOAA: "It is a blatant lie to put forth in the media that makes it seem there is only a fringe of scientists who don't buy into anthropogenic global warming."

- James Peden, atmospheric physicist formerly with the Space Research and Coordination Center in Pittsburgh: "Many [scientists] are now searching for a way to break out (from promoting warming fears), without having their professional careers ruined."

- Apollo 17 astronaut/geologist Jack Schmitt, formerly with the Norwegian Geological Survey and USGS: "The 'global warming scare' is being used as a political tool to increase government control over American lives, incomes, and decision making. It has no place in society's activities."[37]

In conclusion, we might recall remarks offered by Czech president Vaclav Klaus during a speech at the Ambrosetti Forum, Villa d'Este, Italy, in 2007:

The threat I have in mind is the irrationality with which the world has accepted the climate change (or global warming) as a real danger to the future of mankind, and the irrationality of suggested and already implemented measures because they will fatally endanger our freedom and prosperity, the two goals we consider—I do believe—our priorities.

We have to face many prejudices and misunderstandings in this respect. The climate change debate is basically not about science; it is about ideology. It is not about global temperature; it is about the concept of human society. It is not about nature or scientific ecology; it is about environmentalism, about one—recently born—dirigistic and collective ideology, which goes against freedom and free markets. I spent most of my life in a communist society, which makes me particularly sensitive to the dangers, traps, and pitfalls connected with it.[38]

And what are the consequences of this subterfuge? They are costly. Consider that billions of dollars are spent annually on climate science, only to have much of the most important information distorted for ideological and political purposes. American industries, jobs, and revenues may be forced to relocate overseas because of irrelevant CO_2 emission regulations that other countries freely ignore. Environmentalism predicated on false premises blocks drilling in US waters, while unfriendly foreign coalitions exploit these oil reserves. Coal plants that provide half of all US electricity are restricted and penalized, while uncompetitive high-cost and low-potential alternatives receive mandates and subsidies. Schemes are justified to price and trade "carbon sin indulgences" along with a regulatory EPA power grab. Then there are also those therapeutic counseling expenses for treatment of pandemic carbon footprint guilt sufferers.

Corrupt science that supports these travesties has many complicit agents. It is perpetrated by sponsors who fail to provide competent oversight; by ideologically, politically, and financially driven authorities who twist and exploit conclusions; and by lockstep, headline-hungry media organizations that emphasize sensationalism over substance. And we can't forget those among us who, through complacency and denial in the face of obvious deception, willingly forfeit demands for accountability. When we abrogate that responsibility, perhaps we become culpable too.

Ladies and gentlemen of the jury, the prosecution rests its case.

Chapter 12
EXERCISING US EXCEPTIONALISM

LARRY BELL

Bearing painful witness to the arrogance of
unwarranted humility on America's behalf.

N ow that we understand the politics and people behind global
warming, what actions can we take to mitigate the potentially disastrous
consequences of such misguided pseudoscience?

First of all, we have to acknowledge the reality of the situation. Anyone who has had an opportunity to visit other countries around the world should recognize America's exceptional environmental, social, and economic achievements. Our environment—compared with the environments of other developed nations, and starkly contrasted with those of communist countries—is remarkable, clean, and improving. Real progress is occurring in the development of highly efficient energy production and utilization, along with power plant emission reductions as a by-product. Based upon the amount of energy used to produce a dollar value in output, the US voluntarily reduced energy intensity by 20 percent over the period between 1992 and 2004, as compared to only 11.5 percent in the EU under a mandatory approach. This has also enabled economic growth, which averaged more than 3 percent annually between 1992 and 2005, compared with about 1 percent in the EU prior to the recent global recession.

Despite our environmental progress, angry views toward the US and other developed countries expressed by detractors in less free and fortunate parts of the world have gained a larger world stage with the advent of the UN's climate-change theater. Eco-guilt associated with demonization of CO_2 emissions has been added to other sins of capitalism, including unfair wealth, consumption, economic influence, and military power. Speaking to like-minded foreign audiences, our own president has apologized for America's imperfections, arrogance, international mistakes, lack of sustained engagement with neighbors, and dark periods of history. And even though Nicaraguan president Daniel Ortega, Venezuelan president Hugo Chavez, and other unfriendly leaders have expressed strong agreement, they still don't like him or us any better for offering these confessions. Apparently, some of those present during the 2009 Copenhagen Summit meetings, where riots broke out, don't either.

Despite expanding world economies embracing globalism through open market capitalism, many would like to turn their international clocks back to what they regard to be the better "good old days." Thomas Friedman, in his book *The World Is Flat*, attributes much of this sentiment to the strongly anti-American and anti-globalization movement that emerged at the 1999 World Trade Organization conference in Seattle. What began as a primarily Western-driven phenomenon has subsequently gained influence throughout the world, and the movement now represents a convergence of several ideological groups.

One motivation is attributed to upper-middle-class American liberal guilt in reaction to the incredible wealth and power the US amassed following the fall of the Berlin Wall and the rise of the dot-com balloon. Old left socialists, anarchists, and Trotskyites, in their alliances with protectionist trade unions, advance another motivation. Particularly strong anti-American sentiments arose in Europe and the Islamic world over disparities between American economic, cultural, military, and political power versus those in other countries after the implosion of the Soviet empire. Groups concerned with governance influence, ranging from environmentalists to trade activists to NGOs, became part of populist antiglobalization. Others, who constituted a more amorphous group, were more generally concerned about the speed at which the "old world" was disappearing and becoming globalized.

Many of the same people who are behind the global warming hysteria are also strongly opposed to economic globalization. They perceive globalization as a tool by which wealthy nations exploit poor nations in the same way they exploit the environment. They view the American capitalist free market engine as an evil machine that drives globalism, and the economic prosperity it yields as a sin against "social justice."

Let's briefly review those claims on the basis of the real social justice that such detractors purport to care so much about.

According to the World Bank, about 375 million people in China lived in extreme poverty (on less than an equivalent of $1/day) in 1990. The number of impoverished Chinese dropped to 212 million by 2001. If the current trend holds, only about 16 million Chinese will live on less that $1/day by 2015.

In Southeastern Asia—primarily India, Pakistan, and Bangladesh—the number of people living on less than $1/day dropped from 462 million in 1990 to roughly 431 million by 2001, and that number is projected to be 216 million by 2015.

Now, compare those numbers with those in sub-Saharan Africa, which has been slow to become part of globalized markets. There, about 227 million people lived on less than $1/day in 1990. By 2001, there were 313 million people living in poverty, and the World Bank expects the number will grow to 340 million by 2015.

Friedman argues that the world's poor don't resent those who are rich nearly as much as left-wing parties in the developed world imagine. Rather, what they really resent is not having a pathway to get richer and cross the line into the world's middle-class opportunities.

As Deng Xiaoping declared when he released the Chinese economy from its communist shackles and opened it to a free market system, "To get rich is glorious."

He justified those actions with one sentence: "Black cat, white cat, all that matters is that it catches mice." India and Russia have followed the same road since the early 1990s, and together with China, they have become competitive economic and technology forces.[1]

Ironically, Americans are now having to combat attacks from within the very same economic system that offers hope and progress to other countries now following our successful model. If a greater example of true social justice exists elsewhere, where is that place? Those who believe they know might do well to expand their travel experiences abroad.

America's Abundant Opportunities: Capitalizing on Capitalism

Our nation remains a land of unique and enviable opportunity, the home of the American Dream. Our history—and those participants who provided the foundational visions, courageous sacrifices, and tools of science and industry that created this nation—warrants no apology. We have learned from past mistakes and are better for having recognized them and applying those valuable lessons. We are also blessed with vast and diverse resources, natural and human, and we share them generously as good and concerned global citizens. Our position as leading world power is regarded as both a privilege and an often-thankless obligation.

Yes, we care about our environment, and we acknowledge the need for legislative and regulatory incentives and controls to protect it. Yet this will not be accomplished by undermining the economic system that provides the financial, technical, and social resources needed to make improvements. Nor are these goals served by irresponsible climate crisis fearmongering and exaggerated alternative energy capacity projections, which, when exposed, only destroy confidence in the honest science and reporting that are essential as a basis for sound decisions.

And that fearmongering and fraudulent reporting is definitely being revealed: through exposure of damning words and writings of false prophets and profiteers; through direct observable testimony presented by Mother Nature; and through conscientious efforts of some who have dared to challenge dogma served up by high priests of gloom-and-doom orthodoxy. These dedicated and valiant people include Senator Inhofe, Stephen McIntyre, Ross McKitrick, Richard Lindzen, Fred Singer, Roy Spencer, Anthony Watts, and many others previously discussed in this book, plus the hundreds more who aren't.

Rediscovering America

We have historically taken pride in "American know-how," an ability to recognize marketable opportunities in problems, unlimited capacities for invention, and willingness to proactively accept investment risks in pursuit of uncertain rewards. We are a culture of creativity that is recognized, envied, and resented around the world, as exemplified by our music, fashions, movies, sciences, and technologies. We have advanced medicine, expanded agricultural and industrial productivity, and opened new frontiers beyond our planet for peaceful purposes.

America is a nation without ethnic, racial, gender, or class boundaries. Excellent educational opportunities are accessible to all who truly seek them. These resources include public and private institutions at all levels, technical specialization programs, community colleges, and an enormous number and variety of distinguished universities for advanced studies that attract international scholars.

So far, that's the good news. But there are some more sobering aspects regarding America's education and innovation circumstances as well. Many of the technical programs in top-ranked US universities are now dominated by a majority of students from Asia and India, who are often supported by their own nation's scholarships. These are the advanced math, science, and engineering fields that tend to drive innovation in today's technologically competitive world. Foreign attendees, as a general rule, also tend to enter our institutions with stronger math and science backgrounds, achieve higher class rankings, and return to their home countries enriched by their US experiences.[2]

Asians, in particular, appear to be setting the international pace for advanced science and math at all educational levels. Some indication of this is revealed by results of the 2003 international Trends in International Mathematics and Science Study involving half a million fourth- and eighth-grade students from forty-one countries, including the US. The assessment concluded that 44 percent of all eighth-graders in Singapore scored at the most advanced level in math, as did 38 percent from Taiwan. At an IntelScience Fair in 2004, Chinese students won thirty-four awards, more than any other Asian country, including three top global awards.[3]

In China, strong math and science backgrounds are prerequisites for admittance to the best universities or to be hired by foreign corporations operating there. The Microsoft research center in Beijing is one of the most sought-after work-places there, and the competition is fierce. There is a popular saying, "If you are one in a million, there are 1,300 people just like you."[4]

Do leaders of our national government subscribe to this philosophy? Here is what John Holdren, director of the White House Office of Science and Technology Policy, told students attending a meeting on April 10, 2010, sponsored by the American Association for the Advancement of Science: "We can't expect to be number one in everything indefinitely." Apparently, that goal would be overreaching, and it is no longer encouraged in our young people. Maybe social justice promoted by Marx and the UN embodies a need for globally distributed scientific and technological equality as well.

Whereas most Chinese policy makers have engineering and science backgrounds, the majority of ours are lawyers. Perhaps this raises a question regarding which nation will be best prepared for future leadership: one that innovates or one that regulates? If China is now embracing principles that led us to where we are today, perhaps we might turn our attention to relearning from our past . . . and from the Chinese. We need to get educated.

Free Market Entrepreneurship

And what about "rugged American individualism," the spirit where anything you can dream is possible, Horatio Alger rags-to-riches stories, Dale Carnegie confidence, and all that? Is that kind of thinking still legal? Will it unfairly tilt the playing field to favor those who lust for success over those who are less willing to compete? Will it create income disparities and exploit labor markets? Those who imagined that such arguments were settled with the collapse of the Soviet Union and the embrace of capitalism by China and Russia would be wrong. It seems that many people who enjoy the products and prosperity created by entrepreneurship—the jobs it creates, and the services it provides—aren't comfortable with the ambitions of those who practice it. Instead, they are more inclined to place faith in government regulatory mechanisms rather than market forces to provide economic equilibrium, progress, and social justice.

Government interventions into free market mechanisms can have unfortunate consequences, as evidenced by US energy policies where Congress is now picking the winners and losers. Examples are the ethanol debacle promoted under an "energy security" banner; price controls that led to the gasoline crisis of 1974; CO_2

emission restrictions that are blocking development of fossil-fueled power plants; mandated alternative fuel purchases that drive up consumer costs; and restrictions on offshore drilling that afford competitive advantages for foreign-owned companies operating in our Gulf of Mexico neighborhood. Michael Economides speaks of some penalties in his book *The Color of Oil*: "Regulations, unless imposed as part of a well-thought-out, long-term national policy, stifle rugged individualists and capitalists. Worse even in developed nations, regulations can make local industry comfortable with, and then dependent on, government-mandated market reforms. This, of course, is tremendously destructive because it thwarts competition and entrepreneurialism, two of the most important elements of economic success."[5]

Real or imagined crises can provoke knee-jerk, stopgap government regulatory responses that are painfully costly and ineffective. Global climate change/CO_2 alarmism is being used to block development and use of fossil resources through a variety of legal and political actions, including the Endangered Species Act listing of polar bears and the Supreme Court characterization of CO_2 as a pollutant. The latter decision now enables the EPA to regulate CO_2 emissions under the Clean Air Act.

The premises underlying virtually all this are the unproven IPCC climate model apocalyptic scenarios and political agenda–tweaked summaries that have never developed quantifiable links or consequences, either human or natural, between CO_2 and global warming. Even if this were not the case, we can learn much from (1) failed EU attempts to achieve Kyoto Protocol emission reduction targets, (2) EU nations' inabilities to meet escalating energy needs through renewables, and (3) resulting shifts among EU members toward fossils and nuclear energy. Why repeat their earlier mistakes?

Globalization versus Global Governance

It is time to differentiate between energy security and energy independence as well as between international partnering and subordination to international authority. National pride is no cause for shame, and strength, both economic and military, needs no apology. Many have worked successfully and sacrificed greatly to endow America with these gifts. It is our responsibility to preserve them, apply them, and pass them along to the generations that follow. Quite understandably, some other nations have the same idea, and we must respect that fact.

America will continue to depend upon oil imports for the foreseeable future.

We are not alone in this regard, nor do we have the purchasing leverage we once enjoyed. The largest US oil company, ExxonMobil, controls only about 1 percent of global oil reserves, putting it far behind many large nationally owned companies such as Saudi Aramco, NIOC (Iran), Pemex (Mexico), PDVSA (Venezuela), and CNPC (China). As world demands increase, so do the power and influence of Arab and Islamic states (i.e. Saudi Arabia, Dubai, and Iran), along with the economic purchasing power of China, India, and other developing countries.[6]

Global oil competition has become the dominant forcing factor driving world trade and international military alignments. Accordingly, we must realize that national security and energy security are codependent priorities. Energy security is essential if the US is to maintain the economic strength necessary to compete in all world trade markets, along with the military strength to protect our national and allied interests from aggressors. In this regard, our energy industries are the first and arguably most vital line of defense.

Just like other nations, we must diversify our access to energy sources of all types. One aspect of this pertains to geographical sourcing, where we work to reduce dependence upon oil from the Middle East, Venezuela, and other volatile parts of the world. Doing so, however, does not preclude all possible efforts, including diplomacy, economic support, and antiterrorist actions, to enhance stability in those regions. Our security is linked to theirs.

We can participate in helping other nations develop energy resources as trading partners, just as other countries are doing. Examples are investment and assistance in oil and gas drilling and operations (e.g., China); refinery development and services (e.g., India); and advances in nuclear electric technologies (e.g., France, South Africa, and Japan). A key opportunity is to provide technologies and assistance in reprocessing spent nuclear wastes into fuels that cannot therefore be used against other nations for weapons.

The US can reduce dependence upon foreign oil and demands upon our croplands by importing ethanol from Brazil. Produced from sugar cane, it is a much more energy-efficient alcohol source than is corn. This will once again encourage American farmers to diversify crop production, relieve consumer food costs, and accommodate lucrative and humanitarian export advantages.

Yes, America can and should continue to develop and expand use of renewable wind, solar, and biotech capacities, along with hydropower, geothermal, and hydrogen energy to the extent this makes sense. We should not be misled, however, to imagine that these sources will promise any degree of energy security or independence, however greatly we might wish that to be the case. Much greater potential lies in developing improved methods to optimize use of our large coal and shale reserves through clean coal technologies and transportation-fuel derivatives. These will become even more attractive as foreign oil and gas demands continue to add market pressures, which will also make support for expanded domestic drilling a survival necessity for political aspirants.

Rational Environmentalism

All responsible people care about human impacts of energy practices and other activities upon the natural environment. Terrible examples include the inexcusable Chernobyl nuclear reactor failure, the massive pipeline leaks in Russia that spilled 10 percent or more of the oil en route, and horrendous air pollution conditions in China. It is also responsible to recognize a need to preserve energy resources for future generations through conservation efficiencies. Who can argue with that?

Just as everything humans have done in the name of industrial progress hasn't been kind to the environment, it shouldn't be assumed that everything is bad either. Yet the modern-day environmental activist movement tends not to see it that way. If there is a perceived climate change, then it must be our fault, and the consequences must be dire. Since industry creates pollution, then all emissions, including CO_2, must be pollutants. If glaciers appear to be melting more rapidly than they were a few decades before, then we must be responsible, and the condition must be irreversible.

Maybe it's time to apply some constructive hindsight. Not so many decades ago, the glaciers advanced, and times were not really good at all. And while industrialization has changed our planet, the technologies and progress that accompanied it have not been entirely negative. As civilizations have evolved, so have sanitary conditions. Life expectancies have more than doubled since the times when raw sewage was heaped upon the streets of grand Greek and Roman empires and plagues and famines devastated rural populations.

So much for the romantic visions of a peaceful, nirvana-like agrarian life in balance with nature. There are big differences between environmental stewardship ideals, which most of us subscribe to, and the ideologically moralistic, antidevelopment, obstructionist activism that exemplifies much of today's environmental zealotry. Premised on pseudoscientific rationale, publicized through expensive ad campaigns and mainstream media messages, and lawyered up for battle, today's green activist movement has asserted dangerous influences over our energy-driven social, economic, and security prospects.

What can we do to preserve and advance the energy priorities we care about? It's not going to be easy, but there is some hope.

To begin with, we can seek and demand objective and informed news sources so that we know the facts and keep abreast of what is going on around us. The Internet—blog sites and all—is a tremendous resource for data and opinions that cover all sides of events and issues. It's remarkable what the mainstream media doesn't tell us, and equally amazing how often they get the facts wrong in what they selectively present.

We can exert influences over who represents our interests in the arena of politics, and we can tell them what we care about. We can support those we trust through campaign participation, funding contributions, and votes. And we can hold them accountable to earn that continued trust.

We can prepare our children for the future through education and example. We can encourage them to develop survival knowledge in math and sciences and to appreciate the importance of US and world history as well. We can become involved with their schools and take interest in their classroom and homework activities to find out what they are learning. Some of that may prove to be alarmingly misguided.

Responsible Resourcefulness

Americans will experience increasing market pricing pressures to practice more effective energy conservation. In this regard, we must work to do more with less, not simply try to do less using less, applying retrogressive, utopian, ideological fantasies. If we can't drill or dig our way out of fossil-fuel energy dependence, imagining that we can starve our way out doesn't make any sense either. Fossil-fuel energy currently drives our economy and progress. It finances the development of technologies and applications that are more efficient and environmentally friendly. It provides jobs—yes, for coal miners and oil field workers, but also for environmentalists who are supported by energy industry–dependent revenues.

Conservation is not just a matter of using less to do more; it also involves using less of what is most limited so that it can be preserved for uses that are more important. Why, for instance, should we use so much natural gas for electricity if that power can be generated by nuclear plants that are even cleaner? That natural gas can be used for transportation fuel to reduce drains on petroleum reserves and imports.

How can we characterize wind power as "free energy" if its use consumes lots of natural gas as a spinning reserve? And why would we want to use natural gas as a source for hydrogen when the direct use of that gas is so much more efficient and safe? If we switch to electric plug-in cars, where will that energy needed to recharge the batteries come from? How does biofuel reduce fossil-fuel demands if it requires nearly an equal amount to grow and process the plants?

It's time to look beyond green slogans and pursue real solutions. The marketplace, not politics, will ultimately determine which technologies will succeed. Allowing this to happen may be one of the biggest energy security challenges of all.

Transformational Trends

Can America do better? Yes, we can, and we are doing better. A major report released in May 2008 by the American Council for an Energy-Efficient Economy (ACEEE) observes that US energy consumption, as measured per dollar of GDP, has been slashed by half since 1970.[7] The report, prepared with support from the Civil Society Institute, the Kendall Foundation, and the North American Insulation Manufacturers Association, projected that use of cost-effective technologies can reduce US energy consumption by an additional 25 to 30 percent or more over the next 20 to 25 years.

The ACEEE report cites strong evidence of progress in a variety of energy conservation arenas. Annual investments in energy efficiency technologies currently support 1.6 million US jobs, and the $300 billion invested in 2004 was three times the amount spent on the traditional energy infrastructure. The resulting energy saved that year was roughly equivalent to operations of forty midsize coal-fired or nuclear plants. Since 1970, energy efficiency improvements have met about three-fourths of new energy-related service demands. The annual energy efficiency technology market is projected to grow by more than $400 billion by 2030, with investments over that period approaching $700 trillion.[8]

Can we interest you in a bargain price new or used SUV? Either one should be pretty easy to find. Consumers were gradually edging away from big gas-guzzlers as gasoline prices were rising over the past couple of years, but when pump pain reached $4 per gallon, many began to run. According to the *Kelley Blue Book*, the resale value of a 3-year-old Cadillac Escalade SUV plummeted 24 percent in 2008, to $24,500, about twice the rate of decline two years earlier. During that time a 3-year-old Honda Civic lost only 8 percent of its value.[9]

America is becoming energy-conservation conscious because there is no other choice. Many of the adjustments we can make to dramatically reduce fuel and power use will be relatively inexpensive and painless relative to the much-larger burdens of not doing so. We can purchase smaller and more fuel-efficient cars without any real sacrifice of convenience or mobility. We can modify our driving habits and opt for public transportation in many instances, particularly as services improve—and they most certainly will. We can downsize our homes, plan new ones that apply natural conservation principles, and upgrade windows and insulation to control heat transfer. We can reduce energy consumption for pool heating through simple devices, and the simplest of all is by not heating them. We can use solar water and space heating, and geothermal heating and cooling in locales where that possibility is available. We can install power-efficient illumination and other devices, adjust thermostats, and turn off air conditioners and lights when we don't need them. We can recycle aluminum and other reusable materials, and we can consume a lot less water, too. These things are already beginning to happen, but some transitions—building infrastructure redesigns and retrofits, automobile replacements, and upgraded public transportation services, for instance—will take some time, and will never entirely alleviate sustained energy demands.

None of these adaptations need impose significant hardships or seriously compromise satisfying lifestyles. And as they increasingly become common practice, even small changes will make big differences on a national scale. Imagine the significance of reducing transportation fuel use by 50 percent and potentially doing the same through residential energy economies. No, that won't happen overnight. But the process is already beginning.

Demographic pressures, technology developments and energy challenges will profoundly transform many aspects of future American life. Failure to prepare for those changes will have unacceptable consequences. Fuel and power shortages resulting in higher costs will accelerate relocations of households and businesses to warmer locales, particularly those with good access to energy sources. The result will be to leave poorer and older residents behind. These shortfalls will amplify competition among important user sectors and groups, including military, manufacturing, agriculture, and transportation. International relationships and commerce will be impacted in major ways, such as shifts in production and trade, business travel and tourism, and geopolitical tensions and alignments. The circumstances we face are daunting.[10]

The US population more than tripled during the 20th century to reach 300 million in 2006, up from 200 million 39 years earlier; it is expected to grow to more than 390 million by 2050. Although this growth rate is nearly six times lower than that of many less developed countries, consumption of energy, food, and natural resources continues to expand, and the amount of land available for agricultural production continues to decrease. While population growth due to birth rates is relatively slow, people are tending to live longer, adding to costs for medical services that compete for energy and food budgets. About 40 percent of our country's growth is from immigration—both legal and illegal—contributing more than 1 million persons of all ages annually.

A large number of the baby boomers who are now entering retirement are downsizing from detached single-family dwellings to much smaller apartments, condominiums, and patio homes. In 2006, this generation of more than 50 million began turning sixty at the rate of one every eight seconds. Condominiums are becoming very popular in suburban as well as metropolitan settings for a variety of reasons, both for empty nesters and for younger purchasers. One reason is the recent and severe downturn in the economy and job market. Such moves also avoid costs and responsibilities associated with building and lawn maintenance, and they provide "lock-and-go" security convenience that frees residents to travel. Newer units, whether converted from existing structures or built from the ground up, tend to feature quality construction with improved weatherproofing and insulation.[11]

Across America, passenger and freight trains are gaining appeal. June 2008 witnessed 2.5 million Amtrak riders, a record for any month and up 12 percent from the previous year.[12] Throughout the US, the number of commuters who abandoned cars for trains increased by about 15 percent in some major cities during 2007 as gasoline prices soared above $4 per gallon.

Many local transit systems are rushing to add train cars and tracks to accommodate escalating demands. A new rail tunnel is planned to pass under the Hudson River from New Jersey to lower Manhattan, and an entirely new line in New Jersey will connect Newark to coastal suburbs to the south and east. The Washington, DC, Metro is considering extended service from Georgetown across the Potomac River to Rosslyn, Virginia, and on to Dulles Airport. Salt Lake City is looking to add 70 miles of new rail to its commuter suburbs. Houston proposes to quadruple its existing new 8-mile rail network over the next few years, and Dallas plans to double its 35-mile local system. Seattle proposes to add 40 miles of new track beyond the 16 miles now under construction, and new cars are being added to Southern California lines, which occasionally operate at standing-room-only capacities.

Sky-high jet fuel costs will increasingly discourage discretionary airline travel due to higher ticket prices and service cutbacks. Airlines are already reducing numbers of flights and eliminating less profitable destinations, leaving many cities without regular links. These conditions are likely to influence more and more Americans to vacation within the contiguous forty-eight states rather than abroad, and they will promote a greater market for passenger train services in general.

Trains offer many inherent advantages. They are energy efficient when they attract high ridership rates. And unlike cars, they are unencumbered by congested freeways, delays, stress, and parking problems. They also allow passengers to avoid long walks and waits in crowded airline terminals, flight delays and cancellations due to weather, and uncertain arrival times.

America must develop a modern, expansive, and seamless passenger rail infrastructure with nationwide high-speed services. Other countries are doing the same. France is expanding its high-speed TGV network, and Spain and Italy are creating new ones. Germany plans to sell 24.9 percent of Deutsche Bahn, a government-owned railway operator, in a public offering, with two-thirds of the proceeds earmarked for track expansion and other upgrades. Russia intends to add more than 5,000 miles of track by 2015, including a new Trans-Siberian service.

China has completed a record-breaking high-altitude rail link between Qinghai and Tibet, with a section that runs at 16,500 feet above sea level and thus requires pressurized cars. Beijing plans to invest $160 billion over the next 3 years to add 10,000 miles of new track to an existing 56,000-mile network. About half of the expansion will be dedicated to rapid trains that will operate at speeds of up to 200 miles per hour.

America's rail freight industry has been doing very well since legislation was passed nearly 30 years ago allowing companies the freedom to set rates competitively and sell off money-losing lines. This legislation prompted mergers that have improved operating efficiencies and implementation of such new technologies as computer-controlled loading at freight yards that have significantly lowered costs.

One of the most important fuel economy breakthroughs and trends may prove to be outside the energy production, building construction, and transportation sectors, which get most of the attention. The recent development and exploding popularity of personal computers and Internet-based telecommunications can be expected to impact future US commuting and long-range transportation habits in important ways.

Telecommunications and teleconferencing have already begun to make much business travel unnecessary altogether. More and more Americans are now working from home or other locations of their choice with little or no need to commute anywhere, saving time, energy, and money in the process. This advantage also applies to corporations that can utilize teleconferencing to dramatically reduce their need for national and international business travel as well as for large, centralized management infrastructures that are costly to maintain.

Advanced real-time video and data transfer technologies have opened up remarkable new domestic and global enterprise opportunities for people and organizations everywhere. Included are individuals who purchase or sell personal items on eBay; small manufacturers and consultants that market products and services; businesses that conduct meetings with overseas divisions, affiliates, and clients; and scientific and professional organizations engaged in workshops and conferences. These activities and more can occur without the need to purchase extra gasoline or airline tickets, book expensive hotel rooms, pick up meal and entertainment tabs, or spend days or longer periods away from families and obligations that compete with a work/travel schedule.

Just as necessity is the mother of invention, innovation is a parental agent of intervention and adaptation. Notwithstanding some adjustment challenges, societal conservation responses born out of necessities and technological progress can ultimately be assimilated into painless and satisfying lifestyles. Advancing information and communication networks may not fully substitute for physical travel and face-to-face interpersonal contact, but they may free many to live and work where they choose, avoid fuel- and time-costly transport, and wirelessly connect us at all times to global contacts and markets. We may downsize our homes and cars and realize that we live just as comfortably and arrive just as soon. As we turn to public transportation, it is likely that the services will improve, becoming more seamless and convenient.

Embracing Changes and Challenges

Two realities are quite clear: (1) that the short era of inexpensive energy resources is nearing an end; and (2) that there are no single or simple solutions. No known technology advancement or combination of advancements will satisfy the needs of uncontrolled consumption. The future we experience and introduce to those who follow will depend instead upon our human resources of vision, intellect, creativity, and discipline. We must apply all available means to expand the development and use of renewable as well as other resources, yet recognize their realistic limitations. We must strive to implement efficient processes and systems that minimize, recycle, and reuse wastes. We must apply personal and corporate lifestyles that do more with less, recognizing that this makes good economic and moral sense.

Our human ability to gain knowledge about changes we are imposing upon our planet provides opportunities to adapt our living habits, industries, and technologies to prevent avoidable surprises that lead to unfortunate events. Earth-sensing satellite observations and advancements in information technology are yielding a better understanding of nature's complexities and intricacies. This better understanding provides us with lessons we can apply to be more positive contributors. Humans are also blessed with gifts of curiosity, intelligence, and compassion, all of which enable us to recognize our responsibilities and interdependencies within a larger world community.

There is inescapable evidence that human activities are impacting Earth's environment and ecosystems, often not for the better. Air, water, and land pollution are an expanding global reality. Scientists who study these matters do us great service in pointing such things out and helping us to do better. We are not beneficially served, however, by exaggerated statements—purporting to be based upon science—that are calibrated to get maximum public attention. Alarmism, however well intentioned, is not conducive to sound judgment and reasoned responses.

Failure to rapidly develop essential energy capacities will have widespread, destructive social and economic consequences that will be particularly burdensome upon the poorest among us. A 3-decade-long blockage of US nuclear power development has already caused depletion of natural gas that could have been conserved or applied for other, more appropriate fuel and feedstock purposes. This has contributed to high natural gas prices that have forced many US energy- and chemical-intensive industries overseas, along with the jobs and tax revenues they might have otherwise provided.

Expansion of existing energy production capacity infrastructures, and creation of new ones, requires lots of time and investment in a friendly legislative environment. This applies to nuclear plant licensing; fossil drilling; refinery construction;

clean coal and coal shale development; organic and fossil synthetic liquid fuels; and yes, wind farms. While coal is our most abundant long-term fossil source, onerous and unwarranted CO_2 sequestration mandates, in combination with prospective carbon caps, will continue to kill incentives to build new coal-fired plants. US coal use decreased in relation to oil and gas over a 50-year period between about 1910 and 1940,[13] and transitioning back to cleaner and liquid derivative technologies may require decades under the best circumstances. Time is very much of the essence.

Some groups and individuals advertised as "environmentalists" seem to want society to return to what they regard as the simpler, ecologically superior lifestyle of the past. This is neither possible nor desirable. Looking back, earlier tribes may have had lighter ecological footprints only because there weren't nearly as many feet then. Their lives were much harder and shorter than ours, and they used substantially more land per capita to survive and raise larger families.

We can, however, learn much from the past. From a truly "big picture" time perspective, we can readily observe that Earth's climate has changed often and dramatically over long, short, and irregular cycles, with no influence from our ancestors. From a human perspective, we can take heart that our species has adapted to rapid and severe climate shifts on numerous occasions, and the worst by far were periods of cold. We can relearn ways that indigenous peoples in all climate zones have applied logical conservation principles in dwelling construction that make resourceful use of sunlight and natural ventilation.

There should be no doubt that we humans are highly resilient creatures with remarkable abilities to survive in difficult times. In 2002, a report issued jointly by the Ocean Studies Board, the Polar Research Board, and the Board on Atmospheric Sciences and Climate of the National Research Council—titled "Abrupt Climate Change: Inevitable Surprises"—advocated preparation without panic: "The climate record for the past 100,000 years clearly indicates that the climate system has undergone periodic and extreme shifts, sometimes in as little as a decade or less . . . Societies have faced both gradual and abrupt changes for millennia and have learned to adapt."[14]

The report went on to advise: "It is important not to be fatalistic about the threats of abrupt climate change . . . Nevertheless, because climate change will likely continue in the coming decades, denying the likelihood or downplaying the relevance of abrupt changes could be costly."

How do we prepare for rapid climate change? Consider that the most important impact, whether average temperatures rise or drop, will be upon energy demands. A warmer climate will increase crop yields, just as it always has, along with power consumption for air-conditioning. A cooler climate may further accelerate population shifts from US northern states to the Sun Belt, also increasing air-conditioning demands but increasing fuel consumption for winter heating in much of the country as well. Those who pay attention will have noticed that US temperatures, which had warmed until the mid-1940s, then cooled through the late 1970s, warmed until the late 1990s, and now seem to be cooling again, potentially for decades to come. All this is despite steady and "alarming" increases in human CO_2 releases and other activities.

Apart from climate, each of us affects the course of human events, adaptation, and technological, social, and economic progress through our choices and actions. Individually and collectively, we change the world for better or worse in a variety of important ways. We determine which businesses and products will be successful in the marketplace through our purchasing power. We decide how many resources we will consume, how much waste will be created, and whether waste will be recycled, based upon priorities that guide how we live. We influence our children and others around us through our conservation outlooks and the examples we put into practice. And we determine whom we trust to lead us and implement policies we believe in through active participation and informed votes in local, state, and national electoral processes that affect the political climate. That's the climate crisis that we urgently need to address.

NOTES

Introduction

1 Steven Mosher and Thomas W. Fuller, *Climategate: The Crutape Letters*, vol. 1 (CreateSpace, 2010).

2 Ibid.

3 "When Scientists Become Politicians," *Investor's Business Daily*, December 1, 2009.

4 James M. Taylor, "Global Cooling Continues," *Environment & Climate News*, March 1, 2009.

5 "New England Digs Out after Record Snowfall," Reuters, December 14, 2007.

6 "Alarmists Still Heated Even as World Cools," *Investor's Business Daily*, November 5, 2008.

7 "Snow, Wind Batter US East Coast in 2nd Storm," Reuters, February 11, 2010.

8 "NYC Snow Storm Sets Record, Stops Flights, Cuts Power," *Business Week*, February 27, 2010.

9 "What summer? Record cold at LAX as July gloom continues," *LA Times*, July 10, 2010. Available at http://latimesblogs.latimes.com/lanow/2010/07/record-cold-at-lax-airport-as-july-gloom-continues-in-southern-california.html.

10 "Cold wave kills six million fish in Bolivia," *USA Today*, August 4, 2010. Available at http://content.usatoday.com/topics/article/Places,+Geography/Countries/Bolivia/01125Gn5ByaOh/0.

11 Michael Asher, "Temperature Monitors Report Widescale Global Cooling," DailyTech, February 26, 2008. Available at http://www.dailytech.com/Temperature+Monitors+Report+Widescale+Global+Cooling/article10866.htm.

12 Dorell, Oren, "The world is hotter than ever-NOAA," *USA Today*, July 16, 2010. Available at http://icecap.us/index.php/go/joes-blog/the_world_is_hotter_than_ever_noaa2/.

13 Ian Wishart, *Air Con: The Seriously Inconvenient Truth about Global Warming* (HATM Publishing, 2009), 220.

14 Brant McLaughlin, "NASA Admits 1934, Not 1998 Was Warmest Year on Record," Associated Content, August 14, 2007.

15 Alan Carlin, "Comments on Draft Technical Support Document for Endangerment Analysis for Greenhouse Gas Emissions Under the Clean Air Act." Available at http://www.heartland.org/policybot/results/25557/Comments_on_Draft_Technical_Support_Document_For_Endangerment_Analysis_For_Greenhouse_Gas_Emissions_Under_The_Clean_Air_Act.html.

16 Fred Langon, "Polar Bears 'Thriving as the Arctic Warms Up'," *Telegraph*, March 9, 2007. Available at http://www.telegraph.co.uk/news/worldnews/1545036/polar-bears-thriving-as-the-arctic-warms-up.html.

17 Richard Freeman and Merry Baker, "Carbon Trade Swindle Behind Gore Hoax." Available at http://www.larouchepub.com/eiw/public/2007/2007_10-19/2007_10-19/2007-13/pdf/29-34_713_gorehoax.pdf.

Chapter 1

1 Brendan O'Neil, "Global Warming: The Chilling Effect on Free Speech," Spiked-Online.com, October 6, 2005. Available at http//www.spiked-online.com/index.php?/site/article/1782/.

2 Michael Hewitt, "Agonizing Over the Icecap or Frantic about Floods? You May Be Suffering from 'Eco-anxiety,'" March 20, 2008. Available at http://www.independent.co.uk/environment/ climate-change/agonizing-over-the-icecap-or-frantic-about-floods.

3 Bjorn Lomborg, *Cool It: The Skeptical Environmentalist's Guide to Global Warming*, 1st ed. (Knopf, 2007), 127.

4 "Time Bomb," *Investor's Business Daily*, April 21, 2008.

5 Lomborg, 125–27.

6 S. Fred Singer and Dennis T. Avery, *Unstoppable Global Warming* (Rowman & Littlefield Publishers, 2007), 117.

7 Lowell Ponte, *The Cooling: Has the Next Ice Age Already Begun?* (Prentice-Hall, 1976).

8 Bull, Peter, "Hot Politics," *Frontline*, 2007, PBS.org. Available at http://www.pbs.org/wgbh/pages/ frontline/hotpolitics/etc/script.html.

9 Richard Lindzen, "Global Warming: The Origin and Nature of the Alleged Scientific Consensus," *Regulation*, vol. 15, no. 2 (Spring 1992). Available at http://www.cato.org/pubs/regulation/ regv15n2/reg15n2g.html.

10 Amanda Griscom Little, "The Sway of the World: Gore-Backed Group Will Spend Big to Convince Americans Climate Change is Real," *Grist*, May 19, 2006. Available at http://grist.org/ news/muck/2006/05/19/gore/.

11 Adam Lashinsky, "Clean Energy Will Make Gore Rich," *Fortune*, CNN Money, November 20, 2007. Available at http://features.blogs.fortune.cnn.com/2007/11/20/clean-energy-will-make-gore-rich/.

12 "Alliance for Climate Protection Launches $300 Million Campaign to Solve Climate Crisis," Philanthropy News Digest, April 2, 2008. Available at http://foundationcenter.org/pnd/news/ story.jhtml?id=210300039.

13 Bill Mesler, "Al Gore: The Other Oil Candidate," CorpWatch, August 29, 2000. Available at http://www.corpwatch.org/article.php?id=468.

14 "Al Gore's Big Investment," *DealBook, New York Times*, March 6, 2008. Available at http://deal-book.blogs.nytimes.com/2008/03/06/al-gores-big-investment/.

15 Ellen McGirt, "Al Gore's $100 Million Makeover," *Fast Company*, December 19, 2007. Available at www.fastcompany.com/node/60067/print.

16 Roy W. Spencer, *Climate Confusion* (Encounter Books, 2008), 7.

17 "US Climate Change Science Program Has Been Undermined by Budget Cutbacks," Climate Science Watch, September 26, 2007. Available at www.climatesciencewatch.org/index.php/ csw/details/ccsp_budget_cutback.

18 S. Fred Singer and Dennis T. Avery, *Unstoppable Global Warming* (Rowman & Littlefield Publishers, 2007), 104.

19 Ibid, 7.

20 Climate Science Watch, ibid.

21 Jesse Jenkins, "The Innovation Consensus: $15 billion for Clean Energy R&D," The Energy Collective, October 29, 2009. Available at http://theenergycollective.com/TheEnergyCollective/50750.

22 Lindzen, ibid.

23 "Climate Expert Says NASA Tried to Silence Him," *New York Times*, January 29, 2006.

24 Mark Bowen, "James Hansen and Mark Bowen on Censored Science," National Public Radio, January 8, 2008. Available at http://www.npr.org/templates/story/story.php?storyId=17926941.

25 Spencer, 93.

26 Singer and Avery, 122–23.

27 S. Fred Singer, *Hot Talk, Cold Science* (Independent Press, 1992), 40.

28 Heidelberg Appeal, released at the 1992 Earth Summit in Rio de Janeiro. Available at http://www.sepp.org/policy%20declarations/heidelberg_appeal.html (accessed August 5, 2007).

29 Text of the Leipzig Declaration on Global Climate Change. Available at http://www.heartland.org/environmentandclimate-news.org/article/9855/The_Leipzig_Declaration_on_Global_Climate_Change.html (accessed August 5, 2007).

30 Steven J. Milloy, "Survey of State Experts Casts Doubt on Link between Human Activity and Global Warming," News Release, Citizens for a Sound Economy (Washington, DC), October 7, 1997.

31 "Policy Statement on Climate Variability and Change," American Association of State Climatologists (November 2001). Available at http://lwf.ncdc.noaa.gov/oa/aasc/AASC-Policy-Statement-on-Climate.htm.

32 Joseph L. Blast and James M. Taylor, "Scientific Consensus on Global Warming," The Heartland Institute, 2007. Available at www.heartland.org/Article.cfm?artId=20861 (accessed August 5, 2007).

33 S. Robert Lichter, "Climate Scientists Agree on Warming, Disagree on Dangers, and Don't Trust the Media's Coverage on Climate Change," April 24, 2008. Available at http://www.stats.org/stories/2008/global_warming_survey_apr23_08.html.

34 "Global Warming Skeptics Raise a Storm in New York," Radio Free Europe Liberty, March 10, 2009.

35 Naomi Oreskes, "Beyond the Ivory Tower: The Scientific Consensus on Climate Change Science," *Science*, 2004. Available at http://www.sciencemag.org/cgi/content/full/306/5702/1686.

36 Singer and Avery, 126.

37 "Poll: Americans Least Worried about Global Warming," Newsmax.com, March 21, 2010.

38 "Global Warming's New Hockey Stick," *Investor's Business Daily*, March 12, 2010.

Chapter 2

1 Roy W. Spencer, *Climate Confusion* (Encounter Books, 2008), 87.

2 S. Fred Singer and Dennis T. Avery, *Unstoppable Global Warming* (Rowman & Littlefield Publishers, 2007), 138.

3 US Environmental Protection Agency, Global Warming—Climate, October 14, 2004.

4 Spencer, 91.

5 "Pioneer Meteorologist Unearthed Mysteries of Clouds, Storms," *Wall Street Journal*, March 12, 2010.

6 Syun-Ichi Akasofu, "Two Natural Components of the Recent Climate Change," March 30, 2009. Available at www.webcommentary.com/docs/2natural.pdf.

7 Roy Spencer, John Christy, et al., "Cirrus Disappearance: Warming Might Thin Heat-Trapping Clouds," University of Alabama–Huntsville, August 9, 2007. Available at http://www.uah.edu/news/newsread.php?newsID=875.

8 Arthur Y. Hou, "'Heat Vent' in Pacific Cloud Cover Could Diminish Greenhouse Warming,"

Bulletin of the American Meteorological Society, March 2001. Available at http://www.science-daily.com/releases/2001/03/010301072351.htm.

9 Graeme Stephens, "Cloud Feedbacks in the Climate System: A Critical Review," *Journal of Climate,* vol. 18 (January 15, 2005): 237–73.

10 "Peer-Reviewed Study Rocks Climate Debate! Nature Not Man Responsible for Recent Global Warming," *Climate Depot* (July 22, 2009).

11 K. Trenberth, "Predictions of Climate," *Climate Feedback: The Climate Change Blog,* June 2007. Available at http://blogs.nature.com/climatefeedback/2007/06/predictions_of_climate.html.

12 Ernst-Georg Beck, "180 Years of Atmospheric CO_2 Gas Analysis by Chemical Methods," *Energy and Environment,* vol. 18, no. 2 (2007).

13 "MIT Researcher Finds Evidence of Ancient Climate Swings," *Science Daily,* April 20, 1998.

14 Beck, ibid.

15 Christopher Scotese, "Paleomap Project." Available at www.scotese.com/climate.htm.

16 Michael McGoodwin, "Notes of a Geobiology Watcher, or How to Love Your Bacteria: Interactions Between Life Forms and the Earth's Physical and Chemical Systems," 2008. Available at http://www.mcgoodwin.net/pages/geobiologyess313.pdf.

17 Robert Berner and Zavaret Kothavala, "GeoCarb III: A Revised Model of Atmospheric CO_2 over Phanerozoic Time," *American Journal of Science,* vol. 301 (February 2001).

18 Ian Wishart, *Air Con: The Seriously Inconvenient Truth about Global Warming* (HATM Publishing, 2009), 35.

19 Wishart, 36.

20 Beck, ibid.

21 Singer and Avery, 118.

22 Ibid.

23 Patrick Michaels, ed., *Shattered Consensus: True State of Global Warming* (Rowman & Littlefield Publishers, 2005), 47.

24 "Russian Temps Turn up Heat on Warmers," *Investor's Business Daily*, December 18, 2009.

25 "To Denmark, From Russia, with Lies," *Investor's Business Daily*, December 21, 2009.

26 "Russian Temps," ibid.

27 Willie Soon et al., *Global Warming: A Guide to the Science* (The Fraser Institute, 2001).

28 Singer and Avery, 140–45.

29 Vincent Gray, *The Greenhouse Delusion: A Critique of Climate Change 2001* (Multi-Science Publishing Co., 2002), 86.

30 Ibid., 86–87.

31 "Endangerment and Cause or Contribute Findings for Greenhouse Gases Under Section 202(a) of the Clean Air Act: EPA's Response to Public Comments," vol. 3—Attribution of Observed Climate Change, page 4, April 24, 2009. Available at http://www.epa.gov/climatechange/ndangerment/downloads/RTC%20Volume%203.pdf.

32 Gray, 3–8.

33 Steven Mosher and Thomas W. Fuller, *Climategate: The Crutape Letters,* vol. 1 (CreateSpace, 2010).

34 Spencer, 48.

35 Gray, 89.

36 Mark Carreau, "NASA Chief Doubts Global Warming Is Front-Burner Issue," *Houston Chronicle*, May 31, 2007.

37 Ibid.

38 Singer and Avery, 140–45.

Chapter 3

1 S. Fred Singer and Dennis T. Avery, *Unstoppable Global Warming* (Rowman & Littlefield Publishers, 2007), 48–51.

2 Ibid., 52–58.

3 Ibid., 6.

4 Ibid., 50.

5 Ibid., 6.

6 Hubert H. Lamb, *Climate, History and the Modern World*, 2nd ed. (Routledge, 1995).

7 Singer and Avery, 50.

8 Willie Soon et al., *Global Warming: A Guide to the Science* (The Fraser Institute, 2001).

9 "The Great Cool-Down," Newsmax.com, March 2010.

10 "Doctor of Lies," *Investor's Business Daily*, March 16, 2010.

11 Henrik Svensmark and Nigel Calder, *The Chilling Stars: A New Theory of Climate Change* (Penguin Books), 17.

12 "Sahara's Abrupt Desertification Started by Changes in Earth's Orbit," *Science Daily*, July 12, 1999.

13 "Apocalypse Sun?" *Investor's Business Daily*, June 3, 2009.

14 Svensmark and Calder, 27.

15 N. Scafetta and B. J. West, "Is Climate Sensitive to Solar Variability?" *Physics Today* (March 2008): 50–51. Available at http://www.fel.duke.edu/~scafetta/pdf/opinion0308.pdf.

16 "Cosmic Rays Hit Space Age High," *Astronomy Now Online*, October 1, 2009. Available at http://www.astronomyreport.com/research/Cosmic_rays_hit_space_age_high.asp.

17 Ibid.

18 Svensmark and Calder, ibid.

19 Stuart Clark, "What's wrong with the sun?" *New Scientist*, Issue 2764, June 14, 2010. Available at http://www.newscientist.com/article/mg20627640.800-whats-wrong-with-the-sun.

20 Douglas Hoyt and Kenneth Schatten, *The Role of the Sun in Climate Change* (Oxford University Press, 1997), 221.

21 Ibid., 11.

22 Ibid., 224.

23 Ibid., 121.

24 Svensmark and Calder, 221.

25 Bjorn Lomborg, *The Skeptical Environmentalist: Measuring the Real State of the World*, 1st ed. (Cambridge University Press, 2001), 260.

26 Svensmark and Calder, ibid.

27 Ibid.

28 John and Mary Gribben, "The Greenhouse Effect," *New Scientist* (July 6, 1996). Available at http://environment.newscientist.com/article.ns?=mg15120377.000&print=true.

29 Ron Miller and Dorothy Koch "An Aerosol Tour de Forcing," RealClimate Guest Commentary, 2006. Available at http://www.realclimate.org/index.php/archives/2006/02/

an-aerosol-tour-de-forcing/. Also Bellouin et al., "Global Estimate of Aerosol Direct Radiative Forcing from Satellite Measurements," *Nature*, vol. 438 (December 22, 2005): 1138–41.

30 Miller and Avery, 52–58.

31 "2000–2009: The Warmest Decade," World Meteorological Organization, December 8, 2009. Available at http://www.wmo.int/pages/mediacentre/press_releases/pr_869_en.html.

Chapter 4

1 Bjorn Lomborg, *Cool It: The Skeptical Environmentalist's Guide to Global Warming*, 1st ed. (Knopf, 2007), 123–24.

2 Ibid., 127.

3 Richard Lindzen, "Global Warming: The Origin and Nature of the Alleged Scientific Consensus," *Regulation*, vol. 15, no. 2 (Spring 1992). Available at http://cato.org/pubs/regulation/regv15n2g.html.

4 "Judge: Al Gore's Nine Inconvenient Truths," *Metro News*, October 10, 2007. Available at http://www.metro.co.uk/news/climatewatch/article.html?in_article_id=69679&in_page_id=59.

5 Andrew Revkin, *The North Pole Was Here: Puzzles and Perils at the Top of the World* (Kingfisher, 2007).

6 "Retraction: Constraints on Future Sea-Level Rise from Past Sea-Level Change," *Nature Geoscience*, February 21, 2010.

7 Agence France-Presse, "New Study Slashes Estimate of Ice Cap Loss," Mother Nature Network, September 7, 2010. Available at http://www.mnn.com/earth-matters/climate-change/stories/new-study-slashes-estimate-of-icecap-loss.

8 "Climate Scientist Slams RealClimate.org for Erroneously Communicating the Reality of How the Climate System Is Actually Behaving," *Climate Depot*, June 30, 2009.

9 US Senate Committee on Environment and Public Works, Minority Report. Available at epw.senate.gov/public/index.cfm?FuseAction=Minority.Blogs&ContentRecords_id=672bfd77=802a.

10 "Observations: Oceanic Climate Change and Sea Level," *Climate Change 2007: The Physical Science Basis. Contribution of Working Group I to the Fourth Assessment Report of the Intergovernmental Panel on Climate Change*, S. Solomon et al., eds. (Cambridge University Press, 2007), 17.

11 Nils-Axel Morner, "Claim That Sea Level Is Rising Is a Total Fraud," interview in *EIR Economics*, June 22, 2008.

12 "Economic Chill," *Investor's Business Daily*, December 10, 2008.

13 Patrick J. Michaels and Robert Balling Jr., *Climate of Extremes* (Cato Institute, 2009); Anker Weidick, *Satellite Image Atlas of the World: Greenland* (US Geological Survey, 1995).

14 Nigel Lawson, *An Appeal to Reason: A Cool Look at Global Warming* (Overlook TP, 2008).

15 Ian Howat, Ian R. Joughin, and Ted A. Scambos, "Rapid Changes in Ice Discharge from Greenland Outlet Glaciers," *Science*, February 8, 2007. Available at http://www.sciencemag.org/cgi/content/abstract/1138478v1.

16 Cliff Harris, "Alaska's Ice Thickens Over Unusual Summer." Available at http://www.longrangeweather.com/ArticleArchives/AlaskaIceThickens.htm.

17 Richard Foot, "Canadian Scientist Says UN's Global Warming Panel Crossing the Line," *Canwest News Service*, January 26, 2010.

18 Keith Fraser, "Canada's Legal Claims to the Arctic," *The Canadvocate*, December 10, 2009. http://www.thecanadvocate.com/2009/12/10/canadas-legal-claims-to-the-arctic/.

19 Tenney Naumer, "January 7, 2009 2008 Year-in-Review" January 12, 2009. Available at http:// climatechangepsychology.blogspot.com/2009/01/nsidc-2008-year-in-review-arctic-sea.html.

20 Marc Morano, "U.S. Senate report Debunks polar bear Extinction Fears," U.S. Senate Environment and Public Works Committee, January 30, 2008. Available at http:// epw.senate.gov/public/index.cfm?FuseAction=Minority.Blogs&ContentRecord_id= d6c6d346-802a-23ad-436f-40eb31233026.

21 Kirk Friederich, "Royal Canadian Mounted police St. Roch 1940-1942." Available at http://www. pbase.com/rocketman2002ca/rcmp_st__roch.

22 "St. Roch II Expedition," Athropolis, August 2000. Available at http://www.athropolis.com/ news/st-roch.htm.

23 "Arctic Ice Extent Underestimated Because of Sensor Drift." Available at http://news.slashdot. org/article.pl?sid=09/02/19/0420255&from=rss.

24 Michael Asher, "Sea Ice Ends year at Same level as 1979," DailyTech, January 1, 2009. Available at http://www.dailytech.com/Article.aspx?newsid=13834.

25 "Ice Sheets Caused Massive Sea Level Change During Late Cretaceous," *National Science Foundation Study, Geological Society of America Bulletin* (March/April 2004).

26 Bjorn Lomborg, "Global Warming and Mt. Kilimanjaro," *Wall Street Journal*, December 7, 2009.

27 Nathan Burchfiel, "Polar Bear Scene Could Maul Energy Production," May 7, 2008. Available at www.BusinessAndMedia.org/printer/2008/20080507104256.aspx.

28 "Polar Bear Proposal Shows ESA Is Broken," speech by Senator James Inhofe, US Senate Committee on Environment and Public Works, Press Release, January 4, 2007. Available at http:// epw.senate.gov/public/index.cfm?FuseAction=Minority.PressReleases&ContentRecord_ id=ef1cdc42-802a-23ad-4428-93559736e2a1&Region_id=&Issue_id=.

29 "Biological Science Report USGS/BRD 2002-0001: Section 8: Polar Bears," USGS, 2002. Available at alaska.usgs.gov/BSR-2002/pdf/usgs-brd-bsr-2002-0001-sec08.pdf.

30 Burchfiel, ibid.

31 Sterling H. Burnett, "ESA Listing Not Needed for Polar Bears," *Environment News*, March 2007.

32 Scott Whitlock, "ABC's Sam Champion Hypes Global Warming for Eight Minutes," NewsBusters. org, March 28, 2008. Available at http://newsbusters.org/blogs/scott-whitlock/2008/03/28/ abcs-sam-champion-hypes-global-warming.

33 H. Sterling Burnett, "The Polar Bear Extinction Myth," 2008. Available at http://www.savethisnation.org/polarbears.htm.

34 "Interior Secretary Kempthorne Announces Proposal to List Polar Bears Under Endangered Species Act," US Department of Interior, Press Release, December 26, 2006. Available at http:// www.doi.gov/archive/news/06_News_Releases/061227.html.

35 Michele Bachmann, "Governor Palin Blasts Senator Harry Reid," September 3, 2008. Available at http://townhall.com/blog/g/97445152-2071-41fc-9fd8-ccc07e23395f?comments=true#comments.

36 Ben Lieberman, "Don't List the Polar Bear under the Endangered Species Act," WebMemo, no. 1781, January 25, 2008, The Heritage Foundation. Available at http://www.policyarchive.org/ handle/10207/bitstreams/13223.pdf.

37 "Senate Hearing Should Approach Polar Bears Cautiously," January 29, 2008. Available at http:// cei.org/news-releases/senate-hearing-should-approach-polar-bears-cautiously.

38 Robert Ferguson, "Penguins and Climate Change," Science & Public Policy Institute, December 12, 2007. Available at www.ScienceAndPublicPolicy.org.

39 "Climate Change Impacts on the United States, The Potential Consequences of Climate Variability and Change," National Assessment Synthesis Team, US Global Change Research Program, 2000. Available at http://www.usgcrp.gov/usgcrp/Library/nationalassessment/overviewclimate.htm.

40 Curt H. Davis, Yonghong Li, Joseph R. McConnell, Markus M. Frey, Edward Hanna, "Snowfall-Driven Growth in East Antarctic Ice Sheets Mitigates Recent Sea Level Rise," *Science*, vol. 308, no. 5730, pp. 1898-1901, June 24, 2005. Available at http://www.sciencemag.org/cgi/content/full/308/5730/1898.

41 Erik Stokstad, "Boom and Bust in a Polar Hot Zone," *Science*, vol. 315 (March 16, 2007): 1523. Available at http://www.sciencemag.org/cgi/reprint/315/5818/1522.pdf.

42 Gary Sharp, "Coral Bleaching: What (or Who) Dunnit?," *Technology Commerce Society Daily*, April 26, 2006. Available at www.tcsdaily.com/article.aspx?id=042606B.

43 Paul Reiter, "Global Warming Won't Spread Malaria," *EIR Science & Environment* (April 6, 2007): 52–57.

44 Mark Carreau, "NASA Chief Doubts Global Warming Is Front-Burner Issue," *Houston Chronicle*, May 30, 2007.

45 Ibid.

46 "Earth's Fidgeting Climate," *NASA Science News*, October 20, 2000. Available at http://science.nasa.gov/headlines/y2000/ast20oct_1.htm.

47 Lawrence Solomon, "The Deniers, Part III—The Hurricane Expert Who Stood Up to UN Junk Science," *National Post*, February 2, 2007.

48 Ibid.

49 David Stipp, "The Pentagon's Weather Nightmare: The Climate Could Change Radically, and Fast," *Fortune*, February 9, 2004. Also Drunvalo Melchizedek, "Dry/Ice: Global Warming Revealed." Available at http://www.spiritofmaat.com/announce/ann_dryice.htm.

50 Singer and Avery, 153–54.

51 David Rind et al., "Effects of Glacial Melt Water in the GISS Coupled Atmosphere-Ocean Model 1, North Atlantic Deep Water Response," *Journal of Geophysical Research*, vol. 106 (2001): 27335–353.

52 Singer and Avery, 155.

53 Rind et al., ibid.

54 Singer and Avery, ibid. Also Peili Wu et al., "Does the Recent Freshening Trend in the North Atlantic Indicate a Weakening Thermohaline Circulation?" *Geophysical Research Letters*, vol. 31 (2004). Available at http://www.agu.org/pubs/crossref/2004/2003GL018584.shtml.

55 Andy Rowell and Peter Moore, "Global Review of Forest Fires," WWF/IUCN Report. Available at http://data.iucn.org/dbtw-wpd/edocs/2000-047.pdf. Also D. C. Nepstad et al., "Large-scale Impoverishment of Amazonian Forests by Logging and Fire," *Nature*, vol. 398 (1999): 505.

56 "IPCC Rainforest Eco-tastrophe Claim Confirmed as Bunk," *Aftermath News*, March 12, 2010.

57 "The Great Cool-Down," Newsmax.com, March 2010.

58 "New Climate Modeling of Venus May Hold Clues to Earth's Future," *Science Daily*, February 23, 1999.

59 Frazer Cain, "Climate of Venus," *Universe Today*. Available at www.universetoday.com/guide-to-space/venus/climate-of-venus.

60 Richard Lindzen, "Deconstructing Global Warming," Competitive Enterprise Institute, Lecture,

October 26, 2009. Available at http://www.globalwarming.org/wp.content/uploads/2009/10/lindzen-talk.pdf.

61 "More holes in the GW consensus: a chronology," Citizens Electoral Council. Available at http://cecaust.com.au/main.asp?sub=global_warming&id=more_holes_consensus.html.

62 Richard Lindzen, "Global Warming: The Origin and Nature of the Alleged Scientific Consensus," *Regulation*, vol. 15, no. 2 (Spring 1992). Available at http://cato.org/pubs/regulation/regv15n2g.html.

63 Lewis Smith, "Al Gore's Inconvenient Judgment," *Business Times*, October 11, 2007. Available at http://business.timesonline.co.uk/tol/business/law/article2633838.ece.

64 "Judge: Al Gore's Nine Inconvenient Truths," *Metro News*, October 10, 2007. Available at http://www.metro.co.uk/news/climatewatch/article.html?in_article_id=69679&in_page_id=59.

65 Burchfiel, ibid.

66 Roy W. Spencer, *Climate Confusion* (Encounter Books, 2008), 15.

Chapter 5

1 S. Fred Singer and Dennis T. Avery, *Unstoppable Global Warming* (Rowman & Littlefield Publishers, 2007), 125.

2 Richard Lindzen, "Global Warming: The Origin and Nature of the Alleged Scientific Consensus," *Regulation*, vol. 15, no. 2 (Spring 1992). Available at http://cato.org/pubs/regulation/regv15n2g.html.

3 "125 Scientists' Statement on Global Climatic Disruption," *Ozone Action*, June 6, 1997.

4 Singer and Avery, ibid.

5 Roy W. Spencer, *Climate Confusion* (Encounter Books, 2008), 147.

6 Lindzen, ibid.

7 Bryan Walsh, "Science: Top 10 Green Ideas; Top 10 of Everything, 2007," *Time* in partnership with CNN, December 9, 2007. Available at: http://www.time.com/time/specials/2007/article/0,28804,1686204_1686252_1690221,00.html. Also USDOE Pacific Northwest National Laboratory. Available at http://www.pnl.gov/news/release.aspx?id=277.

8 John McLean, "The IPCC's dubious evidence for a human influence on climate," October 2007. Available at http://mclean.ch/climate/docs/IPCC_evidence.pdf.

9 Spencer, ibid.

10 IPCC 1996A:5, "Are Human Activities Contributing to Climate Change?" Available at http://www.gcrio.org/ipcc/qa/03.html.

11 IPCC 2001D:6, "A Report of Working Group I of the Intergovernmental Panel on Climate Change," 10. Available at http://www.ipcc.ch/pdf/assessment-report/ar4/wg1/ar4-wg1-spm.pdf.

12 Bjorn Lomborg, *The Skeptical Environmentalist: Measuring the Real State of the World*, 1st ed. (Cambridge University Press, 2001), 318.

13 Fred Pearce, "Hot Warning," *New Scientist*, vol. 13 (January 22, 2001): 57.

14 Bjorn Lomborg, "Global warming-are we doing the right thing?" Available at http://image.guardian.co.uk/sys-files/Guardian/documents/2001/08/14/warming.pdf.

15 Lomborg, 319.

16 N. Winton, "Global Warming Theory Just Hot Air, Some Experts Say," Reuters World Service, December 20, 1995. Available at http://cei.org/PDFs/Costs_of_Kyoto_Part3.pdf.

17 Spencer, 88.

18 Vincent Gray, *The Greenhouse Delusion: A Critique of "Climate Change 2001"* (Multi-Science Publishing Co., 2002), 2.

19 Spencer, 85.

20 IPCC Climate Change 2000, Chapter 8, "Model Evaluation," 475. Available at http://www.grida.no/climate/ipcc_tar/wg1/pdf/TAR-08.pdf.

21 Ibid., 774.

22 J. T. Houghton, G. J. Jenkins, and J. J. Ephraums, eds., *Climate Change: The IPCC Scientific Assessment* (Cambridge University Press, 1990).

23 IPCC Second Assessment Climate Change 1995, Chapter 8, "A Report of the Intergovernmental Panel on Climate Change." Available at http://www.ipcc.ch/pdf/climate-changes-1995/ipcc-2nd-assessment/2nd-assessment-en.pdf.

24 Singer and Avery, 122; IPCC Climate Change 1995, Chapter 8.

25 Singer and Avery, 118.

26 Ibid., 120.

27 T. P. Barnett, B. D. Santer, P. D. Jones, R. S. Bradley, and I. R. Briffa, "Estimates of Low-Frequency Natural Variability in Near-Surface Air Temperatures," *The Holocene,* vol. 6 (1996): 96.

28 Singer and Avery, 122.

29 "Coverup in the Greenhouse," *Wall Street Journal,* July 11, 1996.

30 Frederick Seitz, "A Major Deception on Global Warming," *Wall Street Journal,* June 12, 1996.

31 Ibid.

32 John Tierney, "The Skeptical Prophet," *The New York Times,* April 15, 2009. Available at http://tierneylab.blogs.nytimes.com/2009/04/15/the-skeptical-prophet/.

33 House of Lords Select Committee on Economic Affairs, "The Economics of Climate Change," 2nd Report of Session 2005–2006. Available at http://www.publications.parliament.uk/pa/ld200506/ldselect/ldeconaf/12/12i.pdf.

34 H. Sterling Burnett, "Climate Panel on the Hot Seat," *Washington Times,* March 14, 2008. Available at http://www.washingtontimes.com/news/2008/mar/4/climate-panel-on-the-hot-seat/?page=1.

35 Burnett, ibid.

36 Philip V. Brennan, "Global Warming Claims Unsupported by Facts," Newsmax.com, March 14, 2008.

37 Steven Mosher and Thomas W. Fuller, *Climategate: The Crutape Letters,* vol. 1 (CreateSpace, 2010).

38 Jeffrey Ball and Keith Johnson, "Push to Oversimplify at Climate Panel," *Wall Street Journal,* February 26, 2010.

39 Ibid.

40 Richard Foot, "Canadian Scientist Says UN's Global Warming Panel Crossing the Line," *Canwest News Service,* January 26, 2010.

41 Paul Joseph Watson, "IPCC Boss Unhinged as Greenpeace Demands Resignation," PrisonPlanet.com, February 4, 2010. Available at http://www.prisonplanet.com/ipcc-boss-unhinged-as-greenpeace-demands-resignation.html.

42 "Cool-Down Phase," *Investor's Business Daily,* August 31, 2010. Available at http://www.investors.com/NewsAndAnalysis/Article/545647/201008311913/Cool-Down-Phase.htm.

43 Anthony Watts, "IPCC's Chairman Pachauri Conflicted," Watts Up With That?, May 11, 2010. Available at http://wattsupwiththat.com/2010/05/11/ipcc%E2%80%99s-chairman-pachauri-conflicted/.

44 Watson, ibid.

45 Foot, ibid.

46 Speech by Jacques Chirac, French president, to the VIth Conference of the Parties to the United Nations Framework Convention on Climate Change, November 20, 2000. Also US Senate Committee on Environment and Public Works, "Global Carbon Tax Urged at UN Climate Conference." Available at http://epw.senate.gov/public/index.cfm?FuseAction=Minority.Blogs&Content Record_id=d5c3c93f-802a-23ad-4f29-fe59494b48a6.

47 Bjorn Lomborg, *Cool It: The Skeptical Environmentalist's Guide to Global Warming*, 1st ed. (Knopf, 2007), 140.

48 Maurine Marton, "Junk Science Begets Junk Lawsuits," *Investor's Business Daily*, March 5, 2010.

49 "Panel on Climate Change Faces Challenges," *Wall Street Journal*, February 8, 2010.

50 Rebecca Terrell, "Congress Launches Climategate Investigation," November 27, 2009. Available at http://www.thenewamerican.com/index.php/tech-mainmenu-30/environment/2415-congress-launches-climategate-investigation.

51 Mark Goldberg, "Member of Congress Introduces Bill to Cut US Funding for IPCC," *UN Dispatch*, July 9, 2009.

52 "Controversies Create Opening for Critics," *Wall Street Journal*, February 17, 2010.

Chapter 6

1 "United Nations Framework Convention on Climate Change: 2002." Available at http://unfccc.int/resource/docs/convkp/conveng.pdf.

2 Harry Lamb, "Maurice Strong: The New Guy in Your Future!", January 1997. Available at http://www.sovereignty.net/p/sd/strong.html.

3 Rosett, Claudia, "The UN's Man of Mystery," *Wall Street Journal*, October 11, 2008. Also "Maurice Strong named in UN oil-for-food report," CTV News website, September 8, 2005.

3 S. Fred Singer and Dennis T. Avery, *Unstoppable Global Warming* (Rowman & Littlefield Publishers, 2007), 210.

4 "Beyond Interdependence: The Meshing of the World's Economy and the Earth's Ecology," Task Force Report #40 (Oxford University Press, 1991). Available at http://www.questia.com/googleScholar.qst;jsessionid=MQlLGBkL6nv3Ywv8bwYvPGrHGK9ynXyTDBNZLRJsQmtJJ W1JKQ7n!-150223949!-1933696167?docId=98252172.

5 "Environmental Scientist: Timothy Wirth," *Dossier*, The National Center for Public Policy Research, April 4, 1996. Available at http://nationalcenter.org/dos7130.html.

6 Zbigniew Jaworowski, "CO_2: The Greatest Scientific Scandal of Our Time," *EIR Science*, March 16, 2007, p. 3, 16. Available at http://www.warwickhughes.com/icecore/zjmar07.pdf.

7 Singer and Avery, ibid.

8 Ibid.

9 Roy W. Spencer, *Climate Confusion* (Encounter Books, 2008), 149.

10 Patrick L. Barry and Dr. Tony Phillips, "Good News and a Puzzle," Science@NASA, May 26, 2006. Available at http://science.nasa.gov/headlines/y2006/26may_ozone.htm.

11 Singer and Avery, 140.

12 Richard S. Lindzen, "Global Warming: The Origin and Nature of the Alleged Scientific Consensus," *Regulation*, vol. 15, no. 2 (Spring 1992). Available at http://www.cato.org/pubs/regulation/regv15n2/reg15n2g.html.

13 Singer and Avery, 234–36.

14 Ibid., 10.

15 John Rosenberg, "Problems with the Protocol," sidebar to "The Great Global Experiment," *Harvard Magazine* (November 2002). Available at www.harvardmagazine.com/on-line/1102199.html.

16 Singer and Avery, ibid.

17 Rosenberg, ibid.

18 Bjorn Lomborg, *Cool It: The Skeptical Environmentalist's Guide to Global Warming*, 1st ed. (Knopf, 2007), 116–18, 146.

19 Singer and Avery, 227.

20 Lomborg, ibid.

21 Singer and Avery, ibid.

22 Spencer, 95.

23 James Taylor, "Kyoto? Nyet!" *Environment and Climate News* (The Heartland Institute), November 21, 2003. Available at http://www.heartland.org/policybot/results/13693/Kyoto_Nyet.html.

24 Singer and Avery, 229–31.

25 Ibid.

26 Darrel Bricker, "Support (74%) Remains High for Kyoto Protocol," Press Release, Ipsos-Reid poll, November 8, 2002. Available at www.ipsos-na.com/news/pressrelease.cfm?id=1667. Also Frank Graves and Christian Boucher, "Public Attitudes Towards the Kyoto Protocol," Ekos Research Associates, June 10, 2002. Available at www.ekos.com/admin/articles/10june02kyotoprot.pdf. Also "Business Leaders Call for Climate Change Action," CBCNews, November 17, 2005. Available at www.cbc.ca/money/story/2005/11/17/kyotobiz-051117.html. Also "Canada-Kyoto Timeline," CBCNews, February 14, 2007. Available at www.cbc.ca/news/background/kyoto/timeline.html. Also "2006 Report of the Commissioner of the Environment and Sustainable Development," Office of the Auditor General of Canada. Available at www.oag-bvg.gc.ca/internet/English/oss_20061003_e_23771.html.

27 Judy Dempsey, "New German Rule Could Increase Greenhouse Gas Emissions," *New York Times*, June 29, 2006. Available at http://www.nytimes.com/2006/06/29/business/worldbusiness/29green.html.

28 Singer and Avery, 234–36.

29 Ibid.

30 Ibid., 227.

31 Lomborg, 23.

32 Singer and Avery, 234–36.

33 Ibid., 227.

34 Lomborg, 136–38.

35 Warren McLaren, "Britain's Stern Report Spurs Action on Climate Change," *Treehugger Science & Technology*, October 30, 2006.

36 Heather Timmons, "Britain Warns of High Costs of Global Warming," *New York Times*, October 31, 2006. Available at http://www.nytimes.com/2006/10/31/world/europe/31britain.

html?_r=1&scp=1&sq=Britain%20warns%20of%20high%20costs%20of%20global%20 warming&st=cse.

37 Bjorn Lomborg, *Cool It: The Skeptical Environmentalist's Guide to Global Warming*, 1st ed. (Knopf, 2007), 136–38.

38 "Is It Hot in Here?" *The Washington Post*, September 9, 2007. Available at www.washingtonpost. com/wp-dyn/content/article/2007/09/06/AR2007090601979.html.

39 Jim Giles, "How Much Will It Cost to Save the World?" *Nature*, November 2, 2006. Available at http://www.nature.com/nature/journal/v444/n7115/full/444006a.html.

40 Lomborg, 22.

41 Ibid., 32.

42 Alessandro Torello and Selina Williams, "Developing Nations Call for Rich to Aid Emissions Cuts," *Wall Street Journal*, December 9, 2009.

43 Jeffery Ball, Guy Chazon, Stephen Power, and Elizabeth Williamson, "Showdown at Climate Talks: Obama Jets to Denmark, U.S. Backs $100 Billion Annual Aid to Clinch Carbon Deal," *Wall Street Journal*, December 18, 2009. Available at http://online.wsj.com/article/SB126104774041695279.html.

44 Christian Wienberg, "Blizzard Dumps Snow on Copenhagen as Leaders Battle Warming," Bloomberg.com, December 17, 2009. Available at http://www.bloomberg.com/apps/news?pid =20601130&sid=a5wStc0K6jhY.

45 "The Copenhagen Concoction," *Investor's Business Daily*, December 8, 2009.

46 Illinois Federation for Right to Life, "Copenhagen: China Pushing Population Control as the Final Solution," LifeSiteNews.com, December 11, 2009. Available at http://groups.yahoo.com/group/IFRL/message/8262.

47 Ellen Goodman, "Human Factor Goes Missing in Copenhagen," *Investor's Business Daily*, December 10, 2009. Available at http://www.investors.com/NewsAndAnalysis/Article/514805/200912091831/Human-Factor-Goes-Missing-In-Copenhagen.aspx.

48 Father John Flynn, "The Re-birth of Population Control: Human Life Seen as a Carbon Problem," Zenit, December 12, 2009. Available at http://www.zenit.org/article-27826?l=english.

49 Lomborg, 41–47.

50 Singer and Avery, 229–31.

51 William D. Nordhaus and Joseph G. Boyer. "Requiem for Koyto: An Economic Analysis of the Kyoto Protocol," February 8, 1999. Available at http://www.econ.yale.edu/~nordhaus/homepage/Kyoto.pdf.

Chapter 7

1 Joseph Romm, "Is the Chicago Climate Exchange Selling Rip-Offsets?" *Climate Progress*, October 6, 2008. Available at http://climateprogress.org/2008/10/06/is-the-chicago-climate-exchange-selling-rip-offsets/.

2 Deborah Corey Barnes, "The Money and Connections Behind Al Gore's Carbon Crusade," *Human Events*, October 3, 2007. Available at www.humanevents.com/article.php?id=22663.

3 Nicolas Loris, "CBO Grossly Underestimates Cost of Cap and Trade," The Heritage Foundation, June 22, 2009. Available at http://blog.heritage.org/2009/06/22/cbo-grossly-underestimates-costs-of-cap-and-trade/.

4 Margo Thorning, "The Impact of America's Climate Security Act of 2007 (S. 2191) on the US Economy and on Global Greenhouse Gas Emissions," American Council for Capital Formation (November 8, 2007), 11. Available at http://www.accf.org/pdf/test-climate-security.pdf.

5 "The Carbon Recession," *Wall Street Journal*, May 10, 2010.

6 Fred L. Smith Jr., "Testimony Before the United States Senate Committee on Environment and Public Works: On the US Climate Action Partnership Report," Competitive Enterprise Institute (February 13, 2007), 8. Available at http://cei.org/pdf/5762.pdf.

7 Patrick J. Michaels, "Why Enron Wants Global Warming," Cato Institute, February 6, 2002. Available at http://www.cato.org/pub_display.php?pub_id=3388.

8 Ken Ring, "The Kyoto Conspiracy: How Enron Hyped Global Warming for Profit," *Investigate*, October 2005.

9 Ian Wishart, *Air Con: The Seriously Inconvenient Truth about Global Warming* (HATM Publishing, 2009), 220.

10 Lisa C. Baker, "International Carbon Action Partnership." *The Christian Environmentalist*, October 29, 2007. Available at http://www.thechristianenvironmentalist.com/2007/10/international-carbon-action-partnership.html.

11 Warren Giles, "Al Gore's Fund to Close After Attracting $5 Billion," Bloomberg.com, March 11, 2008. Available at http://www.bloomberg.com/apps/news?pid=20601103&sid=ahCy2aU0Wd1I&refer=us.

12 Ibid.

13 "The $10 Trillion Climate Fraud," *Investor's Business Daily*, April 10, 2010.

14 Robert Yoon, "Goldman Sachs Was Top Obama Donor," CNN.com, April 20, 2010. Available at http://www.cnn.com/2010/POLITICS/04/20/obama.goldman.donations/index.html?htp=Sbn.

15 Paul Driessen, "For Full Disclosure of Climate Change Risks," *Investor's Business Daily*, March 10, 2010. Available at http://www.investors.com/NewsAndAnalysis/Article.aspx?id=526842.

16 Ross Kaminsky, "Potential Costs to America from Cap-and-Trade," *Human Events*. Available at http://www.humanevents.com/article.php?id=26621#continueA.

17 Jacob Bunge, "ICE Agrees to Buy Climate Exchange for $603 Million," *Wall Street Journal*, May 1, 2010. Available at http://online.wsj.com/article/SB20001424052748703871904575216150636656916.html.

18 Richard Freeman and Marcia Merry Baker, "Carbon Trade Swindle Behind Gore Hoax," *Executive Intelligence Review*, March 30, 2007. Available at www.larouchepub.com/other/2007/3413carbon_swindle.html.

19 "Levin Introduces Bill to Close Enron Loophole and Prevent Manipulation and Excessive Speculation in Energy Markets," Office of Michigan senator Carl Levin, September 17, 2007. Available at http://levin.senate.gov/newsroom/release.cfm?id=283456.

20 Freeman, ibid.

21 Ibid.

22 "Sandor Exits CO_2 Trade, Sells Climate Exchange to ICE," Bloomberg.com, August 30, 2010. Available at http://bloomberg.com/apps/news?pid=20601087&sid=a0y1uKkJBhKQ.

23 "Have You Heard of Shore Bank," MarketWatch, June 27, 2010. Available at http://community.marketwatch.com/groups/us-politics/topics/have-you-heard-shore-bank.

24 "Re: ShoreBank: The Change America Voted In/True but Sad at the Same Time..." *Project World Awareness*, July 27, 2010. Available at http://projectworldawareness.com/2010/07/re-shorebank-the-change-america-voted-in-true-but-sad-at-the-same-time.

25 Sean Higgins, "Kerry: Don't Call It Cap-and-Trade Anymore," *Capital Hill Blog,* Investors.com, January 27, 2010. Available at http://blogs.investors.com/capitalhill/index.php/home/35-politics/1252-kerry-dont-call-it-cap-and-trade-anymore.

26 Sean Higgins, "Climate Bill Backers Hope New Label Will Ease Passage: Don't Call It Cap-and-Trade," *Investor's Business Daily*, April 26, 2010.

27 "Kerry's Powerless America Act," *Investor's Business Daily*, May 13, 2010.

28 Smith, ibid.

29 Katie Fehrenbacher, "Note to BP: Don't Push Green Ads, Then Toxic Waste," August 20, 2007. Available at http://earth2tech.com/2007/08/20/note-to-bp-dont-push-green-ads-then-toxic-waste.

30 Tom Bergin, "BP Sees No Gain from Green Energy," Reuters UK, February 27, 2008. Available at http://uk.reuters.com/article/businessNews/idUKWLB778620080227.

31 Driessen, ibid,

32 Fehrenbacher, ibid; Bergin, ibid.

33 Chris Mooney, "Some Like It Hot," *Mother Jones*, May 2005. Available at http://www.motherjones.com/news/feature/2005/05/some_like_it_hot.html.

34 Stephen Power and Ben Casselman, "Defections Shake Up Climate Coalition," *Wall Street Journal*, February 17, 2010. Available at http://online.wsj.com/article/SB10001424052748704804204575069440096420212.html.

35 Power and Casselman, ibid.

36 Clifford Krauss, "Exxon Rejects Proposals Backed by Rockefellers," *New York Times*, May 29, 2008. Available at http://www.nytimes.com/2008/05/29/business/29exxon.html.

37 Joe Nocera, "At Exxon's Can't-Miss Meeting," *New York Times*, May 31, 2008. Available at http://www.nytimes.com/2008/05/31/business/31nocera.html.

38 Mooney, ibid.

39 David Derbyshire, "Every Adult in Britain Should Be Forced to Carry 'Carbon Ration Cards,' Say MPs," *Daily Mail*, May 27, 2008. Available at http://www.dailymail.co.uk/news/article-1021983/Every-adult-Britain-forced-carry-carbon-ration-cards-say-MPs.html.

40 Ibid.

41 "Europe's Carbon Mafia, and Ours," *Investor's Business Daily*, May 7, 2010.

42 "EPA Delays Emissions Regulations," *Wall Street Journal*, February 23, 2010.

43 "Democrats Revolt over Energy," *Wall Street Journal*, March 5, 2010.

44 "EPA Delays Emissions Regulations," *Wall Street Journal*, March 5, 2010.

45 "EPA's Climate Train on Track," Sean Higgins, *Investor's Business Daily*, August 12, 2010. Available at http://www.investors.com/NewsAndAnalysis/Article.aspx?id=543503&utm_source=feedburner&utm_medium=feed&utm_campaign=Feed%3A+PoliticRss+(Politic+RSS).

46 "We, the EPA," *Investor's Business Daily*, March 16, 2010.

Chapter 8

1 Roy W. Spencer, *Climate Confusion* (Encounter Books, 2008), 98–99.

2 Ibid.

3 Geoff Metcalf, "Scientists Debunk Global Warming," NewsMax.com, December 15, 2008. Available at www.newsmax.com/metcalf/global_warming_hype.2008/12/15/161919.html.

4 Frank James, "Al Gore Slips on Arctic Ice; Misstates Scientist's Forecast," National Public Radio, December 15, 2009. Available at http://www.npr.org/blogs/thetwo-way/2009/12/al_gore_trips_on_artic_ice_mis.html.

5 Steven Goddard, "Arctic Ice Refuses to Melt as Ordered: There's Something Rotten North of Denmark," *Register*, August 15, 2008.

6 Tim Graham, "A Non-Melting Arctic Ice Update," NewsBusters.org, January 7, 2009. Available at http://newsbusters.org/blogs/tim-graham/2009/01/07/non-melting-arctic-ice-update.

7 "Low ice extent in Barents Sea and Hudson Bay," National Snow and Ice Data Center, Twitter.com, December 7, 2009. Available at http://nsidc.org/arcticseaicenews/2009/120709.html.

8 Michael Asher, "So Much for Flooded Cities: Greenland Ice Loss Not Increasing," DailyTech, July 4, 2008. Available at http://www.dailytech.com/article.aspx?newsid=12277.

9 Sharon Begley, "Sounds good, but . . . we can't afford to make any more mistakes in how to 'save the planet.' Start by ditching corn ethanol," *Newsweek*, April 5, 2008. Available at http://climate-diet.blogspot.com/2008/04/jonathan-harrington-interviewed-by.html.

10 Christopher Booker, "The World Has Never Seen Such Freezing Heat," *Telegraph*, November 16, 2008. Available at http://www.telegraph.co.uk/comment/columnists/christopher-booker/3563532/The-world-has-never-seen-such-freezing-heat.html.

11 "Climate Bombshell: NASA and the Media Knew of Temperature Data Issues Nearly Three Years Ago," *Conservative American News*, March 11, 2010.

12 Anthony Watts, "A Little-Known 20-Year-Old Climate Change Prediction by Dr. James Hansen That Failed Badly," *Watts Up With That?*, October 22, 2009. Available at http://wattsupwiththat.com/2009/10/22/a-little-known-but-failed-20-year-old-climate-change-prediction-by-dr-james-hansen/.

13 Spencer, 94.

14 Bjorn Lomborg, *Cool It: The Skeptical Environmentalist's Guide to Global Warming*, 1st ed. (Knopf, 2007), 142–43.

15 Ibid.

16 Ibid.

17 James M. Taylor, "Geothermal Power Would Harm California, Claims Lawsuit," The Heartland Institute, July 1, 2004. Available at www.heartland.org/article.cfm?artid=15261.

18 Spencer, 135.

19 "National Acid Precipitation Assessment Program, Version 2 (NAPAP)," January 19, 2010, NASA: Goddard Space Flight Center. Available at http://gcmd.nasa.gov/records/GCMD_EPA0141.html.

20 William K. Stevens, "Researchers Find Acid Rain Imperils Forests over Time," *New York Times*, December 31, 1989. Available at http://www.nytimes.com/1989/12/31/us/researchers-find-acid-rain-imperils-forests-over-time.html.

21 Spencer, ibid.

22 Spencer, 122.

23 "Court Strikes Down EPA Clean Air Mercury Rule," Center for Environment, Commerce & Energy, February 2008. Available at http://cenvironment.blogspot.com/2008_02_01_archive.html.

24 "The Glaring Truth about Compact Flourescent Bulbs," *Liberty's Logic* (February 1, 2008). Available at http://libertyslogic.blogspot.com/2008/02/glaring-truth-about-compact-fluorescent.html.

25 Spencer, 144.

26 Spencer, ibid.

27 E. Worrel, A. Rietveld, and C. Delacollette, "The Burden of Malaria Epidemics and Cost-effectiveness of Interventions in Epidemic Situations in Africa," *American Journal of Tropical Medicine and Hygiene*, vol. 2 suppl. (2004): 36–40.

28 Spencer, ibid.

29 Spencer, ibid.

30 Spencer, 3.

31 "Obama's Czars: The Hidden Government You Must Know About," Newsmax.com, December 2009. Available at http://www.fourwinds10.com/siterun_data/government/obama_government/news.php?q=1262193521.

32 John Holdren, Gretchen C. Daily, and Paul Ehrlich, "The Meaning of Sustainability: Biophysical Aspects," Distributed for the United Nations University by the World Bank Washington, DC, 1995.

33 John Holdren, Anne Ehrlich, and Paul Ehrlich, *Human Ecology Problems and Solutions* (W. H. Freeman and Company, 1973).

Chapter 9

1 Michael Heberling, "Mandating Renewable Energy: It's Not Easy Being Green," *Freeman Ideas on Liberty*, vol. 56, no. 8 (October 2006). Available at http://www.thefreemanonline.org/featured/mandating-renewable-energy-its-not-easy-being-green/#.

2 Lynn M. Fountain, "Johnny-Come-Lately: Practical Considerations of a National RPS," *Connecticut Law Review*, vol. 42, no. 5, July 2010. Available at http://connecticutlawreview.org/documents/LynnM.Fountain.pdf.

3 Heberling, ibid.

4 Senator Kay Bailey Hutchison, "Undoing America's Ethanol Mistake," April 28, 2008. Available at http://hutchison.senate.gov/opedEthanol.html.

5 Robert J. Michaels, "Hot Air and Wind," CATO Institute. December 20, 2007. Available at http://www.cato.org/pub_display.php?pub_id=8858.

6 James Eaves and Stephen Eaves, "CATO: Is Ethanol the 'Energy Security' Solution?" *Washington Post*, October 3, 2007. Available at www.cato.org/pub_display.php?pub_id=8730.

7 Paul Roberts, "The Seven Myths of Energy Independence: Why Forging a Sustainable Energy Future is Dependent on Foreign Oil," *Mother Jones*, May 1, 2008. Available at http://www.motherjones.com/news/feature/2008/05/the-seven-myths-of-energy-independence.html.

8 Roberts, ibid.

9 Hutchison, ibid.

10 Jeff Goodell, "The Ethanol Scam: One of America's Biggest Political Boondoggles," *Rolling Stone*, vol. 1032 (August 9, 2007). Available at http://robalini.blogspot.com/2007/08/ethanol-scam.html.

11 Benjamin Senauer, "How Biofuels Could Starve the Poor," *Foreign Affairs*, May/June 2007.

12 Senauer, ibid.

13 Dennis Keeney and Mark Muller, "Water Use by Ethanol Plants," Institute for Agriculture and Trade Policy, October 2006. Available at www.iatp.org/iatp/publications.cfm?accountID=258&refID=89449.

14 Sea Stachura, "Ethanol vs. Water: Can Both Win?" Minnesota Public Radio, September 18, 2006. Available at http://minnesota.publicradio.org/display/web/2006/09/07/ethanolnow.

15 Stachura, ibid.

16 Tom Davies, "Ethanol Comes with Environmental Impact, Despite Green Image," *USA Today*, May 5, 2007. Available at http://www.usatoday.com/money/industries/environment/2007-05-05-ethanolenvironment_N.htm.

17 Davies, ibid.

18 Noel Sheppard, "Will Media Remember Gore's 1994 Tie-breaking Vote Mandating Ethanol?" NewsBusters.org, April 22, 2008. Available at http://newsbusters.org/blogs/noel-sheppard/2008/04/22/will-media-remember-gores-1994-tie-breaking-vote-mandating-ethanol.

19 Keith Johnson, "Spin This: Booming Wind Industry Still Seeks Subsidies," *Wall Street Journal*, May 7, 2008.

20 Goodell, ibid.

21 "Subsidies for Corn Ethanol," zFacts, September 9, 2007. Available at http://zfacts.com/p/63.html.

22 David Coltrain, "Economic Issues with Ethanol," Risk and Profit Conference, Kansas State University, August 16–17, 2001.

23 Goodell, ibid.

24 Ibid.

25 Robert Bryce, *Gusher of Lies: The Dangerous Delusions of "Energy Independence"* (Public Affairs, 2008), 125.

26 Ibid., 223–29.

27 Johnson, ibid

28 Bob Keefe, "US Sees More Potential of Wind Power by 2030," Cox News Service, May 13, 2008.

29 "Electricity from Wind Turbines" (Part 3, Chapter 2), zFacts. Available at http://zfacts.com/p/416print.html.

30 Richard Chapo, "Wind Farms: Limitations as Energy Platforms," Ezine Articles, May 18, 2007. Available at http://ezinearticles.com/?Wind-Farms---Limitations-as-Energy-Platforms&id=200914.

31 Bugsy, "John Kerry Falls Off the Fence" *Cape Cod Living*, March 31, 2007. Available at www.capecodliving.blogspot.com/2007_03_01_archive.html.

32 Bryce, ibid.

33 James M. Taylor, "Geothermal Power Would Harm California, Claims Lawsuit," The Heartland Institute, July 1, 2004. Available at www.heartland.org/article.cfm?artid=15261.

34 Glenn Schleede, "'Big Money' Discovers the Huge Tax Breaks and Subsidies for Wind Energy While Taxpayers and Electric Customers Pick Up the Tab," Alternative World Energy Outlook, April 14, 2005. Available at www.aweo.org/Schleede.html.

35 Ibid.

36 "The Big Wind-Power Cover-up," *Investor's Business Daily*, March 12, 2010. Available at http://www.investors.com/NewsAndAnalysis/ArticlePrint.aspx?id=527214.

37 Ibid.

38 "President Obama Awards $2.3 Billion for New Clean-Tech Manufacturing Jobs," White House Press Release, January 8, 2010. Available at http://www.whitehouse.gov/the-press-office/president-obama-awards-23-billion-new-clean-manufacturing-jobs.

39 "The Big Wind-Power Cover-Up," ibid.

40 "The Obama Administration's Alternative Energy Cover-up," BrookesNews.com, March 15, 2010. Available at http://www.brookesnews.com/101503energy.html.

41 "DOE E-mails to Wind Energy Lobbyists Cast Cloud Over Green Job Proposals," *Investor's Business Daily*, March 11, 2010.

42 Andrew Revkin, "Solar Power Wins Enthusiasts but Not Money," *New York Times*, July 16, 2007. Available at http://www.nytimes.com/2007/07/16/business/16solar.html.

43 Mark Clayton, "Wind, Solar Tax Credits to Expire: Green Energy Advocates Urge Sustained Support through Inclusion in Stimulus Package," *Christian Science Monitor*, January 22, 2008. Available at http://www.csmonitor.com/2008/0122/p03s05-usec.html.

44 Paul Davidson, "Forecast for Solar Power: Sunny," *USA Today*, August 28, 2007. Available at http://www.usatoday.com/weather/climate/2007-08-26-solar_n.htm.

45 Robert L. Bradley Jr, "Renewable Energy: Not Cheap, Not 'Green,'" CATO Institute, Policy Analysis, August 27, 2007. Available at: http://www.cato.org/pubs/pas/pa-280.html.

46 Ibid.

47 Ibid.

48 Gwyneth Cravens, *Power to Save the World: The Truth About Nuclear Energy* (Knopf, 2007), 249–50.

49 William M. Welch, "Air Force Embraces Solar Power," *USA Today*, April 18, 2007. Available at http://www.usatoday.com/tech/science/2007-04-17-air-force-solar-power_n.htm.

50 Bradley, ibid.

51 "Next Gen SeaGen," Modern Power Systems, July 19, 2006. Available at http://www.modern-powersystems.com/story.asp?sc=2037525.

52 John W. Lund, "Characteristics, Development, and Utilization of Geothermal Resources," *Geo-Heat Center Bulletin of the Oregon Institute of Technology*, June 2007. Available at http://geoheat.oit.edu/pdf/tp126.pdf.

53 Charles F. Kutscher, "The Status and Future of Geothermal Electric Power," *National Renewable Energy Laboratory*, August 2000.

54 Ibid.

55 Diane S. Katz, "The Trade-Offs of Renewable Energy," *Michigan Science*, November 15, 2006. Available at http://www.mackinac.org/8074.

56 Taylor, ibid.

57 Michelle Kubik et al., "The Future of Geothermal Energy: Impact of Enhanced Geothermal Systems on the United States in the 21st Century," Massachusetts Institute of Technology, 2006. Prepared under Idaho National Laboratory Subcontract No. 63 00019 for the US Department of Energy, Assistant Secretary for Energy Efficiency and Renewable Energy, Office of Geothermal Technologies, under DOE Idaho Operations Office Contract DEAC0705ID14517. Available at http://www1.eere.energy.gov/geothermal/pdfs/future_geo_energy.pdf.

58 Jeremy Griggs, "Thesis Study: A Reevaluation of Geopressured Geothermal Aquifers as an Energy Source," Louisiana State University, Craft and Hawkins Department of Petroleum Engineering, 2004.

59 P. C. Novelli et al., "Molecular Hydrogen in the Troposphere: Global Distribution and Budget," *Journal of Geophysical Research,* vol. 104, no. D23 (1999): 104–30, 427–30.

60 "Price-Anderson Act Provides Effective Nuclear Insurance at No Cost to the Public," Nuclear Energy Institute, June 2010. Available at http://www.nei.org/keyissues/safetyandsecurity/factsheets/priceandersonact/.

61 "International Energy Outlook 2010," Energy Information Administration. Available at www.eia.doe.gov/oiaf/ieo/electricity.html.

62 Susan Moran and Anne Raup, "A Rush for Uranium: Mines in the West Reopen as Ore Prices Reach Highs of the 1970s," *New York Times,* March 28, 2007. Available at http://select.nytimes.com/search/restricted/article?res=F30A1EFB38540C7B8EDDAA0894DF404482.

63 Uwe R. Fritsce, "Comparing Greenhouse Gas Emissions and Abatement Costs of Nuclear and Alternative Energy Options from a Life Cycle Perspective," Institute for Applied Ecology (Oko-Institut), 1997. See also Jan Willem Storm, "Nuclear Power: The Energy Balance." Available at www.stormsmith.nl. Also "Energy Analysis of Power Systems," World Nuclear Association, July 2009. Available at www.world-nuclear.org/info/inf11.html. Also "Nuclear Power, Climate Change, and the Energy Review," Friends of the Earth, June 2006. Available at www.foe.co.uk/resource/briefings/nuclear_power.pdf. Also "Supply of Uranium," World Nuclear Organization, September 2009. Available at www.world_nuclear.orginfo/inf75.html. Also Mohamed El Baradei, "Nuclear Power: Preparing for the Future, International Atomic Energy Agency. Available at http://www.iaea.org/NewsCenter/Statements/2005/ebsp2005n004.html.

64 "State Carbon Emissions Data for the United States: 1990–2001," Mongabay.com, June 21, 2006. Available at http://news.mongabay.com/2006/0621-co2.html.

65 "Endangered Species: US Army Corps of Engineers," Public Notice, June 9, 2005. Available at www.savejonesbeach.org/full-public-notice-lioswp.pdf. See also Eleanor Tillinghast, "Many Costs, Few Benefits of Wind Power," Berkshire Eagle (Industrial Wind Action Group), March 4, 2006. Available at www.windaction.org/articles/1864.

66 "Greening of Paradise Valley," Modesto Irrigation District. Available at www.mid.org/about/100-years/chpt_19.htm>. See also Thomas Raymond Wellock, *Critical Masses: Opposition to Nuclear Power in California,* 1958–1978 (University of Wisconsin Press, 1998).

67 Jesse H. Ausubel, "Renewable and Nuclear Heresies," *International Journal of Nuclear Governance, Economy and Ecology,* vol. 1, no. 3 (2007). Available at http://nucleargreen.blogspot.com/2008/02/renewable-and-nuclear-heresies.html.

68 Nicholas A. Vardy, "Investing in Uranium: the Bull is Back?," The Global Guru. Available at http://www.theglobalguru.com/article.php?id=164&offer=GURU.

69 Rebecca Smith, "Carbon Caps May Give Nuclear Power a Lift," *Wall Street Journal,* May 19, 2008.

70 "Greening of Paradise Valley," ibid. (See also Wellock, ibid.)

71 Steve Tetreault, "Yucca Radiation Limits Unveiled," *Las Vegas Review Journal,* August 10, 2005. Available at http://www.reviewjournal.com/lvrj_home/2005/Aug-10-Wed-2005/news/27026244.html. See also Leo S. Gomez, "Executive Summary: Ultra-Low-LevelRadiation Effects Summit Final Report," January 15–16, 2006. Available at www.orionint.com/ullre/report-2006.pdf. Also "Electricity from Coal," US Environmental Protection Agency, December 28, 2007. Available at http://www.epa.gov/cleanenergy/energy-and-you/affect/coal.html. Also "Nuclear Waste Disposal: High Level," Nuclear Energy Institute.Also Matthew Bunn,

"Preventing Nuclear Terrorism," Belter Center for Science and Public Affairs, John F. Kennedy School of Government, Harvard University, September 24, 2002. Also "Military Warheads as a Source of Nuclear Fuel: Information and Issues Briefs," World Nuclear Association, October 2009. Available at http://www.world-nuclear.org/info/inf13.html.

72 "Wind Power Has Been Promoted: Wind Power Report 2006," Industrial Wind Action Group & ABS Energy Research. Available at www.windaction.org/documents/4446. See also Bernard Benoit, "Berlin Open to Liberalizing Energy Market," *Financial Times*, January 12, 2007. Available at http://www.ft.com/cms/s/507d626a-a1e1-11db-8bc1-0000779e2340,Authorised=false. html?_i_location=http%3A%2F%2Fwww.ft.com%2Fcms%2Fs%2F0%2F507d626a-a1e1-11db-8bc1-0000779e2340.html&_i_referer=http%3A%2F%2Fsearch.ft.com%2Fsearch%3F queryText%3DBerlin%2BOpen%2Bto%2BLiberalizing%2BEnergy%2BMarket%26aje%3Dt rue%26dse%3D%26dsz%3D%26x%3D8%26y%3D5. Also Paul Lorenzini, "A Second Look at Nuclear Power," *Issues in Science & Technology*, vol. 295, no. 3 (March 22, 2005). Available at www.issues.org/21.3/lorenzini.html.

73 "Nevada Loses Decision on Atomic Waste," *New York Times*, August 9, 2006. Available at http://epw.senate.gov/public/index.cfm?FuseAction=Hearings.Testimony&Hearing_ID=da19acbe-802a-23ad-4357-2f58816a73f0&Witness_ID=ce5b02ed-1a66-4b18-a9a7-21b63db6be53. See also Harry Reid, "Press Release of Senator Reid: Reid Statement on Falsification of Yucca Mountain Documentation," March 16, 2005. Available at http://reid.senate.gov/newsroom/record.cfm?id=233737.

74 Ibid.

75 Ibid.

76 "Obama to Announce Loan Guarantee for Nuclear Plant," Associated Press, February 16, 2010.

77 Rebecca Smith and Stephen Power, "Democrats Revolt over Energy," *Wall Street Journal*, March 5, 2010.

78 Sean Higgins and Reinhardt Krause, "New Nuclear Plants Are on Their Way, with Federal Help," *Investor's Business Daily*, June 20, 2008. Available at http://investorshub.advfn.com/boards/read_msg.aspx?message_id=30167445.

79 Larry Bell, "Alternative Energy Options: Getting a Real Grip on 'Green,'" *Energy Tribune*, July 2008.

Chapter 10

1 Nao Nakanishi and Niu Shuping, "China Builds Plant to Turn Coal into Barrels of Oil," Reuters, June 4, 2008. Available at http://www.reuters.com/article/rbssIndustryMaterialsUtilitiesNews/idUSSP13361320080604.

2 Committee on Coal Research, Technology, and Resource Assessments to Inform Energy Policy, *Coal: Research and Development to Support National Energy Policy* (The National Academies Press, 2007). Available at http://www.nap.edu/openbook.php?record_id=11977&page=44.

3 "Coal Power Goes on Trial," MSNBC, January 14, 2008. Available at http://www.msnbc.msn.com/id/22652908/.

4 Eileen O'Grady, "Coalitions Geared to Block US Coal Development," Reuters, January 15, 2008. Available at http://uk.reuters.com/article/oilRpt/idUKN1530481720080115.

5 Rebecca Smith, "Coal's Doubters Block New Wave of Power Plants," *Wall Street Journal*, July 25, 2007. Available at http://www.mindfully.org/Energy/2007/Coal-Power-Plants25jul07.htm.

6 Jeffrey Ball, "Wall Street Tells Big Coal Not So Fast," *Wall Street Journal*, February 4, 2008. Available at http://blogs.wsj.com/environmentalcapital/2008/02/04/wall-street-tells-big-coal-not-so-fast/.

7 Rebecca Smith, ibid.

8 Julie Ruggiero, "DOE Announces Restructured FutureGen Approach to Demonstrate CCS Technology at Multiple Clean Coal Plants," US Department of Energy, Office of Public Affairs, January 30, 2008. Available at http://fossil.energy.gov/news/techlines/2008/08003-DOE_Announces_Restructured_FutureG.html.

9 "Georgia Court Blocks Coal Plant," *Washington Post*, July 1, 2008. Available at http://www.washingtonpost.com/wp-dyn/content/article/2008/06/30/AR2008063002134.html.

10 Lisa Mascaro and Phoebe Sweet, "Reid Has Plan to Leave Coal in the Dust," *Las Vegas Sun*, August 5, 2007. Available at http://www.lasvegassun.com/news/2007/aug/05/reid-has-plan-to-leave-coal-in-the-dust/.

11 "Early Days of Coal Research," US Department of Energy, Fossil Energy Office of Communications, January 10, 2006. Available at http://www.fe.doe.gov/aboutus/history/syntheticfuels_history.html.

12 Ibid.

13 Ibid.

14 Dennis Behreandt, "The Promise of Synthetic Fuel: Coal-to-Liquid Technologies, Pioneered Almost 80 Years Ago, Have the Potential to Free America from Its Dependence on Foreign Oil," *New American*, November 27, 2006. Available at http://findarticles.com/p/articles/mi_m0JZS/is_24_22/ai_n24996859/.

15 Ibid.

16 Deborah Paulus-Jagric, "Global Warming: A Comparative Guide to the EU and the US and Their Approaches to the UN Framework Convention on Climate Change and the Kyoto Protocol," Hauser Global Law School Program, March 2007. Available at http://www.nyulawglobal.org/globalex/Climate_Change_Kyoto_Protocol.htm.

17 "Climate Facts," Natural Resources Defense Council, February 2007. Available at http://www.nrdc.org/globalWarming/coal/liquids.pdf.

18 Ibid.

19 Ibid.

20 Keith Arterburn, "INL Study Demonstrates Environmental Advantages of Baard Energy's Coal to Liquid (CTL) Fuel Process," Idaho National Laboratory, June 18, 2007. Available at http://www.inl.gov/featurestories/2007-06-18.shtml.

21 Nakanishi and Shuping, ibid.

22 Ibid.

23 Robert Bryce, "The Democrats' No-Drill Energy Plan," *Energy Tribune*, July 2008. Available at http://www.energytribune.com/articles.cfm?aid=936.

24 "Senator Boxer: Preventing Offshore Drilling in California," Press Release, February 21, 2006. Available at http://www.boxer.senate.gov/en/press/updates/022106.cfm.

25 "West Coast Senators Introduce Bill to Protect the Pacific Coast from Offshore Oil Drilling," Press Release of US Senator Barbara Boxer, May 13, 2010. Available at http://boxer.senate.gov/en/press/releases/051310.cfm.

26 Margaret Sheridan, "California Crude Oil Production and Imports," 2006 Staff Report, California Energy Commission, Fuels and Transportation Division, Fossil Fuels Office. Available at http://www.energy.ca.gov/2006publications/CEC-600-2006-006/CEC-600-2006-006.PDF.

27 "Killing the Drilling," *Investor's Business Daily*, June 7, 2010.

28 "Assessment of Undiscovered Oil and Gas Resources of the North Cuba Basin, Cuba, 2004," USGS, February 2005. Available at http://pubs.usgs.gov/fs/2005/3009/pdf/fs2005_3009.pdf.

29 Steven Thomma, "Signers object to changes in report," *McClatchy-Tribune News Service*, June 12, 2010. Available at http://bendbulletin.com/apps/pbcs.dll/article?AID=/20100612/NEWS0107/6120333/.

30 "The Antidrilling Commission," *Wall Street Journal*, June 22, 2010.

31 "Obama's Moratorium, Drilled," *Wall Street Journal*, June 23, 2010.

32 Stephen Power, "Judge Overturns Drilling Ban," *Wall Street Journal*, June 23, 2010.

33 "The Job Moratorium" *Investor's Business Daily*, July 29, 2010. Available at http://www.investors.com/NewsAndAnalysis/Article/541937/201007281900/The-Job-Moratorium.aspx.

34 "Salazar's Ban Is Soros' Bonanza," *Investor's Business Daily*, June 24, 2010.

35 "The Bucyrus Travesty," *Wall Street Journal*, June 30, 2010.

36 Louise Radnofsky and Jean Spencer, "Public Still Backs Offshore Drilling," *Wall Street Journal*, May 13, 2010.

37 "Petroleum Inputs to the Sea," Oil in the Sea III: Input, Fates, and Effects (2003), The National Academies Press. Available at http://www.nap.edu/openbook.php?record_id=10388&page=2.

38 Monica Showalter, "In Alaska, the Bid to Drill Oil Means Beating Off Myths, Too; Gov. Sarah Palin Seeks to End Misconceptions in Lower 48 About Oil," *Investor's Business Daily*, July 14, 2008. Available at http://www.freeconservatives.com/vb/showthread.php?t=61366.

39 "Alaska's 'Frustrated' Governor Palin on Our 'Nonsensical' Energy Policy," *Investor's Business Daily*, July 14, 2008. Available at http://omgili.com/newsgroups/talk/environment/C49F02AA10FDCleonard78spprimusca.html.

40 Showalter, ibid.

41 Kate Anderson Brower, "Obama Says US Can't Lag Behind on Energy Technology" (Update 2), Bloomberg.com, May 26, 2010. Available at http://www.bloomberg.com/apps/news?pid=20601103&sid=aWpF05HrToN8.

42 Steven Mufson and Michael Shear, "Obama Hopes Oil Spill Boosts Support for Climate Bill," June 3, 2010. Available at http://washingtonpost.com/wp-dyn/content/article/2010/06/02/AR2010060200380.html.

43 Sean Higgins, "Climate Bill, in Shifting Political Winds, Would Further Restrict Offshore Drilling," *Investor's Business Daily*, May 13, 2010.

44 "War vs. Big Oil Goes Beyond Drilling Ban," Bernard L. Weinstein, *Investor's Business Daily*, August 5, 2010. Available at http://www.investors.com/NewsAndAnalysis/Article/542784/201008051824/War-Vs-Big-Oil-Goes-Beyond-Drilling-Ban.aspx.

45 "Official Energy Statistics for the US Government: Petroleum Basic Statistics," Energy Information Administration. Available at http://www.eia.doe.gov/basics/quickoil.html.

46 Bryce, ibid.

47 David Ivanovich, "Are Speculators Fueling Oil Run-Up?" *Houston Chronicle*, May 25, 2008.

48 Jon Birger, "The Politics of Oil Shale," CNN Money, June 6, 2008. Available at http://money.cnn.com/2008/06/06/news/economy/birger_shale.fortune/?postversion=2008060617.

49 James T. Bartis, Tom LaTourrette, Lloyd Dixon, D.J. Peterson, and Gary Cecchine, "Oil Shale

Development in the United States, Prospects and Policy Issues," Rand Infrastructure, Safety, and Environment, 2005. Available at http://www.rand.org/pubs/monographs/2005/RAND_MG414.pdf.

50 "About Oil Shale," Oil Shale and Tar Sands Programmatic EIS Information Center. Available at http://ostseis.anl.gov/guide/oilshale/index.cfm?printversion=true.

51 Birger, ibid.

52 Ibid.

53 "Daniel Gross, "The Great Refinery Shortage: America needs oil. You'd rather have a beach condo," *Slate*, June 8, 2004. Available at http://www.slate.com/id/2102031.

54 "Will to Drill Is Strong, Poll Finds; Climate Change Pales as Concern," *Investor's Business Daily*, July 14, 2008. Available at http://www.climatechangefraud.com/editorials/1641-will-to-drill-is-strong-poll-finds-climate-change-pales-as-concern.

55 Sergy Paltsev et al., "Appendix D: Analysis of the Cap and Trade Features of the Lieberman-Warner Climate Security Act (S. 2191)," MIT Joint Program on the Science and Policy of Global Change, Report 146 (2007). Available at http://web.mit.edu/globalchange/www/MITJPSPGC_Rpt146_AppendixD.pdf.

Chapter 11

1 "E-mails of climate researchers buttress case of warming fraud," *Investor's Business Daily*, November 30, 2009. Available at http://www.brookesnews.com/093011globalwarmingemails_print.html.

2 "The UN's Global Warming Muzzle," *Investor's Business Daily*, December 11, 2009.

3 Robert Costa, "Inhofe: CRU Scandal Bigger than ACORN Flap," National Review online, November 24, 2009. Available at http://corner.nationalreview.com/post/?q=N2QzZDQ0YjNmMmU3NTQwOWM2M2M0YmE2NGY4YTQzMjc=.

4 Ibid.

5 Keith Johnson and Guatam Naik, "Lawmakers Probe Climate E-mails," *Wall Street Journal*, November 24, 2009. Available at http://online.wsj.com/article/SB125902685372961609.html.

6 Christopher Monckton, "Viscount Monckton on Climategate: 'They Are Criminals,'" Pajamasmedia, November 23, 2009. Available at http://pajamasmedia.com/blog/viscount-monckton-on-global-warminggate-they-are-criminals-pjm-exclusive/.

7 Peter C. Glover, "Europe: Five Minutes to Midnight," *Energy Tribune*, July 2008.

8 Ibid.

9 "The Future of Oil," Institute for the Analysis of Global Security. Available at http://www.iags.org/futureofoil.html.

10 Robert Bryce, *Gusher of Lies: The Dangerous Delusions of "Energy Independence"* (Public Affairs, 2008), 4–6.

11 "The Future of Oil," ibid.

12 Gal Luft, "Fueling the Dragon: China's Race into the Oil Market," Institute for the Analysis of Global Security. Available at http://www.iags.org/china.htm.

13 "Russia: Background," US Energy Information Administration: Independent Statistics and Analysis, May 2008. Available at http://www.eia.doe.gov/cabs/Russia/Background.html.

14 Sergei Blagov, "Russia Pursues Energy Partnership with China," *Eurasia Daily Monitor*,

August 1, 2008. Available at http://www.jamestown.org/single/?no_cache=1&tx_ttnews%5Btt_news%5D=33853.

15 "Russia: Background," ibid.

16 Bryce, 38–40.

17 Ibid., 109–10.

18 Kevin Yamamura, "Gov. Schwarzenegger, Google Unveil Climate Risk Report," *Sacramento Bee*, December 3, 2009. Available at http://www.mcclatchydc.com/2009/12/03/79969/gov-schwarzenegger-google-unveil.html.

19 "How Cronyism Is Infesting Cap-and-Trade," *Investor's Business Daily*, May 6, 2010.

20 "California Should Copy Texas," *Investor's Business Daily*, December 8, 2009.

21 John Goldberg, "Global Warming as a Political Tool," *National Review Online*, December 11, 2009. Available at http://article.nationalreview.com/417683/global-warming-as-a-political-tool/jonah-goldberg.

22 "Greens' Real Target: US Economy," *Investor's Business Daily*, December 8, 2009. Available at http://www.investors.com/NewsAndAnalysis/Article-aspx?id=514619.

23 Ibid.

24 "President-Elect Barack Obama Announces Key Members of Energy and Environment Team," News Room Press Release, December 15, 2008. Available at http://change.gov/newsroom/entry/president_elect_barack_obama_announces_key_members_of_energy_and_environmen/.

25 "Crisis of Climate Change," The Clinton School Speaker Series: Carol Browner, November 16, 2006. Available at http://www.clintonschoolspeakers.com/lecture/view/crisis-of-climate-change/.

26 "Senate Holds Hearing on Legality of Presidential Czars," Judicial Watch Blog, October 7, 2009. Available at http://www.judicialwatch.org.foiablog/45?page=3.

27 Josie Garthwaite, "Todd Stern's Strategy for Climate Negotiations: Not Another Kyoto," January 26, 2009. Available at http://earth2tech.com/2009/01/26/todd-sterns-strategy-for-climate-negotiations-not-another-kyoto/.

28 "Congressman Issa (R-CA) Now Targeting John Holdren in 'ClimateGate' Hacking Scandal," *EnviroKnow: The Politics of Sustainability*, November 23, 2009. Available at http://zikkir.com/z0001/52067.

29 "Boxer, Holdren Defend Motley CRU," Yahoo! News, December 12, 2009. Available at http://a2zbreeds.info/boxer-holdren-defend-motley-cru-yahoo-news.

30 Ian Talley, "EPA Declares Greenhouse Gases a Danger," *Wall Street Journal*, December 8, 2009.

31 Keith Johnson, "Steven Chu: 'Coal Is My Worst Nightmare,'" *Wall Street Journal*, December 11, 2008; comments by Stephen Chu at the National Clean Energy Summit convened by the University of Nevada–Las Vegas, Senator Harry Reid (D-NV), and the Center for American Progress Action Fund, summer 2008. Available on YouTube, "Dr. Stephen Chu at National Clean Energy Summit."

32 "Acceptance Speech by Hilda Solis," John F. Kennedy Library Foundation, Courage Award Ceremony, May 22, 2000. Available at http://www.jfklibrary.org/Education+and+Public+Programs/Profile+in+Courage+Award/Award+Recipients/Hilda+Solis/Acceptance+Speech+by+Hilda+Solis.htm.

33 Statement of Nancy H. Sutley at Hearing on Nominations for the Committee on Environmental and Public Works, United States Senate, January 14, 2009. Available at http://epw.senate.gov/public/index.cfm?FuseAction=Files.View&FileStore_id=2f7ac97a-042b-4f9a-bd1f-ca7d5f4faa46.

34 "Antarctic Ice Melt at Lowest Levels in Satellite Era," *World Climate Report,* October 6, 2009.

35 "A Matter of Facts," *Investor's Business Daily*, July 29, 2009.

36 "Inhofe recycles long-debunked denier talking points—will the media be fooled (again)?" Climate Progress, December 11, 2008. Available at http://climateprogress.org/2008/12/11/inhofe-morano-recycles-long-debunked-denier-talking-points-will-the-media-be-fooled-again/.

37 "Former NAC Chair Jack Schmitt Quits Planetary Society Over New Roadmap," Keith Cowing, NASA Watch, November 17, 2008. Availlable at http://nasawatch.com/archives/2008/Former-nac-chair-jack-schmitt-quits-planetary-society-over-new-roadmap.html.

38 Vaclav Klaus, "Global Warming Hysteria or Freedom and Prosperity?" Ambrosetti Forum, Villa d'Este, Italy, September 9, 2007. Available at http://www.euportal.cz/Articles/1852-global-warming-hysteria-or-freedom-and-prosperity-.aspx.

Chapter 12

1 Friedman, Thomas L. *The World Is Flat: A Brief History of the Twenty-First Century* (Farrar, Straus, and Giroux, 2005), 314–15.

2 Ibid., 271.

3 Ibid., 265.

4 Michael Economides and Ronald Oligney, *The Color of Oil* (Round Oak Publishing Company, 2000), 121.

5 Ibid.

6 "PIW Ranks the World's Top Oil Companies," *Petroleum Intelligence Weekly Special Supplement* (December 22, 1997): 1–4.

7 Karen Ehrhardt-Martinez and John A. Laitner, "The Size of the U.S. Energy Efficiency Market: Generating a More Complete Picture," May 2008, Report Number E083, American Council for an Energy-Efficient Economy. Available at http://aceee.org/pubs/e083.pdf?CFID=1664432&CFTOKEN=20896320.

8 Rachel Halpern et al., "Energy Policy and US Industry Competitiveness," US Department of Commerce, International Trade Administration, Office of Energy and Environmental Industries. Available at http://www.ita.doc.gov/td/energy/energy%20use%20by%20industry.pdf.

9 "Carmakers Accelerate Efforts to Build Next-Generation Hybrid," *Investor's Business Daily*, July 10, 2008.

10 "Abstracts of BES Workshop and Technical Reports," Basic Energy Sciences Workshop Reports, 1999–2010. Available at http://www.er.doe.gov/bes/reports/abstracts.html.

11 "Scaling Down the Nest," NuWire Investor (April 1, 2007). Available at http://www.nuwireinvestor.com/articles/scaling-down-the-nest-51020.aspx.

12 Jay Palmer, "Ticket to Riches," *Barron's*, August 4, 2008.

13 John W. Lund, "Characteristics, Development, and Utilization of Geothermal Resources," *Geo-Heat Center Bulletin of the Oregon Institute of Technology*, June 2007. Available at http://geoheat.oit.edu/pdf/tp126.pdf.

14 Committee on Abrupt Climate Change, Ocean Studies Board, Polar Research Board, Board on Atmospheric Sciences and Climate, Division on Earth and Life Studies, National Research Council, *Abrupt Climate Change: Inevitable Surprises* (The National Academies Press, 2002). Available at http://www.nap.edu/openbook.php?isbn=0309074347.

INDEX

A list of abbreviations and acronyms is located on pages xvii–xix.

A

"Abrupt Climate Change: Inevitable Surprises" joint report, 253
"An Abrupt Climate Change Scenario and Its Implications for United States National Security" (Global Business Network), 79
acid rain, 56, 149–50
aerosols, 56, 86
Africa, 48–49, 68, 76, 152, 239
Ahlbeck, Jarl, 234
Ahluwalia, Arun, 234
Ainley, David, 74
Akasofu, Syun-Ichi, 31
Alaska, 66, 70–71, 97–98, 205–6.
  See also ANWR
Alcoa, 135
Alliance for Climate Protection (ACP), 8, 19
alternative energy. *See* "green" energy
Alvarez, Gabriel Calzada, 168–69
Amaranth hedge fund, 132
Amazon rain forest, 81
Ambrose, Rona, 111
America. *See* United States
American Association of State Climatologists (AASC), 25
American Clean Energy and Security Act of 2009, 139–40
American Council for an Energy-Efficient Economy (ACEEE), 247
American Council on Renewable Energy, 164
American Electric Power, 131
American Geophysical Union, 24
American Meteorological Society, 25
American Petroleum Institute, 210
American Power Act, 134–35
American state climatologists survey, 25
American Wind Energy Association (AWEA), 168–69, 180
Amstrup, Steven, 69
Amtrak, 131
Amundsen, Roald, 67
An Inconvenient Truth (Gore)

on CO_2 levels, 39
disease predictions, 76
global warming dramatizations, 9, 63, 69, 70
"hockey stick" graph usage, 36
proceeds recipients, 19
thermohaline convection, 79–80
UK response to, 83
Annan, Kofui, 101
Antarctica, 63–64, 67–68, 72–74, 86, 104, 232
anthropogenic global warming. *See* human sources of global warming
ANWR (Arctic National Wildlife Refuge), 2, 8, 9, 71, 197, 204–5
Apple Inc., 19–20
Arch Coal, Inc., 195
Archer Daniels Midland Company, 162
Arctic region
  Gore on, 145–46
  polar bears, 9, 68–72, 205
  sea ice, 66, 67, 71, 232
  sea levels, 64
  temperature patterns, 31, 146–47
Argonne National Laboratory, 195
Arizona, 213
Armstrong, J. Scott, 94
Atlantic Multidecadal Oscillation (AMO), 33, 52
Atlantic Ocean, 33, 52, 79–80, 232
Audubon Society, 174
Australia, 109, 116
automotive companies, 137
automotive fuel, 192–93
auto values, 247
Avery, Dennis T., xi
aviation fuel, 134, 192–93, 250
Ayres, Bill, 133
Aziz, Tariq, 101

B

Baard Energy, 194
Bailey, Ron, 112
Ball, Timothy, 216

Barents Sea, 66, 146
Barrasso, John, 98
Bartells, Carlin, 131
Bay Area Environmental Research Institute, 81
Bayh, Evan, 142
Bechtel Corporation, 192
Beinecke, Frances, 201, 202
Benedick, Richard, 102
Bering Sea, 66
Beyond Interdependence (Trilateral Commission), 102
"Beyond the Ivory Tower" (Oreskes), 26
biofuels, 158–62, 180, 193, 195, 208–9, 212, 219
birds, 165–66, 174
Blair, Tony, 108
Blood, David, 10, 20, 130
Blum, Richard, 20
Bodman, Samuel W., 193, 204
Boesch, Donald, 201
Booker, Christopher, 147
Boxer, Barbara, 198
BP, 137–38, 199, 200–203, 213
Brazil, 161, 203, 211, 244
Brekke, Pål, 234–35
Briffa, Keith, 3, 94–95
British Coal Union, 108
Britton, Dave, 38
Brown, Gordon, 113
Browner, Carol, 228–29
Bruck, Robert, 149–50
Brundtland Commission, 101
Bucyrus International Inc., 203
Bulletin of the American Meteorological Society, 32
Bullock, Mark, 82
Bureau of Transportation, 208
Burnett, H. Sterling, 94
Burton, Sir Michael, 83
Bush, George H. W. administration, 150, 174
Bush, George W. (and administration), 21, 23, 79, 106, 109, 150, 198, 205–6, 210
butterfly effect, 43

C

California
   AB32 implementation costs, 223–25
   economic environment, 224
   "green" energy, 163, 166, 171–72, 176, 181, 224
   oil industry, 198–99, 212
   tree ring research, 37

California Energy Commission, 223
California Small Business Roundtable, 223
California State University at Sacramento, 223
Canada, 67, 69, 110–11, 196, 210–11, 221
Canadian tar sand reserves, 211
Cantwell, Maria, 198
cap-and-trade
   carbon brokers, 8, 130–33
   as climate change solution, 19
   corporate beneficiaries, 128–30, 135–39, 180–81
   costs, 9, 139–40, 142, 184, 228
   Democratic support for, 209
   description, 126–28
   fraudulent activities, 140–41
   Holdren as supporter of, 153
   legislation, 134–35, 141–42, 206
   mercury emissions, 150–51
   Obama administration policy, 9, 26, 133, 135, 137, 138, 141
   rationale, 125–26
   ShoreBank connections, 134
Capellan, John, 41
Cape Wind project, 165, 166
capitalism
   entrepreneurship and, 242–43
   free markets and, 97, 98, 126, 127, 214, 227, 239–40, 254
   government interference and, 126, 127, 196, 216, 225–26, 242–43
   innovation and, 137
   opponents of, 238–39
Capps, Lois, 198
Capricorn Investment Group, 19
carbon brokers, 8, 130–33
carbon capture and storage (CCS), 191
carbon dioxide. See CO2
carbon-emission trading. See cap-and-trade
Carlin, Alan, 8–9
Carson, Rachel, 151
Carter, Jimmy administration, 183
Caterpillar, 138
Center for American Progress (CAP), 131, 168–69, 229
Center for Data Analysis (CDA), 140
Champion, Sam, 69
change adaptation, 251–54
Chapman, Bill, 146
Chavez, Hugo, 117, 221, 228, 238
Chernobyl accident, 179
Chevron, 199
Chicago Climate Exchange (CCX), 10, 130–33

China
coal industry, 195–96
economic trends, 239, 240
educational standards, 241–42
Kyoto Protocol and, 100, 107, 111–12, 117–18, 121
oil consumption, 196, 208, 209
oil industry, 200, 211, 220–22, 221, 244
Chirac, Jacques, 97
chlorofluorocarbons (CFCs), 86, 87, 104
Christy, John, 77, 87
Chu, Steven, 230–31
Chukchi Sea, 205, 206
Churchill, Winston, 138, 140
Cinergy, 136
Citigroup Inc., 190–91
Citizens for a Sound Economy, 86
Civil Society Institute, 247
Clapp, Philip, 44
Clean Air Act
CO2 emissions regulation, 9, 98, 126, 141–42, 191, 230, 243
fossil fuel restrictions, 213
mercury restrictions, 150
origins, 129
SO2 emissions regulation, 150
"clean coal," 189, 190
Climate Action Network, 104
Climate (and Energy) Bill, 134–35, 206
climate change
cyclical nature of, 2, 7, 20–22, 25, 48–50, 144, 231–32, 253
definition, 45
human influences on, 33–35
natural causes, 32, 33, 34, 51
solar activity effects, 52–54, 232
Climate Change and World Affairs (Tickell), 16
Climate Change Science Program (CCSP), 21
"Climate Change Summary for Policymakers."
See IPCC
Climate Exchange, 132
climate forcings, 27, 34, 51, 115, 232
"Climategate" e-mail scandal. See also CRU
data manipulation, 2–5, 8
Hansen and, 3–4, 233–34
importance of, 216–18
Mann and, 3–4, 36, 38, 230
Russian climate data, 37–38
climate models
on CO2 levels, 16–17
cost/benefit correlations, 115–16
CRU data as basis for, 38, 147–48, 217, 234

GCMs, 30–31
IPCC predictions and, 77, 90–91, 232, 234–35, 243
ocean circulation data, 64, 80
as polar bear extinction source, 70–71
temperature monitoring and, 43
uncertainty of, 30–33, 51–54, 90–91, 121, 232
Climate Research Unit (CRU). See CRU
Climate Science Watch, 21
Climate Stewardship Act, 136
Clinton, Bill (and administration)
ANWR veto by, 204
global warming campaign, 92
"hockey stick" graph usage by, 36
hydro development, 174
Kyoto Protocol rebuff, 105–6
Mount and Wirth appointments by, 92
as ShoreBank investor, 133
Stern's role, 229
Wirth's role, 102, 129
Clinton, Hillary, 117, 133, 228
clouds, 31, 32, 52, 55
CO2 (carbon dioxide). See also human sources of global warming
biofuels emissions of, 160–61
coal and, 188, 189
data manipulation, 88–89, 216, 230
emission increases, 110–12
Enron and market for, 129–30
EPA regulation of, 8, 9, 98, 126, 141–42, 191, 228, 230, 243
EU emission levels, 107, 108, 110, 111
EU reduction effort results, 110, 111, 218–19, 220, 243
fossil fuel emissions, 188, 189, 190, 191, 193, 194–95, 213, 214
Gore's views of, 39
Hansen on, 24
IPCC reports on, 36
levels of, 17–18, 33–37, 40, 55–56
natural sources of, 2, 33–35, 39
ocean pH claims, 75
pollutant designation, 2, 8, 126, 129–30, 187–88, 214, 243, 245
temperature correlation with, 2, 5, 7, 33–35, 39, 40, 50, 232
coal, 108, 110, 111, 142, 157, 188–92, 219, 231
coal-to-liquid synthetic fuel, 192–97, 253
Cogan, John, 204
Coleman, John, 83–84
Coletti, Miriam, 15
Colorado, 210–12

The Color of Oil (Economides), 243
Columbia River, 174
Committee on Abrupt Climate Change
    (National Research Council), 80
commodities speculators, 209–10
Commonwealth Scientific and Industrial
    Research Organisation, 72–73
communication sector trends, 250–51
compact fluorescent lighting (CFL), 150–51
Competitive Enterprise Institute, 168
Comprehensive Energy and Climate Bill,
    134–35, 206. See also cap-and-trade
computer models. See climate models
Congressional Budget Office (CBO), 139–40
Conoco Phillips, 138
consensus claims, 17, 24–27, 62, 88, 98
conservation efforts, 128, 238, 246–51
Constellation Energy Group, 181
"Constraints in Future Sea-Level Rise from
    Post Sea-Level Changes," 64
Cook, Edward, 3
The Cooling: Has the Next Ice Age Already
    Begun? (Ponte), 16
cooling trend, 4, 5–7, 8–9, 15–16, 50, 53, 57
Copenhagen Consensus, 119–20
Copenhagen Summit, 38, 99–100, 116–18, 226,
    228
coral reefs, 74–75
corporate average fuel economy (CAFE), 137
costs. See also "green" energy costs; subsidies
    cap-and-trade, 9, 139–40, 142, 184, 228
    energy production, 8, 10, 191, 193, 207–10,
    211, 214
    global warming research, 216, 224–26, 236
    Kyoto Protocol implementation, 115–16, 121
    to taxpayers and consumers, 8, 108, 113–14,
    116, 126, 135, 225
"Coverup in the Greenhouse" (Wall Street
    Journal), 93
Crichton, Michael, 143–44
CRU (Climate Research Unit). See also
    "Climategate" e-mail scandal
    Jones on temperatures, 50
    Lamb on climate shift, 49
    models based on data from, 38, 147–48,
    217, 234
    political influences on, 94–95
Cuba, 200, 220–21, 222
Cuccinelli, Kenneth T., 98
Current TV network, 20

D

Danish Center for Politiske Studier, 168
data. See climate models; CO2; temperatures
data manipulation. See also "Climategate"
    e-mail scandal
    CO2, 88–89, 216, 230
    in IPCC reports, 4, 22, 32–33, 41, 87–91
    perpetrators, 236
DDT and malaria, 152
Deep Space Climate Observatory (DSCOVR),
    23
Deepwater Horizon accident, 138, 198–203
Defenders of Wildlife, 69–70
Democratic Party
    climate research budgets, 21
    energy policies, 198, 206, 207, 209, 210–11,
    222
    green legislation, 129, 134–35, 206
    wealth redistribution agenda, 22
dengue, 76
Deng Xiaoping, 239–40
Denmark, 117
Deutsche Bahn, 250
Devon Energy, 199
DeVore, Chuck, 224
Diamond Offshore, 203
Di-Aping, Lumumba Stanislaus, 116
DiPerna, Paula, 131
Discover magazine, 89–90
diseases, 76–77, 119–20
DKRW Advanced Fuels, 195
Doerr, John, 161
Douglas, William O., 151
Dow Corning, 131
Duffy, Geoffrey, 235
Duke Energy, 136
DuPont, 131, 136–37
Durbin, Richard, 198

E

Earth
    atmosphere, 2, 16, 39, 52, 55–56, 73, 86, 104
    orbital wobble, 51–52
    Venus compared/contrasted with, 82
Earth Charter (Strong and Gorbachev), 226
Earth Summit conference, 100–103, 104,
    226–27
Easterbrook, Donald, 50
Ebell, Myron, 71

eco-anxiety or ecopsychology, 14–15
economic consequences. *See* costs
economic globalization, 238–40
economic growth versus environmentalism, 149–51, 240
Economides, Michael, 243
Ecoscience: Population, Resources, Environment (Holdren and Ehrlich), 153, 230
education trends, 241–42
Edwards, David, 173
Edwards, Sarah, 15
Ehrlich, Paul, 104, 152–53, 230
Eizenstat, Stuart, 130
Electric Power Annual (US Energy Information Administration), 174
Electric Reliability Council of Texas, 164
El Niño conditions, 32–33, 52, 72
emissions, 150–51. *See also* CO2; greenhouse gases; Kyoto Protocol
Endangered Species Act (ESA), 9, 68, 71, 205, 243
energy conservation, 128, 238, 246–51
energy efficiency trends, 247–51
Energy Independence Act of 2007, 209
energy industry. *See also* fossil fuels; "green" energy
    business migration and outsourcing, 9, 10, 142, 202–3, 224, 236, 252
    challenges, 155–58
    diversification of, 244
    sustainable energy claims and, 10, 156, 218–19
Energy Information Administration (EIA), 128, 179, 207–8
energy policy, US, 179, 220–23, 242–45. *See also* capitalism; fossil fuels; "green" energy
Energy Policy Act of 1992, 174
Energy Policy Act of 2005, 156, 210
enhanced geothermal systems (EGSs), 176–77
Enron, 128–30
Enron Loophole, 132, 209
Entergy Corp., 181
entrepreneurship, 242–43
environmental activism, 1–2, 149, 151–53, 206, 208–9, 245–46
Environmental Audit Committee, 140
Environmental Defense Fund, 18
environmental impact criticisms, 194
Environmental Protection Agency (EPA)
    administrators, 228–29, 230

on climate forecasts, 30–31
    climate research funding, 22–23
    CO2 emissions regulation, 8, 9, 98, 126, 141–42, 191, 228, 230, 243
    CRU data usage by, 217
    SO2 emissions regulation by, 150
environmental stewardship, 245–46
EPA. *See* Environmental Protection Agency
ethanol, 158–62, 212, 244
European Carbon Exchange (ECX), 133
European Space Agency, 54
European Union (EU)
    cap-and-trade, 140–41
    CO2 emissions levels, 107, 108, 110, 111
    CO2 reduction effort results, 110, 111, 218–19, 220, 243
    Copenhagen Summit concessions by, 116
    DDT ban, 152
    GDP, 227
    green party anger with US, 227–28
    Kyoto Protocol and, 97, 107–9, 121
    NGOs in, 104
    temperatures, 49–50
Excelsior Energy Inc., 190
"Excessive Speculation in the Natural Gas Market" (Senate Subcommittee on Investigations), 132
Exelon Corp., 181
ExxonMobil, 109, 138, 139, 195, 244

F

Fast Money magazine, 20
FCCC (Framework Convention on Climate Change), 38, 45, 100, 105, 116–18, 120–21. *See also* Kyoto Protocol
Federal Trade Commission, 209
Feinstein, Dianne, 20, 198
Feldman, Martin L. C., 202
Felmy, John, 210
Ferguson, Mark, 130
FirstEnergy Corp., 181
Fischer, Doug, 192
fish, 67, 174, 224
floods, 145, 147–48
Ford Motor Company, 131
forecasts. *See* climate models
forests, 81
Fortune magazine, 79
fossil fuels. *See also* natural gas; oil
    coal, 108, 110, 111, 142, 157, 188–92, 219, 231

liquid coal, 192–97, 253
  political environment, 213–14
  responsible resourcefulness, 246–47
  strategic dilemma, 197
FPL Group Inc., 181
France, 97, 182, 219, 244, 250
Francis, Diane, 118
Friedman, Thomas, 238, 239
Friends of the Earth, 174
FutureGen project, 191

G

Ganguly, Sangram, 81
Garcia, Terry, 201
Geithner, Tim, 133
general circulation models (GCMs), 30–31
General Electric, 137, 151, 195
Generation Investment Management (GIM),
  10, 20, 130, 134
The Genesis Strategy (Schneider), 16, 89
Geophysical Fluid Dynamic Laboratory, 16
Geophysical Research, 32
Geophysical Research Letters (GRL), 38, 68
Georgia, state of, 132
geothermal energy, 157, 175–77
Germany, 108, 110, 111, 141, 192, 219
the Geysers (California), 176
GHGs. See greenhouse gases
Giaever, Ivar, 144, 234
Giorgi, Fillipo, 95
GISS (Godard Institute for Space Studies), 7,
  23–24, 30, 32, 147–48
Gisseloe, Henning, 117
glaciers, 15–16, 48, 65–66, 68, 79, 95
Global Business Network, 79
globalization, 238–40, 243–45
"Global Review of Forest Fires" (WWF), 81
global warming. See also climate change;
  human sources of global warming
  alarmism about, 7, 9, 14, 61–63, 113–14,
  145–46, 208–9, 243, 252
  anti-American sentiment and, 226–28,
  238–40
  benefits of, 56–58, 70, 73–74, 89
  crisis emergence, 16–18, 86–87
  definition, 44
  Enron and, 128–30
  marketing strategies, 18–20
  public opinion about, 27
  religious references to, 143–44
  socialist agenda and, 226–27

global warming skeptics. See also scientists
  Gore on, 18, 24–25
  Holocaust denier comparisons, 68, 148–49
  number of, 26–27, 98, 217, 234–35
  Pachauri on, 96
Global Warming: The Complete Briefing
  (Houghton), 114
Godard Institute for Space Studies (GISS), 7,
  23–24, 30, 32, 147–48
Goldberg, Stanley, 235
Goldman Sachs, 130–31, 133
Goldman Sachs Asset Management (GSAM),
  130–31
Google, 20
Gorbachev, Mikhail, 226–27
Gordon, Jim, 165
Gore, Al. See also An Inconvenient Truth
  Alliance for Climate Protection, 8, 19
  business activities, 10, 18–20, 233
  cap-and-trade and, 129, 134
  as CCX shareholder, 131
  Center for American Progress, 229
  Deep Space Climate Observatory, 23
  energy policy, 161, 188
  Enron and, 129
  Generation Investment Management, 10, 20,
  130, 134
  on global warming, 39, 44, 73, 75, 145–46,
  233
  as global warming authority, 82–83
  on global warming skeptics, 18, 24–25
  Hansen and, 7, 17, 23
  "hockey stick" graph usage, 3
  Kyoto Protocol and, 105–6
  mentioned, 15, 153
  net worth, 19–20
  Nobel Prize, 3, 14, 19, 83
  Science, Technology and Space committee,
  17, 22, 62
  scientist criticisms of, 83–84
  US presidential campaign, 105–6
  Wirth and, 17, 92
  government
  interference by, 126, 127, 196, 216, 225–26,
  242–43
  regulatory environment, 198–200, 222–25,
  230, 236, 240, 242–43
Government Accountability Project, 24
Graham, Bob, 201
Graham, Lindsey, 134
Gray, Vincent, 88
Great Britain. See United Kingdom

The Greatest Global Warming Swindle (film), 76
Great Famine of 1315-1317, 49
The Great Global Warming Blunder (Spencer), 87
Greece, 111
Green, Kesten, 94
"green" energy. See also "green" energy costs
   abundance claims, 10
   alternative options, 8, 10, 19
   biofuels, 158–62, 193, 195, 208–9, 212, 219, 244
   corporate beneficiaries of, 137–38
   geothermal, 157, 175–77
   hydrogen, 177–78
   hydropower, 157, 163, 173–75, 183
   nuclear, 137, 157, 164, 172, 179–84, 219, 252
   overview, 155–58
   pollution from, 150–51, 160, 172, 176
   public policy decisions, 157–58
   renewable portfolio standards, 156, 167
   solar, 169–73
   sustainability claims, 10, 156, 218–19
   wind, 163–69, 180, 219
"green" energy costs
   ethanol production, 159, 162
   in general, 156–57
   land requirements, 180
   solar power, 170
   wind power, 163, 166–67
greenhouse gases (GHGs). See also CO2
   aerosols, 56
   chlorofluorocarbons, 86, 87, 104
   data manipulation, 88–89
   emissions levels, 108, 110–12, 128
   water vapor, 39, 52, 55–56, 232
Greenland, 33, 41, 49, 63–64, 65–66, 80, 146–47, 147–48
Greenpeace, 95, 163, 164
Green River Formation, 211, 212
Griffin, Michael, 43–44
Griggs, Jeremy, 177
Group of 77, 227–28
"Guidance Paper on Uncertainties" (IPCC), 89
Gulf of Mexico, 138, 197, 198–203, 205, 206, 221, 222, 223, 243
Gulf Stream, 79–80

H

Hadley Centre for Climate Change, 6–7, 30, 37–38, 80
Hanna, Edward, 41

Hansen, James
   alarmism of, vii, 7, 24, 44, 63, 233–34
   as Bush administration critic, 23–24
   climate models and, 32, 44
   CRU e-mails and, 3–4, 233–34
   as Enron consultant, 129
   as global warming expert, 84, 147–48, 233–34
   Heinz Foundation and, 23, 129
   US Senate testimony, 17, 23, 62
Harris, Peter, 130
Hasnain, Syed, 66–67
Hatch, Orrin, 212
Heartland Institute, 25, 26, 84
hedge funds, 10, 20, 130, 132
"Heidelberg Appeal" statement, 25
Heinz, John, 129
Heinz, Teresa (Kerry), 23, 129
Heinz Foundation, 23, 129
Hemingway, Ernest, 68
Heritage Foundation, 71, 140
Herrera, Victor Manuel Velasco, 235
Higham, Tim, 88–89
Himalayan glaciers, 66–67, 95
HIV/AIDS, 119
Hochberg, Fred, 203
"hockey stick" graph, 3, 36–37, 41
Holdren, John, 153, 230, 242
Hornbeck Offshore Services, LLC, 202
Horner, Christopher, 147, 168, 169
Houghton, Mary, 133
Houghton, Sir John, 92, 114
housing trends, 249
Howat, Ian, 66
"How Warming Is Being Made: The Case of Russia" (IEA), 37–38
Hudson Bay, 69, 146
human sources of global warming
   climate models and, 33–35
   CO2 misconceptions, 38–42, 44–45, 215–17
   cost/benefit models, 115–16, 121
   crisis emergence, 86–87
   as Earth Summit rationale, 100
   IPCC reports on, 22, 40–41, 88–89, 91–93
   petitions and surveys on, 25–26
   political influences, 88–89, 91–93, 225
   as socialist agenda, 226–27
Hume, Mike, 62, 114
Hunt, Jack, 165
hurricanes, 4, 77–78, 97
Hussein, Saddam (government), 101
hydrogen power, 177–78
hydropower, 157, 163, 173–75, 183

I

ice
  glaciers, 30, 48, 65–66, 68, 79, 95
  polar caps, 24, 64, 145–47, 232–33
  sea, 66, 67, 69–70, 145–46
  sheets, 30, 63–64, 68–71, 79–80
Ice Ages. *See also* Little Ice Age
  predictions, 5, 15–16, 62, 120, 231–32
  Younger Dryas episode, 79–80
Iceland, 50
Idaho National Laboratory, 194
Illarionov, Andrei, 38
Illinois, 131
Independent Petroleum Association, 207
India
  economic trends, 239, 240
  educational standards, 241
  fossil fuel energy, 203, 208, 213, 221
  Kyoto Protocol and, 100, 111–12, 118, 121
Indian Ocean, 65
Inhofe, James, 26, 98, 134, 142, 193, 217, 234,
  240
INQUA Commission on Sea Level Changes
  and Coastal Evolution, 65
Institute for Public Policy Research (IPPR), 14,
  61–62
Institute for the Analysis of Global Security,
  184, 194
Institute of Economic Analysis (IEA), 37–38,
  221
integrated gasification combined cycle (IGCC)
  power plants, 191
InterAcademy Council, 95
Intercontinental Exchange, Inc. (ICE), 132–33
Intergovernmental Panel on Climate Change.
  See IPCC
"Internal Study on Climate" (EPA), 8–9
International Arctic Research Center, 66
International Association of Drilling
  Contractors, 202
International Atomic Energy Agency, 179
International Carbon Action Partnership
  (ICAP), 130
International Community for Ecopsychology,
  14–15
International Conference on Climate Change,
  83–84
International Journal of Climatology, 68
International Monetary Fund (IMF), 117
International Paper, 131

International Petroleum Exchange (IPE), 132,
  133
Invest, 136
IPCC (Intergovernmental Panel on Climate
  Change)
  alarmism of, 63
  calls for reform of, 95–96, 98
  climate models, 31–33, 77, 90–91, 120–21,
  232, 234–35, 243
  CRU data usage by, 234
  data manipulation by, 4, 22, 32–33, 41, 87–91,
  216
  EPA action based on reports from, 142
  establishment of, 86–87
  Himalayan glacier prediction by, 95
  human influences on warming, 40–41
  Kyoto Protocol cost/benefit models, 115–16,
  121
  lawsuits based on summary reports, 97–98
  members, 88
  Nobel Prize and, 3, 83, 98
  objectivity of, 3, 22, 37, 87–90, 93–95
  peer review process, 4, 87, 94
  political advocacy of, 22, 88, 91–98
  report author qualifications, 8, 22, 36, 37, 65,
  77
  report creation process, 87–90, 93–96
  roles, 3, 8, 87–90, 93–94
  on SO2 emissions, 150
  temperature data, 41–42
  US Senate investigation of, 98
  wealth redistribution agenda, 226
  working groups, 88–89, 92–93, 97
IPCC 1990 Climate Change report, 42, 91
IPCC 1995 Second Assessment Report (SAR),
  22, 40, 76–77, 78, 91–93, 102
IPCC 2001 Third Assessment Report (TAR),
  41, 76, 78, 88, 89, 91, 94
IPCC 2007 Fourth Assessment Report (AR4)
  computer models criticism, 31–33, 53
  data manipulation, 4, 36, 41
  on global warming devastation, 63–64, 66–67,
  77, 78, 81
  political influences, 88, 94, 95
  scientist opposition to, 78, 95–96, 217
  on solar activity, 53
Iran, 244
Ireland, 111
Irving, David, 149
"Is There Still Time to Avoid Disastrous
  Effects?" (Hansen speech), 24

Italy, 219
Itoh, Kiminori, 217, 234

J

Jackson, Lisa, 141–42, 230
Japan, 111, 244
Jarrett, Valerie, 130, 134
jet fuel, 134, 192–93, 250
Jobs, Steve, 19
Jones, Philip, 3, 4, 38, 50
Jones, Van, 134
Journal of Climate, 32
Journal of Geophysical Research (JGR), 38
Joy, Bill, 20
Joyce Foundation, 130–31, 133
JP Morgan Chase & Co., 190

K

Kapitsa, Andrei, 235
Kaser, Georg, 68
Kelley Blue Book, 247
Kellogg Graduate School of Management, 130
Kelly, Mick, 3
Kendall Foundation, 247
Kenedy Ranch, Texas, 165
Kennedy, Robert F., Jr., 164
Kennedy, Ted, 165
Kerry, John, 23, 134, 165, 207
Kerry, Teresa Heinz, 23, 129
"Key Vulnerabilities Cross-Cutting Theme"
   (IPCC), 89
Khoska, Vinod, 19
King Juan Carlos University, 167–68
King Ranch, Texas, 165
Klaus, Vaclav, 26, 226, 235–36
Kleiner Perkins Caufield & Byers, 19, 161
Kullen, N. J., 68
Kyoto Protocol
   Copenhagen Consensus on, 119
   cost/benefit models, 115–16, 121
   economic impacts, 107–9, 112
   Enron support of, 128–30
   European agendas, 97, 107–9, 121
   GHG reduction goals, 100, 102–3, 105, 121
   GHG reduction results, 110–13, 218–19, 220, 243
   lessons learned, 127–28
   member countries, 103
   motivation for, 93, 120–21
   NGOs role, 104

political hype over, 120–21
Russia's role, 103, 109–10, 121
Strong's role, 100–102
US objections, 105–7, 108, 109, 227
wealth redistribution agenda, 104–5, 226
world governance goals, 97

L

Lai, Marari, 67
Lamb, Hubert, 49
Lamont-Doherty Earth Observatory, 80
Landis+Gyr, 223
Landrieu, Mary, 142
Landsea, Christopher, 4, 78
La Niña conditions, 52
Las Vegas, Nevada, 6, 172–73, 183
Lauer, Matt, 69
Lave, Lester, 17
Lay, Kenneth, 128, 129
Lee, Robert, 54
Leer, Steve, 191
Lehr, Jay, 7
"Leipzig Declaration on Climate Change," 25
Levin, Carl, 132
Lewis & Clark College, 15
Lieberman, Ben, 71
Lieberman, Joe, 134, 136, 193, 207
Lincoln, Blanche, 142
Lincoln-Pipestone Rural Water System, 160
Lindzen, Richard, 82, 240
liquid coal, 192–97, 253
Lisbon Declaration, 227
Little Ice Age (LIA), 37, 50, 52, 57, 67, 79, 109, 232
lobbyists
   biofuels, 193, 208–9
   as climate debate beneficiaries, 7, 156, 165, 181, 182
   crisis emergence and, 86–87
   energy industry, 135, 167, 168–69
   environmental, 174, 181, 191, 195, 204
   Obama administration and, 168–69
   power shifts to, 228
Lomborg, Bjorn, 89, 119, 149
Lotero, Francisco, 15
Louisiana, 202, 207
Louisiana Mid-Continent Oil & Gas
   Association, 202
Luetkemeyer, Blaine, 98
Lunn, Nick, 68
Lu Xuedu, 112

M

MacArthur Foundation, 21
MacLaine, Shirley, 101
Macy, William H., 19
Maddox, Sir John, 94
Madrid Plenary conference, 92, 235
"A Major Deception on Global Warming" (Seitz), 93
malaria, 76, 119, 152
malnutrition, 119–20
Manitou Foundation, 101
man-made global warming. See human sources of global warming
Mann, Michael, 3–4, 36–37, 38, 95, 230
Mao Tse-tung, 101
Marshall, Andrew, 79
Maslowski, Wieslaw, 145–46
Massachusetts, 165, 166
Matteoli, Altero, 112
Maunder Minimum, 52, 53–54
McCain, John, 136
McIntyre, Steve, 37, 38, 240
McKitrick, Ross, 37, 96, 240
McLean, John, 32–33
media
    alarmism in, 9, 14, 68–69, 126, 129, 145, 146, 147–48, 226, 236
    on global cooling, 15–16
    responsible journalism and, 225–26, 246
Medicine Lake Highlands, California, 176
Medieval Warm Period (MWP), 37, 41, 49–50, 52
Menendez, Robert, 207
mercury pollution, 150–51
Merkley, Jeff, 198
meteorologists, definition of, 30
Mewald, Richard, 53
Mexico, 118, 199–200, 210
Microsoft, 241–42
Middle East, 71, 192, 204, 211, 213, 244
Milankovitch cycles, 51
Miliband, David, 113
Milikin, Paul, 70
Milken Institute study, 224
Minnesota, 160
MIT, 32, 177
Mitchell, George, 62
MMA Renewable Ventures, 173
"Model Evaluation" (IPCC), 91
Mojave Desert, 171–72
Molnia, Bruce, 66

Monckton, Christopher, 84, 218
MoneyWeek magazine, 193
Montreal Protocol on Substances That Deplete the Ozone Layer, 86, 87, 104
Moore, Patrick, 180
"More Than 700 International Scientists Dissent Over Man-made Global Warming Claims" (Senate Committee on Environment and Public Works), 98
Morgan Stanley, 190
Mörner, Nils-Axel, 65
Morris, Michael, 183
mosquito-borne diseases, 76–77, 152
Motorola, 131
Mount, Day Olin, 92
MOX fuel fabrication, 181–82
Mt. Kilimanjaro, 68
Munich Re, 96
Municipal Gas Authority of Georgia, 132
Murkowski, Lisa, 141
Murphy, Philip, 20
Murray, Cherry A., 202
Murray, Patty, 198

N

Nantucket Sound, 165, 166
Napoleon, 52
NASA (National Aeronautics and Space Administration). See also Hansen, James
    climate research funding, 22, 23
    data collection and analysis, 43–44
    GISS, 7, 23–24, 30, 32, 147–48
    sea ice data, 146
    on solar activity, 53, 54
    space program funding, 23
    temperature data, 6–7, 147
NASA Science, 77
Nash, Bob, 133
National Academy of Sciences, 16, 17–18, 21–22, 57, 106, 139, 203
"National Assessment of the Potential Consequences of Climate Change" (Clinton administration), 36
National Association of Manufacturers, 140
National Center for Atmospheric Research, 4, 30
National Center for Environmental Economics (NCEE), 8–9
National Center for Policy Analysis, 94, 213
National Climatic Data Center, 7, 148
National Coal Council, 193

National Geographic magazine, 70
National Religious Partnership for the
  Environment, 227
National Research Council, 21, 53, 80, 253
National Science Foundation, 17, 22
national security issues, 78–79
National Snow and Ice Data Center, 66, 146
natural gas
  in Alaska, 8, 9, 71, 197, 204–5
  depletion of, 223, 252
  "green" alternatives to, 208
  hydrogen power from, 177–78
  liquid fuel from, 196
  Obama administration policies, 205–6
  prices, 132, 222–23, 252
  regulatory issues, 222–23
  responsible use of, 246–47
  strategic dilemma, 197
  US reserves, 188, 197, 205
  worldwide competition for, 220–23
Natural Resources Defense Council (NRDC),
  158, 194–95, 202, 213
Nature Conservancy, 129
Nature Geoscience, 64
Nature journal, 34, 81, 93
Nellis Air Force Base, Nevada, 172–73
Nelson, Ben, 142
Nevada, 6, 172–73, 182–83, 191–92
Newell, Reginald, 17
New International Economic Order (NIEO),
  226
New Mexico, 131–32
Newsweek magazine, 147
News World International (NWI), 20
New York Board of Trade, 132
New York Times, 16, 17, 24, 113
Nigeria, 210
Nilles, Bruce, 191
nitrogen dioxide, 129, 189
nitrogen oxide, 160–61, 189, 195
nitrous oxide (N2O), 136, 189
NOAA (National Oceanographic and
  Atmospheric Administration), 6–7, 22, 30,
  42–43, 75, 147
nongovernmental organizations (NGOs), 92,
  104
Nordhaus, William, 121
Norris, Richard, 68
North America, 50
North American Insulation Manufacturers
  Association, 247
Northern Hemisphere, 6, 40, 42, 48, 50, 51

Northern States Power Company, 190
The North Pole Was Here (Revkin), 63
Northwestern University, 130
Northwest Passage, 67
NRG Energy, Inc., 181
nuclear energy, 137, 157, 164, 172, 179–84, 219,
  252
Nuclear Energy Institute, 179
Nuclear Regulatory Commission, 183
Nunavut territory, Canada, 9, 69
NV Energy, 173

O

Obama, Barack (and administration)
  cap-and-trade policies, 9, 26, 133, 135, 137,
    138, 141, 206, 207
  clean energy policies, 168, 203
  climate research funding, 23
  Copenhagen Summit concessions by, 117,
    118, 228, 238
  on gasoline prices, 209
  Goldman Sachs campaign contributions, 131
  Holdren's role, 153
  as Joyce Foundation director, 130
  key environmental players, 228–31
  lobbyist influences on, 168–69
  nuclear power policies, 182–83
  oil drilling policies, 198, 201–2, 205–7
  stimulus tax credit recipients, 223
  wind energy policies, 167, 168
oceans
  Atlantic, 33, 52, 79–80, 232
  coral reefs, 74–75
  El Niño and La Niña conditions, 32–33, 52,
    72
  Pacific, 32, 52, 64, 232
  polar bear habitat, 68–72
  sea ice, 66, 67, 69–70, 145–46
  sea levels, 24, 63–65, 68
  temperatures, 64, 74–75, 232–33
  thermohaline convection, 79–80
  wave and tidal energy, 174–75
Ocean Studies Board, 253
O'Donnell, Frank, 161
Office of Health, Safety and Security (DOE), 22
Office of Management and Budget (OMB), 21
offshore drilling, 198–203, 205, 206, 207
Ohio River Clean Fuels project, 194
oil
  in Alaska, 2, 8, 9, 71, 197, 204–5
  biofuel comparison with, 161–62

Deepwater Horizon accident, 138, 198–203
"green" alternatives to, 208–9
imports, 159, 208
Obama administration policies, 198, 201–2, 205–7
offshore drilling, 198–203, 205, 206, 207
prices, 132, 134–35, 207–10, 222–23
refinery capacity, 212–13
regulatory issues, 198–200, 222–23, 243
shale oil, 210–12
strategic dilemma, 197
US reserves, 188, 197, 205
worldwide competition for, 220–23, 243–44
Oil-for-Food program, 101
Open Society Institute (OSI), 24
Oppenheimer, Michael, 18
Optimum Population Trust, 118
Oreskes, Naomi, 26
Organization for Economic Cooperation and Development (OECD), 103
Ortega, Daniel, 238
"Our Common Future" (Brundtland Commission), 101
Outer Continental Shelf (OCS), 197–98, 205
outsourcing, 9, 10, 142, 202–3, 236, 252
Ozone Action, 86
ozone layer, 86, 104

P

Pachauri, Rajendra, 67, 95–96, 98, 149
Pacific Decadal Oscillation (PDO), 52, 64
Pacific Northwest National Laboratory, 88
Pacific Northwest region, 173–74
Pacific Ocean, 32, 52, 64, 232
Palin, Sarah, 71, 204–5
Paulson, Hank, 131
Peden, James, 235
Pelley, Scott, 68, 148
Pemex, 199, 244
penguins, 72–74
Perdido oil drilling platform, 199
pesticides, 152
Petrobras, 203
Pew Center, 129
Pew Charitable Trust, 74, 75
PG&E, 137
physicists, definition of, 30
Physics Today, 53
Pielke, Roger, 95
Piercy, Jan, 133
Pittman, Bill, 20

Podesta, John, 169, 229
polar bears, 9, 68–72, 205
Polar Bears International, 69, 70
polar ice caps, 68, 69–70, 79, 145–47, 232–33
polar regions, 43
Polar Research Board, 253
politics and climate science, 21–22, 88–89, 91–98, 120–21, 213–14, 225
pollution. See CO2; "green" energy
Ponte, Lowell, 16
The Population Bomb (Ehrlich), 104, 152–53
population control, 118, 152–53, 230
Portugal, 111
Power (Climate) Bill, 134–35, 206
Princeton University, 16
"Problems with the Protocol" (Harvard Magazine), 107
production tax credits (PTCs), 166–67
Project 88, 129
Pryor, Mark, 142
Public Service Enterprise Group Inc., 181
Pulkovo Observatory (Russia), 53
Putin, Vladimir, 109

R

Raines, Franklin, 131
rain forests, 81
Ramesh, Jairam, 118
Raymo, Maurine, 34
Reagan, Ronald administration, 150
Redford, Robert, 18, 191
regulatory environment, 150, 196, 198–200, 222–25, 230, 236, 240, 242–43. See also Environmental Protection Agency
Reid, Harry, 182, 191
Reilly, William, 201
Reiter, Paul, 76
Reliance Power Ltd., 203
religion and climate, 143–45
Renewable Fuels Act, 158
renewable portfolio standards (RPSs), 156, 167
Republican Party, 21, 23, 138, 193, 206, 207
research. See also scientists
data repression, 4, 8–9, 17, 83, 91, 93, 230
funding for, 20–24, 62, 65, 216, 224–26, 236
peer review process, 4, 87, 94
politicization of, 21–22, 91–98, 120–21
skepticism and, 231–33
tree ring, 3, 36–37
Revelle, Roger, 83
Revkin, Andrew, 63

Reyes, Oscar, 141
Rezko, Tony, 133
Roberts, David, 148
Rockefeller, David, 102
Rockefeller, Jay, 141, 142
Rockefeller, John D., descendants, 139
Romm, Joseph, 127
Royal Dutch Shell, 138, 199, 210, 211–12
Royal Society (UK and Commonwealth), 109
Rudd, Kevin, 116
Runge, C. Ford, 159
Russia, 4–5, 37–38, 53, 103, 109–10, 116, 147, 221–22, 240
Russian Academy of Sciences, 109

S

Sahara Desert, 51–52
Saiers, James, 4
Salazar, Ken, 200, 202, 205–6, 210
Salerno, Elizabeth, 168
Samanta, Arindam, 81
Sanders, Kerry, 69
Sandor, Richard, 131, 132
San Joaquin Valley, 224
Santer, Ben, 93
Sasol, 196
satellite data
    Antarctic ice, 232–33
    polar ice caps, 146–47, 232–33
satellite technology, 42–43, 67
Saudi Arabia, 71, 204, 211
Saudi Aramco, 244
Sauven, John, 95
Scafetta, Nicola, 53
Schmidt, Gavin, 84
Schmitt, Jack, 235
Schneider, Claudine, 18
Schneider, Stephen, 16, 89–90
Schumer, Chuck, 204
Schwarzenegger, Arnold, 223
science. *See also* data manipulation; research
    government interference in, 126, 127, 196, 216, 225–26, 242–43
    religion and, 143–45
    trust in, 231–33
Science, 26, 147, 161
Science Daily, 31–32
Science Digest, 15–16
Science News, 16
"Scientific and Economic Analysis Report" (UK House of Lords), 94
scientists. *See also* research

censure of, 4, 8–9, 17, 83, 91, 93, 129, 148–49, 216, 225–26, 230
consensus claims, 17, 24–27, 62, 88, 98
as global warming critics, 78, 83–84, 95–96, 217
politicization of, 21–22, 94
"Scientists' Statement on Global Climactic Disruption" (Ozone Action), 86
Scripps Institution of Oceanography, 68
Sea-Gen, 175
sea ice, 66, 67, 69–70, 145–46
sea levels, 24, 63–65, 68
seals, 70, 71, 73
Sechin, Igor, 221
Securing America (NRDC and Institute for the Analysis of Global Security), 194
Seitz, Frederick, vii, 93–94
Senauer, Benjamin, 159
Serious Materials, 223
shale oil, 210–12
Shapiro, Harold T., 95
Sharp, Gary, 74
Shell, 138, 199, 210, 211–12
Shenhua Group, 196
Shine, Keith, 89
Shmatko, Sergey, 222
ShoreBank, 133
Sieberg, Daniel, 69
Sierra Club, 164, 171, 174, 181, 190
Silent Spring (Carson), 151–52
Simmons, Adele, 133
Simon, B. Kenneth, 229
Simpson, Joanne, 31
Sinclair, Upton, 114
Singapore, 241
Singer, S. Fred, x–xi, 93, 240
Singh, Manmohan, 111
Sinopec, 200
The Skeptical Environmentalist (Lomborg), 89
Skoll, Jeffrey, 19
Snow, Kate, 69
The Snows of Kilimanjaro (Hemingway), 68
socialism
    in Europe, 107–8
    United Nations and, 226–27
    wealth redistribution and, 7–8, 22, 104–5, 116–17, 226–28, 238–39
The Socialist International, 229
solar activity, 52–54, 232
solar power, 157, 169–73, 180
solar system, 52, 82
Solis, Hilda, 231

Soros, George, 19, 24, 116–17, 131, 169, 203, 229
"The Soros Threat to Democracy" (Investor's Business Daily), 24
South Africa, 192, 196, 244
South America, 81, 221
Southeast Asia, 49, 239
Southern Hemisphere, 6, 51
Spain, 167–68
Spalding, Matthew, 229
Spencer, Roy, 31–32, 87, 240
Stanback, Howard, 133
Stanco, Whitney, 138
Stanford University's Global Climate and Energy Project, 139
"Statement of Atmospheric Scientists on Greenhouse Warming," 25
"State of the World 2009" (Worldwatch Institute), 81
Statistical Assessment Service (STATS) survey, 25–26
Statoil ASA, 199
Stena Drilling, 203
Stephens, Graeme, 32
Stern, Sir Nicholas, 113–14
Stern, Todd, 229
"Stern Review on the Economics of Climate Change" (Stern), 113–14
Storch, Hans von, 217–18
Streep, Meryl, 18
Streisand, Barbra, 18
Strong, Hanne, 101
Strong, Maurice, 100–102, 130, 226–27
subsidies
    alternative energy, 19, 126, 156–57
    ethanol production, 159, 162
    liquid fuel, 196
    solar power, 9, 169, 170, 172–73
    wind power, 9, 163, 166–68
sulfur dioxide (SO2), 129, 149–50, 189
Superior Renewable Energy, 166
sustainability, 10, 144, 153, 156, 218–19, 220
Sutley, Nancy, 231
synthetic fuel, 192–93

T

Taiwan, 241
Tapping, Kenneth, 53
tar sands, 196
Tata Energy Research Institute, 96
Tata Group, 96

Taylor, Mitchell, 9, 69, 70
technology sector trends, 251
Tegan, Suzanne, 168–69
temperatures
    climate change adaptation, 254
    CO2 correlation with, 2, 5, 7, 33–35, 39, 40, 50, 232
    cooling, 3, 4, 5–7, 8–9, 15–16, 50, 53, 57
    current favorable conditions, 43–44, 56–58
    Earth's orbital wobble and, 51–52
    historical data, 3, 12, 13, 15–16, 34–35, 40, 48–50, 68
    "hockey stick" graph, 3, 36–37, 41
    IPCC reports on, 41–42
    Little Ice Age, 37, 50, 52, 57, 67, 79, 232
    Medieval Warm Period, 37, 41, 49–50, 52
    monitoring methods, 42–43, 57
    ocean, 64, 74–75, 232–33
    solar activity and, 52–54
    warmest, 5, 6, 7, 41, 56–57, 72–73, 147
Tennekes, Hendrik, 64
Texas, 98, 163–64, 165–66, 169, 224
Thatcher, Margaret, 108
thermohaline convection, 79–80
Three Mile Island accident, 179
Tickell, Crispin, 16
tidal power, 174–75
Tide Foundation, 131
Tillerson, Rex, 139
Time magazine, 14, 16, 18, 69–70, 88
Tomlinson, Daniel, 173
Topolanek, Mirek, 219
transportation sector trends, 249–50
tree ring research, 3, 36–37
Trenberth, Kevin, 4, 33, 77, 78
Trends in Mathematics and Science study, 241
Trilateral Commission, 102
tropical diseases, 76–77
Trout Unlimited, 174
Turner, Ted, 19
Twain, Mark, 82–83
TXU Corp., 191

U

Ulmer, Fran, 201
Union Carbide, 192
Union of Concerned Scientists (UCS), 17–18, 168–69
United Kingdom
    An Inconvenient Truth response by, 83
    cap-and-trade activities, 140–41

coal industry, 108, 110
  Department of Environment, Food and Rural
    Affairs, 96
  Freedom of Information Act, 4
United Kingdom (*cont*)
  GHG emissions, 108–9
  IPCC concerns by, 94
  nuclear energy, 219
  Stern Review, 113–14
United Nations. *See also* Copenhagen
    Summit; IPCC; Kyoto Protocol
  Earth Summit, 100–103, 104, 226–27
  FCCC, 38, 45, 100, 105, 116–18, 120–21
  Madrid Plenary, 92, 235
  Montreal Protocol, 86, 87, 104
  Oil-for-Food program, 101
  wealth redistribution agenda, 7–8, 22, 104–5,
    116–17, 226–28
  world governance goals, 96–97, 98, 102
UN Conference on Environment and
    Development (UNCED), 100–103, 104,
    226–27
UN Environment Programme (UNEP), 86, 88,
    93, 100, 226
UN World Commission on Environment and
    Development (WCED), 101
UN World Meteorological Organization
    (WMO), 38, 56–57
United States. *See also* fossil fuels; government;
    "green" energy; Obama, Barack
  anti-American sentiment toward, 226–28,
    238–40
  budget deficit spending, 228
  education trends, 241–42
  energy economies, 128
  energy policy, 179, 220–23, 242–45
  GDP, 227
  Kyoto Protocol and, 105–7, 108, 109, 128, 227
  monetary concessions by, 117, 118, 228, 238
  power shifts within, 228–31
  resource abundance, 240
  Western European countries contrasted with,
    108
US Agriculture Department, 22
US Air Force, 172–73
US Army Corps of Engineers, 174
US Bureau of Mines, 192, 193
US Bureau of Transportation, 208
US Carbide and Carbon Chemical Company,
    192
US Chamber of Commerce, 142

US Climate Action Partnership (USCAP),
    135–39
US Commerce Department, 22
US Defense Department, 78–79
US Energy Department (DOE), 22, 88, 168,
    169, 179, 191, 208
US Export-Import Bank, 174, 203
US Fish and Wildlife Service, 69, 71
US Geological Survey (USGS), 69, 183, 188,
    200
US Interior Department (DOI), 9, 68, 70–71,
    204, 210
US Labor Department, 231
US Navy, 145
US Senate
  Committee on Science, Technology and
    Space, 17, 22, 62
  on Enron Loophole, 132
  on global warming research, 21, 217–18
  IPCC investigation by, 98
  on Kyoto Protocol, 105–7
US State Department, 92, 203
US Transportation Department, 208
US Treasury Department, 203
University of California–San Diego, 68
University of East Anglia. *See* "Climategate"
    e-mail scandal; CRU
University of Illinois Arctic Climate Research
    Center, 67
Unstoppable Global Warming (Singer and
    Avery), xi
uranium, 179–80
Utah, 210–12

V

Venezuela, 220–21, 222, 244
Venus, 82
Vermeersen, Bert, 64
Virginia, 205–6
volcanic eruptions, 32, 33, 34, 40–41, 51, 54

W

Wal, Roderick S. W. van de, 147
Washington, George, 52
Waste Management, 131
water, 159–60, 212, 224
water pollution, 160
water vapor, 39, 52, 55–56, 232
Watson, Robert, 87
Watts, Anthony, 42, 84, 240

wave energy, 174–75
Waxman-Markey Bill, 139–40
wealth redistribution agenda, 7–8, 22, 104–5,
  116–17, 226–28, 238–39
Weaver, Andrew, 95
Wegman, Edward J., 94
Weiss, Daniel, 207
West, Bruce, 53
whales, 166
Wiesel, Elie, 148
Wigley, Tom, 4
Wildavsky, Aaron, 104–5
Wilderness Society, 171–72
Will, George, 168
wind energy, 163–69, 180, 219
Wirth, Timothy, 17, 92, 102, 129, 227
Woods Foundation, 133
Working Group on Global Warming (Bush
  administration), 106
World Bank, 227, 239
World Commission on Environment and
  Development (WCED), 101
World Energy Council, 179
World Health Organization (WHO), 119

The World Is Flat (Friedman), 238, 239
World Meteorological Organization (WMO),
  38, 56–57, 86, 93, 100
World Nuclear Association, 179
World on Fire (Mitchell), 62
World Trade Organization (WTO), 110, 238
Worldwatch Institute, 81
World Wildlife Fund (WWF), 72, 74, 81, 201
Wyden, Ron, 198
Wyoming, 195, 210–12

X

Xcel Energy, Inc., 190

Y

Yeo, Tim, 140
Younger Dryas episode, 79–80
Yucca Mountain nuclear waste repository,
  182–83, 191

Z

Zhao Baige, 118
Zoi, Cathy, 223

ABOUT THE AUTHOR

Larry Bell is a professor of architecture and an endowed professor of space architecture at the University of Houston, where he founded and directs the Sasakawa International Center for Space Architecture (SICSA). SICSA is globally recognized as a leading academic organization for research, planning, and design of habitats in extreme environments. These include orbital and planetary space facilities, polar research stations, offshore and underwater accommodations, and shelters for populations impacted by natural and man-made disasters. SICSA sponsors the world's only graduate program in space architecture, where a central priority is to explore and apply sustainable design and living approaches that can prevent unnecessary extreme conditions from occurring everywhere on our planet. In this regard, Larry believes that a "Spaceship Earth" perspective is entirely realistic. Municipalities, states, and nations are beginning to realize that we are all in that tiny, fragile spacecraft together. All of us depend upon the same limited support systems and share a vital mission that will determine the future of all life.

Larry and SICSA are frequently featured in national and international broadcast media and print presentations. Examples include the History Channel (*Modern Marvels Series*), the Discovery Channel-Canada (*Daily Planet Series*), NASA Select, PBS, the *BBC TV World Business Report*, the National TV Network of Italy, the Swedish Educational Network, the NEC TV Broadcast Network-Japan, Radio Moscow, and National Geographic TV-UK. Larry has been interviewed and quoted in lead *Time* magazine and *Christian Science Monitor* features. He has also written dozens of technical conference papers and professional journal articles addressing a broad range of space and terrestrial design issues and has written about the environment, energy, and technology for *Energy Tribune*, an international magazine.

Larry has cofounded several high-tech companies. One, a commercial aerospace corporation, grew to more than eight thousand professionals through various mergers and acquisitions and was purchased by General Dynamics. A spin-off of another company he cofounded designs and manufactures drive systems for hybrid-electric buses and other vehicles that are on the roads in several cities.

In addition to NASA headquarters achievement certificates awarded to SICSA, Larry has received important international honors. Among those are the Space Pioneer Award from the Kyushu Sanyu University in Japan and two of the highest honors awarded by the Federation of Astronautics and Cosmonautics of the former Soviet Union—the Yuri Gagarin Diploma and the Konstantin Tsiolkovsky Gold Medal—for his contributions to international space development. His name was placed on the Russian rocket that launched the first crew to the International Space Station. Three major professional aerospace engineering societies in the NASA Johnson Space Center/Texas region jointly selected him for the Technical Educator of the Year Award in 2003.